THE HANDY COMMUNICATION ANSWER BOOK

THE HANDY COMMUNICATION ANSWER BOOK

Lauren Sergy

Detroit

THE HANDY COMMUNICATION ANSWER BOOK

Visible Ink Press®
43311 Joy Rd., #414
Canton, MI 48187-2075

Visible Ink Press is a registered trademark of Visible Ink Press LLC.

Most Visible Ink Press books are available at special quantity discounts when purchased in bulk by corporations, organizations, or groups. Customized printings, special imprints, messages, and excerpts can be produced to meet your needs. For more information, contact Special Markets Director, Visible Ink Press, www.visibleink.com, or 734-667-3211.

Managing Editor: Kevin S. Hile
Art Director: Mary Claire Krzewinski
Typesetting: Marco Divita
Proofreaders: Larry Baker and Shoshana Hurwitz
Indexer: Larry Baker

Cover images: Shutterstock.

Cataloging-in-Publication Data is available at the Library of Congress.

10 9 8 7 6 5 4 3 2 1

About the Author

Lauren Sergy is a speaker, writer, coach, and trainer on public speaking and communication. Since 2012, she has worked with professionals, managers, and executives to ramp up their public speaking and interpersonal communication skills. She is known for her highly practical approach that combines rigorous content development methods with disciplined, dynamic performance, and presentation techniques. A member of the Canadian Association of Professional Speakers, Lauren engages, educates, and entertains audiences with talks on public speaking, communication, rhetoric, and critical thinking. Her clients and audiences include the government of Alberta, Northern Trust Corporation, the University of Alberta, Meeting Professionals International, Alberta Blue Cross, and numerous professional associations. Lauren holds a master's degree in library and information studies and a bachelor of arts in English and classics, as well as additional education and experience in acting, radio, business, management, and staff instruction. Her articles have been published in *Library Journal,* and her blog posts are featured on sites such as Duct Tape Marketing, The Wealthy Gorilla, and Young Upstarts. Lauren regularly posts original content on public speaking and communication on her website at laurensergy.com. She lives in Edmonton, Alberta.

Also from Visible Ink Press

The Handy African American History Answer Book
by Jessie Carnie Smith
ISBN: 978-1-57859-452-8

The Handy American History Answer Book
by David L. Hudson, Jr.
ISBN: 978-1-57859-471-9

The Handy Anatomy Answer Book, 2nd edition
by Patricia Barnes-Svarney and Thomas E. Svarney
ISBN: 978-1-57859-542-6

The Handy Answer Book for Kids (and Parents), 2nd edition
by Gina Misiroglu
ISBN: 978-1-57859-219-7

The Handy Art History Answer Book
by Madelynn Dickerson
ISBN: 978-1-57859-417-7

The Handy Astronomy Answer Book, 3rd edition
by Charles Liu
ISBN: 978-1-57859-190-9

The Handy Bible Answer Book
by Jennifer Rebecca Prince
ISBN: 978-1-57859-478-8

The Handy Biology Answer Book, 2nd edition
by Patricia Barnes Svarney and Thomas E. Svarney
ISBN: 978-1-57859-490-0

The Handy Boston Answer Book
by Samuel Willard Crompton
ISBN: 978-1-57859-593-8

The Handy California Answer Book
by Kevin S. Hile
ISBN: 978-1-57859-591-4

The Handy Chemistry Answer Book
by Ian C. Stewart and Justin P. Lamont
ISBN: 978-1-57859-374-3

The Handy Civil War Answer Book
by Samuel Willard Crompton
ISBN: 978-1-57859-476-4

The Handy Dinosaur Answer Book, 2nd edition
by Patricia Barnes-Svarney and Thomas E. Svarney
ISBN: 978-1-57859-218-0

The Handy English Grammar Answer Book
by Christine A. Hult, Ph.D.
ISBN: 978-1-57859-520-4

The Handy Geography Answer Book, 3rd edition
by Paul A. Tucci
ISBN: 978-1-57859-215-9

The Handy Geology Answer Book
by Patricia Barnes-Svarney and Thomas E. Svarney
ISBN: 978-1-57859-156-5

The Handy History Answer Book, 3rd edition
by David L. Hudson, Jr.
ISBN: 978-1-57859-372-9

The Handy Hockey Answer Book
by Stan Fischler
ISBN: 978-1-57859-513-6

The Handy Investing Answer Book
by Paul A. Tucci
ISBN: 978-1-57859-486-3

The Handy Islam Answer Book
by John Renard Ph.D.
ISBN: 978-1-57859-510-5

The Handy Law Answer Book
by David L. Hudson Jr.
ISBN: 978-1-57859-217-3

The Handy Math Answer Book, 2nd edition
by Patricia Barnes-Svarney and Thomas E. Svarney
ISBN: 978-1-57859-373-6

The Handy Military History Answer Book
by Samuel Willard Crompton
ISBN: 978-1-57859-509-9

The Handy Mythology Answer Book,
by David A. Leeming, Ph.D.
ISBN: 978-1-57859-475-7

The Handy New York City Answer Book
by Chris Barsanti
ISBN: 978-1-57859-586-0

The Handy Nutrition Answer Book
by Patricia Barnes-Svarney and Thomas E. Svarney
ISBN: 978-1-57859-484-9

The Handy Ocean Answer Book
by Patricia Barnes-Svarney and Thomas E. Svarney
ISBN: 978-1-57859-063-6

The Handy Personal Finance Answer Book
by Paul A. Tucci
ISBN: 978-1-57859-322-4

The Handy Philosophy Answer Book
by Naomi Zack
ISBN: 978-1-57859-226-5

The Handy Physics Answer Book, 2nd edition
By Paul W. Zitzewitz, Ph.D.
ISBN: 978-1-57859-305-7

The Handy Politics Answer Book
by Gina Misiroglu
ISBN: 978-1-57859-139-8

The Handy Presidents Answer Book, 2nd edition
by David L. Hudson
ISB N: 978-1-57859-317-0

The Handy Psychology Answer Book, 2nd edition
by Lisa J. Cohen
ISBN: 978-1-57859-508-2

The Handy Religion Answer Book, 2nd edition
by John Renard
ISBN: 978-1-57859-379-8

The Handy Science Answer Book, 4th edition
by The Carnegie Library of Pittsburgh
ISBN: 978-1-57859-321-7

The Handy State-by-State Answer Book
by Samuel Willard Crompton
ISBN: 978-1-57859-565-5

The Handy Supreme Court Answer Book
by David L Hudson, Jr.
ISBN: 978-1-57859-196-1

The Handy Technology Answer Book
by Naomi Bobick and James Balaban
ISBN: 978-1-57859-563-1

The Handy Weather Answer Book, 2nd edition
by Kevin S. Hile
ISBN: 978-1-57859-221-0

PLEASE VISIT THE "HANDY ANSWERS" SERIES WEBSITE AT WWW.HANDYANSWERS.COM.

Contents

Photo Sources

ABC Photo: p. 94.

Acme News Photos: p. 45.

Chris Charabaruk: p. 174.

Glauco92 (Wikicommons): p. 67.

Harris & Ewing Collection, Library of Congress: p. 27.

Ladies' Home Journal: p. 264.

Library and Archives Canada: p. 51.

Library of Congress: p. 42.

NASA: p. 147.

National Archives and Records Administration: p. 25.

National Museum of Rome: p. 65.

Lauren Sergy: pp. 3, 137, 190.

Shutterstock: pp. 6, 8, 10, 12, 15, 17, 21, 23, 29, 32, 33, 35, 38, 56, 58, 59, 61, 72, 74, 78, 88, 98 (top and bottom), 100, 101, 103, 104, 108, 112, 114, 117, 123, 125, 128, 129, 130, 133, 135, 139, 149, 151, 153, 155, 158, 160, 163, 167, 169, 171, 179, 181, 186, 193, 198, 200, 202, 204, 208, 212, 213, 215, 221, 223, 225, 228, 232, 235, 236, 238, 243, 245, 247, 249, 252, 257, 259, 262, 267, 269, 271, 274, 277, 280, 282, 286, 288, 294, 296, 299, 300, 307, 308, 311, 313, 318, 325, 327, 331.

Public domain: pp. 41, 46, 49, 53, 70, 76, 172.

Dedication

For dad, who told me years ago that he wanted me to write books. And for mom, who is a big enough geek to understand why I started by writing a book like this.

Acknowledgments

No one writes a book in a vacuum, and I wish to extend my heartfelt thanks to those who helped me out. In particular, I would like to thank Zubia Mumtaz and Karen Van Der Meer for helping with their expertise and setting me straight on some important facts. Thanks to Shannon de Bruin for being an additional set of eyeballs and a great source of feedback in this book's formative stages. To Etta Verma at *Library Journal,* thank you so much for recommending me as a prospective author for Visible Ink Press—this book was a direct result of that connection. My very deep gratitude goes to publisher Roger Jänecke and editor Kevin Hile at Visible Ink Press; your direction, feedback, and patience were a critical part in the creation of this book.

To my parents, Rudy and Jackie de Bruin, and my mother-in-law, Dianne Sergy, thanks for putting up with my whining and insecurities throughout the writing process. And above all, thank you to my husband, Glen, who not only ensured our children remained fed, watered, and played with while I was in the thick of writing, but who also provided me with encouragement, commiseration, and bags of chocolate chips—all with impeccable timing. As cliché as this expression may be, I truly could not have done this without you.

Introduction

Communication is a subject that fascinates and frustrates people. It is a skill that is absolutely fundamental to our ability to survive and thrive. One would think, therefore, that it's also a skill we would develop intuitively. Alas (or happily for people in my line of work), this is not the case.

"Communication" can be difficult to define. It encompasses a huge number of activities, which all generate meaning in different ways. Communication is messy and complicated. It's buffeted by every kind of culture imaginable—social, ethnic, generational, professional—and is subject to the whims of fashion. It is highly individual, affected by personal tastes and contexts. Words and expressions change on a regular basis, often with more speed than we realize. Communication rarely sticks to any hard-and-fast rules. What works in one form, medium, or context might not work in another. Becoming a skillful communicator takes patience, attention, and a willingness to experiment and take risks.

My goal in writing this book was to make it easier for people to hone their skills and to provide a guide to the kinds of communication questions people deal with on a regular basis. At the same time, I wanted to give a behind-the-scenes glimpse into the incredible world of human communication. Learning the rich history of how we exchange information and ideas is not only entertaining, it enables us to become better communicators. Still, it's important to keep a focus on applied communication—on helping people better navigate our increasingly complex communication landscape. In order to accomplish all this, this book is a hybrid of practical, peculiar, historic, contemporary, beginner, and expert issues and applications of communication.

In this book, I sought to address the practical questions that people actually ask about communication. To accomplish this, I called in the proverbial troops, both offline and online. I went directly to my clients, audiences, colleagues, and online communities to solicit their questions. Many of the questions have come from my own work and experience, and others draw on the experience of experts who kindly allowed me to grill them on their area of knowledge. The audience for which this book is intended is the same as those who submitted questions: business people, professionals, academics, post-secondary students, and anyone who wants to develop a quicker tongue, more graceful expression, and more persuasive communication in everyday life.

The questions I received and developed fell into several distinct categories, and I've organized the contents accordingly:

- The Big Picture—these "big picture" questions look at communication from a broad topic—what it is, how it developed, communication history, and important communication strategies.
- Practical Writing—this section encompasses not only questions about how to write well, but also communication environments in which writing is strongly emphasized, such as email communication and social media. While this section doesn't dive deeply into grammatical issues, some common grammar and style traps are addressed.
- Public Speaking—the questions I received most frequently (and that were usually the most anxious in tone) were related to public speaking. This isn't surprising, as many people are terrified of public speaking. This section deals with all angles of public speaking, from the psychology behind it to vocal techniques to body language to presentation technology.
- Communicating in Specific Environments—even though most communication skills cross from one environment to the next, certain questions were clearly in the domain of business, social, or academic communication. The business section is the heftiest, and contains lots of information that is of use outside the business world. Don't be afraid to wade in!

Communication is a massive topic, one far too vast to completely address in a single book. Because so many issues in communication appear in multiple contexts, I have cross-referenced questions within the book itself. This book focuses on communication within a Western context, and on the United States in particular.

I hope this book ignites a new curiosity and appreciation for communication in your own life. This book won't have all the answers, but it has a lot of them! And it might help you come up with answers of your own. Dig in, have fun, and keep your eye open for opportunities to practice your newfound knowledge and skills. When it comes to communication, the results are always worth the effort.

—Lauren Sergy

WHAT IS COMMUNICATION?

GENERAL COMMUNICATION

What is communication?

Communication is the intentional transmission or sharing of a message or information between two or more people.

Communication takes place through a variety of means, which can include but are not limited to:

- Verbally: using spoken words
- Nonverbally: using gesture, vocal tone, and other non-word indicators
- Written: e.g., books, blogs, pamphlets, graffiti, and more
- Visually: e.g., aesthetic expression and visual art
- Symbolically: e.g., "language of flowers," popular in the Victorian period, "fan signals," popular during the English Regency period, or Morse code
- Chemically: e.g., through involuntary secretions of pheromones or intentionally through use of perfume and scents

The lines distinguishing different forms of communication can be blurry and up to interpretation. Chemical and symbolic communication could, for instance, be classified as subsets to nonverbal communication. There is also debate as to whether sign language is a visual language or an unspoken verbal language.

Different types of communication can be combined. When we speak, we use both verbal and nonverbal elements. Someone on a hot date might use all the communication means at his or her disposal: sending a salacious text message before meeting the date, engaging in witty conversation, using flirtatious body language and dress, bringing a rose (a common symbol of romance), and tying the whole package together by dousing him- or herself in perfume or cologne.

In this book, we'll be focusing on verbal, nonverbal, and written methods of communication.

What conditions need to exist for communication to happen?

All communication happens through a system—a series of steps and conditions that allow the communication process to work. A simple communication system has three components: a way to emit the message (to get the message out), a channel by which to transmit the message (to get the message from point A to point B), and a way to receive or take in the message.

For example, if you were speaking to someone on the phone, you would emit your message by talking. The channel would be the telephone, and the person you were speaking with would receive the message by listening.

If you were reading a book, then the author emitted his or her message by writing words. The channel was the printed book, and you received the message by reading it.

There are two additional elements that need to be present if communication is going to happen. First, the sender must be able to *encode* the message—to transform thoughts and ideas into a form that can be sent, like words or signals. Next, the receiver must be able to *decode* the message—to then process that message into understanding.

Let's say you wanted to communicate a complicated emotion but couldn't find the words to express it. You would fail to *encode* the message, and the communication would fall apart. Similarly, if you spoke to someone who didn't understand your language, then the receiver would have failed to *decode* your message, and the communication would fail.

What is one-way communication?

One-way communication occurs when the person receiving the message can't or won't give *feedback* (a response or reply) to the person sending the message. Examples of one-way communication include watching television, reading books, taking orders, and listening to music.

The path of one-way communication looks like this:

Sender (e.g., journalist) → Channel (e.g., newspaper article) → Receiver (e.g., reader)

Should the receiver take the time and effort to respond to the sender and the sender receives the response, then two-way communication might be initiated. A newspaper reader who writes a letter to the editor in response to a particular article would be initiating two-way communication.

What is two-way communication?

Two-way communication happens when the receiver is able to give feedback to the sender, and the sender receives that feedback. The people involved in the communication are interacting with and responding to one another. In contrast to one-way com-

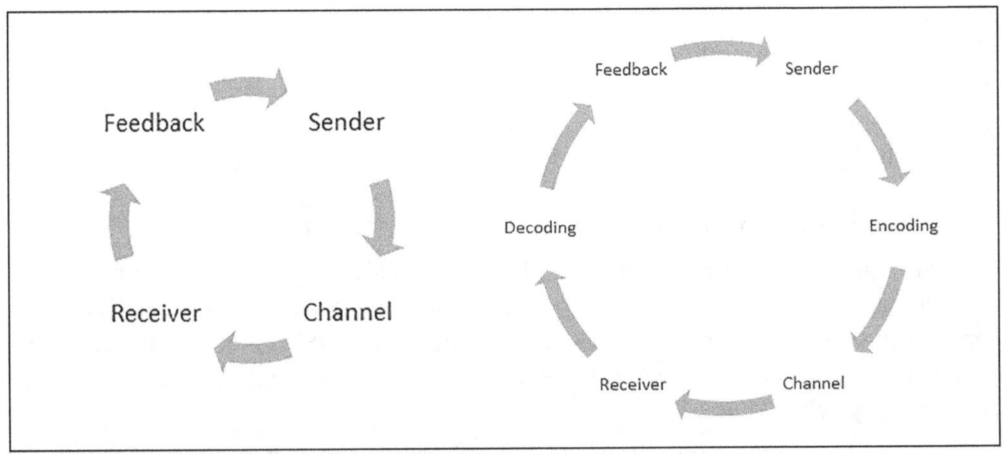

The illustration at left shows how two-way communication ideally works, while the one on the right shows the communication cycle.

munication, two-way communication forms a loop that looks like that shown in the illustration.

What is the communication cycle?

The communication cycle is a model that includes all the elements of communication: sender, encoding, channel, receiver, decoding, and feedback. The communication cycle is useful when developing a full communication plan, creating a new method of communication, or trying to figure out where a communication breakdown may have happened. The communication cycle follows this pattern: a breakdown at any of these points means that the communication cycle couldn't occur. We can use transmitting a message over the Internet as a good example for different breakdowns in the communication cycle:

- Sending error: The sender doesn't have a keyboard with the proper characters to type a message
- Encoding error: The original message data is corrupted and can't be encoded into a format that the computer can understand
- Channel error: Problems with the Internet connection prevent the message from being transmitted
- Decoding error: The receiver got the message but doesn't have the correct computer program to open it
- Feedback error: The receiver was able to understand the message but didn't want to spend the time giving the sender any feedback

How do we learn to communicate?

Learning to communicate begins in infancy, and children learn communication and language skills by interacting with and imitating other people. The caregiver's role in childhood communication and language development is crucial. Children with parents who have strong communication skills usually develop stronger communication skills themselves. When parents and caregivers repeat or imitate the sounds and words a child says, the baby is encouraged to speak, is told that his or her words have meaning, and feels listened to. These positive interactions all encourage further communication.

What behaviors do young children show as they learn to communicate?

The development of communication skills in children's early years follows fairly predictable markers. Babies cry to signal needs and quickly develop different kinds of cries depending on what it is they want. Social smiling is another important early communication signal, and around two months of age, babies begin smiling to show pleasure and to engage with others.

Between three and six months of age, babies learn that certain noises and actions will get certain reactions from others, and they will repeat these actions to get the response they want. Around this time, they also begin to nonverbally express their emotions and begin to recognize facial and vocal cues from others. At this point, babies are able to make inferences about the emotional state and even the intentions of other people.

At the six- to twelve-month stage, babies engage in pre-language behavior—babbling and repeating sounds as they learn to speak. Even though they might not be able to speak yet, babies in this age group can understand some words and phrases. After the one-year mark, children's language acquisition becomes more rapid and regular with them gaining more words every month and beginning to string together simple sentences.

At three and four years of age, some complex and crucial communication skills start to develop. Children typically begin following their language's grammar conventions, start to identify and describe their feelings with more detail, use humor, tell stories, and exaggerate the truth.

What factors can delay the development of communication skills?

When children are raised in environments that have fewer language and interaction opportunities, their communication skills will not develop as quickly. Children who live in emotionally unsupportive or unstable environments often demonstrate delayed communication skills and may be reluctant communicators as they grow older. Many physical and cognitive disabilities also delay the development of communication skills to various degrees.

What is language?

A "language" is a method of communication made up of a system of words with regular grammatical and syntactic structure. Language is used by a group of people. Usually, these people come from a particular community, country, or culture.

Other forms of communication that don't fit the definition of true language are sometimes referred to as "language," but this does not mean that they have the characteristics of an actual language. These non-languages are usually clearly labeled. Examples of this are physical expression being called "body language" or systems of computer programming code being known as "computer language" or "programming language."

The term "language" is sometimes also expanded to include a unique subset of expressions, signals, or vocabulary shared by a very specific group of people. These groups are usually social or professional in nature, and their expressions and vocabulary may either exist only within their group or have special meaning when used in their group.

What are dialects?

Distinct and consistent variations within a language are called *dialects*. Dialects are usually regional—existing in a certain geographic area—but can also develop from factors like social class. They develop gradually over a long period of time. Dialects of languages can differ from their mother language in pronunciation, grammar, spelling, and vocabulary. English has a huge number of dialects; American English and Australian English, for instance, vary considerably. Dialects exist within specific regions of countries, as well. Within the United States, there are many distinct dialects and accents, such as Cajun, Eastern New England, and Texan.

Can dialects hinder understanding between two people who speak the same language?

Dialects can significantly affect the ability of two speakers of the same language to understand each other. Because dialects can vary so much, it is possible for two people to speak the same base language but find it difficult to understand one another. A conversation between someone speaking with a thick Canadian Newfoundland accent and expressions and someone speaking rich Boston English would be entertaining to listen to but probably very difficult for the people involved.

How do we acquire dialects?

People tend to speak the dialect they learned naturally during childhood. However, some speakers may adopt the dialect of a region they move to while others may formally learn a specific dialect. Received pronunciation was considered a highly desirable marker of upper-class status in England and in early twentieth-century America. This dialect was taught in exclusive private schools as part of a student's education.

Thanks to technology and the spread of more standard forms of English, dialects are becoming less regional in nature. However, they still exist and are increasingly developing among different social groups of people, reflecting shared cultural identities rather than shared geographic identities.

Is slang the same thing as a dialect?

Slang is not the same thing as a dialect. While dialects form gradually and are typically centered within a certain geographic region, slang is a deliberate and conscious change

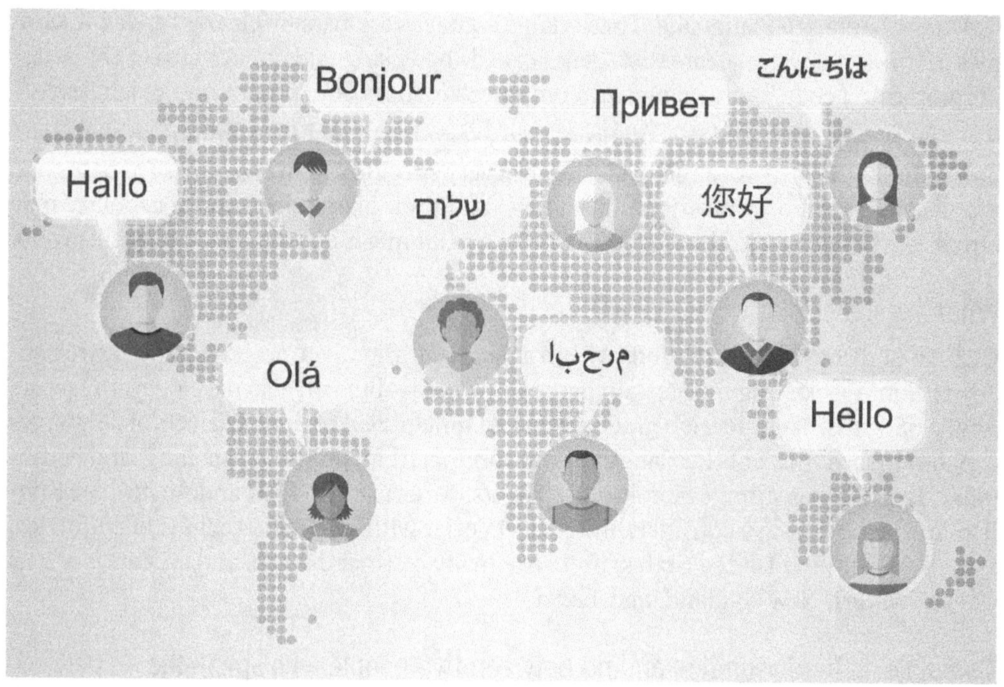

A "language" is a method of communication made up of a system of words with regular grammatical and syntactic structure.

of word meaning more associated with a specific demographic or subculture (e.g., teenagers, hip-hop, geek culture). Linguist Susie Dent identifies motivation and choice as the main distinguishing elements between slang and dialect. We tend to speak the dialect that we were raised with, but we select the slang we use to communicate identity and belonging with a certain group.

How does slang develop?

Slang words develop differently from dialectic vocabulary. Slang purposefully changes or subverts word meaning. It can also involve creating new words and shortening or abbreviating existing words. Slang words and meanings are often vulgar, rude, or have a distinctly uneducated or counterculture feel. Some contemporary slang examples are:

Sick—Excellent, awesome. Usually used by teenagers and young adults. "That party last night was sick!" This is word inversion slang.

On fleek—A compliment. Nice, fashionable. Popular among teenagers. "Your dress is totally on fleek!" This is word creation slang.

OMG—Surprise, shock, disbelief. Acronym for "Oh My God/Gosh/Goodness." Made popular through texting and Internet use. Widely used across age demographics. "My manager asked if I could fiddle with the numbers to make them prettier, and I was like OMG, are you serious?" This is word abbreviation slang.

Expressions may be used broadly in different populations or be restricted to a very small group of people. Slang also tends to be transitory in nature; its use can change in a short period of time and slang terms will follow fashion cycles, often rising or falling in popularity within one or two decades. The Internet has accelerated the life span of slang terms. They now spread very rapidly across different groups and can go in and out of fashion in a very short period of time, sometimes only lasting one year before falling out of favor.

What are some common barriers to communication?

Communication barriers can happen in both written and verbal communication. While there isn't a formal classification of the types of communication barriers, they can be lumped into several categories. Some common barriers that affect overall communication include:

- Language barriers—When lack or poor knowledge of a common language prevents the people communicating from understanding one another. Language barriers can also be created by using obscure or overly formal language, not using clear language, and miring the communication in jargon.
- Physical disability—Conditions such as deafness, hard of hearing, or vision impairment that make the physical actions involved in communication difficult or impossible.
- Attention barriers—When distraction, lack of interest, disengagement, fatigue, or attention-related dysfunctions make it difficult for the receiver to pay proper attention to the person or medium sending the message.
- Mental barriers—When someone's emotional/mental state (e.g., anger, frustration, elation) or habits (like jumping to conclusions) significantly affects either the communication abilities of the sender or receiver of a message. In the case of the sender, he or she may unintentionally muddle his or her message. In the case of receivers, he or she may misunderstand the message or simply "tune out" the sender altogether.
- Contextual barriers—Contextual barriers occur when the sender's and receiver's contexts, such as social or educational, are so different that they are unable to under-

Can slang become a normal part of a dialect or language?

It is possible for slang to cross into dialect. When a slang term endures and enters into common use among all or most speakers, it may get absorbed into the unique vocabulary of a dialect or even into a whole language. The lines between what is slang and what is dialect can be very blurry, however, and that can lead to a great deal of debate over whether a piece of vernacular is slang or a consistent part of a whole dialect.

stand or empathize with one another's circumstances. This is, essentially, an inability to see things from another person's point of view. These barriers may result from differences in culture or etiquette, stereotypes, and preexisting beliefs. A student with no knowledge of cultural or etiquette norms of Regency-era England would have a contextual barrier to understanding Jane Austen's *Pride and Prejudice.*

- Cultural barriers—Socially directed norms of behavior that prevent or hinder communication. Cultural barriers can exist within an ethnographic group, such as when class or caste make it unacceptable for two people to communicate directly. Cultural barriers can also exist within organizational cultures, such as companies with strong hierarchies where it would be taboo for a junior worker to directly speak to an executive manager.

VERBAL COMMUNICATION

What is verbal communication?

Verbal communication is when voiced speech is used to convey messages and meaning between two individuals.

What technology do we use for verbal communication?

Verbal communication technology is focused on catching and transmitting audio messages. Technology can be used to either enhance in-person verbal communication, allow for long-distance real-time verbal communication, or to record audio for playback at a later time. Many communication devices serve more than one purpose and can be used for more than one kind of communication.

Common in-person verbal communication technologies are microphones and speakers, used to enhance and amplify voices.

Common long-distance verbal communication technologies are radio and telephony, which includes telephones and other technology used to perform sound transmission such as VoIP (Voice over Internet Protocol) and mobile phones. Software that allows for inexpensive alternatives to traditional phone lines are popular for both business and personal use, as are web conferencing and video conferencing software.

The most familiar type of verbal communication technology is, of course, the telephone.

Recording and recorded playback technology includes radio, telephony, a huge range of computer software, hardware such as microphones and speakers, and audio-video devices like televisions and projectors.

What are some common barriers to verbal communication?

In addition to the common communication barriers outlined earlier in this chapter, people may experience barriers that specifically affect verbal communication. As with general communication barriers, people may experience more than one verbal communication barrier at the same time. Barriers that are peculiar to verbal communication include:

- Speech barriers—Barriers that make the intelligibility of speech difficult. This may include heavy accents that are difficult to understand and physical or neurological conditions that make it difficult to form words.
- Auditory barriers—When conditions like deafness or being hard of hearing, or environmental conditions such as noise, impede the receiver's ability to hear the message.
- Technological barriers—When technology intended to relay audio or audio/visual messages fails or performs suboptimally, causing the message to be garbled or inaccessible. This could include a poor telephone connection, a static-filled radio channel, or an online video that won't load. Other barriers created by technology occur when short delays in voice transmission break the flow of conversation or cause people to interrupt one another.

Technology also tends to amplify other problems, making speech barriers like heavy accents more difficult to understand, or auditory barriers like a windy or noisy environment even more problematic. It's no fun trying to talk on a cell phone in a windstorm to someone with a thick lisp.

Identifying a type of barrier is not always straightforward. Although people often call accents a "language barrier," they may be more characteristic of a speech barrier. It is possible for someone with an excellent command of a second language to find it physically difficult to pronounce the words. Pronunciation is strongly affected by physical habit and so-called "muscle memory." Many people who have superb written English and can understand native English speakers perfectly can still have poor spoken English.

How do deaf and hard-of-hearing individuals overcome verbal communication barriers?

Many deaf and hard-of-hearing people use sign language in place of voiced speech.

What is sign language?

Sign languages are unique visual languages. Sign language is completely distinct from nonverbal communication like informal gestures or body language. Standardized sign languages such as American Sign Language (ASL) and British Sign Language are true languages with all the necessary linguistic rules and features of syntax, grammar, and vocabulary.

Is sign language a form of verbal communication?

No, sign language is not the same as verbal communication. Verbal communication is voiced and uses sound to convey language. Standardized sign languages such as ASL are visual-spatial communication.

Is American Sign Language a gestural or visual form of language like English?

No, ASL and other sign languages are not gestural forms of English or other languages. They are entirely unique languages with their own grammar, syntax, and vocabulary. While some users of sign language do attempt to incorporate the grammatical rules of their local spoken language, this can result in choppy, stilted, slowed signing that does not always work with the structure of a sign language.

Users of sign languages like ASL who also read and write in other languages are bilingual or multilingual. They learn and use the written form of languages like English separately from sign language. This is similar to someone who learns to use more

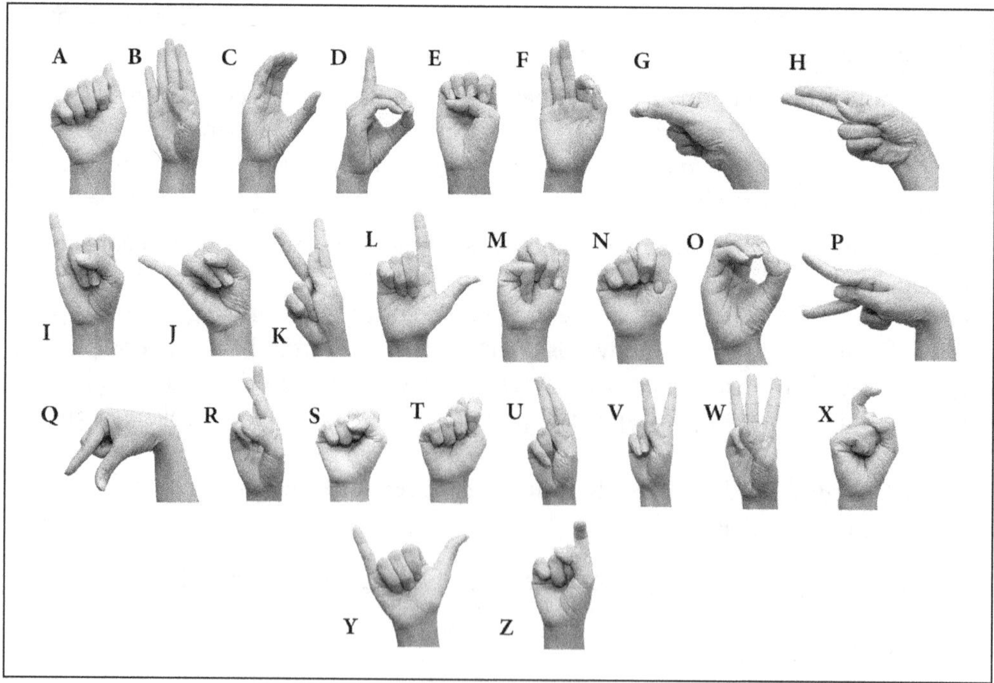

These hand positions represent different letters in American Sign Language. Sign languages also use gestures to communicate whole words, ideas, or concepts.

than one language. For example, a native English user who learns to speak, read, and write Japanese learns the vocabulary, grammar, and syntax of Japanese separately from their knowledge and use of English.

How can I communicate with someone who is deaf or hard of hearing if I don't know any sign language?

The most straightforward way to overcome communication barriers with someone who is deaf or hard of hearing is to write down what you want to say to them. Unless the person is unable to read or write in the same language as you, then this is both effective and convenient.

What technologies have improved the ability for the deaf and hard of hearing to communicate over distances?

Telephone use for the deaf and hard of hearing has been assisted through teletypewriter (TTY) for several decades. Invented in the 1960s, TTY allows for the relay of typed messages. Initially, TTY communication could happen between two TTY devices. To overcome this problem, Telecommunication Relay Services (TRS) were developed, in which a TTY communication assistant converts text messages to voice and vice versa.

In the United States, nationwide 24/7 TRS became mandated through Title IV of the Americans with Disabilities Act. Although Internet services have broadened communication options for many deaf and hard-of-hearing people, TTY and TRS remain crucial for those without reliable Internet connections and for the provision of 911 emergency services. TRS can be accessed from any telephone or TTY in the United States by dialing 711.

Developments in mobile services such as text messaging and Internet software like Skype or FaceTime videoconferencing services have significantly improved the ability for deaf and hard-of-hearing persons to engage in distance communication. These technologies have been embraced by the deaf and hard-of-hearing communities, as they are quick, convenient, and easy to use in areas that have reliable mobile or Internet services. Additionally, the cost of devices like smartphones, computers, webcams, and the necessary software is significantly lower than that of older technologies like TTY or videotelephones.

Captioning is an assistive technology that provides a text transcription of audio information in television and video media. Captions may be written by a live speech-to-text reporter or created prior to broadcast directly from the film or video's transcript. Online automated captioning services that don't rely on a human speech-to-text reporter have been released on sites such as YouTube with varying degrees of success. The subtleties of capturing the nuances of speech and sound can make speech-to-text software somewhat unreliable in its translations.

NONVERBAL COMMUNICATION

What is nonverbal communication?

Nonverbal communication is the sending of unspoken messages or enhancement of verbal communication through body language, gesture, facial expression, attire, vocal tone, and other forms of physical expression. It adds significant and sometimes even incongruent meaning to something that is being said. Tone of voice can be used to convey irony, rolling your eyes might indicate sarcasm, and a touch can elevate a simple statement of "I'm sorry" to a big-hearted expression of sympathy.

How important is nonverbal communication to understanding?

Nonverbal communication plays a critical role in understanding. Much of the meaning conveyed in communication is inferred from nonverbal cues. When nonverbal cues are stripped out, errors in understanding typically increase dramatically because the receiver does not have the same ability to interpret ambiguous words or phrases.

Is sign language nonverbal communication?

No, sign languages are a distinct style of visual-spatial communication and are completely distinct from nonverbal communication. Sign languages are true languages with rules governing grammar, syntax, and vocabulary. Gesture and "body language," on the other hand, do not have the markers of language. They do not have standardized vocabulary and do not use specific grammar or syntax. In contrast to standardized sign languages, gesture and body language enhance verbal messages by conveying feeling, emotion, and tone. Users of sign language will employ additional nonverbal communication signals to enhance their message.

How much of our communication is nonverbal?

While a significant portion of our communication is nonverbal, the amount will vary from person to person and situation to situation. A specific percentage cannot be tied to the amount of communication we do nonverbally.

Over half of what we communicate when we are in visual situations is expressed through our body language.

What is the seven percent rule?

There is a popular idea that seven percent of our communication is verbal, thirty-eight percent is vocal tone, and fifty-five percent is body language. This is a misinterpretation of studies in nonverbal communication conducted by psychologist Albert Mehrabian (1939–) in the late 1960s. On his website, Mehrabian himself states that this figure is not applicable in the way it is frequently represented in the media and only reflects the extremely narrow communication situation created in his studies. The notion that only seven percent of our communication is verbal should not be broadly applied to all communication.

What is paralanguage?

Paralanguage consists of nonword utterances and sounds we make that convey additional meaning to the words we use when we speak. These sounds can include vocal tone, intonation, volume, pitch, prosody (the melodic qualities of our speech), stress, and so on. Paralanguage can indicate grammatical elements (e.g., English speakers use an upward intonation at the end of their sentences when asking questions), or it can be used to give more nuanced meanings like emotion or irony.

Do we choose what nonverbal signals we send when communicating?

Most nonverbal communication is done either subconsciously or without significant planning or strategy. However, nonverbal communication can be done consciously by choosing what nonverbal cues to use or suppress at any given point in time. This is a strategic form of communication and is often seen during presentations and speeches.

When nonverbal communication is planned and used with skill, it appears to be natural and unpracticed; listeners absorb the additional information with ease and aren't distracted by it. When done badly, however, the nonverbal cues come across as overly rehearsed, formal, or unnatural. This can give the audience the impression that the communicator is being untruthful, patronizing, or untrustworthy.

When do we make use of nonverbal communication?

We engage in nonverbal communication continuously, often without realizing it. We may avert our eyes to indicate lack of interest, gesture to indicate that someone can move ahead of us, or choose clothes that let us blend in or stand out. Many people wear headphones as a signal that they don't want to be interrupted. Paralinguistic signals like pitching our voices upward to dissipate conflict or convey excitement provide critical information to listeners and have a profound impact on social interaction. Without nonverbal cues like tone and body language, a communicator's true meaning and intention can be easily misinterpreted.

An excellent illustration of the importance of nonverbal communication is the effect of its absence. Using nonverbal signals and paralanguage is so important to human communication that when someone doesn't give these signals, others become uneasy. People who give very few nonverbal cues, such as speaking in a flat tone or not showing facial expression, tend to come across as cold, aloof, secretive, or untrustworthy. Statements like "I didn't know how to respond—I just couldn't read him" specifically refer to a person's lack of nonverbal communication.

Lack of nonverbal communication is strongly felt in written communication. Unintentional offense or misunderstanding of intent is a common problem in text-only media such as email or text messaging. Readers will often fill in missing paralanguage by mentally "hearing" the writer's tone of voice or "seeing" their body language or facial expression. Imposing paralanguage that the writer never intended can drastically change the meaning or emotionality of a text. To fill in missing nonverbal cues, many email and text messaging users employ emoticons—such as smiling or winking faces—to indicate a friendly or joking vocal tone.

Does nonverbal communication differ across cultures?

Nonverbal cues can vary significantly across different cultures. Specific gestures can carry vastly different meanings. Thumbs-up, thumb-and-forefinger OK signs, and palm-out gestures, while perfectly acceptable in North America, have very rude meanings in many countries. Less deliberate nonverbal cues, such as making eye contact, may also carry heavy cultural significance. In many Western cultures, absence of eye contact is considered rude and inattentive, while in several Asian cultures, it is a signal of deference or respect.

Are there any universal nonverbal cues?

While most nonverbal communication is strongly influenced by cultural factors, there are some traits that appear to have meanings accepted across cultures. Vocal depth is a commonly accepted signifier for dominance, power, and authority. Researchers Paul Ekman and Wallace Friesen have conducted multiple influential studies of facial expression showing strong evidence that the facial expressions for fear, disgust, anger, sadness, and happiness are universal. Certain body postures also have strong universal indicators; slumped shoulders, a caved-in chest, and a downcast gaze typically indicate submission, while squared shoulders, a thrust-out chest, and glaring eyes show aggression.

WRITTEN COMMUNICATION

What is writing?

Linguistic anthropologist Henry Rogers defines writing as "the use of graphic marks to represent specific linguistic utterances." Writing conveys meaning by visually representing specific sounds used in language. This distinguishes writing from other forms of visual communication.

Is writing language?

Like language, writing relies on conventions of grammar, syntax, and vocabulary, along with accepted symbols or marks, to communicate. Writing, however, isn't language; it exists *within* a language and is used to represent it. Different types of writing are broken down into *writing systems*.

Are drawings or images like illustrations and cave paintings considered writing?

True writing is conventional and systematic, meaning that the writers and readers adhere to specific rules regarding the marks they use, the way they make them, the structure of the text, and the way it is read. Proto-writing such as drawings, symbols, and illustrations don't have conventions for things like syntax or grammar the way true writing does.

Additionally, writing specifically represents utterances—the sounds we make when we speak. While pictures or proto-writing can communicate information like emotions, broad ideas, specific notions, and other thoughts, they don't represent utterances or sounds.

That being said, it is sometimes useful and reasonable to include proto-writing as a form of written communication. This is especially true when dealing with common picture-based communication forms like traffic signs. In some cases within this book, the term *written communication* will include proto-writing such as illustrations or wayfinding signage.

For an explanation of proto-writing, please see below.

What are writing systems?

A writing system is writing that has been standardized or that adheres to certain conventions. All writing systems have two components: meaning and sounds. Readers are able to derive meaning from the marks and are able to utter the sounds that those marks convey. Writing systems contain a combination of logograms (single images that represent a complete grammatical word) and phonetic indicators. Even systems that are largely graphic, such as hieroglyphs or Chinese characters, contain phonetic elements. Similarly, writing systems that are predominantly phonetic will use logograms for certain words, such as "$" or "%" in English writing.

Writing systems have internal structures that are independent of the language they represent. This structure governs the actual way the marks are written down and the way in which they are read. English's internal structure is to write and read in horizontal rows from left to right. Chinese characters are most frequently written in vertical columns with each character filling a certain size of space regardless of the number of strokes in that character.

Some writing systems, such as the Maya glyphs shown here, use one symbol to convey a word or idea.

What technologies do we use for writing?

The most fundamental writing technology is something used to make a mark and a material for receiving that mark. Pens, pencils, and paper may not seem like a form of writing technology, but they do fit that description. For further discussion of the development of writing technology, see the chapter "A Brief History of Communication."

Electronic means of writing include word-processing software, email programs, text-messaging software, and publishing software such as blog platforms. Spell- and grammar-checking software are popular writing aids, and word-prediction software is particularly popular for users of mobile devices. Writing input methods technologies include keyboards, touch screens, and voice-to-text dictation software.

What are some common barriers to written communication?

Barriers to written communication are those that are specific to the individual's ability to read or write. For a broader discussion of general communication barriers, refer to the General Communication section of this chapter. Written communication barriers include illiteracy, low literacy, and print disability.

What is illiteracy (including functional illiteracy and low literacy)?

While there are many definitions, the concept of illiteracy, functional illiteracy, and low literacy usually centers on a person's ability to navigate basic and common printed materials necessary to function normally in the society in which they live. This can include an inability to read basic, simple sentences, common signs, and warning labels. Illiteracy may be caused from a lack of education, cognitive disability, or a lack of knowledge of the predominant language where a person lives. Many immigrants may experience a period of illiteracy or low literacy while they learn the language of their new home.

What is a print disability?

A print disability is a condition or combination of conditions that prevent someone from being able to read conventional print despite the person's ability to read adaptive print or despite receiving literacy instruction. Print disabilities can be caused in several ways. Learning disabilities, such as dyslexia, prevent people from understanding printed materials despite literacy instruction. Visual disabilities and vision impairment prevent people from clearly seeing the printed material. Physical disabilities make it difficult for someone to hold or otherwise handle printed material. Print disability does *not* include low literacy or poor reading skill stemming from a lack of education.

What is Braille?

Developed by French educator Louis Braille (1809–1852) in the 1820s, Braille is a system of writing that uses raised dots that can be felt with the fingertips. Braille notation is made up of six dots in a cell, which are raised in different combinations to indicate letters, numbers, or sounds. Braille can be used to write words, numbers, and music. It is one of the most recognized adaptive writing and reading systems for people with visual impairment.

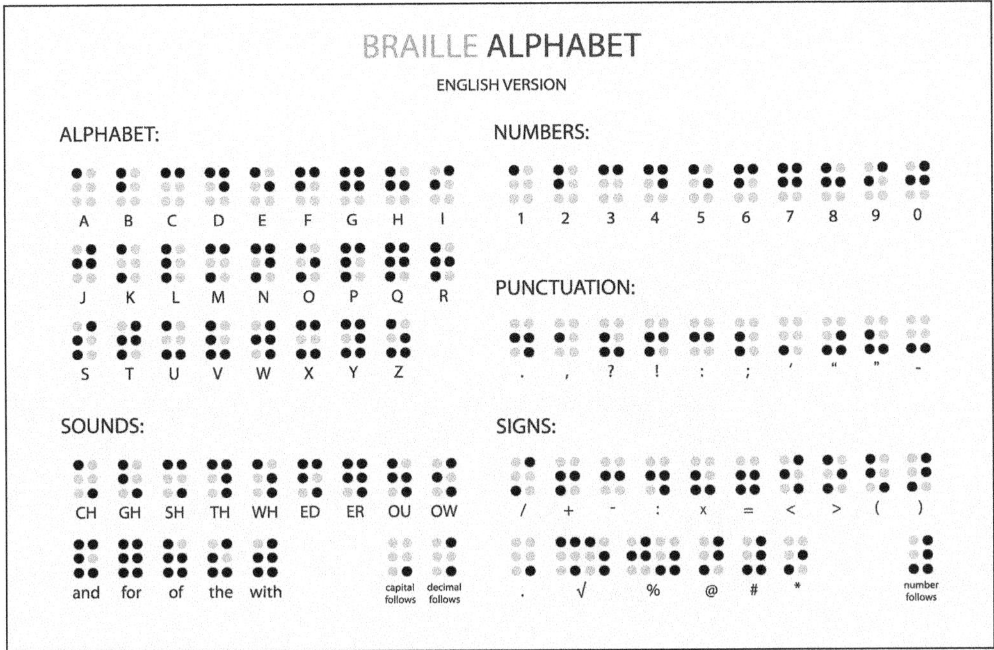

The Braille system uses raised dots to communicate symbols via touch.

What technologies exist to help people overcome print disabilities?

Many assistive technologies exist specifically to help people with print disabilities. Text-to-speech technology converts digital text to audio. Magnifiers or magnification software enlarge text. Literacy support software improves comprehension through a variety of means, including bringing text to the foreground, highlighting phonemes and word segments as they are read, or changing the colors or contrast of print on a screen. Manual assists can help to hold printed materials and turn pages.

People with print disabilities may use these technologies in combination depending on their needs. These technologies may also be used by people with vastly differing print disabilities. Text contrast and color enhancement, for example, can be beneficial to someone with a visual impairment as well as to someone with a learning disability.

A BRIEF HISTORY OF COMMUNICATION

What is true writing?

True writing, also known as full writing, is the use of a conventional system of marks to represent language and spoken word. For a full definition, refer to the first chapter, "What Is Communication?"

What is proto-writing?

Proto-writing refers to graphical marks that are capable of partial or specialized communication. The term "proto-writing" doesn't refer to the time when some graphical marks were made but rather to the degree of functionality that a mark has. Marks used in writing systems such as the English alphabet are highly functional; they can be rearranged and used in many inventive ways to create words and utterances. Pictures and symbols, however, are more limited in their function. Musical notes and mathematical symbols can't be used to spell words or to indicate phonemes, but letters can be used to spell out a musical note or mathematical symbol.

There are huge varieties of proto-writing, and they continue to play an important role in modern communication just as they did in ancient communication. Cave drawings are a form of proto-writing, as are simple tally-sticks (notched bits of bone or wood) and more complex encoding systems like the knotted cords of Inca Peru (called *quipu*). Modern examples of proto-writing are international transportation symbols, computer icons, and mathematical notation.

When did writing develop?

The earliest examples of writing date back over five thousand years to approximately 3300 B.C.E. in Sumeria. Other cultures developed writing after these dates. Notably, the Chinese invented their writing system in approximately 1200 B.C.E., while Meso-American writing begins to appear around 900 B.C.E. Most cultures did not independently invent their writing system but rather borrowed the writing systems of other cultures. Many scholars accept the Sumerian, Chinese, and Meso-American writing systems to have been the major independent inventions of writing.

What were the first examples of true writing?

The earliest example of true writing is the Sumerian cuneiform script. This writing system used wedge-shaped marks usually made by pressing a reed implement into a wet clay tablet. These tablets were baked purposefully or accidentally, preserving the marks. These early writing fragments are accounting records—tallies of goods bought, sold, traded, and owned. These writing samples demonstrate a thriving and growing economy that became too complex to be administered by memory or simple pictograms.

Who learned how to read and write?

Throughout much of history, literacy—the ability to read and write—was the realm of the social, political, or religious elite. These were the strata that have access to the necessary education, time, and materials, and the administrative, cultural, or religious impetus to learn how to read and write. While being illiterate in a largely illiterate society would not carry the same degree of stigma that it would today, societies such as the Greeks viewed the ability to read and write as being one of the characteristics that clearly divided the upper classes from the lower classes and barbarians.

Roman literacy rates were exceptionally high compared with other classical civilizations. Basic education for children was widespread, and wealthy Romans often owned slaves or hired freedmen as their personal scribes and secretaries. The quantity of conversational graffiti within ruins of cities such as Pompeii and Herculaneum indicate that literacy was not out of reach for the ordinary Roman. It should be noted, however, that modern definitions of literacy do not necessarily reflect ancient notions of literacy. What was considered "literate" for an average tradesman—who may have only needed to be able to read and write a handful of words in the course of his business—might not have counted as literacy for a more high-born Roman male who received extensive schooling in reading, writing, and composition. Differences in expectations and education ran along gender, class, and ethnic lines, preventing us from developing a complete understanding of the average rate of functional literacy within Roman society.

Literacy in medieval Europe continued to be the purview of the upper class and clergy. In England during the early Middle Ages, the ability to read and write was restricted almost exclusively to those belonging to religious orders. Literacy was such a distinguishing mark of clergy that people charged with a crime could take a literacy test and, if successful, be tried for their crime in the ecclesiastical courts where there was no capital punishment.

What are pictograms?

Pictograms are simple pictures that represent objects. Pictograms are a form of proto-writing and appear in cultures across the world. While pictograms were precursors to true writing, they are still in use today. Signs such as male and female figures on bathroom doors are modern uses of pictograms.

What are hieroglyphs?

Hieroglyphs are a form of writing that combines pictograms and phonographic marks that indicate specific sounds. A hieroglyph character can represent the literal object it depicts, or it could indicate a speech sound or grammatical component.

While Egyptian hieroglyphics are the most famous form of this writing style, many cultures used hieroglyphs, including the Phoenicians, Hittites, and Mayans.

Hieroglyphs, such as these found in Egypt, use pictograms and photographic marks instead of lettering.

What are Linear A and Linear B?

Linear A and B are the earliest examples of writing scripts found in Europe. Linear B has been deciphered into Mycenaean Greek. Linear A has not been successfully deciphered and seems to write an unknown language.

The Linear A and B tablets were discovered in 1900 by archaeologist Arthur Evans (1851–1941) during his excavations in Knossos. The clay tablets that bear both the Linear A and B scripts appear to be bureaucratic records accidentally preserved by a fire. The Linear B texts have been dated between 1550 and 1200 B.C.E., while Linear A dates back to 1750–1450 B.C.E.

What are alphabets?

Alphabets are writing systems that rely on marks that indicate basic phonemes (smallest unit of sound, such as a single consonant or vowel) of a language. Alphabets have signs that indicate all phonemes, both consonants and vowels, which distinguish them from writing systems like abjads, where only consonants are represented.

Alphabet-based writing systems are not purely phonemic. Marks like punctuation, numbers, symbols, and even spaces are used to convey written meaning when using alphabets.

There are many alphabets in use today. Many alphabets, including the English alphabet, are descendants of the Latin alphabet, which itself evolved from the Greek alphabet. Widely used modern alphabets include Arabic, Cyrillic, Greek, and Hebrew.

What tools were used for early writing?

Innumerable tools have been used for making and preserving writing and other marks. Cave paintings were made by brushing, wiping, scratching, or spraying natural pigments onto walls. As writing developed, a wide array of both mark-making tools and materials for receiving were developed. Common implements used for early writing were the stylus—a pointed implement made from materials like reed, bone, or metal—to make marks on wet clay or soft wax tablets and brushes and reed pens dipped in ink or paints were used to write or paint marks on plant material such as papyrus rolls and slips of bamboo or wood. More permanent or monumental writing was often recorded by chiseling or engraving stone or metal.

Around the second century B.C.E., parchment and vellum began to be used in the Mediterranean. Parchment is an extremely thin sheet of goat- or sheepskin that has been stretched, limed, and dried. Vellum is a similar material made from calfskin. Parchment and vellum can receive marks on both sides, unlike papyrus, which can only carry writing on one side. More flexible and durable than papyrus and other plant-based materials of the time, parchment and vellum could be folded and bound down one side, allowing for the creation of books. From the second to fifteenth centuries C.E., it remained the standard writing surface material in Europe.

Paper, made of pressed pulp from plant materials or rags, is traditionally attributed to having been invented in the Chinese imperial court around 100 C.E. This date, however, may be much later than the actual invention of paper. Archaeological evidence for papermaking going back to the second century B.C.E. and even as far back as the sixth century B.C.E. have been found in other regions of China.

The use of paper did not diffuse into Europe until the tenth century C.E., having been brought to Spain via trade routes that stretched to Asia. Use of paper continued to spread, reaching Germany by the fourteenth century C.E. and supplanting parchment as the primary writing surface across Europe by the fifteenth century C.E.

Pens have been popular writing implements for centuries. Initially created from cut reeds that were then dipped in ink or paint, reed pens eventually gave way to the finer and more versatile quill pens cut from the flight feathers of large birds. The use of fountain pens with ink reservoirs is recorded in European literature from as early as the fifteenth century C.E.

When was the printing press invented?

There is evidence for the invention of movable-type printing presses as early as the eleventh century in China. The huge range of individual characters required for such a press, however, meant that it was not taken up as a viable means of reproducing printed text.

When people refer to the invention of the printing press, they are usually referring to the invention of the movable-type press by Johannes Gutenberg (c. 1400–1468), c. 1440 in Mainz, Germany. A goldsmith by trade, Gutenberg developed movable and reusable cast type that could be set into a matrix on a basic screw press. Gutenberg also created an oil-based ink that released from the type more easily and penetrated the paper more effectively.

This system, which Gutenberg continued to refine, allowed for the production of printed text at a rate unfathomable in its day. Gutenberg began to use his printing press commercially in 1454, and in 1455 printed a forty-two-line Bible, the first book to be printed in this fashion. The success of this press was such that its basic mechanics remained in use within the printing industry until the nineteenth century.

This reproduction of an antique press is similar to the one developed by Gutenberg to mass produce the Bible.

What effect did Gutenberg's printing press have on literacy in Europe?

The ability of printing presses to produce texts and books cheaply and quickly certainly helped prompt an increase in literacy. Prior to the printing press, the only texts available were laboriously copied by hand—a painstakingly slow and expensive process. Access to books was limited, and without a variety of texts available to read, most people had limited means by which to practice this skill.

After the invention of the printing press, literacy spread rapidly as both access to and demand for books expanded. Additionally, the printing press helped create more consistent grammar and spelling due to the reduction of the inconsistencies that naturally came with individually scribing copies of texts. While Europe was made up of many literate societies before the printing press came along, Gutenberg's movable-type press helped pave the way for mass literacy.

It must be noted, however, that the printing press was not the only factor in growth of literacy during the fifteenth century. Other social factors, such as the rise of Protestantism with its emphasis on individual study of the Bible, the expansion of schooling, and the rise of vernacular languages such as English and German as acceptable languages in which to read and write, also contributed to the rise in literacy after Gutenberg created his press.

ORALITY, ORAL TRADITIONS, AND ORATORY

What is orality?

Orality is a culture's use of oral communication to preserve and communicate ideas. Different cultures at different times in history have relied on different degrees of orality as the dominant method of sending and receiving messages as well as preserving history and traditions. Orality can exist within a culture despite members of that society having use of reading and writing.

Communications scholar Walter J. Ong (1912–2003) developed a useful method of distinguishing the degree to which a culture or society depends on orality for preservation of history, knowledge, culture, and traditions. *Primary orality* is "the orality of a culture totally untouched by any knowledge of writing or print," while *secondary orality* is the orality of more high-tech cultures in which a "new orality is sustained by telephone, radio, television, and other electronic devices that depend for their existence and functioning on writing and print."

By Ong's definition, many cultures that are no longer primarily oral can still sustain very strong oral traditions.

What is oral tradition?

Oral tradition is oral communication that serves to preserve, share, and reproduce a group's history, knowledge, and culture through multiple generations. The generation-to-generation sharing and preservation of information is a key marker of oral traditions, and they separate traditional oral material from popular culture or passing pieces of knowledge like a testimonial. Oral tradition takes many forms, including but not limited to poetry, song, stories, folklore, sayings, expressions, and proverbs.

Oral tradition is always present in cultures with primary orality (where the entire culture is illiterate), but it also exists within literate societies. Oral traditions and writing are not mutually exclusive; many literate cultures, such as some indigenous North American tribes, continue to preserve oral records as part of their living histories. It is worth noting, however, that oral and written record-keeping are distinct means of preserving knowledge and rely on different mechanisms for both information retention and communication. The mechanisms and processes by which a group preserves its knowledge in an oral fashion are not always analogous to written record-keeping and are not always easy for people who rely on written records to fully grasp.

How reliable is oral tradition in passing down practical information like history or environmental knowledge?

Oral cultures and traditions produce reliable, complex, sophisticated banks of knowledge. While oral tradition was long thought to be inherently subjective and unreliable, this notion has shifted over the years as understanding of the means through which oral tradition is passed down increases. The means by which this knowledge is shared and preserved in the group's collective memory involves a complex intellectual framework and memory skills. Cultures with strong oral traditions integrate fact-checking activities within their storytelling or information sharing that help increase the reliability and consistency of the information—much like a spoken peer-review process. It is worth noting that authors of written materials are no less subject to the biases, contexts, flawed reasoning, and gaps in knowledge than are the keepers of oral traditions.

What is oratory?

Oratory is the discipline and practice of the delivery of persuasive speeches to audiences. While rhetoric is the theory and craft of argument and persuasion, oratory refers specifically to the craft of delivering and performing persuasive speeches. It utilizes rhetoric as well as vocal and physical performance skills.

While an oration is delivered to a live audience and is responsive to people's reactions, the impact of an oration can last well beyond the time it was delivered. Famous orations such as African American civil rights leader Dr. Martin Luther King Jr.'s (1929–1968) "I Have a Dream" speech, U.S. president Abraham Lincoln's (1809–1865) Gettysburg Address, and Athenian statesman Demosthenes's (384–322 B.C.E.) Third Philippic had major impacts regarding the path of important historical events. Major historic orations such as these continue to be studied, analyzed, and imitated by scholars and speakers today.

Are oratory and public speaking the same thing?

Oratory is a branch of public speaking. While all oratory is public speaking, not all public speaking is considered oratory. Public speaking can encompass a wide variety of activities—giving a toast at a wedding reception, delivering a pep talk to a sports team, presenting an educational lecture, telling a story, and more. Oratory, on the other hand, focuses specifically on the skilled delivery of persuasive speeches. An orator is seeking to move his or her audience toward a specific action or way of thinking.

Martin Luther King Jr. is shown here giving his "I Have a Dream" speech in Washington, D.C., in 1963. The combination of his writing and oratory style have made it a model of inspirational public speaking ever since.

Oration often incorporates more performance art than other styles of public speaking. Eloquence, passion, and expressiveness are always hallmarks of famous orators. Oratory uses the personal beliefs of the orator as one of its persuasive tools and plays on audience emotion to reinforce its stances.

How is oratory different from storytelling?

Oratory deals with persuasive speaking on nonfictional or practical topics. While good oratory has a strong narrative component and the orator may choose to incorporate some storytelling, an oration always has a real-world focus. Storytelling may be used to persuade, instruct, or entertain and may include factual events or fiction in its style.

How did formal oratory develop among Western cultures?

Oratory as Western cultures perceive it became more formalized in Greece in approximately the fifth century B.C.E. as a result of the Athenian judicial system. This system required that both prosecutors and defendants give speeches pleading their case. Most evidence of Attic and Hellenistic oratory can only be found in texts concerning rhetoric, and as rhetoric forms the content of an oration, the two of them seem to have developed side by side in Greece.

Romans incorporate the practices of Greek oratory and rhetoric into their own political and educational culture. Oratory was one of the ways a Roman could forge a political career, and military officers could be expected to address troops or foreign dignitaries. The ability to speak persuasively—sometimes for hours on end—had significant impact on a politician's effectiveness, particularly in a society where literacy was far from universal and access to written records could be difficult to obtain.

Oratory formed a significant part of Roman education and remained a significant skill throughout the Roman period, particularly during the Republic and early Empire. While the study of oratory in Europe blended with the study of rhetoric, the practice of oratory continued to be critical for politicians and religious leaders. The legacy of grand Roman oratory as a means to sway and persuade large numbers of people remain obvious today in political speeches and religious preaching and sermonizing.

How has television, radio, and the Internet affected modern oratory?

Television, radio, and Internet communications have made it possible for oratorical performances to be recorded and shared. Vocal tone and physical performance are both strong factors in a speech's impact. We may have transcripts from famous orations dating back to antiquity, but without knowledge of the tone of voice or gestures used by the original speaker, we are missing a significant amount of information regarding the speech's hidden messages and true impact. Modern communication technology allows for those nuances to be preserved.

Radio and television distribution allowed for a dramatic increase in an orator's reach. While the full impact of both the content of a speech and the way a speech was delivered was previously only available to people watching the speaker in person, developments in telecommunications allowed for that impact to be experienced by an exponentially larger, geographically diverse audience. Radio was the first communication method that made oratory widely available to distant audiences, and it played a critical role in times of significant tribulation such as during World War II when British prime minister Winston Churchill was able to make his famous and inspiring speeches heard to a battered, beleaguered population. Similarly, radio and television allowed for the wide dissemination of the orations of Indian spiritual leader Mahatma Gandhi (1869–1948), Martin Luther King Jr., and many other influences—both good and evil—of modern history.

The Internet, through its capabilities of both preserving orations and allowing on-demand access to them, has further expanded the audiences to which great speeches are available. Orations and grand speeches are resurging in popularity outside of their traditional confines of politics and religion. By increasing access to and awareness of historical and contemporary speeches, websites such as TED.com and YouTube are reinvigorating interest in the speech arts, including the grand, soaring styles and techniques that are the markers of oratory.

What are some stylistic differences between an oratorical speech and other forms of speeches?

Oratorical speeches tend to be grand in style. While the language and word choices often trend toward straightforward words at a relatively moderate level of vocabulary, the manner in which they are delivered is dramatic and charged. Oratory relies on a buildup of anticipation and energy far more than any other style of speech. A superb summary of this effect was given by Sir Winston Churchill in an 1897 essay on oratorical delivery: "The climax of oratory is reached by rapid succession of waves of sound and vivid pictures." Churchill's speeches and orations to the British parliament and public in the 1930s and 1940s demonstrate the grand, soaring language and patterns used in oratory. These can be directly compared to U.S. president Franklin D. Roosevelt's (1882–1945) "Fireside Chats" delivered during the same period, which were not oratorical in style but instead used a friendlier, intimate, casual tone for radio listeners.

Oratory makes an extremely strong appeal to the emotions of the audience. A skilled orator will achieve this in different ways, but when comparing an oratorical speech to other types of public speeches, such as lectures, toasts, or reports, the emotional tone of an oration is undeniable. President Barack Obama's (1961–) statement following the October 1, 2015, shootings on the campus of Umpqua Community College in Roseburg, Oregon, demonstrates heightened emotional appeal through the use of personal restraint.

Photographers and radio broadcasters are shown in this 1939 picture recording one of President Franklin D. Roosevelt's "Fireside Chats" to the American people.

Oratory demonstrates stronger awareness and use of prosody (the use of rhythm, patterns, stress, and intonation) within the delivery than other styles of speaking. This is what gives the words of an orator power, emotion, interest, and variety. Use of prosodic devices such as pauses, drawn-out words, enunciation, and speed are more obvious in oratory than in other speeches. Superb examples of oratorical prosody can be heard in Martin Luther King Jr.'s "I Have a Dream" speech on August 28, 1963, and in Winston Churchill's VE Day speech on May 8, 1945.

COMMUNICATING OVER DISTANCES

What is long-distance communication?

Long-distance communication is the practice of issuing a message from one geographic location that can be received by someone at another geographic location. Smoke signals, lighthouses, and telephones may all be considered long-distance communication. A signpost, however, would not be considered long-distance communication as the person leaving the message and the person receiving the message do so in the same location, even though the sending and receiving happen at different times.

What were the earliest methods of long-distance communication?

Prior to the invention of telecommunications, long-distance communication was limited to signaling systems and postal systems. Signaling was used to send relatively simple, straightforward messages while longer or politically important messages would be sent via a postal system using messengers.

What forms of signals were used in ancient long-distance communication?

Signaling was carried out in a wide variety of ways. Smoke signals, fire signals, horns, noise-making, lighthouses, and mirrors can all be employed to transmit coded signals to someone at considerable distances.

Variations on these methods can be found in archaeological and historic evidence in cultures throughout the world. Famous examples of ancient signaling systems include:

- North American aboriginal smoke signals
- Chinese smoke and fire signal towers along the Great Wall of China
- Fire signals of Lachish, Israel

What are some examples of modern signaling distance communication?

Communication by signal continues to be in use, particularly in military or emergency circumstances. Examples include:

- Semaphore flags
- Naval signal lamps
- International maritime signal flags

Semaphore is a system of using two flags (or lights) held in various positions to indicate letters or other symbols. The system was commonly used to communicate between sailing vessels before the era of electronic communications.

Who created the first postal system?

It is difficult to determine which culture developed the "first" postal system. Postal, or messenger relay systems, have been independently developed by different cultures throughout history. Ancient states that covered a large territory and retained some semblance of stability over long periods of time all had robust postal systems. Some of these systems were more successful than others and garnered admiration even from competing states. Greek historian Xenophon wrote favorably of the Persian postal network in his *Cyraopaedia* (VIII 6.17–18), as quoted in Karen Radner's *State Correspondence in the Ancient World: From New Kingdom Egypt to the Roman Empire:* "It is plain that this is the fastest land travel on earth. And it is excellent to be appraised of everything as quickly as possible so that one can deal with it at top speed."

Written records dating to approximately 2000 B.C.E. refer to an early postal system in Egypt. Records from the Chinese Zhou dynasty dating to approximately 1000 B.C.E. provide evidence for another early postal system. Truly effective ancient postal systems relied on the presence of well-maintained, relatively secure roads to allow for the couriers to travel at some level of speed. Well-organized postal systems were remarkably efficient; the Roman *cursus publicus* (public post) ranked messages according to urgency, and those deemed important enough could travel up to 270 kilometers (170 miles) in twenty-four hours.

The Roman *cursus publicus* was an organizational and administrative feat of communication. Aspects of this system were widely adopted by other cultures and remained in use for centuries after the decline of the Roman Empire.

How secure was ancient postal communication?

Being a courier has been a dangerous profession throughout history. Ancient postal communication could be plagued by spies, robbers, highwaymen, and accidents. Important couriers or messengers were often accompanied or preceded by guards who could ensure that the roads were clear of threat and the postal relay stations were ready to receive them. Many postal systems restricted access to relay stations or resources to official couriers, which allowed for even greater speed, efficiency, and security.

Securing the documents themselves was also highly important. Seals played a considerable role in identifying the sender of a letter, and there were some truly ingenious ways of creating seals beyond the old "glob-of-red-wax" cliché. Assyrians, for example, would bake their clay message tablets inside thin, clay envelopes that bore the seal of a sender and had to be smashed open to retrieve the actual message.

When was postal service first available in America?

The first official colonial American postal service dates to 1639 and was established in Boston, Massachusetts. Primarily used for sending and receiving mail overseas, the service operated out of a tavern owned by Richard Fairbanks by decree of the General Court of Massachusetts.

When was the first U.S. postal service created?

The U.S. postal system was initiated during the American Revolution. The second Continental Congress created a postal system outside of colonial rule in 1775 and named Benjamin Franklin (1706–1790) as the first postmaster general.

The 1781 ratification of the Articles of Confederation set out Congress's exclusive right to establish post offices, and governmental monopoly on mail and mail services was solidified by Congress in 1782.

What was the Pony Express?

The Pony Express was a private mail service that operated between 1860 and 1861. Recognizing a need to open up lines of postal communication between the East and West coasts of the United States, businessmen William Hepburn Russell (1812–1872), William Bradford Waddell (1807-1872), and Alexander Majors (1814–1900) started the Pony Express as a subsidiary company of their Central Overland California and Pikes Peak Express Company operation.

The Pony Express covered a route of approximately two thousand miles that stretched from St. Joseph, Missouri, to Sacramento, California. The Pony Express utilized approximately 190 way stations spaced ten to fifteen miles apart, which allowed riders to have a steady supply of fresh, rested horses for the entire duration of their journey. Through their relay system, the Pony Express could deliver a message overland from coast to coast in less than ten days. Despite its efficiency, the Pony Express was burdened by high operating costs that did not cover expenses and failed to secure key government contracts for mail delivery. After just nineteen months in operation and approximately three hundred round trips, the Pony Express ceased operations.

Much of the ongoing fame of the Pony Express, including tales of the exploits of the couriers themselves, may be attributed to the Pony Express's prominence as a permanent part of William "Buffalo Bill" Cody's show entitled Buffalo Bill's Wild West and Congress of Rough Riders of the World. This show replayed the derring-do of the Pony Express riders, grossly exaggerated and mostly untrue. Nevertheless, Buffalo Bill's show, along with artists and later filmmakers, helped preserve the memory of the Pony Express as a fixture in American Wild West lore.

What is telegraphy?

There are two forms of telegraphy: optical and electrical. Optical telegraphy is a system by which messages are sent through coded visual signals that are seen by a receiver across a clear sightline. Semaphore is a form of optical telegraphy.

When most people think of telegraphy or a telegraph, what they picture is the electrical telegraph—a device that sends messages through electrical impulses over a wire. The electrical impulses are picked up by a receiver, which operates in an on-off (also known as binary) capacity. The receiver transmits a signal—such as a beep, a click, or dots and dashes—based on the electrical impulses it receives.

Throughout this section, the terms "telegraph" and "telegraphy" will refer to the electrical telegraph unless otherwise stated.

How did telegraphy change the way we communicate?

The creation of electrical telegraphy was also the creation of telecommunications. It was the first medium by which humans could communicate instantaneously across hundreds of miles. While optical telegraphs such as the semaphore had been in use since the mid-1700s, the electrical telegraph was not in development until the mid-1800s. The advantages of electrical telegraphy over optical telegraphy are immediately evident: electrical telegraphy requires no sightline and can operate at any time of day or night in any kind of weather—a feat not possible through optical telegraphy.

Who invented the telegraph?

As with many inventions, there were several scientists and inventors working on similar technology at the same time. In the 1830s, telegraphs were independently created in England and in America. In England, British inventors Sir William F. Cooke (1806–1879) and Sir Charles Wheatstone (1802–1875) invented a Ouiji boardlike telegraph that received messages through a series of magnetized needles that pointed at letters and numbers on a panel. Meanwhile in the United States, inventors Samuel F. B. Morse (1791–1872), Leonard Gale (1800–1883), and Alfred Vale (1807–1859) developed a single-circuit system that worked by an operator pushing down a key, which then sent an electrical signal to a receiver, which also pushed down a key that created impressions of dots or dashes on a strip of paper.

When was the first telegraph built?

The first functional telegraph demonstration line was built by Samuel F. B. Morse and Alfred Vale in 1844 between Washington, D.C., and Baltimore, Maryland. As the electric signals sent over the wire could only travel slightly over thirty-two kilometers (nineteen miles) before becoming too weak to receive, this system used relay apparatuses along the

Students in New York City are shown here taking a Marconi class in telegraphy in 1912.

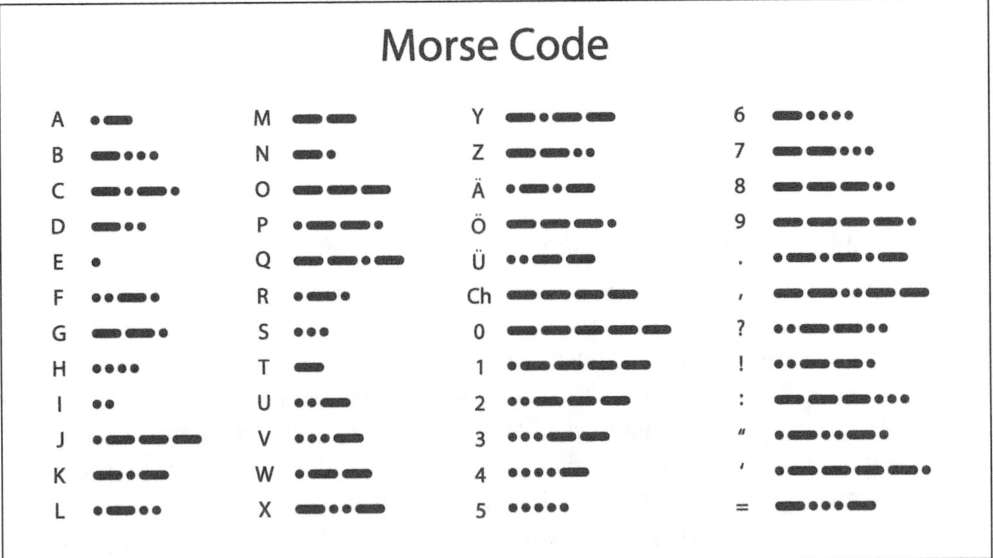

Morse code uses a system of dots and dashes.

telegraph wire to receive and resend the signals every thirty-two kilometers. The first official telegraph transmission was sent on May 24, 1844, from Morse in Washington to Vale in Baltimore.

What is Morse code?

Morse code is the code system created by Morse and Vale for use over their telegraph. It translates the alphabet into a series of dots and dashes, the complexity of which is determined by the frequency that the letter is used in communication. The more common the letter, the shorter and less complex the code for that letter is. Initially, Morse code signals were marked on paper by the telegraph receiver. As operators became adept at understanding the code, the paper marks were replaced by audible beeps that the operators were able to immediately translate.

How did the telegraph change the way people consumed information?

The telegraph had a profound effect on information consumption through newspapers. Newspapers and news agencies could receive dispatches from reporters in geographically distant locations and immediately release the information to eager news consumers.

The speed of telegraph news reporting significantly altered the news cycle and people's notions of what was timely and newsworthy. The news cycle was shortened considerably as reports from all over America could be transmitted in hours or minutes instead of days or weeks. Telegraph receiving stations at telegraph offices, hotels, and post offices could attract crowds of people waiting to receive the newest information from across the country. The activity of anxious crowds waiting outside telegraph stations for battlefront news during the U.S. Civil War is somewhat analogous to the real-time "news tickers" that came into widespread use on cable news networks over a century later during the events of September 11, 2001. Both the Civil War and 9/11 crowds were ravenous for swift reporting of the news, as quickly as possible. Furthermore, both events signaled a sharp increase in public demand for almost impossibly swift, up-to-the-minute news reporting.

How are the telegraph and the American Civil War connected?

The Civil War was the first war that relied on telecommunication for military purposes. The Union had significant advantages in telegraph resources over the Confederates, and at the start of the war, commercial telegraph lines were co-opted by the military. The U.S. Military Telegraph (USMT) Corps was established and worked in partnership with commercial telegraph operators; however, the USMT remained independent from military control and used civilian operators. Many of the officers and managers within the USMT were also employees of various private telegraph companies.

Prior to the Civil War, there were no telegraph lines to the War Department or White House. President Abraham Lincoln and his advisors needed to use the clerks at commercial telegraph stations to relay messages. This created high risk of security breaches, so in early 1862, telegraph lines were run directly to the War Department offices in Washington. As the military also laid huge lengths of telegraph lines to battlefronts and other military stations, President Lincoln was able to immediately communicate with his officers and generals at the warfront. This enabled the off-site president to keep close tabs on the activities of military commanders, prevent them from making unilateral decisions, issue direct orders to the field, and assert his leadership. Lincoln's use of the telegraph as a real-time communication tool for military operations had no precedent, and it played a significant part in the outcome of the war.

The Civil War affected the landscape of the telegraph as much as the telegraph affected the war. The USMT laid fifteen thousand miles of telegraph wire in order to conduct military communication. Although the wire was initially intended to be disposable, the creation of insulated copper wire meant that it would remain in place and in use for long after the war's conclusion. During the war itself, commercial telegraph companies cooperated with the USMT and gave priority to all military telegraph communication coming over their wires. In return, not only did the government defray many costs of the shared military-commercial telegraph offices, but it also allowed cooperative commercial telegraph companies to use the military lines to send private, paid communication when the lines and operators weren't busy.

The combination of low-cost operations and additional reach of private telegraph communication played a part in the considerable profits reaped by commercial telegraph companies during the Civil War. The commercial telegraph companies continued to benefit even after action and hostilities ceased. After the war, the USMT repaired its telegraph lines along with the badly damaged lines in former Confederate territory. After the work was completed and control of private telegraph lines was returned to their original owners, the USMT sold off its equipment and infrastructure to various commercial telegraph companies at rock-bottom prices. In this way, the Civil War created a sudden, rapid expansion of telegraph lines and capabilities, opening up rapid communication in areas of the country that had previously been relatively isolated.

What is telephone communication?

A telephone transmits sound across distances via electronic signals sent over a wire, cables, or other transmission lines. Telephones convert sound waves into electric signals through a transmitter—a microphone to capture and input sound—and then reconstructs the signals into recognizable speech or audio information through a receiver. Telephones allow for people on either end of the line to speak at the same time.

Early telephones were connected via a direct line. As the technology was adopted, this changed to a switchboard system used to change line connections depending on the telephone numbers people want to reach. The switching system for connecting telephones is known as the public switched telephone network (PSTN).

Mobile phone technology first used radio frequency carriers, which were then switched to the PSTN in order to connect wireless mobile phones with other receivers. This developed into the cellular network architecture for telephone connection. In a cellular network, radio service is divided among specific geographic regions, known as cells, each of which is serviced from a base station in their area. This system allows for transmission of digital information, which makes sending and accessing data such as text messages possible.

When was the telephone invented?

As with most technologies, the invention of the telephone spreads several years and is influenced by several people working around the same time. Work on the electric transmission of tones and voices was taking place between the 1840s and 1870s by an assortment of people, including American engineer Elisha Gray (1835–1901), Italian inventor Antonio Meucci (1808–1889), and German scientist Johann Philipp Reis (1834–1874). It is Scottish-born inventor Alexander Graham Bell (1847–1922), however, who is commonly credited with having invented the telephone and who first received a patent for the telephone in 1876.

While other engineers and inventors had a hand in developing the first telephone, it was Alexander Graham Bell who received the first patent.

What were the legal disputes surrounding Bell's telephone patents?

During the 1880s, several individuals initiated legal action against Bell for his telephone patents. Several inventors came forward claiming to have invented the telephone first and sometimes accusing Bell of having stolen their technology. One major player in the patent lawsuits was telegraph giant Western Union, who claimed that many of Bell's patents were invalid or inoperable. The action taken by Western Union brought forth patent caveats (official notices of intent to file patents at later dates with descriptions and drawings of inventions but no physical invention to inspect) filed by Elisha Gray and Antonio Meucci.

Among these legal disputes and patent filing cases, the courts ruled that Bell had pioneered the invention of telephones. Bell was granted extremely broad rights over telecommunication technology, which gave him a legal monopoly over the industry.

When were mobile phones invented?

Mobile phone development began in the early 1970s with the first mobile phone call being placed on April 3, 1973, by Motorola employee Martin Cooper from Manhattan to the Bell Labs in New Jersey. Ten years later, Motorola's DynaTAC 8000X came onto the market as the first commercially available mobile phone. Within its first year of sales, three hundred thousand units were sold.

What are smartphones?

Smartphones are mobile phones with an interactive display screen and an operating system. These phones function more like computers with telephone capabilities rather than true telephones. With the development of the third-generation (3G) telephone networks in the early 2000s, data exchange rates capable of transmitting photos, emails, and other data-heavy items became available. Prior to this time, smartphones were fairly limited to the transmission of voice and text messages.

What is text messaging?

Text messaging is a method of sending written messages to mobile phones and smartphones using a digital phone network. Text messaging refers to written messages sent over SMS (Short Message Service) and multimedia messages sent over MMS (Multimedia Message Service).

How has text messaging affected language?

As with any new technology, text messaging has introduced new words into our language—such as "emoji" and "texter." Most famously (or perhaps infamously), text messaging has popularized the use of acronyms and "text-speak" expressions in spoken language, such as someone saying "OMG" in a conversation instead of the long form "Oh, my God."

The enthusiastic use of acronyms in text messaging has been the source of some concern regarding a decay in the language skills of youth who use text messaging as their preferred method of contact. Remarkably, however, a similar concern existed when telegraph communication became readily available. Telegraph operators abbreviated and shortened as many words as possible in order to increase the speed and economy of their communication. This created some hand-wringing that telegraph shorthand would infiltrate regular language and butcher it beyond recognition. Needless to say, the concerns were somewhat overblown.

Another contemporary fear regarding the effect of text messaging on our communication habits is that people will become accustomed to a shorter, terser, less elegant form of speech due to the brevity of text messages. It should be noted, however, that throughout history, language style has fluctuated due to fashions in technology, philosophy, and notions of cultural propriety. A "plain" style of speech became hugely popular in the seventeenth century, when philosophers such as Francis Bacon (1561–1626) and Thomas Hobbes (1588–1679) felt that ornamented speech was not fitting with the advancements in scientific thought of the time. Later, the influence of neoclassicism in art and literature rejuvenated interest in emotional, ornamented language. Text messaging may influence a current trend for a terser style of communication, but it is one small shrub in an ever-shifting landscape of language.

What is VoIP?

VoIP stands for Voice over Internet Protocol. VoIP is an alternative method for transmitting voice that converts sound waves into data instead of analog signals. The data is then sent over the Internet to the receiver and converted back into sound. Computers, most mobile phones, and traditional phones fitted with a VoIP adapter are capable of making VoIP calls. Most VoIP providers now allow VoIP calls to be sent to regular telephones. VoIP is becoming a popular alternative to traditional phone lines as the cost for the service is often cheaper.

Why should VoIP users be concerned about calls to 911 or similar emergency services?

VoIP providers don't necessarily connect to 911 or other emergency phone services that use the public safety answering points (PSAP) call routing system the way that non-VoIP phone carriers do. As such, it cannot be taken for granted that a VoIP service will allow 911 or emergency service calls. The U.S. Federal Communications Commission (FCC) has also reported 911 calls placed over VoIP systems being sent to the wrong lines of the PSAP. Furthermore, vital information such as the caller's location are not always correctly sent to the PSAP through the VoIP provider, meaning the operators cannot trace the location of the VoIP call. Finally, power outages may render VoIP services inoperable, meaning that emergency calls cannot be placed at all.

In an effort to minimize risks to people trying to contact 911 and emergency services, FCC requires VoIP service providers to meet specific regulations for such calls, such as providing emergency access to their user's address and location details. However, there still remains the need for VoIP users to be knowledgeable about potential 911 call limitations and to keep their address and location information updated with their VoIP provider.

Similar concerns with VoIP phone access to emergency service numbers have also been reported in countries outside of the United States.

MASS MEDIA: NEWSPAPERS, RADIO, AND TV

What are mass media?

Mass media are communication methods or systems of carrying information to large numbers of people at once. A method or system of transmitting information is called a "medium" (plural "media"). A message conveyed over a mass medium is the same for everyone receiving it.

Mass media generally has the characteristics of being impersonal (not directed at a specific individual), delayed (it takes some time to transmit the message to the audience after it has been created), and one-way. There are exceptions to all these characteristics, especially when considering the many-to-many nature of social media and other highly interactive forms of online media.

What are common forms of mass media?

Mass media can be classified in many ways. Typically, it falls into three distinct categories: print media, electronic media, and new media.

Mass media, just as television broadcasts, are forms of communication that are not directed at any one individual but at a broad group.

Print media includes anything that is put down in writing and accessible to a large number of people simultaneously. It can include formats as varied as direct mail pamphlets and billboards; however, the dominant forms of mass print media are books, magazines, and newspapers.

Electronic media encompasses media that is transmitted through electronic channels that are predominantly one-way and that, at one point, had an analog or nondigital form. Radio and television are electronic media.

New media is an amorphous, rather undefined range of media that includes the Internet, the World Wide Web, Internet-based broadcasting such as podcasts and blogs, video games, social media, and smartphones. New media is digital, usually has an interactive component, and can often be manipulated by an end user. It often contains a component that collects data from its users regarding their behavior or any information they input into the medium. New media also often demonstrates a form of information organization and cross-referencing wherein information sources are connected through hyperlinks or other networking tools. New media and the Internet will be discussed in the section "How the Internet Changed Everything" later in this chapter.

The lines between different forms of mass media can be blurry. For example, Netflix exhibits many of the traits of new media, such as enhanced user selection, digital transmission, and a personalized experience but the content it provides is either taken from television—an electronic medium—or is created following a format and style that is very similar to traditional television shows. So is Netflix new media, electronic media, or both? Are newspapers that publish their content both in a print format and on their website still considered print media, or are they a hybrid of print media and new media? There are no hard-and-fast answers to these questions. As new media continues to develop and the nature of other forms of mass media evolve as well, these questions and others like them will continue to arise.

When did the earliest newspapers appear?

Evidence for a daily written announcement accessible to the public exists from Rome dating from c. 130 B.C.E. Called the *Acta Diurna,* this tablet was posted on a wall during Senate meetings, informing local citizenry of official business in the public interest as well as general interest items. China also had a precursor to newspapers during the Han Dynasty (206 B.C.E.—220 C.E.) through the copies of edicts. These documents contained government news that was circulated to officials.

The earliest versions of newspapers as we conceive of them today are the seventeenth-century *Corantos*. Printed in Germany, Switzerland, Vienna, and Belgium in the early 1600s, these one-sheet papers distributed information about events in Europe. English versions were printed in Amsterdam, then exported to London and Paris.

The true precursors to newspapers began appearing in England in the mid-1600s. Initially these publications were called *Diurnals,* a term that was popularly replaced with "newspaper" around 1660. The earliest true newspaper in England was the *Lon-*

don Gazette, which began publication in 1665 as the *Oxford Gazette.* This was a government-approved publication that provided information on local and foreign affairs, local interest news, and government proclamations. Its format would be recognizable to us today.

What was the first American newspaper?

The first American newspaper was the *Publick Occurrences Both Forreign and Domestick,* printed in 1690 by Boston bookseller and publisher Benjamin Harris. Its print run lasted one day. Harris did not obtain the necessary permissions to publish his newspaper and ruffled political feathers by printing information that was critical of local and international officials. He was arrested and his newspaper suppressed.

The first successful newspaper run was the *Boston News-Letter,* started in 1704 by Boston postmaster John Campbell (1653–1728). It received subsidies from the colonial government and was therefore subject to governmental agenda, but it was instrumental to the establishment of newspapers as a viable medium of communication.

Newspapers began appearing in greater numbers as the Revolution drew near. Independently funded newspapers like Benjamin Franklin's *Pennsylvania Gazette* became major players in promoting revolutionary ideology and propaganda. Many of these early newspapers reflected the political instability of the time and had content that would appear outrageously slanderous to today's readers.

What outcomes did the American Revolution have on newspapers and journalism?

A major action for the first post-Revolution congress was to decide what limits would be placed on expression through media such as newspapers. Freedom of the press was established in the First Amendment of the Bill of Rights: "Congress shall make no law respecting ... abridging the freedom of speech, or of the press."

Despite the passing of the First Amendment, fear of subversion through newspapers and other publications continued. In 1790, Congress passed the Alien and Sedition Acts in response to fears of French foreign nationalists and sympathizers. This act criminalized any writing that could be deemed false or malicious toward the government or the president. This act resulted in many newspaper editors who expressed anti-Federalist views being charged, arrested, and even imprisoned for the contents of their publications. The Sedition Act was highly unpopular and allowed to lapse in 1801.

Debate surrounding the freedom of speech and of the press as outlined in the First Amendment continues today. The full extent of the meaning of this amendment is often debated and redefined. The notion of what constitutes "the press" is unclear and changeable, particularly as disruptive technology changes the face of formal and informal journalism. Additionally, the absolutism with which freedom of speech and expression should be treated is hotly contested. This debate demonstrates the gray area between the ideology of free expression and its real-world practice.

What was the party (partisan) press?

From the late 1700s to approximately 1830, newspapers often received patronage from political parties. These patronages led the newspapers to act more as editorial mouthpieces than sources of journalistic news. Editors would give open support to the patron party's candidates and policies and in turn would receive direct funding or government printing contracts to continue running their newspapers. The tone of these papers was highly biased and very crude, often resorting to outright slander and name-calling of members of opposing political factions.

What was the penny press?

The penny press was the birth of mass newspaper distribution through a low-cost model that drew revenue predominantly from selling advertising. The penny press age launched on September 3, 1833, when Benjamin Day (1810–1889) published the first issue of the *New York Sun*. Available at the price of one penny, the *New York Sun* was an immediate success.

There were several contributing factors that led to this new form of newspaper. Technological advances such as steam-powered and cylinder presses made printing significantly faster and cheaper. A densely packed population, high immigration rates, and rising literacy among the working class created a large readership. The *New York Sun* focused its articles on exciting stories involving crime, entertainment, and human interest topics—subjects that appealed to a broad audience. This contrasted sharply with the more elite topics of business and politics that dominated traditional newspapers.

Publisher Benjamin Day created the *New York Sun*, the first penny press in America.

The true revolution that Day introduced to the newspaper industry was his distribution model. Instead of relying on a subscription model that either required ready cash or credit, Day employed hawkers to sell his newspapers on the street one issue at a time. The *Sun* was cheap, exciting, and readily available to the masses. The huge readership was attractive to advertisers, who bought advertising space directly from the newspaper.

The penny press model was swiftly imitated, and penny papers began appearing in major cities across the United States, notably James Gordon Bennett's *New York Morning Herald* and Horace Greeley's *New York Tribune*.

What was the yellow press?

Yellow press, also called yellow journalism, was a style of journalism that favored sensational stories, large headlines, dramatic illustrations, and gossip and rumor. Its name was derived from the popular Yellow Kid cartoon. This form of reporting—easy to digest, startling, and favoring the lowest common denominator—was a smash hit. This format paved the way for huge growth in circulation figures and advertising revenue for the newspapers that embraced it.

Several prominent and influential newspaper owners were involved in the yellow press. James Gordon Bennett's (1795–1872) *New York Herald,* Joseph Pulitzer's (1847–1911) *New York World,* and William Randolph Hearst's (1863–1951) *San Francisco Examiner* and *New York Morning Journal* all followed this shocking, sensationalist format.

The yellow press eventually fell out of favor as its sex-, crime-, and outrage-saturated pages began to cast journalism in a disreputable light. Its impact on journalism and newspaper culture, however, remains important today. The tactics of the yellow press increased mass circulation of newspapers, and yellow press features such as large headlines and dramatic images remain as a mainstay of both print and digital newspapers today.

What is broadcasting?

Broadcasting is the wireless transmission of a message to many recipients or receivers at once. The transmissions are made available to the listening or viewing public through the standardization of receiver types. Prior to the invention of radios capable of clearly transmitting voices, the only truly mass medium for communication was newspapers. After the viability of radio broadcasting was proven in the early 1900s, radio and television broadcasting was developed and readily available to average people in developed countries in a relatively short period of time.

Italian Guglielmo Marconi is generally regarded as the inventor of the radio though some believe that Nicola Tesla deserves the credit.

The most recent innovations and significant changes in broadcasting come in the form of Internet broadcasting (webcasting). Further discussion regarding the effect of the Internet on mass media can be found in this chapter in the section "How the Internet Changed Everything."

When was radio invented?

Radio communication was preceded by experiments in electromagnetic waves in the mid-1800s. By the 1860s, scientist James Clerk Maxwell (1831–1879) demonstrated via mathematic theory that electromagnetic waves could travel through air. Intentional transmission of an electromagnetic signal was likely achieved by inventor David Edward Hughes (1831–1900) in the early 1880s. In 1888, German physicist Heinrich Rudolf Hertz (1857–1894) conclusively proved the transmission of electromagnetic waves through the air. As the term "radio" was not yet in use, these waves were referred to as Hertzian waves.

There is some argument as to whether Italian Guglielmo Marconi (1874–1937) or Serbian American immigrant Nikola Tesla (1856–1943) "invented" radio as they both filed patents for the technology within a few months of each other. Marconi is generally credited with having invented commercially viable radio and for being the first to transmit sound wirelessly. Marconi sent the first radio signal—a series of telegraph code clicks—in 1885. In 1901 he successfully sent the first transatlantic radio message from a transmitter in Poldhu, Cornwall, England, to a receiver at Signal Hill in St. John's, Newfoundland, Canada.

When were the first successful voice transmissions over radio?

Transmission of voices would not be achieved until 1903 with the invention of the liquid barretter by Canadian inventor Reginald Fessenden (1866–1932). In January 1906, Fessenden made the first successful two-way radio transmission of Morse code between Brant Rock, Massachusetts, and Machrihanish, Scotland. The first public broadcast of music and voices was also made by Fessenden from Brant Rock on Christmas Eve in 1906.

Radio broadcasts became viable with American inventor Lee DeForest's (1873–1961) improvement and amplification of radio signals with his invention of the Audion tube. From the late 1910s to the early 1920s, licensed and unlicensed radio broadcasters proliferated.

What kinds of effects did radio have on society?

When radio became more readily available to the general public in the early 1920s, it was an instant hit. From the start, radio transcended many communication barriers that newspapers and other print media could not. It could be enjoyed despite illiteracy, visual impairment, or infirmity. It overcame many income and class barriers. As radio programming was free and the radio receivers were not onerously expensive, radio allowed people of vastly different income levels to access and enjoy the same entertainment, educational, and informational programming. Not only could this create a way for people previously separated by wealth or class to share an experience, it was also an important morale booster during the Depression years.

Radio created an entirely new form of social activity: gathering one's family and friends around the radio to collectively listen to a radio program. Additionally, radio provided a more intimate medium for people to receive communication—the sense that they were speaking to a friend in their living rooms. The radio's ability to offer an experience that was paradoxically both intimate and shared gave it the power to create communities of listeners—shared experience and camaraderie between people who all sat down to listen to the exact program at the exact same time regardless of geographic location. That an experience like an opera or political oration could be simultaneously experienced by people living on opposite coasts created new paradigms of group identity that could be likened to the experience of being part of a "community" on the Internet over one hundred years later.

How did early radio affect American politics?

As with any new form of media, radio impacted the way in which politicians reached out to voters. Prior to radio's existence, the only options people had for engaging in political discourse was through live events hosted by party representatives or through news received from the newspapers. The power of radio in political affairs, however, was evident from the outset of public radio broadcasting. The first scheduled and advertised public broadcast made in the United States was coverage of the 1920 presidential race between Republican Warren G. Harding (1865–1923) and Democrat James Cox (1870–1957). Following his victory, President Harding enthusiastically adopted radio as a political tool to reach the public, even making international and trans-Atlantic broadcasts to reach an audience outside of America. Use of the radio as a standard political communication tool was cemented by the late 1920s.

Politicians did have to learn the strengths and limitations of the radio. Radio allowed for a very different campaign structure wherein politicians could reach audiences without the need for extensive travel to give the identical speech over and over. Oratorical skill did not have the same advantage with a radio audience as it did with a live audience. Many exemplary orators failed to translate their skills to this new medium. In 1924 Democratic presidential candidate John W. Davis and prominent politician William Jennings Bryan, both renowned for their oratorical skill, could not adapt their speaking skills to the constraints of radio. President Calvin Coolidge, on the other hand, preferred radio and found that it made up for his lack of public speaking ability. According to Coolidge:

> I am very fortunate that I came in with the radio. I can't make an engaging, rousing, or oratorical speech to a crowd ..., and so all I can do is stand up and talk to them in a matter-of-fact way about the issues of my campaign; but I have a good radio voice, and now I can get my messages across to them without acquainting them with my lack of oratorical ability or without making any rhetorical display in their presence.

President Franklin Delano Roosevelt's 1933–1944 "Fireside Chats" radio broadcasts were a masterstroke in connecting with and engaging the American people in politics. President Roosevelt understood the strength of radio as an intimate medium, and he used the "shared intimacy" of radio communication masterfully. Roosevelt used a more casual, plain language style of speaking that appealed to a wide audience and was praised for being able to make his policies and plans more accessible to the common citizenry. His audience was urged to listen to the president's radio program in groups and as a community activity. Historian Jason Loviglio notes that "in examining the popular responses to the chats, it becomes clear that Roosevelt's intimate visits in the homes of the listeners were often experienced as invitations to transform the boundaries of domestic, political, and social space in the service of national renewal."

By the 1940s, most Americans were receiving their political information through the radio, displacing newspapers as the predominant source for politically related communication, debate, and discourse. Radio remained dominant through 1948, the last election year before the introduction of television.

What was the ***War of the Worlds*** broadcast?

On October 30, 1938, actor and director Orson Welles (1915–1985) staged a radio play version of H. G. Wells's *War of the Worlds* as part of the regular radio program *Mercury Theatre on the Air.* Welles told the *War of the Worlds* story of Martian attacks on Earth through a series of phony emergency broadcasts that interrupted more standard, banal programs like fake weather reports and music programs. Welles's brilliant staging of the program convinced many listeners that the fake emergency broadcasts of the Martian attacks were real. Reports of mass panic and hysteria began to circulate, and rumors of stampedes, deaths, and traffic jams abounded. Social historians, however, have uncovered little evidence that this mass panic ever took place.

Orson Welles is shown here addressing the press after the radio broadcast of *War of the Worlds*.

Newspapers and reporters gleefully took up the story and exaggerated the number of people fooled by the broadcast as well as the effects of the so-called mass panic. The perpetuation of this story may have been an attempt of newspaper editors to capitalize on its sensational nature, but it may also have been a way for newspapers to discredit their rival medium of radio. Welles's production, and by extension radio as a whole, was labeled as dangerous, irresponsible, and unreliable.

The reaction to the *War of the Worlds* broadcast spurred increased interest in the effects of mass communication on individuals and society as well as academic interest in topics later known as media literacy. Unfortunately, the earliest studies by researchers such as Hadley Cantril and Paul Lazarsfeld on the effect of the *War of the Worlds* broadcast were marred by unreliable sampling, poor research methodology, and outright manipulation. These studies helped reinforce rather than repeal the "mass hysteria" myth that surrounded the *War of the Worlds* broadcast. However, they still helped pave the way for new inquiry into the effect of mass communication on people and society.

When was television invented?

Early television technology and audiovisual broadcasting were being explored at the same time that radio technology was becoming powerful, stable, and widely adopted by the public. The earliest instance of electrical transmission of a visual scene occurred in 1884 when German scientist Paul Nipkow (1860–1940) used his Nipkow disc to scan elements of a picture—dots he called pixels—and then transmit and recompose them into a viewable image.

German inventor Paul Nipkow created the Nipkow disc, which could scan images, interpret them as pixels, and transmit them, an essential step in developing the TV.

Over the next fifty years, many scientists and inventors worked on nascent television technology. Notable events in television's early development include American inventor Lee de Forest's (1873–1961) development of radio amplification, which made television a more practical prospect, Georges Rignoux's 1909 Paris demonstration of instantaneous transmission of pictures via selenium cells, and Scottish engineer John Logie Baird's (1888–1946) 1925 presentation of televised moving faces. The development of electronic television marked another major phase in television technology. Russian inventor Vladmir Zworykin (1888–1982) contributed several critical developments in the 1920s and 1930s, including his use of cathode ray tubes, electronic transmission of images via his iconoscope tube, and his kinescope cathode-ray receiver, which made pictures suitable for home viewing.

At the same time that Zworykin was developing new television technology, American Philo Farnsworth (1906–1971) was simultaneously working on his own forms of fully electronic television transmission. His invention of the image dissector allowed for the first transmission of an electronic television signal that involved absolutely no mechanical parts. Farnsworth is credited with transmitting the first live human images. Farnsworth's work intersected with that of several other television pioneers, including Zworykin, with whom he would enter several bitter patent battles over who was the true inventor of the electronic television system.

When was television widely adopted by the general American public?

Although television sets were commercially available to the general public in America as early as 1939 and construction of two commercial stations was to begin in 1941, World War II put a halt to further development of television stations. All the same, improvements to television technology continued. After the war ended, public demand for television sets and programming exploded with the number of commercial stations increasing from twenty in 1948 to ninety-eight in 1950. Within ten years, 440 television broadcasting stations were transmitting programs to nearly 90 percent of U.S. households.

How did early television affect American politics?

Just as with radio, the potential for television as a political platform was apparent from the outset. And just as with radio, politicians needed to determine how to best use this new medium. New possibilities for campaigning were now possible. Traditional campaign speeches were televised, mostly in half-hour time slots. These were essentially televised versions of radio speeches. Much more innovative was the "Eisenhower Answers America" ad campaign in 1952. This novel political campaign tactic had Dwight D. Eisenhower's (1890–1969) presidential campaign buying up commercial breaks and advertising spaces to air short TV spots of Eisenhower answering questions from average Americans.

The unusual format and short, focused content of the ads proved to be immensely successful. People found the ads more memorable. Listeners were able to recall specific talking points from the "Eisenhower Answers Americans" ads, while surveys of traditional Eisenhower speeches demonstrated very little audience retention of what the former World War II general had spoken about. Eisenhower and the Republican Party continued their innovations in the 1956 campaign, where they held televised news conferences with predrafted questions asked by audience plants instead of questions from reporters. They celebrated Eisenhower's birthday on TV. They broadcasted coffee talks between Eisenhower and female members of the public. Television could amplify the feeling of intimate connection. It gave the politician the ability to look directly into the camera and therefore into his audience's eyes—as vice presidential candidate Richard Nixon (1913–1994) had done in his 1952 Checkers speech.

What was the "Checkers speech"?

In 1952, Richard Nixon, who was then a candidate for vice president under the Eisenhower ticket, gave a speech defending himself about payments he had received for his political expenses. Nixon did not know the names of those who contributed to the fund, but some suspected millionaires were trying to buy off Nixon (at the time, a U.S. senator from California). While campaigning for Eisenhower, Nixon interrupted his travels to make a half-hour broadcast during which he defended himself, attacked his detractors, and declared that, if he had to, he would give back the money he spent but would not give back a gift from one donor, which was a dog named Checkers that his children had come to love. Nixon's deft handling of the speech and reference to the dog gained him considerable support from the public and became a famous example of a politician using television to gain support during a career crisis.

A screen shot of then-Senator Richard Nixon giving his famous "Checkers speech" in 1952.

In addition to the different nature of the television medium, a new concern cropped up. Politicians didn't just have to worry about having a good voice and manner for radio, they also needed to have the right appearance for television. The importance of image was driven home spectacularly during the first televised debate between the Republican nominee, Vice President Nixon, and his Democratic rival, U.S. senator John F. Kennedy (1917–1963) of Massachusetts, in the 1960 campaign. Kennedy's youth, health, vitality, and good looks shone from the television. Nixon, pale without makeup, skinny from a bout with the flu, and sweating profusely under the lights, appeared weak and nervous in comparison. Kennedy spoke to the camera, while Nixon shifted his gaze around to the journalists, giving the impression that he could not make "eye contact" with the viewer. While the truth of the famous story of radio listeners believing Nixon had won while TV viewers feeling that Kennedy had won is highly debatable, the importance of a politician's looks and appearance on TV is not. Kennedy's good looks were hardly the only reason for his victory in that election, but they certainly helped. Just as television amplified the viewers' sense of intimacy with a politician, so too did it amplify the need for good grooming and skillful TV manners.

What was television's role in McCarthyism?

Television played a pivotal role in both the rise and fall of U.S. senator Joseph McCarthy (1908–1957) of Wisconsin. McCarthy used the television medium to great effect when perpetuating the Red Scare—the anticommunist movement that swept across America and heralded years of media censorship and paranoia. Bombastic and sensationalistic, McCarthy was an electrifying performer in his television appearances, and he sought out as many opportunities as possible to appear on TV. Audiences watched, and many believed the unfounded and sweeping accusations that McCarthy brought forward.

Yet while McCarthy was attacking increasingly high and improbable targets, in 1954 CBS journalist Edward R. Murrow (1908–1965) was chipping away at the Red Scare through his TV documentary program *See It Now.* On March 9, 1954, he dedicated *See It Now*'s entire half-hour program to a feature called "A Report on Senator Joseph R. McCarthy." In this report, footage of McCarthy bullying, attacking, and berating confused witnesses exposed the senator as a liar and demagogue.

Shortly after Murrow's episode on McCarthy aired, the Army-McCarthy hearings began. For thirty-six days, networks televised the hearings to the American public. McCarthy's pugilistic style, which once helped him win high public approval ratings via his TV appearances, now came across as crude, cruel, manipulative, and contemptuous. The combination of the Army-McCarthy broadcasts and Murrow's *Report* brought about the downfall of the senator through the same medium that had initially helped him rise.

How did television impact the Civil Rights Movement?

Television sets were becoming more common in households at the same time the Civil Rights Movement was taking hold. Both segregationists and civil rights activists worked to make the television medium appear in their favor.

Segregationist politicians took to the television to promote their views, while networks in communities and states with segregationist leanings tended to suppress programming featuring African Americans or civil rights topics. While blackouts of civil rights issues were possible at a local level, the programming could be broadcast across the nation, particularly in regions outside the Deep South, where civil rights sympathies were stronger.

Civil rights leaders such as Martin Luther King Jr. (1929–1968) understood the potential of a symbiotic relationship between television media and the Civil Rights Movement. The movement needed awareness and viewers to support its cause, something that television could furnish. TV networks needed dramatic images and stories to attract viewers, and civil rights activities were hotspots of those captivating images. Marches, confrontations, and other events were scheduled for times that worked with the schedules of nightly newscasts. The powerful oratory skills of King and other civil rights leaders were also superbly suited to the audio-visual format of television and to the programming needs of the networks.

A major effect that television had on the Civil Rights Movement was that it was able to transmit images of the violence being endured by the demonstrators in places like Birmingham and Selma, Alabama, to an audience relatively removed from that degree of racial tension. Television coverage of the Civil Rights Movement reached not only a national audience but an international one as well. It not only helped a wide audience witness the events, but it also encouraged and assisted the organization of activists themselves. The combination of powerful (if often simplified) narrative and shocking visuals increased sympathies as well as popular and political pressure to enact change regarding civil rights issues.

It is critical to note that television was only one of the many factors that led to the success of the Civil Rights Movement. Political climate and motives, public opinion, economic considerations, and myriad other factors combined to make this critical event possible.

What were McLuhan's contributions to our understanding of mass media?

McLuhan's work heralded new forms of pop culture and media studies and had a massive impact on communication and communication technology studies. Concepts for which McLuhan is particularly noted include:

- The effect of print technology on human culture, awareness, and thought patterns. Print changed human sense and moved us away from a species whose predominant sense was aural and toward a species whose predominant sense is visual.
- The effect of advertising on public consciousness in that advertising can be used to shape public consciousness. People may derive more pleasure from the information transmitted in the advertisement than in the thing being advertised.
- The "tetrad": McLuhan's four laws of media. Media has four simultaneous effects on the world and on other media around it: enhancement (the amplification of a certain effect), reversal (the effects when a medium is pushed to its limit and its characteristics are reversed), obsolescence (when one medium renders another medium obsolete), and retrieval (what prior forms of service or action are brought back into play by this medium).

Who was Marshall McLuhan?

An exploration of mass media cannot be undertaken without acknowledging Marshall McLuhan. Dr. Herbert Marshall McLuhan (1911–1980) was a Canadian professor of English literature but was most noted for his academic and intellectual contributions in the areas of communication theory and media analysis. He achieved fame in the 1960s for his studies on mass media and the effect they have on human cognition and behavior. His approach to media studies revolved around the concept that a medium is something—usually a technology—that extends a person's physical senses or mental capacities. The lightbulb, print, television, and language are all media. The extension of one sense displaces other senses, and that adoption of a new medium fundamentally changes the way humans function. According to McLuhan, media change the way we think and behave in a large-scale, societal context.

- "Hot" and "cool" media: Media that have more information density and less sensory input, such as print or radio, are high-definition or "hot" media. "Cool" or low-definition media, on the other hand, contain more sensory input and less information density. These different sensory-information densities create new forms of awareness and require different degrees of engagement from the users. The hotter a medium is, the more it spoon-feeds its content to its audience. Print is considered a cool medium. In comparison to print, radio is a hot medium and television is hotter than radio.
- The "Global Village": Through electronic media, experiences from around the world become more available and familiar. Additionally, electronic media drives a strong desire among the audience to participate in its activity. This encourages a retribalization of humanity as people move away from the individualistic activity of reading print and toward more group activities as we all receive the same message and are more concerned with what the group knows and thinks. We behave as a tribe, rather than as individuals. This concept of the Global Village and retribalization is thought to have predicted the effect that the Internet would have on human behavior.
- "The medium is the message": This famous statement of McLuhan deals with the importance of the effect media have on human consciousness and behavior over and above the content that the medium carries. This statement is discussed further in the following question.

What are McLuhan's most well-known works?

McLuhan wrote several books, the most influential of which were:

- *The Medium Is the Massage: An Inventory of Effects* (1967): This book, in which McLuhan teamed up with graphic designer Quentin Fiore, addressed how different media affected the human senses and drives social and cultural change. It was McLuhan's best selling book. The use of the word "massage" instead of "message" in the title was a typographic error. McLuhan found the error interesting, as it described how media can "massage" our thoughts and understanding and also acted as a play on the term "mass age." The misspelling was retained in the title.

Marshall McLuhan was a Canadian professor whose ideas on media theory greatly influenced television and advertising.

- *Understanding Media: The Extensions of Man* (1964): In this book,

McLuhan addresses how electronic media affected communication, thought, context, and life for humans in the twentieth century.

- *The Gutenberg Galaxy: The Making of Typographic Man* (1962): A rich exploration of the effect of print and literacy on human consciousness, this book helped propel McLuhan into international intellectual fame.
- *The Mechanical Bride: Folklore of Industrial Man* (1951): In this book, McLuhan treats advertising, comics, and newspapers as forms of modern folklore. It explores the effect these media, particularly advertising, have on collective consciousness, and it is formative to the field of pop culture studies.

What does "the medium is the message" mean?

McLuhan's most famous statement, "the medium is the message," is an often misinterpreted comment on the effects of media on human thought and behavior. Part of the difficulty in unpacking this statement is that McLuhan used dense, obscure, often contradictory prose and assigned meanings to terms that weren't always transparent or consistent with the meanings most people assigned to them.

In the case of "the medium is the message," "medium" refers to technology in general, and "message" is the effect that the medium has on society. This effect of the medium is entirely independent from the content carried by the medium. It is important to note that McLuhan saw "message" and "content" as being completely separate entities. For example, the medium of printing had the effect (or the message) of setting up a structure of awareness that moved us from a predominantly aural society to one dominated by our visual senses. The printed word created literate man, and this is a far greater effect than the content carried by any one printed book. Similarly, the effect that watching an individual program on TV has on an individual is nothing when compared to the effect (the message) that the environment created by TV technology (the medium) has on that same person.

THE INFLUENCE OF THE INTERNET

What is the Internet?

The Internet is essentially a network of networks. The networks come from a wide variety of sources, both public and private, and include personal, academic, business, and government networks. These networks exchange information through standard protocols known as the Transmit Control Protocol/Internet Protocol (TCP/IP). Through these protocols, data is broken into packets that are transmitted through network operators at various speeds depending on the type of connection being used. The majority of information or data exchanged through the Internet is sent at the gigabit-speed level through high-speed connections.

All forms of information and data are exchanged through the Internet. The Internet is used to deliver a wide array of commercial and noncommercial content, products, and services, which include video and audio streaming, telephony services, peer-to-peer networking, email, and financial transactions, to name just a few.

Who invented the Internet?

As with all other forms of groundbreaking communications technology discussed in this book, the history of the Internet is a many-layered affair involving people from different places working on developing similar technology around the same period of time. Broad data networking technologies were being developed during the 1960s and early 1970s in multiple places—the United States, the UK, France, and elsewhere. However, the lion's share of credit for the creation of the Internet typically goes to the U.S. Department of Defense Advanced Research Projects Agency (DARPA).

Operating in the shadow of the Cold War, DARPA sought to create a network that was robust enough to maintain its security even during a nuclear attack. The results of its effort was the Advanced Research Projects Agency NETwork (ARPANET). The ARPANET system of splitting information into packets and sending them over shared circuits allowed the network to continue to operate even if a computer went down. In 1974, TCP/IP was developed by telecommunications pioneers Vint Cerf (1943–) and Robert Kahn (1938–) and enabled more advanced data and file sharing. The Department of Defense released the TCP/IP communication standard to the public, allowing it to be openly and freely used.

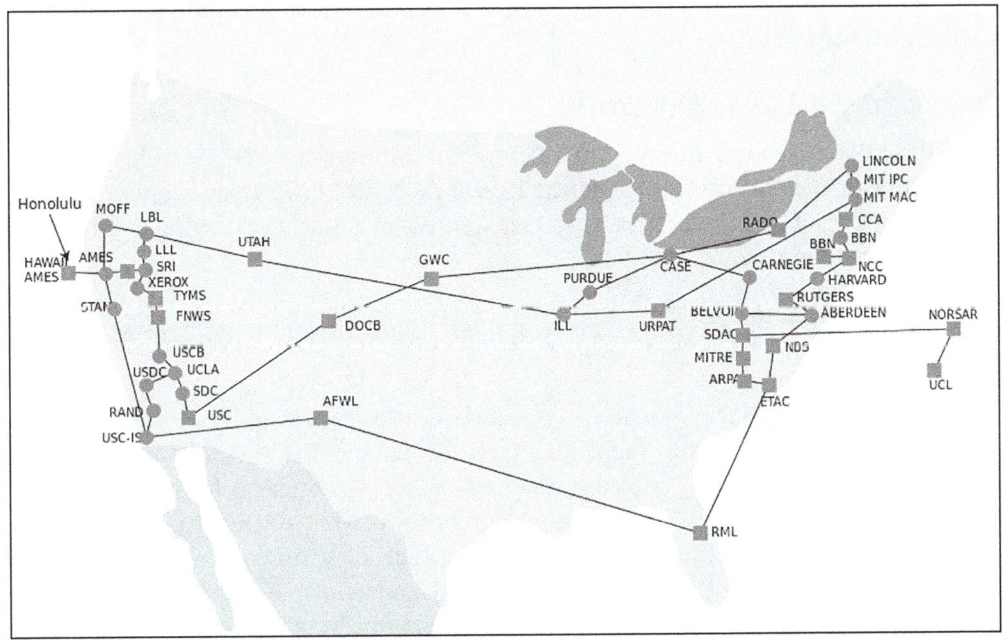

A map showing the universities that were connected to ARPANET in 1977.

ARPANET connected the academic networks of several academic research institutions, and in the early 1980s, a large number of networks were added to ARPANET. The term "Internet"—derived from "inter-networking" as well as Kahn's "Internetting Project" (the project that would give rise to TCP/IP)—started to be used to describe this network. In 1984, ARPANET ceased operations and was shut down. The Internet remained in place, however, and in 1987 the Department of Defense transferred oversight of the Internet to the National Science Foundation.

What is the difference between the Internet and the World Wide Web?

While the Internet is the network that allows connected computers to share data, the World Wide Web (Web) is an application that allows web pages and documents to be created and shared over the Internet. The Web uses hypertext to link together documents in a manner that makes it significantly easier to retrieve information—such as a document—from a larger database. Prior to the 1990s, any activity on the Internet needed to be done through manually entering text-based commands.

The Web uses three specific technologies to retrieve and share information. Hypertext Transfer Protocol (HTTP) is the protocol by which information is formatted, fetched, and transmitted. URL stands for Uniform Resource Locator and provides the address where a resource is located on the Web. HTML, or Hypertext Markup Language, is the language or code used to create viewable documents on the Web. It puts the information contained in a website into a graphic format that is more easily read and understood by humans.

The Web is accessed by web browsers, commonly referred to as "browsers." Browsers make the information on the Web accessible and readable in a graphical, point-and-click interface format.

Who invented the World Wide Web?

The World Wide Web was invented in 1989 by Sir Tim Berners-Lee (1955–), a fellow at the European Organization for Nuclear Research (CERN). Berners-Lee was also responsible for inventing the first web browser, a software application through which people access the World Wide Web.

How has the Internet affected traditional media industries like radio, newspapers, and television?

The Internet's effect on traditional media industries is profound and continues to evolve and develop. The Internet has radically altered people's ability to access media, information, and entertainment. Choice is now one of the top concerns for information or media consumers. We want to be able to pick and choose what and when we watch, read, and listen. The growth of on-demand services, which plays to consumer demand for content when and where they want it, has created a new form of competition for traditional media providers. Free or pirated content has forced media outlets to adapt their profit models and have altered profitability of old subscription service models. The rapid dissemination of information—especially news and rumors—over online channels has also created difficulties for media formats that must respond to a rapid news cycle.

Why has the radio industry been less disrupted by the Internet than the television or newspaper industries?

Not all traditional media industries have been equally affected by the Internet. Radio listenership and profitability has held steady in markets such as Canada, while newspapers across the world are undergoing a rapid decline. The differences in performance in the wake of the Internet can be pegged on various reasons. Radio services can be easily streamed online in both live and archived format, and the technology allows for advertising to play without disruption.

Consumption habits and devices also favor radio; casual listening in the car or on portable devices remains popular. Many devices that access the Internet are also able to access AM/FM radio signals. The radio industry as a whole also embraced the changes brought by the Internet to their industry more readily, moving toward Internet-based radio service delivery rather than clinging solely to terrestrial or satellite radio. The global accessibility of Internet radio stations has allowed stations to expand their audience beyond their former geographic or syndicated broadcast area. People are able to explore more radio listening options, and homesick expatriates or travelers can still tune in online to their favorite hometown morning radio show.

When Internet radio was first finding its legs, it was relatively inexpensive for traditional radio stations to launch their own Internet radio site. In the early years of Internet radio, content licensing laws in most countries did not cover online streaming of content. For years, many traditional radio stations were able to "piggyback" their broadcast content licenses onto their online programming. Such legal loopholes are beginning to be closed, however. For instance, in 2013 the Australian Full Federal Court ruled that terrestrial radio broadcasts and online simulcasts were different services that spanned different geographical areas. This ruling meant that providers of radio services needed two separate content licenses—one license for the content broadcast over radio airwaves and one license for the same content streamed online. Despite the narrowing of these licensing loopholes, their early existence helped radio media providers adapt to the realities of the Internet and establish their online presence more smoothly and firmly.

What are "on-demand" and streaming services?

One area of dramatic change has been seen in the rise of on-demand streaming services, such as Internet radio and television-style content services like Netflix and Hulu. These services are an alternative to traditional radio stations or cable television. Users can view licensed content free of any programming schedule.

How have on-demand services altered traditional television and radio programming?

On-demand services, including services like Netflix as well as online streaming services like Internet radio, have changed audience watching/listening behaviors and program creation and access models. The ability for streaming to allow people to easily access the programs they want whenever they want them has given rise to the popularity of "bingeing," where people will go through multiple episodes of a TV or Internet radio program in a single sitting. Binge-watching in particular has become so popular that streaming television providers such as Netflix are creating their own program series and then releasing an entire season's worth of content at the same time.

Netflix began as a service mailing movies to customers and evolved into a streaming service of movies and TV programs.

How has peer-to-peer file sharing and free online content affected traditional media outlets?

Another way in which the Internet has created change for traditional media industries is in people's willingness to pay for content. Peer-to-peer file sharing and piracy have made it much easier to access content without paying for it, which cuts considerably into the content and advertising sales revenues for traditional television producers. Dealing with piracy is exceptionally difficult. Copyright laws vary from country to country, file sharing happens on a massive scale, and people are divided on the morality of pirating content. The issue of illegal downloading is unlikely to be legislated away.

Content piracy aside, free online resources such as blogs and news sites have also thrown a wrench into traditional media revenue models. Information is becoming an ever-cheaper commodity. This has been particularly disruptive to the newspaper industry. Free classified ad sites such as Craigslist wiped out classified advertisement revenue for newspapers—traditionally one of their more lucrative revenue streams. Subscribership is also in decline, particularly among younger readers who prefer to access their information online and are less likely to be loyal to one particular newspaper or news site.

What the success of paid streaming services like Netflix and Hulu have demonstrated is that consumers are willing to pay for content, but they want the feeling of greater choice over how they access and consume that content. Some television networks are partnering with streaming services and offering their content over alternative pay-per-program sources like YouTube Red. Many newspapers have adopted a model whereby people can freely access a certain number of articles on their website each month but then need to pay for access to more articles or to access certain kinds of news stories. The long-term viability of these "freemium" revenue models in a rapidly changing, choice-flooded market is still being determined.

How have online publishing platforms like blogs challenged the newspaper industry?

The massive glut of information available online, the proliferation of self-publication platforms, and the speed with which information spreads online presents problems for the newspaper industry. With a news cycle shortened by instant online publication, traditional paper newspapers are finding it more difficult to deliver news in what audiences consider a timely fashion. Many newspapers responded to the short news cycle and instant online publication by creating their own websites and regularly posting breaking news. However, the fight to be the first to break a story has also curtailed editorial checks and balances, leading to a perception that journalistic quality has been in decline in many major newspapers.

What are blogs?

Short for "weblog," blogs are websites where one or more authors easily post and share information, commentaries, links, and resources. Anyone with access to the Internet can post and publish their blog, making their thoughts, opinions, and activities available for others to read (or not, depending on the blog's privacy settings). Someone who writes a blog is a blogger, and the activity of writing a blog is called blogging.

Many blogs feel similar to a diary or online journal, and most of them are just that—ways for people to express personal thoughts or activities to an online audience. Blogs, however, have the potential to be powerful vehicles for information dissemination. Several successful for-profit blog sites, such as the Huffington Post and Salon.com, have expanded beyond blogging and into news aggregation, becoming part of the mainstream media landscape. Many large news aggregators and traditional news outlets have their own blogs, which may act as a sort of editorial or opinion column for their bloggers or writers. Blogs exist for every conceivable purpose—from sharing knitting patterns to revealing political atrocities. While a few bloggers have achieved fame and fortune from their activities, the vast majority of blogs are created and maintained for personal reasons, without any prospect or want for financial gain.

Whether or not a website is a blog depends more on the style of the post than on the software used to create the post. Blogs are usually frequently updated and posts typically appear in reverse chronological order. Some bloggers, companies, and organizations program their own blog sites. Many people prefer to use point-and-click blogging platforms like Blogger, TypePad, and LiveJournal to create their own blogs without any website programming knowledge at all.

What is microblogging?

Microblogging is a form of blogging wherein a post is very short—often just a couple of sentences or words long. Simple links, updates, pictures, and videos are popular microblogging content. Most microblogging occurs within the context of social media, taking place over social media platforms like Twitter, Facebook, and Instagram.

What is vlogging?

Vlogging is video blogging—blogging using video instead of text. The ease of publishing and sharing vlog content on websites like YouTube has contributed to the rise of vlogging as a popular form of expression.

What is streaming?

Streaming is the simultaneous downloading and playing of data, usually audio and video, through a network. The data sent by streaming is automatically deleted after playback, meaning no recording or file is kept on the computer. Effective streaming requires a fast, reliable Internet connection to receive the data, otherwise, there are interruptions in the playback. To prevent this, streaming sites create "buffers," small caches of content stored in the program's temporary memory. The buffer is downloaded slightly ahead of the content being played so that the playback isn't interrupted while new content is loading.

Many online content providers are streaming services, including Netflix, Spotify, and YouTube.

What is a podcast?

A podcast is a series of digital audio or video files available for download over the Internet. Podcasts are often recorded like radio shows, and many radio stations offer podcast

An increasing number of people who could never have done so on traditional TV and radio are now creating and broadcasting their own original programs as Internet podcasts.

versions of their programs. Podcasting is different from streaming because streaming requires a constant connection to the Internet while podcasts are downloaded to a computer or device and can be listened to offline.

Podcasts are often distributed through online programs that allow for the uploading, categorizing, and discovery of podcasts through their database and search systems. These systems usually work with a web feed that allows users to subscribe to podcasts they like. iTunes and Stitchr are two popular podcast distribution programs.

What is a "feed"?

A web feed, usually just referred to as a "feed," is an aggregation of updated content from a variety of sources. These updates are then made available to a subscriber through the feed's software. Initially, a "feed" referred specifically to data sent to a feed subscriber from websites that used an aggregation program like RSS (Rich Site Summary). However, popular use of the term has been expanded to include just about any list of real-time information updates, especially on social media sites like Facebook. Facebook explicitly calls the area of a member's page where friend updates are posted the "Facebook news feed."

What is an app?

"App" is short for "application." An application is a software program that is used to perform specific tasks. While the term is most commonly used in reference to apps for mobile devices, desktop computers run apps as well. Some apps run through the device's or computer's operating systems while web apps are run through web browsers.

What are emoticons and emojis?

Emoticons are representations of facial expressions using text symbols like colons, parentheses, and letters. The smiley face :), frowning face : (, and winking ;) emoticons are commonly used.

Emojis are graphical icons that represent feelings and expressions. Popular emojis include smiley faces, hearts, thumbs up, etc. For a computer or mobile device to correctly display an emoji, that emoji set needs to be supported by its program. This means that certain emojis will not display correctly on all devices, whereas emoticons—being created entirely by standard text characters—will display across most devices and computers.

Some common emojis, which are a way to express emotions and reactions quickly without typing them out.

Why do we use emoticons and emojis for text-based communication?

Emoticons and emojis serve a very useful purpose when communicating with text. Writing cannot directly express nuances like vocal tone and other nonverbal signals. These signals can be critical to the correct interpretation of a message. For example, a smiley-face emoticon can indicate intentions like gentleness or a desire to avoid offending someone, while a wink emoticon clearly indicates humor or a joke. A reader's reaction to a message can be drastically different when a wry joke is clarified with a ;) emoticon.

Although emoticons and emojis are useful, they are considered very informal (sometimes even juvenile) and should be avoided in professional communication. Excessive use of emoticons can also be annoying as it may seem childish.

What are memes?

Common use of the term "meme" refers to Internet memes, which are pieces of media, ideas, or activities that are rapidly shared through the Internet. Recaptioning photos is a popular type of meme activity. Internet memes are characterized by their extremely fast spread and huge reach. They typically have a relatively short shelf life, although some meme phenomena like LOLcats have remained in popular culture for years. Memes are typically lighthearted, silly, or sarcastic. They may convey anything from pointless humor to satirical commentary on current issues.

What is a troll?

An Internet troll is a person who posts abusive or purposefully provocative statements on Internet communities, forums, comments sections, or social media with the sole purpose of disrupting conversation or eliciting emotional responses from other users. This activity, known as "trolling," can range from mildly annoying to upsetting to full harassment.

It is important to be aware of trolling behavior as it can seriously impede online communication and even impact some people's sense of safety when communicating in online environments. Trolling is often marked by repetitive personal attacks against other commenters or identifiable groups of people. It does not contribute to any meaningful discussion and does not present reasonable arguments that are open to debate. When reading through online forums or website comments section, it is critical that readers are aware of the possibility of pointless, hateful commentary and to ignore the posts unless there appears to be a real threat. Internet trolls need responses from the people they are trying to infuriate in order to have any power. The best response is generally no response at all. As the popular online saying goes, "Don't feed the troll."

Why are people more aggressive when communicating online?

Aggressive online behavior by people who would not otherwise act in such a way is a phenomenon that has received much attention in academic circles and mainstream media. There are several factors in online communication that increase the likelihood of someone sending inflammatory or uncharacteristically mean messages, along with the chance that a reader will misinterpret a message as being more aggressive than it actually is.

The Internet is an environment that encourages disinhibition—behavior that someone would not engage in under normal circumstances. On the positive side, disinhibition can lead some people to communicate with more openness, honesty, and support than they would offline. On the negative side, it can also lead people to engage in more rude, hostile, or abusive communication than they otherwise would.

How does anonymity and lack of face-to-face contact contribute to aggressive online communication?

Anonymity and the use of online avatars or alternate identities can give people a sense of security when interacting online. Because they can't be identified, they feel safer to act in potentially unacceptable ways. Lack of real-time, face-to-face contact also contributes to disinhibition. When we are unable to see or hear people's nonverbal cues (e.g., eye contact, body language, vocal tone), we can't adjust our communication to suit the signals they are sending us. We are also less likely to worry about how others might respond to us and feel freer to express things we would not normally be willing to say. This removal from the people with whom we are communicating lessens our empathy and can increase our hostility.

Another important factor to online aggression is the unconscious layering of tone and subtext into a conversation. Many people "hear" the tone of the message they are reading and may even conjure up a visual image of the sender's physical expressions. This can easily lead to a misinterpretation of a message's subtext, which can easily scale into a more aggressive online interaction than either party intended.

Because people feel protected behind a mask of anonymity online, they feel they can act in ways they probably wouldn't in face-to-face situations.

There are many other factors that can also lead to increased aggression online, such as an absence of social status cues, ready access to a large volume of aggressive material, social mirroring of aggressive behavior, and ample opportunity for aggressive behavior. However, it must be said that the online world also presents a great deal of opportunity for and demonstration of altruistic, kind behavior—behavior that is often encouraged by the same factors that facilitate aggression.

It is important not to view the online world as a frightening, dangerous place with aggression lurking around every corner and in every comment. It is also important, however, to understand that the online environment can foster behavior in us and others that we would not normally engage in in real life. With this awareness, it becomes possible to be more objective and less reactive to ill-mannered online comments. It also becomes easier to objectively monitor ourselves to ensure that we are being responsible online communicators and are engaging with others in a manner that is clear and respectful.

What are some ways I can ensure I'm not inadvertently being aggressive or sending the wrong message?

It can be very difficult to objectively review our own written material, but it is good practice to double-check anything you are about to post online or send in an email or text message.

When posting in an online community such as a forum or message board, consider the rules of behavior—both written and unwritten—of that community. Certain groups do not allow posting that is hateful, is off-topic, or contains foul language. Other groups may ban messages that are clearly intended to create discord or topics that are contentious in nature such as religion or politics. Rules of behavior are not always clearly defined, so when you are interacting with an online community, pay attention to patterns of posting behavior to see what is acceptable to the majority of people there.

You will need to keep potential readers or audience context in mind. Consider what the person or the group may consider to be funny or in poor taste, what they would think of as topical or irrelevant. Bear in mind the subject of the communication and angle from which a reader might approach it. If addressing a subject that is personally sensitive to the person or people you are interacting with, you may want to be more careful with your language and expression than if you were discussing the same subject with people who were not personally vested in the topic.

Read what you have written out loud. When we speak out loud, we often include nonverbal cues that aren't apparent in the written word. These cues and their meaning can become obvious when you hear yourself speak, and you can check against what you have written to see if you clearly conveyed those meanings.

Read what you have written out loud using different tones and emphases. Consider the emotional or mental state of the person or people who will be reading your words, and say your message out loud with those emotions present in your tone. You may discover that a statement that seems innocuous in a friendly or neutral voice is very provocative when said in an angry or frustrated tone. If the person reading that statement is likely to be frustrated or angry when they read it, then rework your message so that your intention and tone are clear.

RHETORIC

KEY IDEAS AND TERMS

What is rhetoric?

Rhetoric is the art of persuasion and influence. Professor and classicist Angie Hobbs defines rhetoric as "the art of persuading a specific audience to specific actions and beliefs through the use of language." It is a discipline existing primarily within the language arts. While many modern rhetoricians have expanded it to include the visual arts, for the purposes of this book it will be defined in its classical sense and will be referred to in its application to spoken or written language.

Rhetoric is often seen as analogous to oratory, but there is an important distinction between the two. While the root of the word "rhetoric" refers to the act of speaking, the discipline of rhetoric is not limited to its application in public speaking. Rhetoric is concerned with the composition and expression of persuasive thoughts and ideas through language, while oratory is specifically concerned with the art and act of delivering a speech.

A strong component of philosophy has been present in rhetorical study throughout its history. Many scholars and philosophers have investigated how use of rhetoric and language affects our development and understanding of truth, spirituality, science, the natural world, and culture.

What is discourse?

Discourse is the exchange of ideas or expression of thought in spoken or written formats. The term may also be extended to include exchange of thoughts or ideas through other media, such as through visual representation. Advertising, for example, often combines verbal or textual discourse with visual discourse to get its message across. While discourse often refers to a two-way exchange of thoughts and ideas, it may also take place through a one-way exchange of information. Even if the audience is incapable of responding to the person issuing the communication, they are still engaging in discourse by interpreting the message and assigning varied meaning to it.

What is an argument?

Within rhetoric (and in many other contexts), an argument is a compilation of statements, reasoning, or proofs given to establish and defend a position. The purpose of an argument is to either persuade an audience or to explore an idea so as to arrive at a conclusion or truth.

A heated or angry exchange of views or opinions, on the other hand, is a fight.

What is a rhetorical device?

Rhetorical devices are specific uses and arrangements of words intended to have an effect on the audience above and beyond the plain meaning of the words. For example, hyperbole is a rhetorical device in which a characteristic or idea is exaggerated in order to draw the audience's attention to that characteristic or idea. Alliteration is the repetition of an initial consonant sound for emphasis, memory, or artistic effect.

What is a rhetorical question?

A rhetorical question is a question that is asked for effect rather than one asked to generate an answer. Usually these questions imply an answer without ever actually giving one. A rhetorical question is more properly known as an erotesis, and it is one of a great many rhetorical devices.

RHETORIC FROM CLASSICAL TO MODERN TIMES

Where did rhetoric originate?

The formalization and study of rhetoric as a discipline began in Hellenistic Greece. Ancient rhetoricians attributed the development of the discipline to Sicily near the middle of the fifth century B.C.E. In particular, the development of a systematized approach to persuasion was given to the Sicilian Corax. The study and practice of rhetoric then moved to Athens; according to legend, Corax's pupil Tisias moved from Sicily to Athens, bringing rhetoric with him.

While the truth behind the story of Corax and Tisias is debatable and largely legend, the activities of rhetoricians, orators, and Sophist instructors confirm that rhetoric rose to prominence in Greece during this time period.

Why did rhetoric develop in Greece at this time?

During this period, an early form of democracy was established in Syracuse, and in the wake of political change, a large number of litigations arose in the courts. Litigants could present their case to a court and jury, an activity that required the person arguing the case to be an extremely effective speaker.

The Athenian court system also allowed for people to argue their case directly to their peers, who would cast ballots to determine who won the case. Litigants, however, needed to present their own case—there was no option to hire someone else to speak on one's behalf. The need to speak well and persuasively was clearly necessary in a system such as this, and rhetoric was adopted as a means by which to improve persuasive powers. Rhetoric and oratory also opened up the possibility of a political career for any skilled male citizen in Athens, and the demand for instruction rose as more people vied to establish their careers. This demand for rhetorical instruction gave rise to the Sophists, itinerant teachers specializing in rhetoric.

Who were the Sophists?

Sophists were traveling instructors who taught rhetoric and oratory and were frequently hired to write speeches for litigants in the Athenian courts. Sicilian ambassador Gorgias began teaching oratory and rhetoric in Athens in the late 400s B.C.E. and is credited as being one of the founders of Sophism.

Sophists were not limited to teaching rhetoric, but it formed the backbone of most of their instruction. They were relativists, believing that universal truth was not possible. Sophist philosophy and, by extension, rhetoric was heavily criticized by contemporaries such as Plato. Plato was a vociferous opponent of rhetoric and condemned it as being a manipulative art, focused on teaching people how to lie and flatter their audience. Nonetheless, demand for Sophist instruction remained strong among Athenian youth who needed a good grasp of rhetoric to be active players in politics and culture.

The Greek philosopher Aristotle wrote the first important book on rhetoric.

Who was Aristotle?

Aristotle was a Greek philosopher and major influencer of systems of Western philosophy. Born circa 384 B.C.E., Aristotle was the son of a Macedonian court physician. He was sent to Athens as a young adult to further his education and there joined Plato's Academy. Aristotle returned to the Macedonian court in 343 B.C.E. to tutor Alexander the Great (356 B.C.E.–323 B.C.E.). Many of his works, including those on physics, metaphysics, and natural sciences, were profoundly influential on European scholarship from the Middle Ages through the Enlightenment. He was the first person to develop systems and theories of formal logic, which were and remain major influences on the modern study of formal logic. One of his major works, *The Art of Rhetoric*, was the first text to analyze the mechanisms of language and persuasion with a more objective, scientific view rather than through the lens of moral philosophy.

What was Aristotle's influence on rhetoric?

Although he was Plato's pupil, Aristotle's views on rhetoric differed significantly from those of his teacher. While Plato viewed rhetoric as a generally reprehensible art, Aristotle viewed it as morally neutral, its virtue or vice determined by the person using it. He believed that rhetoric and language, when used in an ethical way, could help us arrive at truth through reasoned argument.

In his great work *The Art of Rhetoric*, Aristotle makes a key foundational contribution to the formal study of rhetoric by defining the rhetorical appeals, the three defining components of any rhetorical argument. These elements are:

- Logos—the logic within an argument
- Ethos—the public character of the speaker or author
- Pathos—the emotional element within an argument

For further explanation of rhetorical appeals with examples of how to use them within a persuasive argument, refer to "Useful Rhetorical Terms, Devices, and Concepts" later in this chapter.

Another foundational concept contributed by Aristotle are the three genres, or types of rhetorical persuasion:

- Deliberative (also called legislative)—focused on examining current choices, options, and circumstances to choose a future course of action
- Forensic (also called judicial)—examines past action to arrive at a judgment about things that have happened
- Epideictic (also called ceremonial or demonstrative)—praises or condemns

How was rhetoric important in the Roman republic and early empire?

Romans embraced a more positive view overall of rhetoric. Romans recognized the need to change the manner of address and the choice of language and argument depending on the makeup of their audience. For Romans, rhetoric was a method and system by which to reach an audience on the audience's terms, and it often reinforced shared or cultural notions of value and virtue.

Rhetoric saturated Roman political and legal life. Unlike the courts in Sicily or Athens, the Roman legal system allowed litigants to have other people advocate on their behalf. This meant that there was a tradition of professional oratory that rewarded an advocate's skill in persuasion and communication. In the political arena, addressing crowds—be it the Senate or a crowd of ordinary Romans—was a core activity. Anyone who was to influence the course of politics needed to be able to speak and argue with a high degree of skill.

Romans saw rhetoric as a key factor in men's political and legal careers as it enabled them to compose and deliver persuasive speeches. The importance they placed on rhetoric is reflected in its pinnacle role in Roman education. While many Romans had access to education, only the wealthy elite would progress through schooling long enough to study under a teacher of rhetoric.

Many Greeks (perhaps most notoriously Plato) viewed rhetoric as a manipulative art intended to deceive an audience through grandeur of speech. For Romans, this would have been an affront. Rhetoric and oratory was bound up in a Roman's *auctoritas*—a person's status and reputation. Classicist John Dugan notes in *The Cambridge Companion to Ancient Rhetoric* that "the sort of speech which placed the orator's status in doubt because it appeared to resort to verbal trickery that played upon the audience's emotions implied a deficiency of *auctoritas*."

As the Roman Empire matured, the power of the emperors increasingly outweighed that of the politicians; rhetoric along with oratory declined in political practice and became more of a pedagogical or educational tool.

Who was Cicero?

Marcus Tullius Cicero was a Roman politician, lawyer, and scholar known for his works on rhetoric, oratory, politics, and philosophy. Cicero was born in 106 B.C.E. in Arpinum, Italy, to a wealthy family of no noble lineage. Educated in both Rome and Greece, Cicero modeled much of his work and style after Aristotle and is credited as being key to the preservation of Aristotle's work in Western civilization. Cicero's prowess in oratory was instrumental in his stellar career as a legal advocate and politician. Cicero was killed in 43 B.C.E. after having run seriously afoul of Octavian (later Augustus) and Mark Antony.

Roman scholar and politician Cicero outlined the five canons of rhetoric: invention, arrangement, style, memory, and delivery.

What was Cicero's influence on rhetoric?

Cicero's approach to rhetoric emphasized a strong balance between the form of expression and the content of an argument. Cicero outlined the five canons of rhetoric (invention, arrangement, style, memory, and delivery). Within the canon of arrangement, he broke speeches down into a specific six-part format (introduction, narration, division, proof, refutation, and conclusion). This style of arrangement continues to be used today in strongly persuasive speeches.

In addition to his methods for rhetoric and oratory, Cicero laid the foundation for the philosophical outlook of humanism. In Cicero's philosophy, the rhetorician-orator played a key role in the bettering of a community. Cicero believed that an orator, having mastered rhetoric and being highly educated, was in a position to understand how best to live and, through his power of speech, would be able to instruct his community on how to lead good lives and enact good laws.

For further explanation of Cicero's five canons and the principles of arrangement within a speech, refer to "Useful Rhetorical Terms, Devices, and Concepts" later in this chapter.

How did the study and use of rhetoric change in Medieval Europe?

After the end of the Roman Republic, rhetoric and oratory became less important as decision-making moved away from the politicians and toward the emperor. Rhetoric continued to be an important part of Roman education, but that practice declined along with the Roman Empire itself.

During the decline of the Roman Empire and the early medieval period, rhetorical discourse shifted from a political application and toward religious application. Medieval rhetoric placed little emphasis on oratory but was valuable for creating sermons. At the same time, rhetoric also became more focused on literary arts—especially letter writing and interpretations of texts (namely the Bible). Its application to the written form was a significant evolution of the uses of rhetoric, and medieval poetry and literature demonstrate awareness of the written uses of rhetorical form, figure, and discourse.

Within medieval universities, rhetoric, along with logic and grammar, formed part of the trivium, the foundation subjects of a liberal arts degree.

What developments in rhetoric happened during the Renaissance?

During the Renaissance, study of rhetoric was strongly influenced by humanism in terms of its content and philosophy. Classical, rather than medieval, rhetoric was favored. Notably, texts on the study of rhetoric started to be produced in vernacular languages, rather than solely in Latin. The first English language text on rhetoric, Leonard Cox's *The Art or Crafte of Rhetoryke*, was published circa 1524.

How did rhetoric continue to change after the Renaissance?

During the seventeenth century, the ornamented, intentionally hyperbolic rhetorical styles of the Renaissance were set aside for a clearer, plainer style of expression. Thinkers such as Francis Bacon and Thomas Hobbes felt that excessive focus on eloquence and rhetorical figures was inappropriate to clear communication and scientific inquiry.

RHETORIC TODAY

How has the study of rhetoric developed in modern times?

The study of rhetoric has enjoyed a revival since the early twentieth century. Advances in the field of semantics helped propel interest in the study of formal rhetoric. The explosion of means by which we communicate also contributed to the surge of interest in rhetoric. Advertising, media, and mass media all incorporate significant study of contemporary rhetoric. Additionally, modern rhetoric includes more investigation into the intentions of both communicator and audience, and it places a greater emphasis on the role of the audience in the interpretation of a discourse.

Modern definitions of rhetoric have expanded to include visual rhetoric—the way in which interpersonal communication and meaning are expressed through visual, nonverbal, and nontextual communications. Many modern rhetoricians are interested in communication through symbols. Much like the medieval expansion of rhetoric to include written and literary forms of communication, the inclusion of visual communication represents a significant development in the scope of this subject and opens us up to new ways of thinking about how we communicate.

Is ancient or classical rhetoric still relevant today?

Despite the new dimensions of rhetorical study and the influences of new methods of communicating, rhetoricians today still deal with many of the same concepts, theories, and issues that ancient rhetoricians dealt with. Topics such as ethos, logos, and pathos are as relevant today as they were over two thousand years ago. The means by which we communicate may have multiplied, but at the heart of all new communication technologies are still the ways and means by which humans use language and other forms of communication to influence and persuade one another.

Who are some noted modern rhetorical theorists?

While far from an exhaustive list, the individuals below have made significant contributions to the modern study of rhetoric.

- Kenneth Burke (1897–1993): An American literary critic, Burke was deeply interested in the symbolic nature of literature and, by extension, knowledge. He investigated literature as a form of communication that extended beyond the confines of literary structure and included the contexts of both author and audience. For Burke, rhetoric was a key part of literary interpretation and was not limited to the intentions and goals of the author.
- Ivor Armstrong Richards (1893–1979): Like Burke, much of Richards's work was in the field of literary criticism. Richards was keenly interested in symbolism and helped pioneer the field of semantics (the study of meaning in language). His approach to rhetoric centered on the idea of language being a medium through which

human thought and knowledge developed. Richards felt that traditional rhetoric was too prescriptive and too focused on persuasion. Instead, Richards focused on the use of rhetoric as a means to understand fundamental laws of language and to determine how communicator and audience both created and derived meaning within discourse.

- Marshall McLuhan (1911–1980): Canadian professor of English and mass media theorist, McLuhan proposed new ideas of the role of media and technology in rhetoric and human discourse. For more information on McLuhan's work, refer to the "A Brief History of Communication"chapter.

American literary critic Kenneth Burke was fascinated by symbolism in literature.

- Chaïm Perelman (1912–1984): Perelman, a Polish philosopher and professor of law, was a theorist in argumentation (the process of systematic reasoning in support of an idea or action). He applied formal logic to practical arguments and described a process by which arguments were formed based on the values of the audience. Along with coauthor Lucie Olbrechts-Tyteca (1899–1987), he wrote *The New Rhetoric: A Treatise on Argumentation* in 1958. This work focuses on nonformal arguments and how the communicator achieves acceptance of an audience through the presentation of quasi-logical arguments that appeal to the audience's sense of value and reality. *The New Rhetoric* provides insight into not only the mechanics of argumentation, but why they work.

RHETORICAL TERMS, CONCEPTS, DEVICES

The following is by no means an exhaustive list of rhetorical concepts or devices. Rather, it is a selection of some of those most useful when composing a speech or written work or when delivering a speech.

What are the rhetorical appeals?

The rhetorical appeals were laid out by Aristotle as the foundations of any rhetorical argument. They are known as appeals because they each appeal to a different sensibility within an audience. The appeals are logos (logic), pathos (emotion), and ethos (character). All discourse contains at least one of these appeals, and any combination of the three may appear in a single talk, speech, argument, or communication. These are considered by many to be the most powerful tools of persuasion within rhetoric.

What is logos?

Logos refers to the logic within an argument. The rhetorician generally appeals to the audience's sense of logic—their own understanding and view of the world based on their context. In this sense, logic is less an appeal to formal, mathematical logic and more an appeal to the audience's reason. A skilled rhetorician will determine how to make the logic within his or her argument appeal to the audience's notion of what is logical.

Does using logos mean using facts or known truths in an argument?

Just because an argument uses logos doesn't mean that the logic itself is sound or true. In rhetoric, logos often merely means that an argument is given a logical structure. Consider these two apparently logical arguments:

Socrates is a man.
All men are mortal.
Socrates is mortal.

This statement is true: all men are mortal. Socrates is a man, therefore he is mortal. But if the argument is adjusted slightly, we end up with something completely different:

Socrates is mortal.
All men are mortal.
Socrates is a man.

This statement is flawed logic. While its structure follows the structure of logos and seems reasonable, it falls apart quite easily. Horses and fig trees are also mortal. Perhaps Socrates is a fig tree. But if the audience has been primed to think of Socrates as a man, then they likely wouldn't pick up on the fallacy in the otherwise logical argument. As such, the argument still appeals to the audience's sense of reasonable thinking—that Socrates is a man—and it still counts as an appeal to logos.

What is a logical fallacy?

A logical fallacy is a statement that contains errors in reasoning. These statements are often constructed using a logical framework (*A* is *B*, and *B* is *C*, therefore *A* is *C*) but are flawed and usually lack proper evidence. Logical fallacies appear very often in arguments, especially informal arguments or fights. Even though they present flawed arguments, they can be extremely useful in argument or debate situations where two opponents are battling for the upper hand.

The following are common logical fallacies:

- *Ad hominem*—A fallacy that attacks someone's character rather than their argument. "The candidate might be a brilliant economist, but I have proof that he cheated on his taxes. Do you want a cheater to represent you?" Ad hominem attacks are directed at a person's *ethos*.

- *Argumentum ad populum* (Argument by popularity)—Using the popularity of an opinion as proof that it is true. For instance: "Nine out of ten dentists recommend Brand X toothpaste."
- *Post hoc ergo propter hoc* (After this, therefore because of this)—The assumption that because Thing A happened after Thing B happened, Thing B caused Thing A. This is popularly expressed as "Correlation does not equal causation." Post hoc arguments frequently appear in matters of alternative health.

In a political debate between candidates for office, one often hears examples of *ad hominem* fallacies—more commonly known as "attacks on someone's character."

- Red herring—A statement used to distract people from the real issue. For example: "This pipeline is not going to save our economy, and pipelines are environmental disasters. Don't you care about the environment?" The original topic was the economy, and a red herring was used to switch it to the environment.
- *Reductio ad absurdum* (Reduction to absurdity)—To take a premise beyond its original scope and to an illogical conclusion. A classic, if clichéd, example of reductio ad absurdum is:

Child: "But all my friends are going!"

Parent: "And if all your friends jumped off a bridge, would you?"

- Slippery slope—A slippery-slope fallacy is similar to a *reductio ad absurdum,* except it snowballs consequences of an action into increasingly catastrophic outcomes. "If we legalize gay marriage, next we will be legalizing polygamy, pedophilia, and bestiality too!"
- Straw-man—A straw-man fallacy creates a new argument for an opponent to attack by misrepresenting the original argument. If someone was to protest putting anchovies on a pizza because anchovies taste bad, the other person could set up the following straw man: "I can't believe that you don't want anchovies on the pizza. Anchovies are full of omega 3s—don't you want this meal to be healthy?" The original argument was not about whether or not pizza should be healthy, but rather that anchovies don't taste good. A straw man appears similar to a red herring; however, a straw man creates a new argument within a topic, whereas a red herring introduces an entirely new topic to argue about.

Watch out for logical fallacies in both your own arguments as well as in other people's arguments. They are very common.

What is pathos?

Pathos is the appeal to the audience's emotions. In rhetoric, pathos is what is used to tug at heartstrings, get people riled up, or make them laugh. Pathos also employs visceral feelings and is at use when a speaker is describing experiences such as sounds, smells, or other sensory information. Storytelling makes strong use of pathos by creating a mental picture of a scenario and getting the audience emotionally invested.

Effective speakers demonstrate sympathy with their audiences, mirroring parts of their emotional state or mood. A speaker may also demonstrate the emotions that he or she wants the audience to feel, acting like an emotional role model for those with whom they are communicating.

When in a speech or text should pathos be used?

Pathos is best used toward the end of a speech, argument, or text. People prefer to think that they make judgments based on reason and rationality, and audiences may feel annoyed or manipulated if the emotional card is played too early. On the other hand, pathos tends to solidify people's commitment to a recommendation or course of action. Emotion plays a considerable role in motivation, so when leveraged at the end of a speech, it can result in an audience that is more committed to the speaker's viewpoint or recommendations.

What is ethos?

Ethos is the rhetorical appeal to the character of the speaker (or author, as the case may be). With ethos, an audience is persuaded to the speaker's point of view partially because of the credibility or reputation of the speaker him- or herself. Ethos is more focused on the speaker's public persona rather than his or her personal or individual goodness, virtue, or "rightness." A whole patchwork of individual characteristics can be employed in forming ethos: Personality, credentials, experience, past actions, family history, values, and beliefs are just a few markers that can create or demolish a speaker's or author's ethos with an audience.

Like logos and pathos, it is the audience's sense of what constitutes proper ethos that is at the heart of this appeal. What sort of person does the audience want as a leader? As a pundit? What does the audience feel is the right combination of education and experience for someone to be considered an expert? What constitutes good ethos for one audience will be different for another.

How can someone demonstrate his or her ethos?

A speaker can most directly demonstrate his or her *ethos* verbally by talking about his or her characteristics that fit within the values of his or her audience. When 2016 Republican presidential nominee Donald Trump said, "I'm really rich," this was an argument that appealed to ethos. Many in his audience value and admire wealth and believe that independent wealth is an admirable trait as a leader as it creates fiscal objectivity.

Republican presidential candidate Donald Trump appealed to *ethos* when he declared, "I am really rich."

Ethos can be established indirectly by having someone else praise the qualities of the speaker or author. These character references can take many forms. In public speaking, they often happen when an event organizer or respected member of the audience gives an introduction to the speaker. In advertising, it appears in the form of testimonials. Publishing makes frequent use of this ethos tactic by including samples of praise from reviewers on the book jacket. Even including academic degree letters and accreditations after a name on a business card is a method of establishing ethos.

In addition to verbal and written declarations of *ethos*, nonverbal expressions are also possible. Clothing and etiquette are both important markers of ethos, as they establish that the speaker understands the values and norms of behavior of his or her audience and can fit in with their aesthetics and expectations.

What are the five canons of rhetoric?

Cicero divided rhetoric, and oratory in particular, into five canons for creating and analyzing a speech or any discourse. These canons outline a process for generating a sound argument and then presenting it to an audience. While the canons were originally meant to be applied to public speaking and oratory (especially the canons of memory and delivery), with a bit of creative thinking, they may be applied to other forms of communication. The canons and their applications within rhetoric are:

- Invention (*inventio*)—Invention is the process of coming up with the actual material and content of a speech or written work. During invention, topics are brainstormed, ideas are developed, and arguments are formed. Things to consider when in the invention phase are who is your audience and what is their context, what sort of evidence or proof do you have for the validity of your argument, and how should you organize and present your evidence.
- Arrangement (*dispositio*)—Arrangement is how a discourse is ordered. Ideas and arguments are laid out according to a specific formula that is of the greatest advantage to the speaker. While there are many different ways to successfully arrange a

speech or piece of writing, within the rhetorical canons, arrangement specifically follows this pattern: introduction, statement of facts, division, proof, refutation, conclusion. This arrangement will be further discussed in the following question.

- Style (*elocutio*)—The choices of words and language used to express an idea. While style was at one point equated with excessively fancy speech, it is present in all rhetoric. Word choice conveys subtle meaning is often emotionally charged. The use of the words "pro-life" and "pro-choice" versus "anti-abortion" or "pro-abortion" are weighted down with meaning and innuendo. The same goes for the choice to use "rebel" versus "freedom fighter" or "price" versus "investment." Even the notion of using plain, simple language to express an idea relates specifically to the canon of style.
- Memory *(memoria)*—Methods by which a speaker may commit a speech to memory. Memory tricks include use of mnemonics, storytelling, metaphor, and vivid imagery. While these devices are traditionally used for the benefit of the speaker, they may also be applied with a view to making a discourse more memorable for an audience.
- Delivery (*actio* or *pronuntiato*)—Delivery is concerned with the *way* something is communicated, rather than *what* is being communicated. This relates to the expressive skill of a speaker, his or her ability to use body language, vocal tone, dramatic pauses, and so on. Modern applications of delivery could include the framing choices of a film director or the layout of a print advertisement by a graphic designer.

How should a speech be arranged, according to Cicero's five canons of rhetoric?

Within the canon of arrangement, a speech is organized thusly:

1. Introduction (*exordium*)—The topic of the speech is stated, and the speaker establishes his or her ethos and credibility.
2. Statement of facts or narration (*narratio*)—Provide the context for the speech. Ideally, a story or narrative account is told to explain to the audience the circumstances surrounding the speech and to set up context for the arguments that are to follow.
3. Division (*partito*)—Introduce the audience to the arguments you are going to make with a brief summary of them. The arguments of your opponent may also be briefly or indirectly mentioned here.
4. Proof (*confirmaito)*—Logical arguments are provided to back up your position. This portion is strongly focused on appealing to logos. It often comprises the main body of a speech.
5. Refutation (*refutatio*)—Answer and attack the arguments of your opponent or of anyone who might dispute or question your claims.
6. Conclusion (*peroratio*)—Summarize your arguments and deliver a call to action for your audience. The conclusion is the place to make strong appeals to pathos and is typically the most emotional part of a speech.

What is accumulation (*accumulatio*)?

Accumulation is the building up and summarizing of various points in a speech toward a climax. This is usually used in the conclusion of a speech. The following excerpt from Sir Winston Churchill's famous "We Shall Fight on the Beaches" speech is a superb example of accumulation:

Prime Minister Winston Churchill demonstrated his oratory skills during World War II with his "We Shall Fight on the Beaches" speech.

> Even though large tracts of Europe and many old and famous States have fallen or may fall into the grip of the Gestapo and all the odious apparatus of Nazi rule, we shall not flag or fail. We shall go on to the end, we shall fight in France, we shall fight on the seas and oceans, we shall fight with growing confidence and growing strength in the air, we shall defend our Island, whatever the cost may be, we shall fight on the beaches, we shall fight on the landing grounds, we shall fight in the fields and in the streets, we shall fight in the hills; we shall never surrender, and even if, which I do not for a moment believe, this Island or a large part of it were subjugated and starving, then our Empire beyond the seas, armed and guarded by the British Fleet, would carry on the struggle, until, in God's good time, the New World, with all its power and might, steps forth to the rescue and the liberation of the old.

What is anaphora?

Anaphora is the repetition of a word or group of words at the beginning of a series of phrases or lines. It is a rhythmic, highly memorable technique and often plays strongly on pathos. Civil rights leader Martin Luther King Jr.'s repeated use of "I have a dream" in his speech by the same name is an excellent example of anaphora.

What is decorum?

Decorum is the ability of a speaker to fit in with the values and expectations of the audience. It may be considered a part of a speaker's ethos. The correct choice of words, the right kind of clothing, the proper table manners, and participation in a group's official or unofficial rituals are all acts of decorum.

When a speaker behaves decorously, it often is not noticed. It is used to help a speaker fit in with his or her audience's idea of what is proper. When decorum is violated, it tends to be obvious and can make the speaker a target of satire, mockery, or rhetorical attack from opponents.

What is disinterest?

In rhetoric, to be disinterested does not mean to be *un*interested. Rather, it means that someone is lacking in bias and can behave with impartiality. Like decorum, disinterest builds a speaker's ethos. When a speaker demonstrates disinterest, he or she can give the impression that he or she is able to put the interests of the audience ahead of his or her own agenda.

During his 2015 presidential candidacy announcement speech, Donald Trump frequently used his wealth to demonstrate his disinterest to his audience. His statement "I don't need anybody's money. I'm using my own money. I'm not using the lobbyists, I'm not using donors, I don't care" demonstrates his disinterest when it comes to financial pressure. Here, he is effectively telling his audience that he cannot be bought—unlike other politicians who will succumb to the financial pressures and interests of the groups that help fund their political campaigns and careers.

What is concession (*consessio, paramologia*)?

Concession is a strategy that acknowledges the validity of an opponent's argument. It is used to set up a rebuttal, to make a point sound weaker, to guide the focus of an argument, or to turn an opponent's own point against him or her. For example, if a company has been criticized for having a small staff, an argument using concession could be "Yes, we are small, but that makes us agile. Because there are only a few of us, we don't get bogged down in bureaucracy. We don't have to consult with a million stakeholders—we can make decisions and move ahead quickly."

What is *hypophora*?

Hypophora is to answer your own question. This can be a useful tactic that acknowledges potential arguments against your position or points of skepticism within an audience but then immediately explains them away. It allows the speaker to appear as though he or she is presenting a balanced argument, while at the same time taking away the ability of the audience to make any counterarguments themselves (even if the counterargument was only happening in their own heads).

What is *kairos*?

Kairos is rhetorical timing. An argument, position, or statement can be more effective if it is made at the right time and conveyed through the right medium. An apology delivered via a phone call is more sincere and personal than one delivered through a text message: This is the *kairos* of a communication medium. If you sent a thank-you card to someone very soon after he or she did you a favor, you come across as thoughtful. If you send it months later than you should, you will seem forgetful. Jokes that don't go over well are often the result of poor timing or *kairos*.

What is *litotes*?

Litotes is an understatement used to make a point. It is usually used in irony. Litotes can make a speaker seem more subtle or tactful.

What is metaphor?

Metaphor is a figure of speech that uses one thing to represent something else. Examples of metaphors are expressions like "putting the cart before the horse" (a metaphor for doing things out of order) or "throwing the baby out with the bathwater" (to get rid of something good in order to eliminate something bad).

Metaphor has many uses. It can be used to explain or illustrate a concept by comparing it to something else. It can be used for aesthetic purposes—for the pure enjoyment of creative use and interpretation of language. Many speakers and authors use it to demonstrate their creativity or virtuosity with language. Audiences can become more engaged when a metaphor presents them with the opportunity for creative interpretation. Metaphor is an excellent tool for pathos as it creates powerful emotional effect by painting vivid pictures in the audience's mind.

What is a mixed metaphor?

A mixed metaphor is when two unrelated metaphors are combined. If someone were to say "we need to really step up to the plate and take the bull by the horns," they are mixing the metaphor of stepping up to the plate (to be ready to take action) with the metaphor of taking the bull by the horns (to tackle a difficult situation). The result sounds clumsy or awkward and may even be confusing for the audience, who could have a hard time accurately interpreting the actual meaning.

Elizabethan-era playwright and poet William Shakespeare had a notable gift for composing memorable metaphors.

How can one use metaphor well?

When composing a metaphor, stick to one theme or idea so that the audience can create a clear picture in their heads of what you are saying. Examples of consistency in metaphor are readily found in Shakespeare's works:

> "But, soft! What light through yonder window breaks? / It is the east, and Juliet is the sun." (*Romeo and Juliet* 2.2.3–4)

> "All the world's a stage, / And all the men and women merely players." (*As You Like It* 2.7.138–9)

The Gettysburg Address is another superb example of a clear, consistent metaphor that extends throughout an entire speech. In it, President Abraham Lincoln uses a metaphorical theme of birth, death, and rebirth to create an image of life and immortality in his audience's mind.

What is periphrasis (circumlocution)?

Periphrasis, commonly known as circumlocution, means to "speak around" a subject. A periphrasis uses excessive descriptions of something to imply an opinion rather than directly stating the opinion. A speaker often uses periphrasis to avoid directly offending someone or when he or she is afraid of any reprisals that might occur should he or she say what is really on his or her mind.

"Maggie is an interesting character. She loves playing devil's advocate, and you always know where you stand with her. Take what she says with a grain of salt" is periphrasis for "Maggie is obnoxious, tactless, and abrasive."

Periphrasis may also be used when a person is described, rather than identified, by name. It is often used in a derogatory way, but it may also be used humorously or to protect identities. The character Voldemort in the *Harry Potter* series is referred to by the periphrasis "He Who Must Not Be Named." Someone not wanting to identify who he or she is talking about might say "the person in question."

What is tautology (*tautologia*)?

Tautology repeats the same idea in different ways but in a manner that is tiresome or unnecessary. Repetition can be extremely useful when communicating—it can refocus an audience on the main subject or reinforce a concept. A tautology, however, isn't helpful or meaningful—it's merely redundant. It is very common in politics and debate, and it may be used to intentionally misdirect, confuse, or to buy time.

EFFECTIVE WRITTEN COMMUNICATION

COMMON TYPES OF WRITTEN COMMUNICATION

What are letters?

Letters are a form of written correspondence that directly addresses a person or organization. Informal letters may follow any sort of format and be any length. Formal or professional letters of correspondence typically feature the addresses of both the sender and the recipient, the date the letter was written, a salutation, the body or main content of the letter, a sign-off, and the signature of the writer or representative. Packages of documents, such as a contract or report, are often accompanied by an introductory or summary letter to the recipient.

Letters may be sent in hard-copy format or as emails. As email has become the prevalent form of written communication, certain kinds of hard-copy letters have risen in status. Sending handwritten letters to someone in the mail is considered to be a particularly intimate form of correspondence. Letters containing formal acclamations, official notices, or legal documents are frequently sent by post and may be announced with an email.

What are emails?

Emails are digital messages containing text, pictures, media, or file attachments sent between two recipients through an online connection. For many people, emails are the form of written communication they will use most frequently. For a thorough review on email and its uses, conventions, and other matters, refer to the chapter on "The Email Minefield."

Are letters and emails treated the same?

While the function of letters and emails are often similar, letters (aside from mass mailings and advertisements) often have a more intimate or formal feel than emails. Letters have also become a way to attract attention and increase the likelihood that a piece of correspondence will be read, especially in business-to-business transactions. The overwhelming quantity of emails people receive from day to day makes it easy for a message to be overlooked. As use of hard-copy letters and regular post have decreased, letters now stand out as an attention-grabbing form of communication.

Many writers take more care when drafting a hard-copy letter than when writing an email. While important emails should be treated with the same care as formal hard-copy letters, most emails are more casual in tone and don't need to stick to the same conventions. Abbreviations, informal salutations and sign-offs, and short, chatty messages are more common in email than in letters.

Emails usually demand significantly faster replies than hard-copy letters. Instant sending and receiving of emails have led people to expect responses anywhere from within a couple of hours to within a couple of days. It is considered negligent or discourteous to take more than a few days to reply to an email, whereas the reply cycle of a letter can be a couple of weeks or more.

What are reports?

Reports are documents containing status updates, facts, and data about a given topic or issue. They are usually more direct and technical in language and tone than essays. They are intended to be relatively objective documents, providing verifiable information that helps the reader make sense of an issue or make decisions about a course of action. Reports can be created based on a person's observations or more extensive investigation. Evidence and information are gathered, analyzed, and interpreted for the reader. Conclusions and recommendations are supported by the evidence presented in the report.

How should reports be structured?

Good reports follow a clear structure that leads with the context for the report, followed by the methods used to gather the information, an analysis of the data, and any conclusions or recommendations made based on that analysis. Many reports will also include a summary or abstract that condenses key information and states the main conclusions.

The following is a generic outline for a report. Long or complex sections should be broken down into subsections to keep the content clear and logical for the reader:

- Title
- Terms of reference: The purpose of the report and intended audience. Terms of reference don't always appear in reports but are often useful, especially if the report is going to be broadly distributed.

- Abstract or summary: A brief outline of the report's contents.
- Contents: A table of contents may be necessary for lengthy reports.
- Introduction: An explanation of the objectives of the report, the scope of the information, parameters of the research, and any limitations.
- Methods: An explanation of how information was gathered or research conducted.
- Results: The findings of any research or investigations. This section includes all data and any diagrams or charts needed to illustrate the data or findings. Do not include analysis or commentary in this section.
- Discussions/Analysis: This section contains any analysis or interpretation of the gathered information.
- Conclusion: A statement of the significant findings and interpretations presented in the report. The writer can reinforce his or her opinions or recommendations here, but no new information should be introduced.
- Appendix: Any additional information or data that may be of interest to the reader, such as surveys or lab results.
- Bibliography: A list of any sources referred to in the report as well as additional references that may be of interest to the reader.

What are briefing notes?

Briefing notes are short documents used to keep decision-makers up to date on issues within their area of responsibility. These are often used for communication between employees, managers, and supervisors and are especially prevalent in large organizations and governments.

Briefing notes should be short, usually no more than two pages, and very concise. Every word and sentence must provide clear and useful information without ornamentation. The information should be accurate and reliable, and any limitations such as missing information must be directly stated. The document should be scannable; headers and bullet lists make it easy for the reader to glance at it and pick out the most important information.

How should briefing notes be structured?

There are many variations on briefing notes, and many organizations will have their own structure to follow. A sample outline is:

- Topic: The issue at hand or purpose of the note.
- Statement of Facts: A short description of the issue's background, its current status, considerations, and any next steps or actions that need to be taken. These may each appear as a subheader in order to make the document easy to scan.
- Conclusion: A summary of the information, its meaning, and any recommendations.

What are essays?

Essays are written works that analyze a topic. While essays are one of the more common forms of composition used in academic and educational work, they are also found in nonfiction literature and opinion pieces. They are especially prevalent in humanities, social sciences, and arts disciplines. Many bloggers and online writers regularly create and post essays (with varying degrees of success).

Essays can contain analysis and opinion, and both should be defendable and backed up with evidence. The writer presents his or her stance or position on a topic (a thesis statement) and builds a reasoned argument, supporting it by interpreting texts and finding relevant information and sources. Essays should give the reader more than a simple walk-through of what other people have said about a topic. Rather, the writer uses other sources to create and support a new idea, interpretation, and view, which are presented and defended throughout the essay.

Briefing Note: County Fairgrounds construction status

ISSUE

Construction of new facilities on the Shelbyville County Fairgrounds are significantly behind schedule. The County Fairgrounds has already been booked as the site for the July 2017 All-Counties Festival.

BACKGROUND

The facilities on the Shelbyville County Fairgrounds are undergoing much-needed reconstruction and modernization to meet user needs and safety codes. Construction began in March 2015 and completion was scheduled for November 2016.

CURRENT STATUS

Construction is approximately 6 months behind schedule. It is no longer certain if all the facilities will be open for use in time for the 2017 festival.

CONSIDERATIONS

-The alternative venue used for the 2016 festival was insufficient for the number of visitors. Significant complaints were received concerning driving distance, lack of parking, and overcrowding.
-Vendor and exhibitor registration is already higher than anticipated.
-Due to demographic shifts, more families with young children have been attending the festival. Changing and nursing facilities should be provided, and additional options for children's physical activity centers are recommended.

OPTIONS

-Host festival at multiple locations, according to event type
-Place an early cap on vendor and exhibitor registration
-Investigate alternative or non-traditional venues
-Reduce number of planned events
-Hire mobile services to provide family change/nursing facilities and play spaces

CONCLUSION/PROPOSED MOTIONS/RECOMMENDATIONS

S. Taft will investigate alternative locations and mobile service providers. Decisions regarding registration capping or reduction of events will be made once contingency facilities have been evaluated. Commission members are encouraged to recommend potential venues.

An example of a briefing note.

How are essays structured?

Most essays follow a three-part structure of an introduction, a body, and a conclusion. The introduction lays down the background of the topic and its importance, and it presents the author's position or thesis statement. The body is where the author's argument is developed and supported through interpretation and presentation of sources. The conclusion draws together the points with a final summary and statement to further reinforce the essay's argument. All sources and citations are listed in a bibliography or works cited list at the end of the essay. Longer essays may use headings to improve clarity, though these aren't often used in essays of less than three thousand words.

What are announcements?

Announcements are short communications with the sole purpose of informing people about an important event. They are used in social and professional contexts. Social announcements often relate to a coming-of-age or key life event, such as births, deaths, engagements, anniversaries, and milestones. Professional announcements may inform people of changes in company policy, new partnerships, new hires or layoffs, milestone achievements, new initiatives or products, or any other development of interest to staff, clients, or the general public.

Announcements sometimes precede or are accompanied by invitations to a related event.

How can I craft an effective announcement?

First, consider what the purpose of your announcement is. If you are announcing a serious event, such as a death or a shutdown, keep the tone direct, respectful, and somber. If you are announcing an exciting or joyous event, like a birth, engagement, new initiative, or accomplishment, a suitably light and jubilant mood is appropriate. Let your personal or corporate style dictate your tone. Use more formal language if your style is traditional or elegant, and use more informal or chatty language to seem casual, energetic, or quirky.

If you are issuing a business-related announcement that has implications for staff or stakeholders, briefly state what those implications may be and when people can expect more information. Changes in business or work can often make people nervous, and being upfront about implications and timelines will go a long way to allay any misgivings. If your announcement is related to something on which people might want to take action, inform them of what the appropriate action is and where they can find assistance or more information (such as a hotline or the company website).

Be sure to include all relevant information: important dates, who the announcement is about, and concise details about the event or situation. Avoid lengthy descriptions, opinions, or overly effusive gushing; these are unnecessary and might make it seem like you're trying a bit too hard to get people to agree with or be excited about the announcement.

When should formal, written invitations be issued?

While it might be tempting to use email invitations or social media tools (like the brutally overused "Events" tool on Facebook), hard-copy invitations have a gravitas that can't be matched by electronic invites. Written invitations should be used for events that are

SHELBYVILLE ATHLETICS COMMISSION Board Meeting
6:00 p.m., September 12, 2016
Town Hall, 1001 Main Street, Shelbyville, Anystate

MINUTES

The meeting was called to order by Chair Terry Chambers at 6:03 p.m.

1 . Roll Call, Recording of Attendance
Present: Chair Terry Chambers, Vice Chair Lorne VanHoft,
Commission Members: Sampreet Singh, Elaine Brososki, Shelley Lin
Executive Director Simon Taft, Recorder Tom Arnold
Absent with Regrets: Ron Simmons

2. Call for Requests to Speak from the Public
No requests to speak.

3. Adopt Agenda
MOTION: That the agenda be be adopted as presented.
MOVED: S. Singh SECONDED: S. Lin CARRIED

4. Adopt Minutes from the Previous Meeting
MOTION: That the July 1 1, 2016 minutes be adopted as presented.
MOVED: S. Singh SECONDED: L. VanHoft CARRIED

5 Items Arising from Previous Meeting
There was discussion regarding the office moving expenses listed on the Financial Statement. S. Taft will follow up with Finance and clarify the amounts allocated and update the Commission on his findings.

6 Financial Report
F. Medina is the new auditor for the SAC. Moving expenses after August 27th are not reflected on these statements, and will appear on the following month's statements.
MOTION: That the August financial statement be received.
MOVED: E. Boroski SECONDED: S. Lin CARRIED

7 New Business
Development of promotional campaigns for the All-Counties Festival will begin on September 15th. Members of the commission will be contacted to provide interviews for commercial footage.

Construction of the new county fairgrounds is significantly behind schedule. Alternative locations will be reviewed for availability as contingency venues. Multiple sites may need to be booked to meet space requirements.

8 Date of Next Meeting
The next meeting is scheduled for October 17, 2016, at 7:30 p.m. at Town Hall.

9 Motion to Adjourn
MOVED: That the meeting be adjourned.
The meeting adjourned at 7:45 p.m.

An example of minutes to a meeting.

of special importance or formality, such as traditional weddings, or as a means of inviting VIP guests such as a mayor or important business figure to a professional function.

What are minutes?

Minutes are the written proceedings of a meeting. They are used by many organizations, associations, and committees to track discussions, to remind attendees of the proceedings, and to keep interested nonattendees informed of what was discussed. Some organizations, such as S corporations and C corporations, are required by state law to keep minutes of major meetings.

Minutes are taken during the meeting itself and not composed in retrospect. The minute-taker may wish to bring an audio-recording device to ensure the accuracy of his or her written record. As taking minutes is a very consuming task, the minute-taker should not have other responsibilities during the meeting. Minutes are submitted to key meeting attendees for review and approval. Approved minutes are stored with the organization's records.

What should be included in minutes?

In addition to the record of meeting discussions, minutes must include the details of the meeting, such as time, date, and location, a list of attendees and absentees, and the meeting agenda. A verbatim account of the discussions is not necessary. When capturing the proceedings, the minute-taker should record:

- major points within a discussion
- items to be voted upon
- any decisions made
- next steps or actions, the person or people responsible for them, and their anticipated date of completion
- items to be carried forward to the next meeting
- the date, time, and location of the next meeting

AFFECTING MEANING AND INTERPRETATION

Who is more responsible for communicating meaning in a piece of writing—the writer or the reader?

Literary theorists have long wrestled with how we create and extract meaning from text. Many theories place the onus for creating meaning on the reader. Each reader brings a different context, background, set of biases, and worldview to what he or she reads, and these factors will influence his or her interpretation of a text. The author can do little to influence these factors, especially if he or she wants to leave the reader some chance to do his or her own interpretation.

An excellent and very simple example of readers inserting meaning was the brouhaha over casting a black actor to play Hermione Granger in the 2016 debut of the play *Harry Potter and the Cursed Child.* Some *Harry Potter* fans objected to this choice, insisting that Hermione was white. Other fans applauded the casting, many stating that they pictured Hermione as being from their own ethnic background. *Harry Potter* author J. K. Rowling was quick to point out in interviews and on social media that the only features she described for Hermione were her bushy hair and her cleverness—there was never any comment on Hermione's color or ethnicity. Readers inferred Hermione's ethnicity themselves.

J. K. Rowling, author of the popular "Harry Potter" fantasy novels, noted that she never described the race of her character Hermione Granger. Readers just assumed she was white.

While some theorists do insist that meaning is created by the reader, it is the task of the writer to communicate his or her intended meaning as clearly as possible. Not all the responsibility for meaning and understanding can fall on the reader's shoulders, and misinterpretations are not necessarily the fault of the audience. A large part of a writer's skill is his or her ability to clearly and accurately convey his or her intended message in a manner that can be understood by the largest part of his or her target audience. By the same token, a reader must not discount the writer's context and worldview when interpreting a text. To do so will strip substantial meaning from the text, which might alter how the reader understands it.

Ultimately, meaning and understanding are things to which both writers and readers contribute. The writer can't communicate clearly without keeping in mind the views and realities of his or her intended audience. Nor can the reader dismiss the context of the writer and still create an informed understanding of the work.

What is writing style?

Writing style is the way something is written. It is the artistry and aesthetic of an author's work, and it contributes to the overall feel of a text. Style can be described as the writer's voice. Each author will have a unique style of expression, even when he or she must adhere to specific formats and standards. Some authors' styles are difficult to define, while others' are highly distinctive. Style tends to come out more clearly in creative works where the author has a great deal of agency, rather than in texts that are more utilitarian or technical.

Style can affect meaning by influencing the way a reader engages with a text. Irony, for instance, can be difficult to convey in writing, and the intended implication of an ironic or sarcastic statement might be lost on a reader. A flat or dull style might cause a reader's attention to slip and to overlook meaning. A clear, upfront style can help make it easier to find meaning in complicated texts. The style of writing should match the tastes of the audience for which it's intended as well as the purpose of the text. A business report written for a board of directors, for instance, should have a more formal and technical style than a travel blog post written for a youthful, casual audience.

How does a writer's "voice" or style come through in a text?

Many factors go into a writer's unique style. The overall length of sentences, for instance, can affect the feeling of speed within their text; short, clipped sentences will create a fast pace, while long, compound sentences will slow it down. Big, complicated words can make the author sound more technical or academic (or pompous), while small words can give a feeling of energy. Use of slang can create a voice that is folksy and casual. An absence of contractions will give the author a formal voice. An author will vary his or her tone depending on the seriousness or lightness of a piece, but even within those variations, the overall style will still come through.

Small samples of work taken on their own aren't enough to determine an author's voice. That comes through when looking at a longer piece or several pieces of his or her writing. Readers will be able to see an author's unique patterns and stylistic markers such as sentence composition. An author's style will change as he or she matures and gains experience, and he or she may also adapt his or her voice based on the communication fashions of the day.

What is subvocalization?

Subvocalization is silent, mental speech made when reading. It allows us to "hear" the sound of words in our heads. This is a largely subconscious process, and readers will make miniscule movements with their larynx, tongue, and other speech muscles while subvocalizing. This practice of mentally "hearing" a written text may help the reader develop understanding and reading while improving his or her ability to remember the material.

Subvocalization can significantly slow down the speed of reading as pauses, silences, and variations in speed are important parts of speech and meaning. Speed readers train themselves to avoid subvocalizing words.

How does subvocalization affect the way we interpret text?

Subvocalization allows us to insert nonverbal auditory signals such as tone, diction, and emphasis into written material. These signals are important cues for developing meaning as they can indicate anything from irony to emotional state. Subvocalization also helps us make sense of ambiguous or vague phrases by letting us create different possible meanings through changes in tone. We can then take the meaning variation that best fits the context of the rest of the text.

As useful as subvocalization is, it can also create misunderstandings. It's common to read an email or social media post with the "wrong" tone, creating meaning that is very different from what the author intended. It's difficult for us to turn off this process, so expecting readers to ignore subvocalization is unrealistic.

How does punctuation indicate phrasing and pacing?

Many kinds of punctuation provide us with visual representations of silence and thought transitions. Periods, exclamation marks, hyphens, commas, and semicolons in particular affect our perception of pace and speed when reading. Commas provide a short auditory pause and can give a lengthening effect, especially when they are used to build complex sentences. Periods indicate a slightly longer pause than commas and indicate completion of thought. If most sentences are short, the pause after a period tends to shorten as well, creating a brisk, choppy pace. Semicolons and hyphens can be used to connect and bridge ideas; vocally, they indicate a brief pause without the downward inflection of a period. Exclamation marks make a sentence sound energetic and excited. Other forms of punctuation have different effects on the way we "hear" what we read and when used well provide rich nonverbal meaning to written works.

What is subtext?

Subtext is an implied message that is not directly communicated through the words being used. It's a secondary message—a meaning *behind* the words. It can appear in written and spoken communication, in fiction and nonfiction, and in creative or practical works. What is communicated through subtext varies. It can infer a contrasting message or deeper, alternate meaning to what is presented on the surface. It can convey emotion, mood, and opinion. Subtext also allows for greater play between the writer and the reader as the writer is deliberately leaving information for the reader to interpret in his or her own way. When readers pick up on subtext, it can give them a feeling of being "in" on what the writer is getting at, allowing for a more complex communication experience.

Is it appropriate to use subtext in practical or professional written communication?

While subtext is a mainstay of fiction, nonfiction authors need to treat it with a bit more caution, especially if the piece of writing is intended for practical or professional reasons. Subtext can sacrifice clarity and precision for inference and implication. This can create problems when the communication needs to be transparent, straightforward, or is intended to help with making decisions. On the other hand, subtext can considerably liven up a dry or boring document. A skillful writer can use clever subtext judiciously while still making his or her intended meaning completely clear. Subtext may also be acceptable in situations where the communication is limited to people who are very familiar with the writer and have a good understanding of his or her personal tone, style, and shared context or background information. Even under these circumstances, it should be reserved for nonurgent or casual communications.

How can a writer indicate subtext to a reader?

Subtext can be communicated in a variety of ways, from formatting to grammar to word choice. Unexpected or dramatic formatting, such as a single-line paragraph in a series of longer paragraphs, provides emphasis. The use of an ellipsis demonstrates an unfinished thought or indicates that something has been left unsaid. Dashes connect thoughts and demonstrate the continuation of an idea or a conceptual link. A very obvious and frequently used grammatical device used to indicate subtext is the use of quotation marks around a word to imply that the truth doesn't live up to the substance of the word (e.g.: We consulted with members of the organization's "advisory panel" to get their opinion.)

Word choice is a key component of subtext. Secondary or hidden messages can be sent by choosing words that deliberately overstate or understate a piece of information. People often choose language to express strong opinions delicately. Using euphemisms or saying things "diplomatically" are ways of maintaining a polite face while expressing a negative message through subtext. Experimenting with different words, turns of phrase, and structure is the best way to become a skilled user of subtext.

PERSUASIVENESS

How is persuasive writing different from persuasive speaking?

Writing and speaking are not interchangeable methods of persuasion. As different mediums of expression, they use the tools at their disposal in different ways. Speakers have tone of voice, body language, and other nonverbal cues that are particularly effective when persuading through emotion. Writers are able to use formatting, structure, and other writerly devices to build and reinforce their argument. The methods used by writers don't always translate well into speech and vice versa. A highly persuasive speaker may be useless as a persuasive writer, while the writer might not have talents as a speaker.

How long should a piece of persuasive writing be?

There are different approaches to length in persuasive writing. Some writers prefer to keep their content brief and to the point, using clear, direct evidence to persuade the reader. Short advertisements with catchy sound bites and simple, attention-grabbing statistics demonstrate how effective brief persuasive writing can be. But there is also a place for lengthy persuasive pieces. Some people prefer to state and restate their argument, providing large amounts of evidence and building up emotions to compel their reader. This is a common strategy in Internet marketing, where long-form sales pages can take several minutes to read and combine storytelling with evidence, testimonials, and other persuasive devices. Both these forms have their merits, and different readers will respond to them in different ways. When deciding on the length of your own piece of persuasive writing, consider the reading habits, preferences, and attention spans of your audience along with the amount of information you need to convey to them.

What elements and information should be included?

The elements of a persuasive text and a persuasive speech are very similar. The writer will need to introduce a problem, propose a solution, and provide evidence to support his or her solution. Persuasive pieces strongly benefit from including a call to action: a specific instruction the reader can complete relatively quickly and easily. The information presented should always be completely relevant to solving the problem and make sense with the audience's worldview. Tangents and unnecessary background information must be avoided as they can distract and overwhelm the reader.

How should I organize my content?

Again, there are many similarities between organizing a piece of persuasive writing and a persuasive speech. Two methods of organization work particularly well for persuasion: Ciceronian arrangement and the story arc.

Ciceronian arrangement is outstanding for arguments related to politics, culture, and social matters. For a full outline of Ciceronian arrangement, refer to the "Speeches and Presentations" chapter.

The story arc style of arrangement works very well for motivational or sales-related persuasive pieces. It builds up tension and feelings of urgency in the reader, then presents them with a solution in just enough detail to convince them they want it. To learn about using story arc arrangements to write persuasive documents, refer to the "Speeches and Presentations" chapter.

How does tense affect persuasiveness?

Tense has a very strong subliminal impact on what we are trying to persuade someone of. If you are attempting to persuade someone about culpability—where responsibility, guilt, blame, or credit for something lies—then you should write in past tense. This keeps the reader's focus on a deed that has been done or a thing already accomplished. Present tense is the language of identity and values. If the goal is to convince people to adopt a new point of view, opinion, or belief, you will need to write in present tense. If you want your reader to take action and actually do something, use future tense. This gets them thinking about the next step they must take to achieve a desired outcome or goal.

What persuasive techniques can I use in my writing?

Persuasion in both writing and speaking is related to skill in rhetoric. For a thorough review of persuasive rhetoric as well as useful rhetorical techniques and devices, refer to "Rhetoric."

CLARITY

What affects clarity in written communication?

The ability to express ideas clearly is a core writing skill. Clarity is affected by mechanics such as sentence length, grammatical error, and use of a passive voice. It can also be affected by ambiguous or vague statements, wordiness, and poor organization of ideas.

Many people lack clarity in writing because they did not take the time to review and edit their work. Stepping away from your writing and then reading it again at a later time can help you look at it with fresh eyes and pick out what needs clarifying. Similarly, reading your text out loud may reveal awkward or muddy expressions. It's well worth investing a bit of time in improving your clarity—it often saves you considerably more time than trying to clear up misunderstandings afterward.

What is wordiness?

Wordiness is when a writer uses more words than necessary to make his or her point. The writing becomes cluttered and difficult to understand. Wordiness is different from simply using long words. Some writers use a more ornamented or flamboyant style, but if their writing isn't cluttered and their meaning is clear, then they aren't being wordy. Writers who use simple words but pad out sentences with useless phrases are being wordy. Overstatements, redundancies, passive voice, and vague or indirect words are common culprits of wordiness.

What is plain language writing?

Plain language, also called plain English, is a simple and straightforward way of communicating. It focuses on using short sentences and eliminating inflated vocabulary. Plain language does not dumb down a piece of writing; rather, it's meant to make it clearer and easier for a reader to understand. This makes it especially useful when dealing with very sophisticated or complex matters. Federal agencies are mandated by law to use plain-language practices.

For an outstanding guide to plain writing, especially for governmental use, visit the Plain Language Action and Information Network at www.plainlanguage.gov.

What are active and passive voices?

When using an active voice, the subject of the sentence is taking an action: "The soldier fired the gun three times." In passive voice, the subject is being acted upon instead: "The gun was fired three times by the soldier." Generally, active voice is preferred to passive. Scientific writing, however, uses passive voice as a way of increasing the impression of objectivity while reducing the presence of researchers or authors (and, presumably, their bias or opinion) from the document.

What is ambiguity?

The late great comedian Groucho Marx once provided a perfect example of ambiguity in order to get some laughs when he said, "One morning I shot an elephant in my pajamas. How he got in my pajamas, I don't know."

Ambiguity is when a phrase could have multiple meanings or interpretations. It's easy for a writer to be blind to ambiguity as the intended meaning is clear in the writer's own head. It's also difficult for readers to "see" an ambiguous sentence differently from their first reading as they've mentally committed to their first impression of its meaning.

Ambiguity is created in many different ways. A common cause is when words have multiple meanings, such as synonyms or slang, and either meaning is plausible. For example, if someone were to say "That band is sick!", they could mean that all members of a music band are ill, that they really enjoy a band's music, or that they like a physical band such as a wristband.

A famous—and much debated—source of ambiguity is the use of the serial (or Oxford) comma. In this case, the presence or absence of a comma after the second item in a list of three or more items could change the meaning of a sentence. The phrase "I saw the main course, soup and salad" could mean that the person saw three different dishes—a main course, soup, and a salad. It could also mean that the main course is soup and salad. If a serial comma was used, the phrase would be "I saw the main course, soup, and salad" and the only meaning would be that the person saw three different dishes.

Word order can create ambiguity. Comedian Groucho Marx's famous line from the 1930 movie *Animal Crackers* demonstrates the problems caused by word order ambiguity: "One morning I shot an elephant in my pajamas. How he got in my pajamas, I don't know."

Inference and incomplete information are two areas of ambiguity common in technical and instructional writing. Even when word order is correct, grammar is clear, and all definitions are agreed upon, a phrase can be ambiguous by inference. In "Mary had a little lamb," one person may assume that the sentence referred to Mary once owning a pet lamb, while another person may think that Mary ate a small dish of lamb for dinner. Incomplete information happens when the author assumes the reader shares some preexisting knowledge and so doesn't explicitly provide relevant information.

What is jargon?

Jargon is vocabulary specific to a particular context or situation. It is very common among people who share a profession, trade, or special interest. For example, the term "stat" is medical jargon for urgency or something that must be done immediately. Among video gamers, "zerg" means to swarm or overwhelm a more skilled or powerful enemy with a large number of weaker players.

Although jargon can improve clarity and precision of communication for people who share that vocabulary, it causes confusion for people unfamiliar with it.

Can repetition improve clarity?

Repetition can help create clarity by reinforcing or emphasizing a concept. A word can be repeated to increase its impact or present an idea in different ways to help a reader understand it. Repetition should be used sparingly if it's to be effective; overdoing it will make passages tiresome and annoy the reader.

Redundancy is needless repetition and never serves a purpose. Examples of common redundant expressions are:

- very unique—Something is either unique, or it isn't. There are no degrees of uniqueness.
- added bonus—A bonus is always an added feature.
- advance notice—Notices are, by definition, given before something happens. To say that it's "in advance" is redundant.

What are some methods for clarifying difficult or muddy concepts?

Analogy is an excellent method of describing complex or difficult ideas. Analogies draw comparisons between two things that appear to be quite different in order to explain their nature or meaning. Typically, analogies are created by comparing something that the reader or listener is unfamiliar with to something they know and understand. Analogies can be simple, single-sentence statements or long allegories or parables. In practical and nonfiction writing, the most common forms of analogies used are metaphors and similes. For a more thorough examination of the use of metaphor, refer to the "Rhetoric" chapter in the section "Useful Rhetorical Terms, Concepts, and Devices."

Should I use headings in my document?

Headings can significantly improve the clarity in a document by providing clear focus on thought. They also improve the reader's ability to scan the text for the parts most relevant to his or her interests. Headings break up the information in more easily digestible chunks and help the writer better organize his or her content. Some academic writing styles, such as the American Psychological Association (APA) style, require the use of headings to organize a paper. In the case of formal research or academic papers, the headings might be limited to words like "Introduction," "Methods," and "Discussion." In business documents and articles written for general or informal audiences, more descriptive headings should be used. For example, a business report could use the heading "What Our Customers Are Saying" instead of "Survey Results," or a travel blogger could write "Planes, Trains, and Automobiles" as a heading for a section about transportation instead of the duller heading "Transportation."

How should I format bulleted or numbered lists?

Bulleted and numbered lists can make sequential information easier to read and understand. Numbered lists are used when the order of the list items is important, such as in a sequence of steps, or when a list is ranking the items according to some scheme. Bulleted lists can be used when order or rank is unimportant.

Vertical lists are easier to read and remember than in-line lists. Formatting rules vary, but consistency is important. If the first item in a list begins with a noun, all items in the list should begin with nouns. Use either full sentences with punctuation at the end or sentence fragments with no punctuation; do not blend the two.

If each item in a list requires a lengthy description or discussion, or the list itself is complex, it may be more suitable to organize the items using subheadings instead of a list.

CLICHÉS, RUN-ONS, AND OTHER GAFFES

What are clichés?

Clichés are expressions or phrases that have been used so often that their original meaning or impact is lost. Clichés are not always bad—they can be used as commonplace or folksy wisdom and sometimes for humorous effect. If a writer uses them clumsily or too often, they demonstrate lack of originality or sophistication and can bore or annoy readers.

What are run-on sentences?

Run-on sentences combine two independent clauses into a single sentence. They lack punctuation needed to separate the clauses, such as commas, semicolons, or periods. Length doesn't determine whether or not a sentence is a run-on; excruciatingly long sentences can still be grammatically correct provided they use correct punctuation. Run-ons, either short or long, give a panicked, breathless quality to sentences. To fix a run-on sentence, be sure to separate the clauses either with suitable punctuation, such as a semicolon or period, or with a combination of punctuation and a conjunction such as "and," "but," "for," "so," and so on.

What is the problem with using passive voice?

Passive voice can result in very wordy or awkward sentences as more words are necessary to convey the same meaning. Passive voice can also seem indecisive; the author may sound as though he or she is hedging his or her opinion or attempting to distance him- or herself from what he or she is saying. This can make the writing weak and unconvincing. It may also seem as though the writer is making an effort to avoid assigning any responsibility to the subject of the sentence. As such, passive voice can make statements seem slippery—politicians beware.

How can I avoid being wordy?

To avoid wordiness, pay attention to the meaning and contribution of every word in a sentence. If a word or phrase doesn't contribute to the meaning or help convey your desired feeling, chop it out and rework the sentence. Pay attention for redundancies, roundabout expressions, and passive voice.

What is a vague pronoun reference?

Pronouns (e.g., it, this, he, that, who) must refer to a specific noun and must agree with that noun in number and person. If two nouns appear in a statement and are followed by a pronoun, it might be difficult to figure out to which noun the pronoun is referencing. For example, "Sandra wore her best dress to the wedding. It annoyed her with its excessive formality and huge price tag." In this sentence, "it" could refer to either Sandra's dress or the wedding she attended.

Vague pronouns are fixed by being more specific about which noun the pronoun refers to or by reworking the sentences:

- The pronoun could be replaced with a noun: "The dress annoyed her with its excessive formality and huge price tag."
- The sentence could be reorganized to make the reference obvious: "Sandra wore her best dress to the excessively formal, high-priced wedding."
- The nouns could be broken up into different sentences: "The dress, which was excessively formal and had a huge price tag, annoyed Sandra. She wore it to the wedding anyway."

What are wrong-word errors?

Wrong-word errors occur when a word is misused. Homonyms—words that sound the same but have different meanings—are frequent culprits in wrong-word errors. For example, the sentence "They engaged in gorilla warfare" should actually be "They engaged in guerrilla warfare." Misunderstood expressions are vulnerable to wrong word errors: "I could care less" is a common wrong-word version of the expression "I *couldn't* care less." Many wrong-word errors occur because of lack of understanding of a word's definition or use. *Literally* is often used when the person actually meant *figuratively*.

What are dangling modifiers?

Modifiers add description to a sentence or statement. When it is unclear what a modifier is referring to, it "dangles" as it doesn't connect with a subject or even with the rest of the sentence. Readers may be unclear about the subject of the sentence or the doer of an action. Dangling modifiers create confusion somewhat similar to vague pronoun references.

There's a big difference between guerilla warfare (top) and gorilla warfare (bottom). Choosing the wrong word can make one look foolish, to say the least.

To fix dangling modifiers, be explicit about the subject to which the modifier refers. This may be done by adding the subject to the vague clause, separating the clauses into two different sentences, or reworking the sentence structure so the modifier appears either immediately before or immediately after the subject that it is describing.

What are noun strings?

Noun strings are a series of nouns that describe or modify a final noun. These are problematic because they tend to be overly dense, can infer complex relationships and confusing identities, and can be difficult to interpret. Many noun strings are created with the intention of making a name more accurate, but they often end up confusing or pedantic. In some cases, it can even be hard to figure out which noun is the actual subject.

For example, technical jargon, project names, and committee names are frequent culprits of noun strings:

- Interlibrary single-sign-on shared database
- Amended safe ownership and handling of magical creatures legislation
- Employee safe workplace rights development committee

Reworkings of these noun strings could be:

- Shared databases with single-sign-on
- Amended legislation for the safe ownership and handling of magical creatures
- Committee for the development of safe workplace rights

SPECIALTY WRITING

What is specialty writing?

Some forms of writing require specific and consistent style and methods to be useful. Specialty writing is writing that follows specific conventions of expression and style to fulfill a document's purpose. Technical, instructional, scientific, and legal writing are examples of purpose-driven specialty writing.

What is technical writing?

Technical writing is a direct and efficient style of writing used to give instruction or explanation to different audiences. Technical writing usually refers to writing manuals, instructions, reports, product descriptions, and specifications. The audiences for these works may range in knowledge from beginners to experts, and the author's use of language will change to accommodate the audience's level of knowledge. The subject of the word does not have to be technological or technical in nature. The "technical" aspect refers more to the style of the writing: clear, concise, and effective in simplifying and communicating complex information. Technical writing should be objective and contain little or no reference to the author.

What is science writing?

Science writing is similar to technical writing, except that it focuses on explaining scientific information to different audiences. Science writers are often tasked with translating scientific information into something that is more easily understood by a lay audience and has more broad-based appeal.

Are science writing and scientific writing different?

Both science and scientific writing are forms of technical writing, but they differ in their audience and manner of expression. Scientific writing is technical writing about science, written by scientists for scientists. Science writing involves descriptive narrative, which presents the information in a livelier, more engaging way that makes it suitable for popular media.

What is legal writing?

Legal writing is a type of technical writing that focuses on analyzing legal problems, persuasive argumentation, and creating legally binding documents such as contracts, policies, or bylaws. Many legal writers follow plain language principles, but the complicated nature of their subject can still lead to dense texts that are difficult for a lay audience to understand. Legal citation follows a specific style and standardized format. This format is laid out in *The Bluebook: A Uniform System of Citation* style guide. Institutional contributors to *The Bluebook* are Columbia University, Harvard University, the University of Pennsylvania, and Yale University.

The style and jargon that appears in legal documents such as contracts and wills is often called legalese.

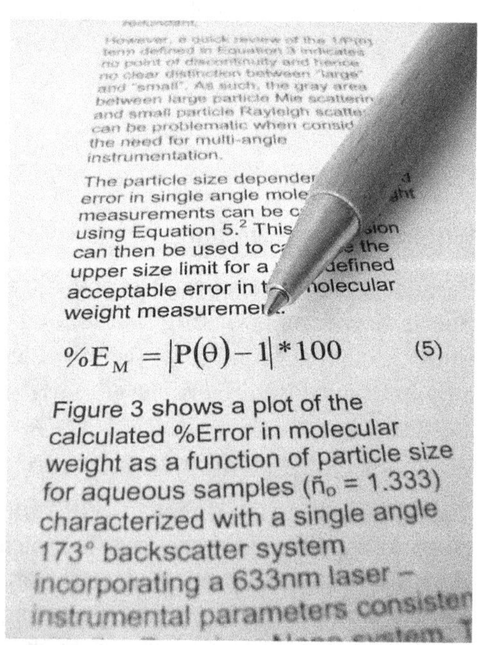

The writing style of science writing differs, depending on whether it is directed at a lay audience or other scientists.

Why is legalese so dense and complicated?

A common complaint regarding legal documents and lawyers themselves is that they are too difficult to understand. Many feel that this is done intentionally to confuse nonlawyers and obfuscate facts. California attorney Richard Silvester explains that the dense, confusing nature of "legalese" is necessary for creating legally sound documents. Legal documents are not created as whole, stand-alone texts. Instead, they are assembled piecemeal with statements and clauses from a wide variety of sources, including books of law, seminars, and court cases. This lengthens documents and can create a disjointed feel to the information. Additionally, the attorney must include explicit details about alternate circumstances that could affect the interpretation of the document. This creates lengthy backup language that addresses many situations and creates a tighter, loophole-resistant document.

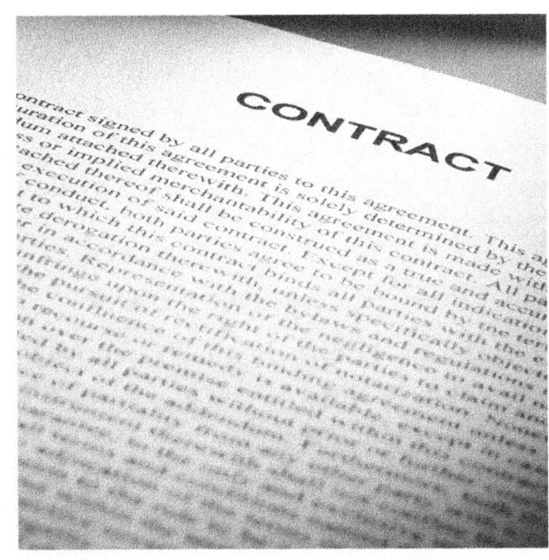

Legal language used in documents such as formal contracts can be difficult for the average person to follow.

While these practices mean that legal documents are difficult to understand, it should be remembered that they are written for people with highly specialized knowledge and language and are not for a general audience. A lawyer, however, should be able and willing to walk a client through a legal document and explain its contents.

What is scholarly writing?

Scholarly writing, also called academic writing, communicates research, analyses, and insights between academics. The style and language assumes that the reader is also an academic with knowledge about the subject at hand; definitions and explanations of background information are rarely provided. The conclusions, insights, and opinions expressed in scholarly writing are expected to be informed and supported with additional evidence cited throughout the text. Sources are presented at the end of the text in a bibliography or works cited section. Different academic disciplines follow different style guides for formatting and citations. For more information on citation guides and style, refer to the "Academic Communication" chapter at the end of this book.

How is a scholarly article different from an article in a regular newspaper or magazine?

Articles in scholarly journals must follow very different standards than those in popular media. In order to be accepted for publication in respected journals, articles submitted to scholarly journals are peer-reviewed for quality and accuracy. The language and style used in newspaper or magazine articles are vastly different from those used in scholarly articles published in academic journals. Scholarly articles are written for an academic audience, use specialized vocabularies, contain detailed findings and statistics, and follow a formal style of formatting and layout.

Newspaper and magazine articles are written for a lay audience and seek to entertain the reader as much as to inform them. Findings are simplified and presented in a manner that a broad lay audience is able to understand. Popular media has often been criticized for overstating findings in scholarly articles, often misrepresenting the facts or conclusions in order to make the magazine or newspaper article more appealing to readers.

What does "peer-reviewed" mean?

Peer review is a form of quality control that vets articles submitted for publication in an academic journal. Experts in the same field as the article's author review the article for the robustness, reliability, and importance of the scholarship being presented. Articles are also evaluated on whether they meet the style and standards of the journal and whether they fit with the journal's publishing mandate.

What is copywriting?

Copywriting is the process of creating content that promotes a product, service, business, or person. It's primarily related to marketing and sales, although the copy itself might not be explicitly promotional in nature. A great deal of online copywriting is done to create useful, informative content on blogs and websites. This content, however, is generally intended for use in "content marketing," where the purportedly useful information is created with the intention of attracting prospective clients. For information on content and content marketing, refer to the websites and social media section of the "Business Communication" chapter.

What is instructional writing?

Instructional writing is a specialized form of technical writing that focuses on the teaching process. It is strongly emphasized in educational fields but is used for many different purposes. Good instructional writing teaches the material from the learner's point of view, breaking down multistep processes into smaller individual components. Steps that may seem obvious to the writer must still be presented to the reader if learning is to take place. Instructional writing makes fewer assumptions about the reader's knowledge, context, or view than many other forms of technical writing.

What are infographics?

Infographics are visual representations of complicated information, often through summarizing or simplifying data and concepts with pictures, symbols, and graphs. They help represent information in a manner that makes it easier for readers to see patterns and make connections between concepts. Infographics are often self-contained, expressing an idea as a whole and not as a part of an accompanying article. More images and icons are used in infographics than in regular statistical graphs. Images are part of the storytelling aspect of this method of communication, and they may impart as much information as any of the facts or figures represented in the infographic's text. The aesthetic appeal and visual design of an infographic is as important to its effectiveness as the information it contains.

While this method of communication has been around for as long as writing has existed, infographics have recently exploded in popularity. Their visual nature makes them appealing, quick to read, and easy to share, and they enjoy considerable popularity on social media.

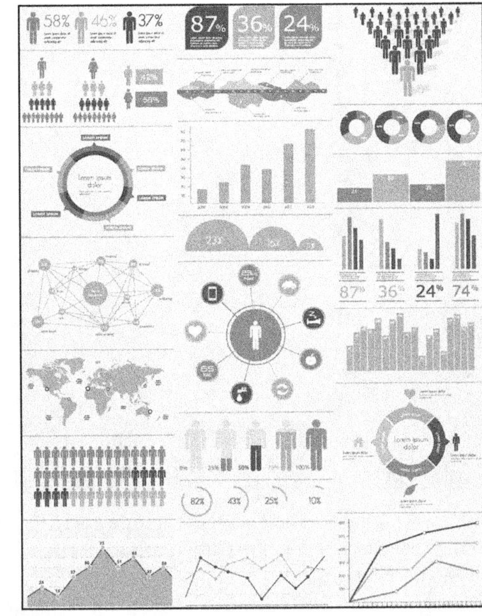

Infographics are images that help convey complicated information in easy-to-understand visuals.

Why are infographics used in instruction sheets, such as the IKEA assembly instructions?

Infographics are especially suited to representing information that would be difficult or overly wordy to explain in text. Instructions for physical tasks are often much clearer when explained with a diagram illustrating the action than through attempts to describe it verbally. Phrases like "attach dongle A into flange B" can be difficult for a reader to visualize, but an illustration demonstrating the dongle being screwed on to the flange is much easier to understand. Infographics also overcome language barriers, resulting in a better customer experience and fewer errors due to mistranslations on the part of the customer and the technical writer.

Why are the IKEA assembly instructions so effective at communication?

IKEA instructions follow standards that emphasize clarity and continuity while taking into consideration the customer's point of view—literally. The illustrations demonstrate clear, step-by-step actions that follow the actual process of assembling the furniture from a single point of view. No assumptions are made as to the skill or handiness of the customer—it's not taken for granted that the person putting together the furniture knows to tighten the screws by inserting the Allen key provided. The perspective stays the same throughout the instructions; although certain parts may have close-up illustrations, the items themselves are never turned or rotated. This allows the customer to easily reorient his or herself whenever he or she needs to move around or away from the piece being assembled.

What is the point of the IKEA Man's expressions of happiness, confusion, and worry?

While the expressions of the iconic IKEA Man are hilarious, they serve an important communication purpose. His expressions reflect and guide us, the customers, through the

IKEA instructions for assembling furniture are an example of effective communication using simple illustrations.

emotional roller coaster that is assembling flat-pack furniture; this actually increases our patience with the assembly process. His happiness with his new purchase and the assembled final product is like a shared celebration. His sadness when he smashes something with a hammer reflects our dismay when we do the same thing. By showing hopeless confusion when reading the instructions, then going to his phone and calling the IKEA help line, he reassures us that it's okay to be completely lost and have to ask for help. These simplified emotions help console, reassure, and encourage customers with an added, tension-releasing dose of light humor.

THE EMAIL MINEFIELD

EMAIL IN BRIEF

What is email?

Email is the transmission of digital messages between two computers with an Internet or online connection. The messages may contain text, images, and files attached to the message. Depending on the speed of the sender and receiver's servers, email may be sent and received almost instantaneously.

Email was first developed in the 1970s within the Advanced Research Projects Agency Network (ARPANET) systems. For a long time, email's use was practical and not personal. During the 1980s, its use increased among the academic, scientific, and business communities. Personal use of email didn't take off until the 1990s as home computers and Internet connections became more common.

What is an email client?

An email client, also called desktop email, is software installed on a computer that is used to read and send emails. Messages are stored locally on the computer the client is installed on. Popular email clients include Microsoft Outlook, Thunderbird, and Postbox.

While messages stored in an email client aren't accessible through a browser-based interface, email clients do offer some advantages over webmail. Offline, local storage of messages means that the user can access his or her messages when not connected to the Internet or if his or her email server goes down. Local storage also lightens the load on the user's Internet connection and can speed up Internet browser use. Email clients provide more robust security and encryption than webmail. Many email clients can integrate with other apps and software, allowing information to be shared and organized between programs.

What is webmail?

Webmail is an Internet-based application that allows email to be accessed through a browser. Webmail can be accessed from any computer with an Internet connection and rarely requires the user to download any programs or software to his or her hard drive. Messages are stored on an off-site server supporting the user's webmail and not locally on the user's computer. The email program can't be accessed if the user's computer is offline or if the server hosting and storing the email is down.

Many Internet providers include webmail as part of their service packages, and webmail programs are easily found online. Popular webmail programs include Gmail, Hotmail, Live, and Yahoo Mail.

What are email protocols?

Protocols are the methods and rules by which email programs send messages to one another. There are three main types of email protocols currently in use:

- Post Office Protocol version 3 (POP3): This type of protocol downloads and saves messages on the user's computer before deleting them from the email server. POP3 can't be used with webmail.
- Internet Message Access Protocol (IMAP): This protocol stores messages on remote email servers and can be used with webmail and email clients.
- Simple Mail Transfer Protocol (SMTP): This protocol is usually used only for sending messages, not for receiving them. It can be used with webmail and email clients who use their own proprietary email protocols and with clients who use POP3 or IMAP to retrieve messages.

According to the laws during the time she was secretary of state, Clinton's email use was not illegal. However, it was acknowledged to be extremely careless and contrary to recommended best practices because it made her emails more vulnerable to hacking. Ultimately, Clinton's actions were not contrary to any laws during the period being investigated. At the end of the July 2016 FBI investigation, neither Clinton nor her aides were found guilty of any criminal wrongdoing.

What is spam?

Spam, also called junk mail, is unwanted email sent to many people at once. Someone who sends spam is a spammer. Most spam is sent as marketing, though many spam messages are also sent as fraud schemes or to spread computer viruses. Email programs contain filters that recognize common elements of spam messages; the program then filters these messages into spam or junk mail folders. The messages are automatically deleted after a period of time. Despite this precaution, spam frequently finds its way into a user's in-box.

Spammers collect databases of email addresses from various sources and send out their messages in bulk. Messages are sent from the spammer's computer or through "zombie" computers that have been hacked to send spam without the knowledge of the

What was the controversy surrounding Hillary Clinton's emails during her time as secretary of state?

While acting as U.S. secretary of state, Hillary Clinton exclusively used a private email address to conduct government business, rather than an official state.gov email address. The email address was hosted on a private server located in Clinton's home, and it was used for both government and personal purposes. Hosting of email on a private server gave Clinton great control over the archiving, preservation, and access to her government emails, including a measure of protection against Freedom of Information Access and other information requests.

Clinton's primary reason for using a private email address for both official and personal correspondence was that of convenience, she maintained. She was not able to access her personal email on her government-issued BlackBerry smartphone and did not want to have to carry around or check two devices.

During her time as secretary of state, it was permissible—though not advisable—for government officials to use personal email addresses to conduct official business. Government-related email correspondences conducted via private address were to be transferred to government servers and preserved for record keeping, as per the Federal Records Act. This law was amended in 2015, after Clinton left office, and now stipulates that government business-related emails sent via personal email address must be transferred to government servers within twenty days of transmission.

In response to a direct request made by the State Department, Clinton turned over 30,490 messages, totaling over 50,000 pages of correspondence. However, Clinton reported that 31,830 personal emails from that address were deleted. In July 2015, Clinton also turned over her email server and a USB flash drive containing government business emails to the U.S. Department of Justice for inspection. This submission was part of an FBI probe into the email affair. During the investigations by the State Department, the Department of Justice, and the FBI, over two thousand emails sent by Clinton and her aides were deemed to have been classified, secret, or confidential.

computer's owner or users. Spammers may hijack email addresses by hacking into an email account or by forging an email account's identifying information. Both these strategies make spam look like it's coming from a trusted source, allowing it to pass more easily through email spam filters.

Many countries have antispam laws which may include fines and jail time for violation. In 2014, Canada implemented one of the world's toughest pieces of antispam legislation, requiring businesses to obtain consent from an email user to send them commercial messages. The Canadian Anti-Spam Legislation (CASL) covers other online activity as well, such as phishing or social media posts. By contrast, the U.S. CAN-SPAM (Controlling the Assault of Non-Solicited Pornography and Marketing) Act of 2003 allows for an opt-out method of consent, only applies to email spam, and is considered to be less robust than CASL.

You can add a spam filter to your email box to help sort through junk mail, but it is not a perfect solution.

What is an attachment?

An email attachment is a digital file sent along with an email message. Attachments can be of any file type, including digital documents, photos, videos, or other media. Attachments are sometimes used to distribute computer viruses or malware. To avoid downloading malicious software (malware), only accept and open attachments that you are expecting to receive or that come from a trusted source. To further protect your computer, use your email program or antivirus to scan the attachment for potential malware before opening it or saving it to your computer. Many email programs automatically scan attachments for viruses and may prevent suspicious email from being delivered to your in-box.

What is a "bounce"?

When an email "bounces," it means that it never reached its recipient. Emails can bounce for a number of reasons, which are documented in the bounce notification. Two common reasons for bounced emails are email address errors and blocked email senders.

If your email message was returned with the comment "user unknown," the bounce is due to an email address error. Email address errors can stem from typos in the address, deleted addresses (such as when someone is no longer with an organization and his or her email has been removed from the system), or from fake email addresses.

Firewalls and security settings may block email from certain senders because the sender's email address or domain has been identified as untrustworthy or as a source of spam. Entire email servers and hosts can be blocked if they are common sources of spam. This might cause messages sent from valid, trusted sources, such as a personal contact, to be rejected by the recipient. This situation tends to happen among institutions with high security features on their email servers, such as academic institutions, research facilities, government departments, and health agencies.

What are autoresponders?

Autoresponders immediately send automatic replies to emails they receive. The auto-responder can be set up to reply to any email it receives or only to messages that meet certain rules—such as those sent from a certain email domain or that come from online contact forms. An "out-of-office" message is a common type of autoresponder.

ADVANTAGES AND PITFALLS OF EMAIL

What are the key strengths of email?

Email is an extremely convenient and cost-effective method of communication. It allows people to send and receive messages on their own time. Messages are delivered almost instantly, which allows for more timely responses to urgent or time-sensitive matters. A single email can be sent to multiple people, creating group conversations where everyone receives the same message at the same time. This creates more efficient and reliable communication strings. Files may be attached to email messages, providing delivery of documents and other files that is faster and less expensive than using traditional mail or courier services.

Communication management is another significant advantage of email. Should a person use a webmail client, he or she can access his or her email from any computer with an Internet connection. Most email services have systems that allow for sorting, filing, and archiving messages. Organizing emails can be automated; users may set up rules in their email program that will automatically file certain kinds of messages into specified folders as they are received. Many people like using email as a way of creating a communication record, a digital "paper trail" of correspondence that can be referenced at a later time.

What are the key weaknesses of email?

Email is limited by the very technology that makes it possible. It is impossible to send or receive email without access to the Internet. Senders and receivers are at the mercy of their email servers; in the case of desktop email clients, messages can be viewed but not sent or received if there is a server error. For webmail users, any server downtime means they can't even read their saved messages until the server is back up and running.

Email users often find themselves bombarded with more emails than they want to deal with. Spam is one culprit of email overload, but so are newsletters, email lists, chain letters, and other unnecessary messages sent from family, friends, and colleagues. Although email systems enable messages to be filed and sorted, it's easy to let the contents of one's in-box get completely out of hand with old messages—both read and unread—piling up into an unmanageable morass of information. When this happens, it's easy to forget to reply to messages or even miss reading important emails altogether.

Security is an ongoing problem with email and will never be fully resolved. It is possible for email accounts to be hacked and used for malicious purposes such as spreading computer viruses or distributing spam. Many people share sensitive information in their emails; this information can be stolen if hackers gain access to an email server. Computer viruses can be spread by email attachments, infecting the computers of unwitting email recipients that open the attachments. Fraud schemes, such as phishing, disaster relief scams, and "Nigerian Prince"- or "Spanish Prisoner"-type scams, are commonly sent through email. For an up-to-date list of current online scams, including email frauds, visit the Federal Trade Commission's Scam Alerts website at www.consumer.ftc.gov/scam-alerts.

Why are emails so easy to misinterpret?

As with any other form of written communication, email is stripped of nonverbal signals like body language and tone. A person's cadence and vocal changes are implied through the way the text is written. Many people don't take this into consideration when composing emails. Messages are often read as being terser than they actually are. Irony is lost, and even polite expressions can seem sarcastic. Even when emails are formal and straightforward, the lack of nonverbal information can cause some people to fret or to insert meaning that was never intended. Some people will use emoticons or emojis to try to make up for this lack of expression, but those are unacceptable in anything other than very casual communication.

The instantaneous nature of email encourages knee-jerk responses and rushed communication. People may respond to an irritating email in the heat of the moment instead of waiting to cool down and compose a more rational answer. The distancing effect of email communication leads people to respond in ways that are more forward, aggressive, or inconsiderate than they would in a face-to-face or even voice-only conversation. For more information on why aggression is increased in online communication, refer to the "A Brief History of Communication" chapter.

How does email create a "paper trail"?

Messages that are sent and received through email are stored either in the desktop client or in the email server. All messages have a time stamp, the sender and recipient are clearly identified, and they are often "nested," meaning that all the messages in a string of emails appear one below the other in reverse chronological order. Everyone involved in an email conversation has a copy of the messages; if one person deletes the emails, the other people still have their own records. These characteristics make email an excellent way to have documented conversations that can be referred to at later dates. Many people choose to communicate through email specifically so they have these records.

How secure is my email?

Security and confidentiality of email are never guaranteed. Email servers can be hacked, ISP providers can release email access to law-enforcement officers, system and network administrators can use their credentials to access email, and employers usually have the right to read any messages their employees send through the organization's email system. An employer's right to an employee's email messages can come as a shock to many employees, who assume that their in-boxes can't be accessed by anyone else and who think their "personal" messages are somehow protected by moral right.

Security can be increased through measures like email encryption software and authentication practices. Encryption "locks" the content of the email as it moves from the sender to the server to the final recipient. If the message is to be read, the correct algorithmic "key" is necessary to unlock the encrypted message. Authentication also helps increase email security. The form of authentication most familiar to average users is the username and password needed to sign in to an email service. Authentication can also happen at a higher level to "prove" that an email really is coming from where it's claiming to be from instead of a different source masquerading as the sender (a "spoofed" email address). None of these systems are foolproof, however, and breaches are more common than many realize.

While email isn't an open-door free-for-all, it's important to be aware that security and confidentiality aren't guaranteed. It's good practice to know your rights regarding email access, to use strong passwords and change them frequently, and to keep an eye open for suspicious activity such as friends receiving spam from your email address.

EFFECTIVE USE OF EMAIL

When should I call someone on the telephone instead of sending an email?

As convenient as email is, there are times when it's better to pick up the phone instead. When a discussion is complex or requires a fair amount of feedback, a phone conversation can be more efficient and significantly clearer than email. When speaking over the phone, we engage in "check-back" behavior—asking the other person if he or she understands us and signaling our own understanding through minor sounds like "uh-huh" and "okay." Clarity is further improved because we can hear the person's tone of voice, which contains important nonverbal information and context. This also makes phone calls more personal and better for relationship building.

Composing emails can take a significant amount of time—often spending much more time than we intended. The natural flow of phone conversations means that we aren't wasting time writing and tweaking emails. Time is also wasted waiting for people to reply to emails. Emails are easy to ignore, and there can be server lags in the transmission. Feedback is instant in a phone conversation, which speeds up the conversation cycle. Many of us have committed silly productivity mistakes like sending twenty-five emails over the course of three hours to make simple dinner plans—plans that could have been made with a two-minute phone call.

Phone calls may also be a better option if the conversation needs to deal with several distinct topics. Verbal conversations tend to follow through to completion; we discuss one idea until satisfied and then move on to the next. In email, however, conversations are more convoluted. Most people will bring up multiple subjects in a single email. This can cause confusion as people try to respond to everything but fail to specifically state which subject they're addressing. Using inline replies can help reduce confusion, but it still creates a choppy flow of information and affects clarity and recall.

What are CC and BCC?

CC and BCC are used to add recipients to an email other than those in the "To" field.

CC stands for carbon copy. This term refers to the past practice of making copies of hand- or typewritten documents by placing a piece of carbon-coated paper in between two blank pieces of paper. When the writer wrote on the top piece of paper, their impressions would transfer through the carbon paper, leaving an exact duplicate of their writing in carbon pigment on the bottom, blank piece of paper.

In the case of email, it simply refers to sending other people a copy of an email. Recipients in the CC field are visible to other recipients in the CC and the To fields. People in the CC list will receive replies if the Reply All function is used.

BCC stands for blind carbon copy. Recipients in this field are not visible to anyone else receiving the message. Most email programs don't send Reply All responses to BCC recipients, but it's important to know whether or not this is the case for your email program.

When should I use a CC or a BCC?

CC is commonly used to keep people informed of email communication to which they don't necessarily need to reply. It's often used as a way of reporting activity to a supervisor or keeping interested parties in a conversation loop without directly involving them. The CC feature is useful but can be overused and contribute to in-box clutter. When using the CC field, ask yourself why the person should be CC'd instead of involved in the conversation by including them in the To field. If you are unsure if they genuinely want or need to receive the email, it may be better to not send it to them at all.

BCC use can be contentious. It is a very good way to protect contact information in group emails and to avoid cluttering up other people's contact lists. It also helps conceal emails from spam programs that harvest email addresses from group messages. However, it is also used to secretly share conversations with other people. This practice is considered backhanded and dishonest unless there is a solid reason for doing it.

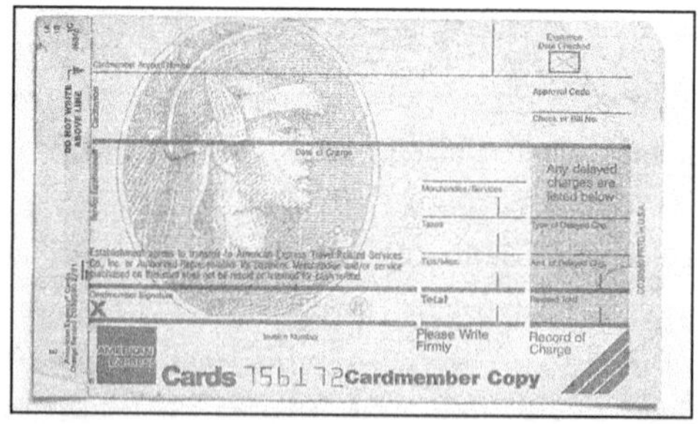

Carbon paper was once used to make copies of documents (such as sales charge card receipts). The term "carbon copy" is still used today to mean duplicate copy, even in electronic communications.

What is Reply All?

The Reply All email tool sends a reply to everybody included in the To and CC fields of an email. It is useful for group email conversations when the response is of interest to everyone participating in the conversation.

Why is Reply All so problematic?

There are many horror stories of snarky or otherwise inappropriate email responses being unintentionally sent out because someone used Reply All instead of Reply. The Reply All function also contributes to in-box clutter when recipients send simple thank-yous, confirmations, or other questions or comments that only the person who sent the original message is interested in. Sometimes Reply All is set as the default reply mode, or the Reply All button is very close to the Reply button and easy to click by accident. If you are replying to a group email and you only want your response to go to the sender or to a few key recipients, double-check that you are *not* using Reply All—it's an easy mistake to make.

What is forwarding?

Forwarding a message copies the content and any attachments of an email you've received into a new message with a blank To field. The subject line of the original message is copied with the prefix "Fwd:" to indicate that it is a forwarded message. A new recipient's email address is entered into the To field.

How do I craft a good subject line?

Subject lines are important as they help the recipient decide whether or not to open an email. Subject lines also help your email stand out among all the other messages in an in-box. Emails should always have a subject line—never leave it blank. To create a good subject line, follow these guidelines:

- Clearly state the purpose or content of the email: Avoid cryptic subject lines such as "Hi" or "Do you have a minute?" Lines like "Wedding anniversary party venue info" or "Application for employee educational grant program" let the recipient know what to expect when he or she opens the email.
- Be concise: Keep the subject line curt and limit yourself to eight words or fewer. Sentence fragments are acceptable.
- Indicate if the email is urgent: If time is of the essence, add a note like "Urgent" to the subject line. Don't overuse this or say a message is urgent or time-sensitive if it isn't; this is the email equivalent of crying wolf, and your recipients may start ignoring your messages.

How long should an email be?

Email is best used as short-form communication. Overly long emails encourage readers to skim or ignore chunks of content. Generally, emails should be kept to no more than two or three short paragraphs. Avoid nonrelevant chit-chat and get to the facts at hand. If you need to have a longer exchange with someone, consider setting up a phone call with him or her instead. If you need to send someone a lot of information, draft it into a document that can be attached to the email.

How can I cut back on the amount of email clutter I get?

Cluttered in-boxes are a serious concern for many people. Many of us are overwhelmed with the volume of email we need to deal with on a daily basis, and processing it is time-consuming. For most of us, a sizable chunk of this email is clutter—things we don't need to read but still take up valuable time and mental bandwidth. To reduce your email clutter, take the following steps:

- Unsubscribe from newsletters and feeds: It's tempting to subscribe to newsletters and feeds that interest us, but these are major contributors to email clutter. Tools such as Unroll.me can help you unsubscribe from unwanted newsletters and will "roll up" those you want to keep into a single daily digest email.
- Change listserv settings to "daily digest": Industry-related listservs are valuable tools for many professionals, but they can swamp in-boxes. Listserv programs allow members to receive emails individually or as a daily digest. Change your account settings to daily digest to reduce the number of listerv emails you get. Contact the list moderator if you need assistance.
- Dedicate specific times of day for processing and replying to emails: By batching your email activity into specific time blocks, you reduce switch-tasking and increase your efficiency. In order to stop forgetting to reply to emails—a major consequence of clutter—either answer your emails as you open them or use email extensions such as Gmail's Boomerang (www.boomeranggmail.com) to send the email back to you at a later date and time for processing.
- Reply to emails by calling the sender: As previously discussed, phone calls are often more efficient than emails. If you receive emails from people you are able to call or to speak to in person (such as your colleague down the hall), do so. This will save time and train them to call or visit you instead of using email.
- Immediately delete chain letters and forwarded jokes: Well-intentioned friends and acquaintances might be trying to send you a smile or some interesting news, but if you are overwhelmed with email, these are an unnecessary and unhelpful time-suck. Get rid of them.

You can cut down on clutter in your inbox by unsubscribing to newsletters that you no longer read regularly.

How can I encourage people to take action on my emails?

Sometimes we never get the response or action we need from an email. Keep in mind that people may be dealing with overcrowded in-boxes and overwhelming to-do lists, and it's easy to forget to respond to an email. If you need a person to take action, make it easy for him or her to do so by explicitly stating at the end of your email what it is you want him or her to do (reply, call, set up an appointment), the time by which you want him or her to do it, and how he or she can do it (give your phone number, a link to a website, or other resource). This will reduce the recipient's need to actively think about what he or she needs to do and how he or she can do it, making it easier and faster for him or her to take the action you want.

How can I check the tone of my email?

As with other forms of written communication, the best way to check the tone of your email is to read it out loud with different inflections and vocal variations. Think about any circumstances or worldviews your recipient might have that could affect how he or she interprets your email. Be sure to use words rather than emoticons to clearly express the mood or tone of your email. Emoticons are not always suitable for use in email, and they can be ineffective at changing the tone of the text.

What sort of formatting, such as fonts and type size, should I use?

The best formatting to use in email is usually whatever appears as default in the email client. Avoid any formatting that may reduce the readability of your message, such as fancy fonts, unusual text, or background colors. Fonts should be no smaller than 11 or 12 points.

Should I use a signature?

Signatures automatically appear at the end of email messages and usually inform the recipient of details like your full name, job title (if applicable), and contact information. Signatures are very helpful, especially if you have different email addresses in use or if the recipient wants to reach you through other methods, like by phone or by postal mail.

How should a signature be formatted?

Signatures should be simple and easy to read. Fancy or novel formatting, such as unusual fonts or colors, should be avoided. Avoid the use of images or signature files, as these don't always appear properly in different email programs.

Most email signatures are used for business or professional purposes. Your organization may have in-house standards or signature templates that you are required to use. If you are putting together your own email signature, include the following information:

> Best Regards,
>
> Kevin Hile
> Managing Editor, Visible Ink Press
> p: (555) 111-2222
> e: khile@vip.net
> 1234 Main Street
> Chicago, IL 42311
> www.visibleinkpress.com

An example of an email signature (note: information here is not actual, except for the Web address).

- Full Name
- Company and job title
- Telephone number
- Email Address
- Postal address (if applicable)
- Website address (if applicable)

You may also include your business's motto, slogan, or tagline, provided it isn't more than one short sentence. Do not add multiple taglines, lists of past awards, or quotations.

EMAIL ETIQUETTE

How promptly should I reply to emails?

The speed of email has increased expectations for prompt replies. While some emails may have more urgency than others, not everything has to be replied to immediately. Replies within twenty-four to forty-eight hours are usually considered quite timely. Depending on the content, a three-to-four-day reply cycle might also be acceptable. Messages can go stale if it takes longer than a week to reply to them. If you aren't able to properly reply to an email within the first week, send a brief note letting the sender know when he or she can expect a more detailed email from you. If you think that you and the sender will exchange a large number of emails within a few hours, it may be better to call him or her instead.

How formal should I be when using email?

The formality of your emails will depend on the context and the people involved. Personal email among friends and family can be as casual as you see fit. Professional emails are usually more proper in nature, although exchanges between friendly coworkers can have the same tone as personal messages. Formality increases along with the corporate rank of the person with whom you are communicating. Group emails tend to be more official in tone than one-on-one exchanges. If you are sending an email about an important matter, such as a contract or a job application, use straightforward, polite language. Match the tone of your email to the tone you would use for a hard-copy letter or a document such as a cover letter.

How do I end an email conversation?

Ending an email conversation can be a tricky point of etiquette. Some people exchange acknowledgments that they received an email and well-wishes out of a desire to be polite. Others will make chatty comments or inquire after some aspects of the other person's life in order to show friendliness. All these habits can lead to email exchanges that carry on far longer than they should. If your email exchange has fulfilled its purpose, sign off with a farewell that makes it clear that no reply is necessary. Closing statements like "I look forward to our next conversation," "Let me know if I may be of further assistance," "Best wishes on your project," or a casual "Talk to you later," are all indications that a conversation has run its course. The person may reply in a similar fashion, but there is no need for you to respond again.

Do I have to acknowledge receipt of an email?

Acknowledging receipt of an email is only necessary if the matter is especially urgent or if the person is justifiably expecting a quick reply but you won't be able to answer him or her until later. If an email is sent to you without need for immediate reply or action, you don't need to acknowledge that you received it.

Should I use the "request read receipt" function?

Some email programs have a function that will send you a message (a "read receipt") when your recipient has opened and presumably read your email. When the recipient opens the email, he or she will get a message that asks whether he or she wants to send a read receipt, and he or she can choose to send the receipt or cancel it. Using this function has fallen out of favor and is considered rude; it's as though the sender is checking up on the recipient in a very parental way. As the sender can choose to cancel the read receipt, there is no guarantee that one will be sent to you, and you risk insulting someone for no purpose.

If you are concerned that someone will not read an important message, include a purposeful question to which they must reply, such as "what are your thoughts on XYZ?" or "does this match your own memory of the conversation?" If the recipient doesn't send you a reply to the question, you will have an excuse to email or call him or her and ask the question again. This is a roundabout alternative to the read receipt, but one that doesn't risk insulting the recipient.

Using all uppercase letters in an email is like screaming insanely at the recipient and is not considered good email etiquette.

Why shouldn't I write in uppercase letters?

Also called typing in "all caps," using uppercase letters to emphasize a sentence or statement is the equivalent of yelling. It is considered rude and can make the person who wrote it seem somewhat unhinged. Consider the difference in tone between the following sentences:

Direct—Replies must be received by Wednesday.

Yelling—Replies MUST be received by WEDNESDAY.

Deranged—REPLIES MUST BE RECEIVED BY WEDNESDAY.

How can I politely add emphasis to some of my sentences?

If you need to strongly emphasize a point in your email, give the statement its own line in the body of the text so it stands out. You can also use italics or bold fonts to draw attention to it. A statement emphasized with bold font is considered slightly stronger than one emphasized with italics:

- *Replies must be received by Wednesday.*
- **Replies must be received by Wednesday.**

Are text-speak abbreviations or slang acceptable, such as "TTYL" for "Talk to You Later"?

Using text messaging-style abbreviations in email is very casual and only acceptable in familiar, personal emails.

Do I need to use salutations and sign-offs?

Salutations and sign-offs are polite ways of starting and ending emails. Without a salutation, an email may seem abrupt. Sign-offs give closure to a communication and help end the email on a pleasant note. If the conversation involves several back-and-forth emails, salutations are dropped after the first two emails are exchanged, and sign-offs are usually dropped until the final email that closes the conversation.

What salutations are appropriate for email?

Email salutations change depending on the purpose of the email and how well you know the recipient. For personal emails or professional emails with colleagues you know well, a simple "Hi," "Hello," or in the case of group emails, "Hello all" work well. If your email needs to be less familiar or more formal in tone, "Dear _____," "Good afternoon," and "Greetings" are acceptable.

Using names in salutations is considerate and friendly. Starting an email simply with the person's name is abrupt—always precede the name with a salutation, such as "Hi Lauren," instead of just "Lauren."

If you are not familiar with the recipient, if they are of high rank in your organization, or if they hold office, be sure to use their last name along with an honorific, e.g.: "Dear Mr. Smith," "Hello Dr. Ahmed," or "Greetings, Minister Galen." If you are sending a formal email to a committee or organization, use the committee's title or organizational name in place of a proper name.

What are some recommended email sign-offs?

As with other rules, personal sign-offs for friends, family, or particularly chummy coworkers, can be just about anything. For all other situations, it is best to be simple and straightforward. Avoid quotes, cutesy expressions or jokes, and unnecessary exclamation marks. If possible, tailor your sign-off so it is specific to the individual and the context of the email. If you are making a request, sign off with "Thank you." If you are sending congratulations or wishing someone well, sign off with "Congratulations" or "Best wishes."

Examples of popular sign-offs for casual emails: Cheers, Yours, Take care, Talk to you soon, Later, Thanks!

Examples of popular and polite sign-offs for professional or formal emails: Best, Regards, Thank you, Sincerely.

Is it acceptable to use emoticons?

Emoticons are useful for expressing some nonverbal cues but are very casual in style and tone. If overused, emoticons can become distracting or could make the reader doubt the sincerity of the email. They should be avoided in formal or professional emails.

How should I introduce people through email?

Before making any introductions, get permission from the people you want to introduce, as not everyone wants their contact information shared. If both parties are interested in the connection, send a group email dedicated to the introduction. You may start the email by introducing one to the other or both at once. Examples of an introductory sentence are:

> Sarah, I'd like to introduce you to Jordan.
>
> *or*
>
> Sarah and Jordan, I'm pleased to connect you two.

Then, address each person separately. Give them a description of the person you are introducing them to and why:

> Sarah, Jordan is the senior accounts manager for Wingdings Unlimited. I've known him for over five years, and he has some very unique insights into the markets you want to explore.
>
> Jordan, Sarah is the chief operations officer for Dongles Worldwide. She has been looking at expanding into the market niche you occupy, and I think there might be potential for collaboration between your companies.

At this point, you may add any information necessary to further their relationship or simply turn the conversation over to them. It is possible that they may choose to include you as the conversation evolves, or they may move to a two-way conversation that doesn't involve you.

SOCIAL MEDIA

SOCIAL MEDIA IN BRIEF

What is social media?

Social media refers to online communication tools that allow people to easily share information, ideas, and creative works in virtual communities run by social media companies. Social media companies operate "platforms"—the specific back-end technologies and front-end user interfaces of a social media site. While many users think of "social media" as being related specifically to social networking sites, social media sites fulfill other purposes as well, such as media sharing, question-and-answer sites, discussion forums, and collaborative content creation.

What are the features or hallmarks of a social media site?

All social media sites focus on user-generated content. The content may vary; media, bookmarks, status updates, blogs, and questions and answers are just a sampling of some of the content found in social media. Users create a profile, which may be searchable by other users or search engines, to interact with other users or post content. Communication between users, often called a "conversation," is encouraged, although the form that the conversation takes varies between different social media platforms.

What are some popular forms of social media?

Social media takes many forms and fulfills many purposes. Many platforms cross over different types of social media functionality but usually have a dominant purpose. There are no straightforward categories or definitions for types or forms of social media, but many share characteristics in terms of purpose or user experience. Some common types of social media sites along with platforms popular in Western countries are:

Networking and Microblogging—These types of social media revolve around connecting with and meeting people. Social networking sites tend to focus on sharing short updates (microblogging), link sharing, and media embedding. Most social media platforms have some element of networking in them, though certain platforms emphasize networking more strongly than others. Examples: Facebook, LinkedIn, Twitter, and Tumblr.

Livestreaming—Livestreaming is real-time video or audio broadcasting. Users can watch other users' live streams or create their own. Some social media live-streaming apps store broadcasts permanently, while others remove the broadcast after a certain period of time. Examples: Periscope, Blab, and Meerkat.

Media Sharing—Videos and photos are the most popular types of media shared on these social media sites. Social media sharing has edged into mainstream entertainment and now competes with traditional television and cable outlets for viewers. YouTube in particular has grown into a juggernaut entertainment platform. Other examples: Instagram, Vine, and Snapchat.

Curation and Bookmarking—These social discovery platforms center on sharing links to online content. Users create categories to organize their links and can share other users' links in addition to their own. Examples: Pinterest, Delicious, and StumbleUpon.

Discussion and Q&A Forums—Supporting conversations about everything from pop culture to family matters to tech support, discussion forums are like big and often baffling cocktail parties. These social media sites focus more on active conversation than on status updates or media sharing. Discussion forums are notorious for harboring social media trolls (aggressive or malicious commenters) but also create strongly supportive and helpful online communities. Examples: Reddit, 4Chan, and Quora.

Educational—Educational social media sites emphasize content creation over user profiles or networking. These sites often have discussion areas, user-to-user messaging, and social networking components, but they are usually intended to be used for improving site content. Many sites allow group editing of shared content. Examples: Wikipedia and Slideshare.

Reviews—Social review sites allow users to rate and rank anything from businesses to people. Engagement and conversation between reviewers and the businesses they review is common. Examples: Yelp, Zomato, and TripAdvisor.

What is microblogging?

Microblogging is a popular social media activity where a user creates very short posts that are shared through a social media platform. Examples of microblogging in social media are Twitter posts, which are restricted to 140 characters, and Tumblr, which functions as an alternative to long-form blogs and encourages short posts and media shares. Many social network platforms have a microblogging component, usually appearing as a "status update" function.

What is engagement?

Engagement is when two or more users interact with one another, such as by replying or commenting on a social media post. Conversations can often involve multiple users, who then engage with one another by responding to each other's comments. Engagement might be very simple and surface-level, usually done through reaction widgets such as "like" or "favorite" buttons. "Sharing" or reposting a user's content is another form of engagement that can significantly increase the audience reach of the original post by exposing it to people in the sharer's network.

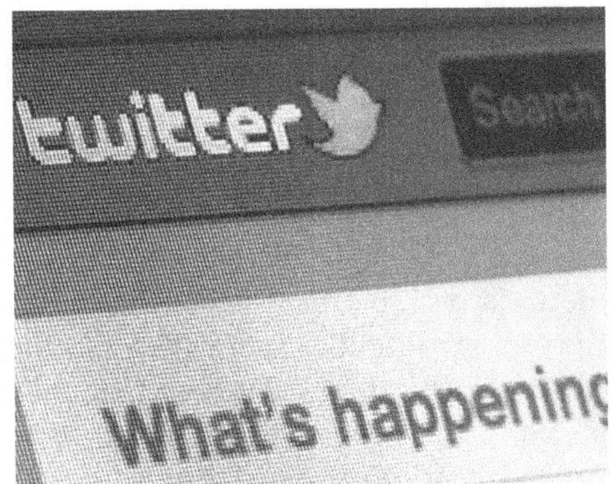

Twitter is a service on which people can microblog: posting short texts and links about themselves and their interests.

What are viral posts?

Viral posts are content that gets viewed or shared by a large number of social media users in a very short period of time. While virality doesn't have to happen on social media platforms alone, the networked nature of these platforms, combined with media and link-sharing capabilities, makes them the most common way for content to go viral. Viral content is usually some kind of digital asset, like a video or photo.

It is extremely difficult to pin down what causes something to go viral. A combination of factors are needed: the right audience needs to see it, it can be easily shared, it is likely entertaining or shocking, and it may be timely to other current events. Attempting to intentionally create viral content has become a hot marketing activity for many organizations. Many brands have successfully created viral campaigns (such as the Old Spice Guy campaign), while many others have spent considerable time and money into failed viral media strategies.

What is clickbait?

Clickbait are links on social media feeds, in emails, and on websites with strongly emotional, shocking, sensationalist, or hyperbolic headlines intended to get readers to click on said link. The actual value or quality of the content that the clickbait headline links to is usually questionable and may redirect viewers to unrelated content or websites. These links often appear as "sponsored content," meaning that they are paid advertisements.

Clickbait headlines are often easy to recognize, following predictable formulas that include numbered lists, a vague hint at the actual content, and statements like "you won't believe what happened next!" Many of the characteristics of clickbait headlines are reminiscent of the strategies used in yellow press or tabloid-style journalism. Backlash against using these strategies to drive online traffic has been rising. Clickbait has been derided as cluttering up social media news feeds to the extent that social media companies like Facebook are changing their technology to reduce user exposure to low-quality content.

What is tagging?

Tagging is the practice of adding keywords to a piece of content's metadata to make it more discoverable. In social media networks like Facebook or Twitter, tagging associates the profile of another user with a specific post or piece of content. This may be to draw a user's attention to the post or to identify the person in a photo. Tagging someone in a post or photo can make that post or photo visible to other people that the tagged user has in his or her network. In order to improve privacy, many social media platforms allow users to limit other people's ability to tag them.

What are hashtags?

Hashtags are a form of keyword tagging used in social media platforms to make a post more discoverable. Anyone can create or use them by applying the "#" symbol in front of a keyword—for example, #communication. If multiple words are being used, the words are grouped together with no spaces in between. Hashtags are not case sensitive. A social media user interested in a topic can run hashtag searches for related posts. For example, a football fan wanting information on the 2017 Super Bowl might search for #SuperbowlLI (Super Bowl LI, or Super Bowl 51). If a fan wants his or her post to be included in conversations about that topic, he or she inserts the hashtag into the post: "Can't wait for #SuperbowlLI in #Houston!"

Hashtags can be placed anywhere within a post. They are often incorporated into a sentence in order to save space, such as "This book on #communication is a must-read!" If the hashtag doesn't incorporate elegantly into a post, it is usually added at the end: "This book on communication is a must-read! #publicspeaking #business #CareerBuilder"

A trending hashtag is one that has become popular among a large number of users. Many websites and social media platforms provide lists of trending hashtags.

ADVANTAGES AND PITFALLS OF SOCIAL MEDIA

How does social media encourage communication?

Social media provides different ways and means for people to connect and communicate with one another. Social media can drastically increase people's ability to reach out and interact with others. This can be especially important for individuals whose social interaction is limited by mobility, geography, or other isolating factors; social media may improve their well-being and quality of life. Additionally, many find the fast, casual style of interaction on social media platforms to be a satisfying way of quickly checking in with friends. This encourages people to exchange brief but frequent communications, which can help strengthen relationships.

Social media provides an easy way for people all over the world to connect and communicate, but it can also encourage the formation of very shallow relationships, limit exposure to different points of view, and leave one vulnerable to unfriendly personal attacks.

The range and breadth of networking possibilities allows users to share their ideas more widely and organize into cohesive online communities. These capabilities have meant that social media now plays an undeniable role in social and cultural movements as well as in civic and political activism. Increased distribution channels have also given people new ways of spreading their thoughts and ideas to a large audience. Creation and distribution of original, media-rich content such as videos, photos, and multimedia posts are encouraged through the easy-to-use interfaces boasted by many social media platforms. Communication through social media tends to be quite open in nature. Information can be shared easily and news spread rapidly, allowing for people to keep up with current affairs.

It should be noted that these and other benefits of social media are most pronounced among skilled users with good offline communication skills as well. When social media use infringes on regular, in-person social activities and daily life, any benefits are quickly lost. As with most things in life, moderation is key.

Why can social media stifle communication?

While social media can provide an excellent way of connecting with others and sharing ideas, there are many ways in which it can prevent the sort of communication it is supposed to encourage. Social media has been criticized for promoting "weak ties"—relationships that don't involve a deep or lasting bond. Weak ties encourage equally shallow conversations and interactions, particularly as communication is reduced to short sound bites that can be easily shared over the limited space of a status update. Many studies have demonstrated that people who spend more time on social media spend less time engaging with others in person. This limits the opportunity for deep, lengthy conversation. While online discussions and exchanges of posts might mimic conversation, these written, asynchronous conversations are not the same experience as real-time, face-to-face exchanges. Without practice in engaging in sustained and complex conversation, communication skills can deteriorate.

Anxiety about other people's reactions to disagreeable or controversial posts can strongly influence what people are willing to post online. The spiral of silence communication theory demonstrates that when someone gets a negative reaction to something he or she shares or when he or she sees other people receiving negative reactions, he or she becomes less likely to express controversial or disagreeable thoughts. Dominant opinions are communicated while minority views become suppressed and made to seem more unusual than might actually be. In social media, where aggressive commenting is more common than in "real life," this effect can seem even greater.

Because it is easy to seek out others who share the same viewpoint, individuals can more effectively limit their exposure to opposing viewpoints. By avoiding opposing opinions, people can become less capable of communicating effectively with those who think differently than they. Studies and analyses by communications professors Sherice Gearhart and Weiwu Zhang demonstrated that these behaviors were more pronounced in people who were relatively unskilled users of social media networks.

How long do social media posts hang around for?

Determining the life span of a post on social media depends on how "life span" is defined and what social media platform is being used. Different platforms make posts visible in different ways, which can affect the life span of a post in terms of how long it may last in someone's social media feed. Social media networking feeds update very quickly, which means that a post is likely only going to be visible in someone's feed for a short period of time before getting pushed out by newer content.

The term "shelf life" refers to the length of time it takes a post to fall to half its initial value in visibility and user engagement. The shelf life of a post on most social media platforms is very short. Social media metrics company Wiselytics calculated the shelf life of a Facebook post at approximately ninety minutes and Twitter posts at sixteen minutes. While these posts are still visible on user profiles and may be searched, after a period of time they become practically invisible to others, lost among the noise in the feed or on the platform.

A short shelf life doesn't mean that a post can't be found at a later time. While social media posts tend to pass out of people's field of view quickly, they remain within the system and are potentially discoverable for years. Some platforms do theoretically delete posts from a user's profile after a certain length of time or a certain number of posts. Snapchat allows users to view other user's posts for only a few seconds before the post becomes inaccessible to that viewer. Twitter only allows a user's most recent thirty-two hundred tweets to be viewed. However, this does not mean that old "snaps" or "tweets" can't be found. Snapchat, Twitter, and other social media platforms keep archives of old posts. These can be requested by the user, access can sometimes be purchased, viewers can take and keep screenshots of posts, and private or archived posts could potentially be hacked.

Is it possible to remove social media posts from the Internet?

Most social media platforms allow users to delete old posts, which will no longer show up in a user's profile or in his or her followers' news feeds. This doesn't mean that the post has not been archived in some form elsewhere. Many public figures have come under fire for poorly thought-out social media posts that they deleted but that were saved by other social media users through screenshots or other archiving systems. If you are attempting to "clean up" your social media presence for one reason or another, always remember: Just because you removed something from your profile doesn't mean that it doesn't exist elsewhere on the Internet.

How does social media improve consumer advocacy and customer service?

Social media provides a very public method for consumers to interact with businesses. The strength of social media networks and review sites has made it easy for people to seek and post customer reviews. Online reviews have significant impact on a consumer's purchasing decisions with negative reviews being particularly influential. When a business has a social media presence, consumers can make their reviews even more visible by posting them directly to that business's social media profiles or by tagging the business in their own posts. Because of the visibility of these posts, many companies will respond to them rapidly. Through social media, consumers have been given more power to hold businesses to account for the quality of their services, products, or activities in a highly visible and public way.

How did social media encourage content consumers to become content creators?

Through intuitive user interfaces and relatively easy learning curves, social media allows people with little technological knowledge about creating websites to post their content online. Publishing content on social media is usually easy and fast, and platforms often support many different kinds of media. This encourages content creation and distribution by significantly reducing technological skill barriers.

Social media also provides people with easier access to audiences. People who create content typically want that content to be viewed by at least a few people, and attracting online attention can be difficult without a means to easily distribute the content to viewers. The networks and communities on social media allow creators to put their content directly in front of prospective viewers through various means, such as user news feeds, searchable hashtags, content recommendations, and front pages with aggregated content from active users.

What is data mining?

Social media data mining is the collection and analysis of massive amounts of information gathered through social media databases to learn about patterns of human behavior. The information gathered includes user profile information, posts, networks, and interactions between users. The behaviors analyzed could be related to anything from consumer buying patterns to online dating. The data created has a wide variety of uses, including the development of software and technology and for marketing and advertising purposes. As social media data includes habits and behaviors that would be impossible to collect through other techniques, it is a veritable gold mine for marketers.

What privacy issues should I be aware of when using social media as a communication tool?

Privacy is a major concern on social media. User accounts often have default settings that allow a user's information, profile, and posts to be viewed publicly. Even when people change their privacy settings to limit access to their posts and profiles, tagging creates privacy problems by letting information about a user—such as a photo—to be shared across other users' networks. Third-party applications that run through social media sites, such as games or content aggregators, frequently require users to grant access to their profile and contacts and may even make posts on behalf of a user. The terms of service on many social media sites can be murky in regards to privacy. Questions as to who "owns" the user profile information and content posted to a social media site often occur. Finally, many social media sites conduct data mining on users. Companies may sell this information to commercial enterprises or even grant third parties access to their user databases for data-mining purposes.

What effect has social media had on news and journalism?

Public communication of news has shifted since the rise of social media, and the effect on news distribution and journalism has been both good and bad. A positive effect has been the increased access to public opinion, sources, and breaking reports. Social media

Software, apps, and websites often require users to acknowledge that some of their data may be collected for marketing purposes before they are allowed to use a service.

has also given news outlets and journalists a new way to communicate with their readership via direct interaction and personalized content. Citizen journalists are able to access readers and viewers with unprecedented ease. This has allowed for a wider variety of narratives and experiences of current events to be shared with news consumers.

On the other hand, social media has presented news communication models with many difficulties. With the huge amount of content and noise on social media sites, attention has become a scarce resource. News outlets and journalists find themselves competing for readership with citizen journalists, freelancers, self-proclaimed pundits, and anyone else sharing news through social media.

Quality and objectivity within news communication have become especially worrisome. In order to cut through the noise and attract attention on social media channels, objectivity has decreased in favor of attention-grabbing headlines and clickable links. Nonprofessional citizen journalists rarely have education and training in objective reporting, which can influence what information and meaning is presented in news stories. Social media has also significantly shortened the news cycle, leading many news providers to favor quickly releasing poorly researched news stories in order to be the first to reach readers.

Has social media contributed to social and political participation?

Social media has often been touted as a contributor to a rise in social and political participation. Favorite case studies for this are Barack Obama's 2012 presidential election campaign and the organization of Arab Spring protests and activities through social media channels. (The Arab Spring was a wave of protests and revolutions throughout many Arab countries from 2010 to 2013 in which people were protesting dictatorships.) Many youths received the majority of their information about society and politics through social media channels. News items are often sent their way by friends or family, which increases the influence these stories have on their readers. The way information is distributed over social media means people have less active searching to do to find stories of interest. Direct individual and mass communication through social media also makes it easier for groups to form and take organized social, civic, or political action.

Arab Spring protests began in Tunisia in 2010 and spread throughout many Arab countries, such as these protests in Alexandria, Egypt, with the help of communication through social media.

Despite the initial hope that online political and social participation through social media would increase offline participation, studies have demonstrated that the effect on participation isn't consistent between different countries. There is evidence that social media and social sharing played a significant role in the events of the Arab Spring. But despite expectations, social media hasn't resulted in a spike in political participation in other countries, such as the United States. While online activism is on the rise, offline activism—especially voter turnout during elections—hasn't changed in a statistically significant way. Peter Dahlgren, an expert on media, communication, and political activism, explains this conundrum: "Access to social media per se usually will not turn people into engaged citizens, [but] .. social media can play an important function in facilitating participation." Social media might not turn nonparticipants into activists, but it does help and encourage people who are already interested in playing a bigger role in social and political affairs.

What is slacktivism?

Slactivism refers to online awareness campaigns and activity that encourage people to demonstrate support for a cause or idea with minimum effort or involvement. These campaigns are most commonly spread through social media and involve actions such as sharing an update with a trending hashtag, signing an online petition, or modifying a user profile picture. Slacktivism has been accused of reducing true actions, such as donating to a cause, by satisfying people's desire to feel like they're participating without actually doing anything meaningful.

The actual civic and political engagement of slacktivists is, however, more complicated than simply clicking on a petition and forgetting about it. More recently, slactivist activity has been shown to act as a sort of gateway to further participation. Campaigns such as online petitions and profile picture overlays help keep social issues top-of-mind for people who would not otherwise be aware of them. Participation in these campaigns helps foster feelings of belonging to a group, which in turn increases the likelihood that someone will participate in more meaningful activities in the future. There's also a social proof aspect of slacktivist campaigns. Seeing a large number of supporters, or seeing friends or family sharing or "liking" an online campaign, can convince skeptical people that an issue is worth supporting (or at least worth thinking about).

Trolling is harassing people on social media for no reason other than trying to upset people.

What is trolling?

Social media trolling is when one or more social media users harass an individual or attempt to create discord in a social media community by posting inflammatory comments. For a discussion on trolling and online aggression, refer to the chapter "A Brief History of Communication" in the section "How the Internet Changed Everything."

What are sockpuppets?

Sockpuppets are false identities and fake social media accounts. Sockpuppets are often used on social media to churn up discord, disagreement, and fighting on online discussions. They are also used to influence online discussion by creating the impression that more people agree with a certain viewpoint or share a certain opinion about something. Some sockpuppets are created for the purposes of deception, fraud, or online harassment. Creating sockpuppets for the purposes of aggressive social media marketing has also become commonplace.

Some sockpuppets are easy to identify. They may follow lots of people while having very few followers themselves, have few posts on a social media platform, and have limited or vague user profiles. Other sockpuppet accounts are more elaborate and may be difficult to distinguish from legitimate social media profiles.

What is a personal brand?

A personal brand is a curated online identity an individual creates for him- or herself for a strategic purpose, often related to career or business aspirations. A personal brand communicates specific aspects about someone's identity, personality, and key strengths. These brands can be fostered in many online spaces, including individual websites and blogs, but are strongly reinforced through social media use. As social media is commonly used by everyone from employers to prospective mates in order to learn about someone's personality, creating brands has become a popular concept for strategically managing one's social media activity. This concept can be used to teach responsible online behavior, as the idea of being a brand illustrates how online activity can affect others' perception of what someone is really like in the same way that advertising affects our perceptions of commercial brands.

What sorts of social media posts or choices affect personal brands?

Personal brands are affected by a wide range of choices concerning what personal and professional information one shares online and where to share it. These choices are influenced by the individual's goals for his or her personal brand (whether he or she is trying to build his or her career, improve his or her business, gain social media followers, etc.) as well as his or her target audience. As it is impossible to appeal to everyone, people building brands select an audience demographic they want to appeal to—e.g., millennials and Gen-Xers in the financial industry, stay-at-home parents, or teenage fashion aficionados. Choices related to purpose and audience will affect other decisions, such as which social media platforms to use, what content to share, and how to craft a user profile.

On social media, the most visible aspect of a personal brand is what someone chooses to post and share. People establishing a brand adopt consistent posting strategies, sharing information and ideas that fit within a defined range of topics. A blend of professional and personal interests is usually represented. This allows a person to demonstrate his or her skill or knowledge in certain areas while making him or her more relatable. Being able to communicate a personality online increases trust, makes someone more identifiable in a crowded online space, and attracts social media followers.

Choice of social media platforms affects brands by placing the user among a certain audience type and associating with a specific style of online communication. All social media platforms have a sort of "personality" created through their purpose, user experience, and the amalgamated personalities of the users themselves. This platform personality influences what people think about the platform's users, so the choice of one social media platform over another does have an effect on a personal brand. Someone who is mostly active on LinkedIn might be perceived as more professional or corporate-minded than someone who exclusively uses Pinterest and Instagram. Snapchat users might be seen as more youthful and less discretionary than someone who distributes his or her videos through Vimeo.

Personal identifiers, especially usernames and profile photos, are another critical choice in personal branding. They communicate a great deal about both the person behind the brand and the audience he or she is attempting to attract. Usernames that involve a variation of the person's first and last name are perceived as more mature, more professional, and more trustworthy than usernames involving clever or cutesy monikers. Similarly, crisp, professional-quality profile photos increase the impression of reliability and trustworthiness than do grainy selfies. More user profile information that can be important to personal branding includes hobbies, interests, and links to the person's other online presences such as additional social media profiles and his or her personal website or blog.

How can social media affect communication between employees, employers, and coworkers?

The lines between professional and personal lives can be very blurry on social media. Many don't distinguish between professional or personal context when posting on social media. As social media profiles provide snapshots into people's personalities, employers are increasingly turning to social media to gain insight into the personalities of prospective employees. Employee social life and nonwork activities can be subject to scrutiny by some employers with possibilities for both formal and informal repercussions for unwanted behavior. It isn't only employers who blur professional and personal social media identities. The general public may do so as well, viewing someone's personal information as a reflection of the values of the organization he or she works for.

Comfort with sharing personal information should be considered when deciding whether or not to connect with coworkers over social media. There may be pressure to add coworkers to one's social media network. Some employees may feel uncomfortable granting coworkers, supervisors, or managers access to their personal posts or photos.

Others may enjoy sharing these slices of their personal lives with the people they work with and find that it helps deepen relationships with coworkers. Should someone decide to connect with coworkers or supervisors over social media, they need to be aware that anything they post might have implications in the workplace. While there are no right or wrong answers as to whether someone should connect with coworkers on social media, practicing discretion when posting is always advisable.

EFFECTIVE USE OF SOCIAL MEDIA

Is everything I do on social media public?

Social media platforms have varying privacy settings, and it's important to become familiar with these settings to know what is public and what is private. Most platforms' default settings have all posts released publicly unless you change those settings. There are often three layers of visibility: public (everyone can see a post), a setting where posts are only visible to people with whom you are connected or "friends," and private. Some platforms allow people to restrict what certain followers can see, allowing posts to be visible to some people with whom you are connected but not others. In addition to the privacy settings for your posts and information, you should decide if you will allow people to tag you in photos or posts. Many platforms allow users to block themselves from being tagged in posts (please refer to the question "What is tagging?" earlier in this chapter). Other privacy settings allow you to block certain users from contacting you or seeing your posts. Check your account settings on your social media platforms to learn more about the privacy options available to you.

Even though there are many privacy settings on different platforms, a good rule of thumb is to assume that nothing you post on social media is private. Be aware of your own comfort levels in relation to private and public information. Some people are comfortable with sharing a great deal of personal information, while others prefer to keep their personal life private. Only post information, photos, and updates that you wouldn't mind showing up in your local newspaper. If you are in doubt whether or not something is "safe" to post in social media, your best option is to avoid posting it at all.

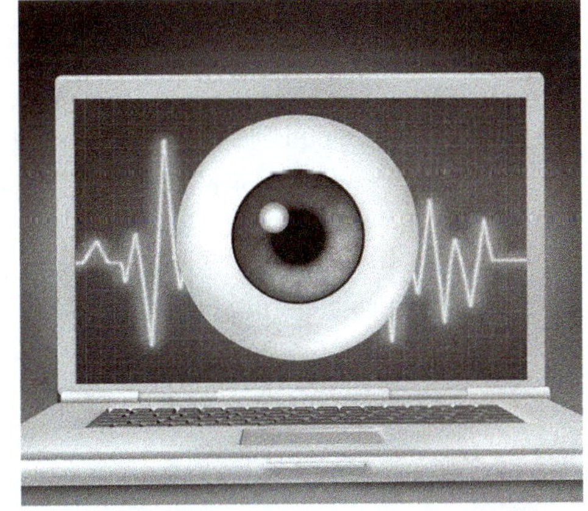

How much of what you do on social media is being observed, even recorded? You can limit eyeballs on your activities by adjusting your privacy settings.

How do I choose which social media platforms to use?

The choice of social media platforms is dizzyingly vast and evolves rapidly. Deciding on which ones to use depends on what you want to use them for, how you prefer to engage with content, and who you want to connect with. The following table lists eight social media platforms popular in the United States, along with some characteristics and strengths for personal and business use.

Facebook

Characteristics: Largest, most populated social media networking site; very broad user base; popular for status updates, personal photo sharing, private messaging, and creating groups or communities of users; supports longer posts

Personal Uses: Find and connect with old and current acquaintances; share personal photos; private messaging; create event invitations; join or create groups of users

Business Uses: Business page for connecting with customers; direct conversation and discussion with customers; run contests, polls, and campaigns; share company culture; advertising

LinkedIn

Characteristics: Majority of users are college-educated adults; intended for professional and work/business-related networking; professional groups and associations may create profiles; publishing platform for articles (*Pulse*); presentation-sharing platform (*Slideshare*)

Personal Uses: Use profile as an enhanced resume; seek employment opportunities; publish and distribute articles and presentations; research employees at different companies; participate in discussion related to your work or area of expertise

Business Uses: Recruitment; establish online company profile; publish and distribute articles and presentations

Twitter

Characteristics: Microblogging; link and news sharing; monitor current trends and breaking news; good for quick "in-and-out" engagement and scanning

Personal Uses: Follow breaking news and developing events; find trending topics; follow topics of interest; create personalized lists; tweets are short and easy to scan

Business Uses: Distribute original content to followers; share content from other people with followers; follow trending issues; attract traffic to business website or blog; frequent but brief communication with followers

Pinterest

Characteristics: Social bookmarking and curation; majority of users are adult women; provides images and links to content elsewhere on the web; create "Pinboards" to organize content

Personal Uses: Popular choice for food, lifestyle, do-it-yourself projects, and crafts; easy to organize and save links to online content for future reference; focus is on sharing other's content—no need for status updates or blog posts

Business Uses: Product image sharing; brand image creation; longer shelf life of posts than most other platforms; communicate corporate culture; track performance of your Pins; issue "behind-the-scenes" snapshots

YouTube

Characteristics: Video-sharing site; huge audience and community; popular alternative to television

Personal Uses: View and comment on videos; find original video content; create personal channel and playlists; upload and share videos; excellent for accessing tutorials and instructional videos

Business Uses: Create and distribute videos; advertising; create playlists for subscribers; search engine optimization—creating and uploading videos increase visibility in Google search results; create links back to business website

Instagram
Characteristics: Media sharing network; photo editing and filtering capabilities; popular among teenagers, young adults, and millennials

Business Uses: Edit and share videos; feed shows all photos of people in your network; emphasis is on sharing images, no need for writing text updates

Business Uses: Communicate corporate culture and personality; share product photos; issue "behind-the-scenes" snapshots; feed shows all photos a user is subscribed to; long shelf life for posts

The social media site Instagram focuses on photo and video sharing and includes editing and filtering capabilities.

What is the best way to use hashtags?

For hashtags to be useful or help promote a social media post, they need to be used with some care. The following best practices apply to hashtags in many social media platforms:

- Don't overuse hashtags—a single post should not contain more than three hashtags. Any more will make the post look like spam.
- Hashtags should be relevant to the content of the post. It is very poor practice to "hijack" trending hashtags for promotional purposes. For example, people would be annoyed if someone posted "#Football is awesome and so is this amazing sale at Bob's Discount Mattresses #SuperbowlLI" during playoffs.
- Don't duplicate hashtags within a single post.
- Keep hashtags straightforward and simple—this makes them easier to search.
- Consider the purpose of your message when creating hashtags. Informational or topical posts tend to use subject-specific hashtags like #business or #personalfinance. Personal, sentimental, and inspirational posts often use hashtags that express feelings and emotions, like #excited or #lovinglife.

How can I increase engagement on social media posts?

Engagement on social media posts is rewarding for individuals and businesses alike. There are many ways to encourage people to comment on or share your posts. Some useful methods for increasing engagement are:

Ask questions—Comments can be increased by soliciting opinions and asking questions that people can respond to. Be sure to follow up and reply to any comments or answers; otherwise, people will think you aren't paying attention to their contributions.

Post "shareable" content—Links to useful articles, short how-to tips, and funny photo memes are easy for users to read and to share. If you don't enjoy creating original shareable content, then share other people's content with your social media followers. If you want to share something, it's likely other people will also want to spread it around.

Comment on and/or share other people's content or posts—Engaging with others encourages them to engage with you in return. Be sure to credit them when sharing their content.

Include photos or other media in your posts—Images draw the eye and encourage people to click on links, read posts, and share content.

Create polls or surveys—Polls and surveys are even easier and faster ways for people to give you their opinions. Many social media platforms have easy-to-use polling or surveying tools.

Do not *directly ask for people to share your content*—This is somewhat tacky and can even result in your post being hidden from social media feeds. Platforms like Facebook and Twitter contain algorithms that bury posts with share or retweet requests.

How frequently should I post on social media?

Recommended posting frequency depends on what platform you are using and why you are using it. Many people "lurk" on social media, using it as a way to keep up with friends, family, or current events without ever posting themselves. If you are a casual user of social media and don't have much interest in how many people follow you or see your posts, then there is no rule as to how often you "should" post. It is considered rude, however, to post with excessive frequency. For more information, please refer to the section on social media etiquette later in this chapter.

Some users, especially those using social media to grow their business, want to actively solicit followers. In this case, you need to post often. On platforms with fast-moving feeds like Twitter and Facebook, posting about two or three times a day can generate the most interest. Platforms with longer post shelf lives include LinkedIn and Instagram, where a posting schedule of once or twice per week may be enough to engage your followers and gain new ones. It's important, too, to post at the right time of day when people are most active on social media platforms. There are many online software services that can calculate your optimal time for posting content on different social media platforms.

A reliable posting schedule is important for gaining and holding on to social media followers. Regularity in posting builds trust and attracts followers; people won't follow a user who is rarely active. Whether you choose to post to Facebook and YouTube three times a day or three times a week, maintain a predictable posting schedule so that your followers know when to expect new content.

What should go into a social media profile?

The type of information that gets put into a social media profile depends on what you are using social media for and what platform you are on. For example, a good LinkedIn profile should list your key skills and attributes along with your current work, past work experience, education, and any other information relevant to your professional identity. Facebook asks for a considerable amount of information in its profiles, but many people choose to leave areas such as "employer" or current place of residence blank (or fill in fake or mildly sarcastic information). Listing hobbies and interests is popular among users of most social media platforms.

When deciding what you should put into a social media profile, use the following questions to guide your decisions:

- What am I using this social media platform for?
- Who will be seeing my profile?
- What impression do I want them to have of me?
- What information is relevant to them?
- What information isn't important?
- What information might create privacy issues?
- What do I like knowing about other people?

What makes a good profile picture?

Your profile picture communicates a great deal of information about you and your personality. It is the most visual aspect of your personal brand. Photos that cast you in a bad or juvenile light, especially those demonstrating juvenile, sophomoric behavior like drinking or suggestive poses, will affect people's impressions of you regardless of the content of your social media posts. For all profiles and platforms, clean images that clearly show your face are recommended. Be sure that the picture is of a size and resolution that works well with the image settings in your chosen platforms. For casual profiles, choose a photo that makes you feel good about yourself or confident in the way you look. For business or work-related profiles, pick something that shows you in appropriate dress and is up-to-date. If your only good business photos are from a professional shoot you did ten years ago, then it's time to take a new picture or book a new photo shoot.

A straightforward, recent, good-quality photo of yourself always makes the best profile picture.

How should I deal with negative comments or a social media troll?

When encountering comments that are negative, malicious, or trolling, it's easy to become angry and want to respond immediately. The best way to respond to such comments often depends on how aggressive the comments are. If you receive a negative comment that doesn't seem overly aggressive or malicious, then try engaging in polite discussion. Strategies like asking the commenter questions or providing simple, straightforward explanations can often turn a negative comment into a useful discussion.

When the comments are malicious or inflammatory, a different approach is necessary. As discussed elsewhere in this book, the best option for dealing with online trolling is to neither respond to nor acknowledge the trolling. People who participate in trolling activity are usually there to incite outrage, and they thrive off reactions. If, after several attempts, no response is given, the troll is likely to take his or her attention elsewhere.

Most online trolling is annoying and may be distressing, but it does not usually signify actual threats against the person being trolled. In recent years, however, there has been increasing concern over especially aggressive trolling and online harassment. Common forms of aggressive trolling include:

- "Doxing": Posting people's telephone numbers and home addresses on public forums
- Threats of physical violence against an individual or an individual's family
- Attempts at blackmail, often threatening release of sexually explicit photographs or private information

This list represents some common forms of aggressive trolling and is by no means exhaustive. If you are the target of aggressive trolling and online harassment or feel that your personal safety is at risk, contact your local law-enforcement agency and document the harassment.

What is newsjacking?

Newsjacking is the practice of referencing a piece of trending news and then inserting personal or corporate messages, ideas, or thoughts about that issue. This is usually done by directly mentioning a current news event, using its related trending hashtags, and inserting a personal comment or a link to related content. Newsjacking is extremely common and may be done intentionally or inadvertently. Individuals may newsjack on social media in order to draw attention to their thoughts or opinions on a current issue, or to build their visibility or personal brand. People in the public eye, such as celebrities or politicians, might newsjack to increase their visibility among fans or constituents. Businesses frequently newsjack as a form of advertising.

A masterful example of newsjacking occurred during the 2013 Super Bowl when an unexpected power outage hit the Superdome. During the blackout, the Oreo cookie social media team took to Twitter, sending out the tweet "Power out? No problem." The tweet included an image of a single Oreo cookie, softly glowing against a black background, and the caption, "You can still dunk in the dark." The tweet was wildly popular. It was shared thousands of times through social media and has been applauded by mainstream and online marketing critics alike as a brilliant stroke of social media marketing.

An example of newsjacking that some found in poor taste was when Sears used the 2012 Hurricane Sandy disaster to try to sell their products on a special Web page.

Why can newsjacking be a controversial practice?

For newsjacking to be effective, the news story being referenced must be actively trending and gaining widespread attention. Many trending stories and hashtags deal with issues that are highly sensitive or solemn, such as memorial holidays or natural disasters. Newsjacking topics like these for the purposes of marketing is perceived as crass, insensitive, and wildly inappropriate. Many people and companies have made this mistake. Hashtags and comments referencing the Boston Marathon bombing in 2013, the 2011 political uprisings in Cairo, Hurricane Sandy, Martin Luther King Day, and Memorial Day have all been newsjacked by major brands to advertise products and sales. Judgment from the court of public opinion was swift, and the offending brands were pilloried on the same social media platforms they used for the newsjacking. People and businesses who run afoul of newsjacking often delete the offending posts and issue apologies. However, it's common practice to take screenshots of offending posts and then repost them to websites and other social media sites.

SOCIAL MEDIA ETIQUETTE

Do I need to accept "friend" or other connection requests on social media?

Some people feel considerable pressure to network with people who send connection requests, particularly if the person is a friend or family member. It is not considered poor etiquette to turn down requests to connect through social media. However, if the person making the request is close to you, you may want to consider how he or she will react if you refuse the request.

One of the most effective and straightforward ways to turn down a request to connect on social media is to simply ignore it. In the bustle and noise of social media, many people forget that they made a connection request. If the person making the request is from your work and feigning ignorance isn't an option, polite refusals that state that you prefer to keep personal and professional social media activity separate are acceptable and keep everyone's dignity intact. Similarly, if you don't want to accept a request from someone outside of work, you could explain that you limit your social media to immediate family or some other easily identifiable group.

Increasing privacy settings can help decrease unwanted connection requests. Other options offered by most platforms include blocking certain people from sending you connection requests or accepting a connection request but using the privacy settings to severely limit what you allow that person to see.

How should I connect with people at work—such as my boss, supervisor, or coworkers—on social media?

Your decision to connect or "friend" professional colleagues through social media will depend on your relationship to them, the social media platform you are using, and the general acceptance of social media in an organization's culture. The safest path to follow is to not send friend or connection requests to people senior to you on the organizational ladder. This is the equivalent of calling your boss on their personal phone and should be especially avoided if the workplace or professional relationship is very formal or traditional. In very small organizations, informal or nontraditional work environments, or among your peers, sending out social media connection requests is more acceptable. Always keep your organization's social media policies in mind; some organizations don't allow supervisors or coworkers to post recommendations on another employee's social media profile and may even discourage employees from connecting on social media at all.

Someone has followed me on social media. Do I need to follow them back?

There are social media platforms that allow users to follow other users and see the other user's posts in their feeds without directly connecting or networking with them. Twitter and Pinterest are examples where users can "follow" other users' activities.

Many people immediately "follow back" any social media user who follows them. This practice can help expose someone to new audiences and expand their circle of influence, and it is considered by some to be polite. Not following people back, however, isn't considered impolite. If a new person decides to follow you on social media, look at that person's user profile to decide if he or she is a real account and if you are interested enough to want updates about him or her in your feed.

Is it acceptable to tag other people in photos posted to social media sites?

While the tagging may be done with the best of intentions, many people don't want pictures of themselves posted to social media either for privacy reasons or because they want to be able to manage their personal brand and online image. If someone has asked you to share an image of them over a social media platform, then it is acceptable to tag them. If he or she hasn't given you permission or if you are uncertain if he or she would be comfortable with being tagged, it is better not to do it. People have the opportunity to tag themselves in your photo should they wish.

How often is too often to post on a social media site?

"Cluttering" someone's social media feed with overly frequent posting is bad etiquette. While it's fine to post several times a day, firing off one post after another in rapid succession forces other stories out of your followers' feeds with what are usually low-quality posts. This disrupts the shared-space nature of social media and can reflect badly on the person posting. Posting several times a day is acceptable, but posts should be spread out over several hours. Occasionally engaging in high-volume posting is acceptable, provided it isn't done too often.

Two exceptions to posting frequency etiquette are when people are posting live reports from an event or function they're attending or if they're having a social media event where they're interacting with followers in real-time through their posts. These two situations happen across many different social media platforms but are best known for occurring on Twitter, where they're often referred to as "live tweeting" or "twitter chats." If you are going to be posting live reports or holding a chat through your social media platform, it is polite to send out notifications to your followers letting them know that you will be doing high-volume posting at a given time.

How can I monitor my tone when posting on social media?

Tone is important on social media, especially when writing text-based posts like tweets or status updates. Irony, sarcasm, and other nonverbal emotional cues don't translate well to text. The fast and casual style of communication in social media, along with the propensity for increased aggression, can easily lead to writing posts that convey the wrong tone.

A good practice for watching your tone in social media posts or comments is to read what you have written out loud, putting different emotional twists on your vocal tone to see how it might be perceived by readers. This usually sorts out most problems and can help create clearer, more meaningful posts. In general, ironic or sarcastic remarks should be avoided. Using emoticons or emojis to express certain emotions can be useful for your readers as they do convey some nonverbal meaning. However, avoid relying too heavily on these. Posting smiley emoticons at the end of sarcastic or potentially insulting statements comes across as very passive aggressive and shouldn't be used as a way to "soften" posts or comments.

What is oversharing?

Oversharing can mean a variety of things. It can refer to overly frequent posting, sharing distasteful information (like the details and symptoms of a bout with food poisoning), posting minutiae from everyday life, or frequent negative posting like complaining. Some forms of oversharing present privacy risks, like posting about leaving for vacation, details of your home, and personal contact information.

What is a humblebrag?

A humblebrag is a comment that is phrased to seem humble or self-effacing but in reality is intended to point out something you are proud of. Humblebrags are also used to solicit approving or congratulatory comments from others. It is a communication behavior especially prevalent on social media and is now considered juvenile or annoying. The disingenuous style of communication is what makes humblebrags so irritating. It's easy to inadvertently post humblebrags, especially if you are not comfortable with celebrating your accomplishments or other positive personal traits. It's completely acceptable to share such things over social media, but it's better to talk about them directly rather than trying to couch them in false humility.

Is it polite to ask people to share my content?

Asking others to share your content may be seen as overly self-promotional or attention-seeking, especially if you do so regularly. While it may be acceptable to ask people to share your material every now and then, doing it too often comes across as needy. Using hashtags or creating memorable, sharable content is a better strategy for spreading your social media content.

How much of my own content should I post versus sharing other people's content?

Sharing other people's social media content is a great way to demonstrate that you are interested in what others have to say as well as in giving interesting information to your own followers. This holds true for both personal and business-related social media use.

A popular guideline for business or professional social media accounts is to limit posting self-promotional content (like links to your latest blog article or new product) to one-third of your total posts. The remaining two-thirds of your posts should share information from other sources.

For personal social media accounts, the etiquette is looser and is more focused on the type of information you choose to share than a ratio of personal versus shared content. Aim for an equal mix of personal updates and sharing of other people's content, such as news stories you find interesting or photos you like. Avoid sharing clickbait-type content, hoaxes such as alarmist updates about the platform's terms of service, vague status updates intended to elicit concern, or excessive complaining.

What is "hijacking" content?

There are two common forms of content hijacking on social media. The first is when someone reposts another person's content on his or her own social media platform without crediting his or her source. This is considered rude—the equivalent of passing off someone else's work as one's own. Avoiding this breach in etiquette is straightforward: When sharing someone else's social media post, mention the source's name or username in the post or provide a link to the original content. Many platforms automatically do this when someone shares content.

The second common type of social media hijacking is when a hashtag is used for a different purpose than it was originally intended—usually for satire or mockery. Celebrities, politicians, and large businesses creating hashtags for self-serving ends or public-relations campaigns are particularly vulnerable to hashtag hijacking. While this form of hijacking can be deeply irritating for the originators of the hashtag, it's usually considered fair game from a user's perspective. Social media is, after all, an interactive, participatory style of communication with a brand audience, and sometimes the audience doesn't respond in the way that a corporate marketing department would like.

THE PSYCHOLOGY OF PUBLIC SPEAKING

HOW PUBLIC SPEAKING AND ORATORY AFFECT COMMUNICATION

How is communicating through public speaking different from communicating through written materials?

The ways we transmit and process information through public speaking are very different from doing so in writing. Even when the same or similar information is available in written format, there are significant differences in language, expression, and the amount of information made available to the audience.

Reading and writing involve different cognitive and neural processes than speaking and listening. This affects the way we extract meaning from written versus spoken content, along with the information we take in to create that meaning. Different people will use different strategies to create meaning from written or spoken texts, and these strategies might vary widely.

Other differences in the way we communicate through public speaking can be found in the inclusion of nonverbal information, the use of sound techniques such as rhythm and volume changes, and in the time-bound nature of speech. All of these create a completely different information and communication experience. The experience of attending a lecture delivered by a famous professor is not the same as the experience of reading a textbook written by the same person. Content written for out-loud performance will not be as effective when read silently from a page. It is difficult to fully appreciate Shakespeare's *Hamlet* simply by reading the text. It's when we hear and see a skillful delivery of the play that we truly appreciate the author's mastery of expression and emotion.

How is public speaking and oratory "time-bound"?

Public speaking and oratory, like music and other forms of live performance, are linear and constrained (or "bound") by the time in which they are performed.

When we read, we can skip around in the book, going back to refresh our memory or confirm understanding, or moving forward to get an idea of where the text is going. Some books, such as this one, are intended to be read out of order as the reader sees fit. When we are speaking or listening to someone speak, however, we can't go back in time and relive a previous moment in the speech. The content of a talk is meant to be delivered and consumed in an uninterrupted progression. Of course, if we are watching or listening to a recording of a talk, we can rewind to a previous moment, but the talk was still created and performed with the intention that it be taken in continuously.

Being time-bound creates some limitations in public speaking. It can be hard to accurately refer to things we've already said. The content and information must be delivered in an extremely organized way if the audience is to be able to follow along. But it also creates unique expressive opportunities for the speaker. A skilled speaker will use time to his or her advantage, changing his or her speed and pace of delivery, or using rhythm and repetition to create more interest, emphasis, or excitement among his or her audience.

How is public speaking a social act?

In contrast to the mostly individual nature of reading, communicating through public speaking is a social act. Public speakers appear in social spaces and typically with gatherings of several people. The speaker is in contact with his or her audience and has a sense of the reactions and receptiveness of the people listening to him or her speak. Speakers will often engage directly with their audience, asking for feedback or simple participation. Similarly, the audience engages with the speaker through cheers, clapping, laughter, and other group responses.

Additionally, the audience is experiencing the speech, talk, or presentation in a social setting and as a social activity among themselves. Like the speaker, members of the audience can get a sense of how other people are responding to the talk and will feed off the energy and responses of the people around them. There is typically engagement between members of the audience as people exchange thoughts about the speech with one another after and even during the presentation. This sense of a shared experience can amplify the persuasive effect of a speech, help form group identity, and take advantage of herd mentality, where individuals get swept up in the opinions and emotions of the larger collective.

What ways can public speaking and oratory be a more powerful way of communicating than writing?

Public speaking, especially dramatic oratorical styles, is especially good for communicating emotion and nonverbal information as well as for creating a sense of connection

President John F. Kennedy giving a 1961 speech about sending Americans to the moon. Public speaking affords ways to communicate a message more powerfully through body gestures and methods of speaking.

and intimacy between the speaker and the audience. As was discussed earlier in this book, nonverbal communication gives us a wide range of information and meaning above and beyond the words we use. This information can be used to create an emotional or even physical reaction in audiences. By speeding up his or her rate of speech, a speaker can cause a listener's heart to beat more quickly. By using lots of visible physical tension, the speaker can amplify tense moods or emotions in the audience.

Many methods of expression that work exceptionally well in public speaking come across as clumsy in written form. Repetitive devices, such as anaphora (repetition of a word or group of words at the start of several sentences) have incredible dramatic power when spoken out loud but can be tedious to read. Similarly, prosody (the melodic and rhythmic qualities of speech) can't be replicated in writing.

When can public speaking be a poor choice for communication?

Public speaking is not always the best way to communicate. Speakers who are unfamiliar with their material or severely lacking in confidence or competence can send signals that cause the audience to have a lack of confidence in what they are saying. Speakers who antagonize their audience through poorly presented material or through content that conflicts with the audience's interests risk having the group outright reject what they are saying. In this way, the herd mentality that may help amplify a speaker's persuasive effect can also turn on the speaker, causing people to feel more hostility as a group than they would have as individuals.

How are power and public speaking related?

Power and public speaking share an intimate, often confusing relationship. Power is a person's ability to direct other people's actions or way of thinking. Power can be expressed very obviously or very subtly. In human relationships, power is always granted to someone by the people around him or her. In every social group, there will be power dynamics. These power dynamics and relationships may be formally defined, as in the case of a company's corporate hierarchy, or they may be informal, such as with a social group where there is typically someone who directs most of the activities or takes over conversations.

People who engage in public speaking tend to be granted a degree of temporary power by the people listening to them. An exception to this is when the purpose of the presentation is for the speaker to be judged or evaluated on some aspect of his or her performance, such as in speaking competitions or during sample presentations for job interviews. In that situation, the speaker is supplicating to the audience or presenting solely to seek his or her approval, which tips the power balance in favor of the audience.

How do speakers take on a position of power when they are presenting?

There are several aspects of public speaking that signal to the audience that the speaker is in a position of power:

- Much like authors, speakers are often considered experts on the thing they are speaking about. If they weren't, we reason, they wouldn't be speaking about it.
- Speakers often physically separate themselves from their audience. This separation may be as simple as standing up when giving a toast or moving to the front of a boardroom table to give a report. It may also be as staged or formal as walking onto a stage or standing behind a pulpit or lectern. This separation makes the speaker the center of attention. It is also a very vulnerable and physically exposed position—a position that, instinctually, only a powerful person would be willing to take.
- Speakers have temporary control of the audience's behavior. They command the audience's attention, and it is expected that the audience remains quiet unless the speaker invites them to speak. The speaker can also give the audience simple instructions, such as asking them to raise their hands or introduce themselves to the person sitting beside them.
- Speakers initiate what is, for the most part, a one-way conversation. This is an indication of authority as the speaker is taking on the active role, and the audience remains relatively passive.

How might taking on a position of power affect the speaker?

Some speakers are unaffected by the idea of taking on a role of authority, and some enjoy the experience. Many speakers, however, are very uncomfortable with the notion

The physical position one takes when speaking can add power to the messages, such as when a preacher stands behind a pulpit, which helps to focus attention on the speaker.

and find that taking control of a room provokes anxiety. This is especially true when being the speaker upsets the power dynamic that the speaker is accustomed to, and they feel out of place or self-conscious about their temporary status.

ANXIETY AND FEAR OF PUBLIC SPEAKING

What is fear of public speaking?

Fear of public speaking, also called speaker's anxiety, is a generalized anxiety triggered by the act or idea of speaking in front of groups. There is no specific size or type of group that triggers this fear. Some people are comfortable speaking in front of groups of complete strangers but are anxious when speaking to friends or family or vice versa. Some people are nervous speaking to small groups, and some are anxious when faced with a large crowd. Many people experience anxiety with any speaking situation, regardless of audience size or makeup.

Speaker's anxiety can range in intensity from mildly nervous to full-blown panic. It is also possible to experience speaker's anxiety outside of public speaking. For many people, the mere thought of giving a talk or presentation is enough to trigger nervousness.

What is glossophobia?

Glossophobia is an intense, overwhelming fear of public speaking. It is related to social phobia and social anxiety but may exist on its own without the glossophobe experiencing other social phobias or anxieties. Many glossophobes experience related anxiety in situations where they must network with unfamiliar people or perform tasks in front of others. Glossophobia can be triggered even when speaking in front of very small groups. People with this phobia may go out of their way to avoid speaking or drawing attention to themselves. This can interfere with school, work, or social interactions.

Why do so many people fear public speaking?

The notion that more people fear public speaking than death is so bandied about that it has become cliché. There is no denying, however, that public speaking is an activity that provokes a huge amount of anxiety in many people, including in professional speakers and performers. This anxiety can be as strong for someone giving a speech to a crowd of five hundred strangers as it can be for someone giving a presentation at a meeting, speaking to a small group of people, or giving a toast to a gathering of family and friends.

There are a number of reasons why public speaking is an anxiety-creating activity. Much of the anxiety relates to experiencing an instinctual sense of immediate danger and a primal fear of being rejected by a social group. When we speak, we become the center of a group's attention, often physically separating ourselves by standing up or taking a position at the front of a room or behind a lectern. This is a vulnerable position to be in, one in which we are relatively defenseless facing a mob of people. This alone is enough to trigger strong anxieties about our ability to survive an attack when outnumbered.

Adding to the anxiety of being vulnerable and the focus of attention is the fact that the speaker is granted a fair amount of power—a state with which many people are uncomfortable. Speakers are often placed in a position of responsibility and expertise, and during their presentation, they have some control over the actions of the audience. They can demand the audience's attention, for example, direct them to do a simple activity, or choose to accept or refuse questions from the audience. If speakers do not feel confident assuming a position of temporary power and control, they may become very nervous about doing so.

A basic fear of rejection is another key player in the reasons we fear speaking. Humans are social animals, and belonging to a group is extremely important to our survival. Any time we give a presentation or speech, we are under a degree of scrutiny. If our performance or the content of our talk fails to meet the expectations of the audience, our status could be diminished, and we may face humiliation and rejection from the group.

Finally, the fear of public speaking generates a host of extremely unpleasant symptoms, all of which increase the likelihood that we will stumble or mess up part of our performance. These symptoms and the mistakes they generate create a cycle of reinforcement and conditioning: We experience symptoms of fear when we present, which lead to mistakes, which lead to unpleasant feelings such as failure or humiliation, which reinforce the idea that public speaking is frightening. Eventually, we come to fear the fear itself.

The anxiety caused by fear of public speaking triggers a physiological state known as fight or flight.

What is the fight-or-flight response?

Fight or flight is an automatic physiological response to dangerous stimuli or circumstances. It physically prepares our bodies to either fight off a threat or flee it, if necessary. While fight or flight is an automatic or involuntary response, it isn't always accurate. It can be triggered by a stimulus that doesn't actually threaten our survival—such as watching a horror film—and can even be provoked by our own imagination.

Fight or flight is a cascade of chemical signals and physiological responses. When our brain perceives a danger, the hypothalamus sends signals to the sympathetic nervous system and the adrenal cortical system to prepare the body for action.

A flood of over thirty hormones is released, including the famous epinephrine (adrenaline) and its companion norepinephrine, causing the following effects:

- Heart rate and blood pressure increase
- Breathing increases to bring in more air for exertion
- Blood is diverted from extremities, such as your fingers and skin, to larger muscle groups (you need strong arms and legs for running and punching, not dextrous fingers for playing the piano)
- Pupils dilate to take in more light
- Muscles tighten and tense in preparation for action
- Glucose is released into the bloodstream
- Digestion shuts down—fighting is more important than food!
- Attention and thought is diverted away from detailed work and toward the larger environment ... all the better to find the best path to escape that marauding tiger.

Fear of public speaking is common. People are afraid of being rejected or embarrassed by a group whose attention is focused on them.

What are some common symptoms of public speaking anxiety?

While different people will experience somewhat different symptoms of public speaking anxiety, the majority of them can be traced back to the physiological effects of fight or flight. Common symptoms and their fight-or-flight-related causes are:

Symptom	Physiological Cause
Racing heart	Increased heart rate
Flushing, hot flashes	Increased blood pressure and blood flow to muscles
Cold hands, chills, tingling sensations	Decreased blood flow to extremities and skin
Hyperventilating, feeling breathless	Increased breathing rate
Nausea, butterflies in the stomach	Slowed/shut down digestion
Tunnel vision	Dilation of pupils
Dry mouth	Slowed/shut down digestion
Forgetfulness, racing thoughts	Attention diverted from detailed work and toward larger environment for escape or survival
Shaking	Increase in blood glucose, muscle tension

One symptom of public speaking anxiety that is not related to fight or flight but still bears mention is procrastination. This is a symptom of psychological avoidance triggered by the desire to avoid the danger or unpleasant stimulus (public speaking) in the first place. Unfortunately, this usually leads people to leave creating and practicing their presentation until the last minute, which just increases their anxiety and feelings of being unprepared. Needless to say, this doesn't help one iota.

Are introverts naturally more afraid of public speaking than extroverts?

There have been several studies investigating the degree to which the personality traits of introversion and extraversion affect people's speaking ability. Overall, extroverts do not seem to have much advantage over introverts when it comes to experiencing public speaking anxiety. Both groups experience nervousness, and both personality types can enjoy public speaking or be terrified by it.

Studies have demonstrated that extroverts experience slightly fewer symptoms of anxiety than introverts. Maria Dietrich and Katherine Verdolini Abbott's 2010 study on vocal function during stressful public speaking scenarios shows that extroverts did not use as much vocal effort when public speaking, but public speaking did still trigger vocal stress in their subjects. Another study, by Peter MacIntyre and Kimly Thivierge, demonstrated that extroverts anticipated being slightly less anxious about public speaking than introverts and were overall more willing to speak.

If MacIntyre and Thiverge's findings represent most extroverts, then the willingness of extroverts to speak may lead them to take more advantage of speaking opportunities than introverts. As repetition and practice are critical to overcoming the fear of public speaking, the real advantage extroverts may have would be that they are likely to engage in public speaking more often than introverts and by doing so further reduce the amount of speaker's anxiety they experience.

Do professional speakers get nervous?

Yes, many professional speakers and performers experience performance anxiety and stage fright, and public speaking is a type of performance. Famous speakers and performers who have spoken publicly about stage fright include investor Warren Buffett, singers Barbra Streisand and Adele, comedian Stephen Fry, and the late actor Sir Laurence Olivier. Stories of using antianxiety medicine, vomiting, and trying to escape before a talk or performance abound.

Speaker's anxiety, performance anxiety, and stage fright are all normal responses to activities where we are vulnerable, exposed, and subject to the judgment of an audience. Many accomplished speakers, presenters, and performers learn to manage to their fear and end up excelling at their art in spite of it.

Even people famous for performing in front of crowds have confessed they get nervous. Singer and activist Barbra Streisand has talked about her personal struggle with stage fright, for example.

How can I manage my fear of public speaking?

Even though fear of public speaking can be crippling, there are several steps that you can take before, during, and after the presentation to help manage your anxiety.

Before Your Presentation

1. View public speaking as a conversation you are having with several people rather than a formal presentation. Most people feel at ease when they are just talking with people, and changing the way they perceive giving a speech or a presentation can help lower apprehension.
2. Don't procrastinate! Procrastination is an avoidance tactic and can only make anxiety worse. Start creating and practicing your presentation as soon as possible, and work on it in small chunks to avoid building up anxiety.
3. Keep your presentation simple. Sticking to only a few short points or one primary message can help you focus and means that you don't need to worry as much about losing your place, missing information, or going over your allotted time.
4. Know your material, but don't memorize it. Memorizing scripts word for word is a very difficult task and creates a huge mental load. It also prevents you from going with the flow and makes it hard to get back on track if you lose your place. Work on being able to speak about the different parts of your presentation in a free-flowing manner and don't bother memorizing exactly what you want to say.
5. Practice, practice, and practice some more. The key to knowing your presentation is practicing it. The more you practice, the better you will be able to remember

your content come presentation time and the more you can focus your attention on connecting with your audience rather than trying to remember your material.

During Your Presentation

1. Limit your use of notes. Pages of notes are awkward to handle and tempt speakers into reading their presentation instead of speaking to the audience. Limit your notes to one page of bullet points in a large, heavy font. Use the bullet points only to cue you as to where you are in your presentation.
2. Breathe fully and deeply. Diaphragmatic breath brings in maximum air to your lungs and body while helping to slow down your heart rate and lower blood pressure. When anxious, many people hyperventilate or hold their breath. Both of these increase feelings of panic. Instead, focus on dragging the air deeply into the bottom of your lungs. You will start to feel calmer.
3. Stand tall and proud with a wide, grounded stance and big gestures. Taking up space increases flows of testosterone and decreases cortisol, which in turn boost feelings of power while decreasing stress. People who slouch and use diminutive postures and gestures tend to experience and project more anxiety than people who use lots of physical space.
4. Move around while you present. Part of the fight-or-flight response tenses your muscles and gets you ready for action. If you stand stock still, that tension can build up. Move your body, walk around the presentation areas, and use big gestures. Doing so will give the physical energy somewhere to go and will help calm you down.
5. Make eye contact with individual audience members. This will increase the feeling of having a conversation rather than giving a presentation. To increase that feeling even more, ask your audience questions. If it is a small group, you can ask for someone to answer a question. If it is a large group, you can ask for a show of hands. Be creative. This will make you feel more connected to and comfortable with your audience.

After Your Presentation

1. Follow up with your audience. If you forgot some piece of information or weren't able to answer a question, follow up with your audience afterward. You can do this by getting the contact information for attendees if it is a small group or by having the person organizing the event send out a mass email to a larger group. You can even post follow-up comments and resources to a website if you have one or share them over social media accounts. This takes away some of the anxiety people experience when they are afraid they will forget a portion of their presentation. You can *always* find a way to follow up with the group, and they will think highly of you for taking the time to do so.

I often forget what I'm supposed to say. What do I do when I get nervous and my mind goes blank?

Writing down the bullet points you want to cover on note cards can help prompt you in a speech and avoid drawing a blank.

Forgetting your material, losing your place, or simply "going blank" is an incredibly common response to speaker's anxiety. Unfortunately, forgetting what you were supposed to say then feeds into the anxiety that made you forget it in the first place, perpetuating a vicious cycle. Physically calming down and refocusing yourself on your content will help you get through this. Come prepared with simple, easy-to-read speaker notes with bullet points outlining the main themes of your presentation. If you forget what you need to say next, pause and take a slow, calming breath. If you bring a bottle of water with you, you can take a sip to justify needing to pause. Glance at your notes to remind yourself where you are in your presentation, picture your next line in full, then begin speaking slowly and calmly. This will help settle down the fight-or-flight state and refocus your mind so that you can again think clearly about your presentation.

CHARACTERISTICS OF A GOOD PUBLIC SPEAKER

What are the characteristics of a good speaker?

Whether or not someone is considered a good speaker depends a great deal on the tastes and preferences of the people listening to them. A speaking style that one person finds energetic and engaging may seem hyperactive and overbearing to someone else. A topic that is dry to one listener is riveting to another. Information that is old news to your colleague may be completely novel to you.

That being said, there are some general characteristics held by most accomplished speakers:

They are experts in or speak about relatively narrow topics. Most speakers are subject matter experts and typically only give talks or presentations about a focused, well-defined area of their expertise. Many of their presentations will have similar content, and they will deliver the same or similar presentations to many audiences.

They spend significant time crafting their presentations and regularly review and update their content. As mentioned above, many speakers use the same presentation many times. However, they invest a significant amount of time creating each presentation; five minutes in a finished presentation could have easily taken two hours of effort to create and polish. Furthermore, they are constantly on the lookout for audience feedback or industry changes that need to be incorporated into their presentation. This means that any given presentation will go through multiple iterations during its lifetime.

They target their presentations to specific audiences. Good speakers understand that their subject is not of interest to everyone and that different audiences will have different information needs relating to that topic. Therefore, many speakers only speak to certain demographics—such as health care workers, or high school students, or accountants, and so on. Additionally, they take into consideration the context of each audience they are speaking to so that they may tailor their presentation to that particular audience. This does not mean that speakers need to create new presentations for each new audience, but it does mean that they take the time to adjust certain details for different audiences so that their presentation is always relevant and appropriate.

They speak at a pace that is comfortable and easy for the audience to listen to. While there are some exceptionally fast professional speakers out there, such as businessman Tony Robbins, most accomplished speakers talk at a moderate pace that is both energetic and easy for the audience to listen to.

They are expressive, using vocal variety and body language to enhance meaning and increase interest. Nonverbal cues like vocal tone and body language play a critical role in speaking. Good speakers will use voice and body-language techniques to keep their audience interested and engaged.

They create well-organized presentations with a narrow point of focus. Good speakers understand that their talk must be well organized if audiences are going to be able to follow it with ease. Additionally, they know to keep the talk focused on a relatively small amount of information. Poor speakers tend to jam too much content into their presentations, which leads to information overload for the audience (not to mention presentations that go over their allotted time—something despised by audiences the world over).

They practice. Speaking is a skill, and like any other skill, it improves with practice and declines without. Accomplished speakers spend a considerable amount of time practicing both their speaking techniques and their presentations.

They speak a lot. This characteristic is related to the one above. Accomplished speakers, whether or not they are famous, actively seek out and welcome speaking opportunities. If a speaker doesn't speak in front of an audience on a regular basis, he or she will experience a decline in his or her ability to relate and respond to a live audience. Smaller speaking opportunities also provide speakers with the chance to test out their material and see how audiences react to it. In this way, they can hone new material they are preparing for a larger upcoming presentation or make adjustments to existing presentations to keep things fresh.

What are some characteristics of a "bad" public speaker?

Many of the traits of poor public speakers are simply the opposite of the good traits listed above. However, it is useful to identify a few particular failings:

They don't try to adapt their knowledge and content to the audience's worldview or context. When speakers don't dig into their audience's worldview, circumstances, or existing knowledge about the subject, they aren't always able to make their own material relevant or interesting to the audience. Speakers should always strive to make it easy for an audience to see how the content of a presentation relates to them.

They don't update their content on a regular basis. There are few areas of expertise that don't require a speaker to update their content. Updating content isn't just about making sure that any related technology or scientific developments are current. It also means adapting the language, expressions, and social or cultural values to contemporary norms.

They make patronizing or insulting remarks about the audience. This tends to occur when the speaker has not taken sufficient steps to learn about his or her audience or approaches the talk with significant overconfidence or arrogance. In all these cases, the speaker fails to treat his or her audience with consideration or respect.

They fail to engage their audience—speaking in monotone, limiting gestures, and/or reading excessively from notes. People who are insecure about their presentation content or are anxious about speaking tend to dampen their expressiveness and rely heavily on their notes. In these cases, the speaker appears disengaged with their content or the audience, and the audience will be uninterested in return.

They don't speak about what they promised to speak about. A common mistake speakers make is to not align the content of the presentation with the title or description of the presentation. When the audience goes to a talk anticipating to learn about a certain topic but is then given something different, their expectations are not met and they can be frustrated. This mistake often happens when a speaker suffers from Shiny Object Syndrome (getting distracted by new ideas and thoughts that prevent them from completing a point that needs to be made) and changes his or her content shortly before his or her talk. It also frequently happens as a bait-and-switch tactic for sales pitches disguised as information sessions.

They jam too much content into their presentation. It is easy to overload an audience with information. Speakers fall into this trap when they aren't able to determine what the most important piece of information is within their presentation, or they feel they need to address every possible angle of their subject within a single presentation.

They go over their presentation time. Exceeding your allotted speaking time is the cardinal sin most pilloried by audiences. When a speaker doesn't narrowly focus their presentation or doesn't time their presentation during practice sessions, they will almost invariably go on longer than they should. Audiences are impatient and unforgiving when speakers run too far over time. Doing so is disrespectful to the audience's time and to any other speakers or items that may be following their presentation. It is better to end on time or early, even if it means cutting out portions of the presentation.

One way speakers fail is when they do not engage their audience.

What role does trust play in public speaking and communication?

Whether in business, the workplace, at home, or among friends, trust is central to successful communication. Public speakers and presenters who build trust with their audience are typically more successful than those who do not develop any particular relationship. Trust allows understanding and consensus to be formed with greater ease, opinions and contrary views to be expressed openly, and creative ideas to be shared. Trust-based communication between people leads to better relationships and less stress. It allows people to better explore mutually acceptable solutions to problems and creates win-win outcomes. For families, it means better outcomes for children. For business, it means more successful deals and increased effectiveness.

How is trust developed?

Trust is created when members of the audience feel that the speaker has their interests at heart and that they can rely on the speaker to follow through with any actions or behavior they speak about. Specific actions that a speaker can take to develop trust are:

- Speak openly and plainly in a way that is easily understood
- Consider the context and worldview of the person he or she is communicating with
- Use polite, respectful language
- Behave with discretion when sharing information
- Behave and respond in a way that is relatively consistent and predictable
- Take action on promises and commitments
- Take responsibility for his or her own words or actions instead of deferring blame to others

Do confident people make better public speakers?

Confident people do not necessarily make better public speakers. While confidence can help people overcome performance anxiety, and the image of confidence makes a great impression on an audience, being a good public speaker depends on much more than mere confidence. Speakers may have false confidence, where they believe they are prepared to give their talk but suddenly get seized by unexpected speaker's anxiety right before they start. Others may believe that their confidence will see them through, and they end up underpreparing for their presentation. Confidence is a key element in public speaking, but it does not replace regular practice on the wide range of skills necessary to be an excellent speaker.

Do outgoing people make better public speakers?

As mentioned earlier in this chapter, extroverts (outgoing people) may have a slight advantage over introverts in terms of handling speaker's anxiety. This, however, does not mean that extroverts make inherently better speakers than introverts. In an analysis of five studies on personality traits and public speaking skills, Clyde Dow found that there was only a very slight favoring of extroverts in public speaking skills. One of the studies in Dow's analysis noted that extroverts trended toward either end of the public speaking-skill scale, with introverts being more consistently represented as "good" speakers.

Attempting to label oneself or someone else as a naturally "good" or "bad" speaker based on the extrovert/introvert personality trait is counterproductive. Individual experiences with public speaking range so widely that skill or anxiety can't be related to a single trait. An introvert may find that the relative anonymity of a large audience makes him or her feel more comfortable and expressive than the intimacy of a small group presentation. An extrovert may be perfectly at ease presenting to a group of colleagues but feels overwhelmed when faced with a large crowd.

Conscientiousness, a willingness to experiment with speaking, a strong focus on the needs of the audience, and regular practice are better indicators as to whether or not someone is or could be a great speaker. One should not be made to feel overly concerned *or* overly confident about one's public speaking skills based simply off a simplified description of one's personality.

What role does listening play in regards to speaking?

A good speaker or communicator must be able to identify and define the needs, goals, and wants of the people with whom they are speaking. Listening skills are critical for the speaker's ability to do just that. A person's or audience's needs, goals, and wants are identified through close listening to the information they are divulging, along with the subtext of what they are saying and the context in which they are speaking. People with good listening skills listen for things like hidden messages, clues as to a person's emotional or mental state when communicating, and what is said *and* left unsaid. They search for meaning above and beyond the strict definition of the words people use.

Based on that information, a speaker can analyze the motives and needs of the people they are speaking to and either deliver a talk or guide a conversation that is strongly focused on serving the needs of the people they are addressing. This allows the speaker to deliver both meaning and value to their audience in a given conversation or speaking scenario.

Without good listening skills, speakers can easily miss the mark in terms of the information they are delivering and end up giving a talk or having a conversation that is not meaningful or even relevant to the person or people with whom they are speaking. Speakers who fall into the trap of not listening to their audience before, during, and after their interaction run the risk of overwhelming their audience with information, giving the wrong information, or even spending large amounts of time talking about themselves.

What is the difference between listening and hearing?

Hearing is an involuntary process that involves an automatic, passive response to sound or noise. It is what happens when sound enters our ears and our brain receives the information, adding it to our experience of the environment that surrounds us. Hearing does not involve any voluntary interpretation or analysis of the sound that we are receiving through our ears.

Listening, on the other hand, is a voluntary, active process. When someone is listening, he or she is focused on the information the other person or thing is giving him or her. It is a purposeful activity we engage in when we want to understand the deeper meanings of the things we hear. The term "active listening" is redundant. All true listening is active—doing anything less is merely hearing.

As many parents of teenagers may know, it is possible for someone to hear what you say but not listen.

Can you "listen" to nonverbal communication?

Yes—not only can a speaker listen to nonverbal communication, it is critical to his or her success as a speaker. A speaker must pay considerable attention to the nonverbal communication flowing to him or her from his or her audience during a speaking situation. The ability to listen to nonverbal communication allows a speaker or communicator to adjust what he or she is saying from moment to moment so that he or she can more effectively engage his or her audience, maintain audience focus, and respond to an audience's needs.

Most speaking scenarios are rarely one-directional; you (the speaker) are usually having a conversation with one or more other people (your audience). Even if your audience can't say much—or anything—in return, nonverbal information like body language, shuffling, whispering, looking away, and other cues can allow you to "listen" to messages they are sending you, such as their level of attention and engagement. Behaviors like shuffling and whispering may indicate boredom or confusion, and the speaker may wish to change direction or spend more time on a difficult concept. Laughter, questions, and other signs of engagement can indicate to a speaker that the audience is on board with what he or she is saying and that he or she can continue with the same energy or line of thought.

How do I know if I'm getting the right messages when I'm listening to nonverbal cues?

There is no specific "correct" interpretation of nonverbal cues. What a speaker thought was engagement could be confusion or vice versa. Sensitivity as to the meaning of nonverbal communication usually comes from experience and practice. Speakers can practice nonverbal listening in a multitude of settings any time during the day. The key is to spend the time and energy thinking about what a person was saying and how he or she was behaving, analyzing it, placing that behavior into the context of the speaking situation or interaction, then thinking about the outcomes of the conversation or talk.

If people ask me questions when I am speaking, does it mean they weren't listening?

Whether a question indicates an audience member's lack of attention or not usually depends on the sort of question he or she is asking. Questions that ask you to repeat basic information or bring up issues that you covered thoroughly or already answered questions about may indicate that the audience member was not listening. Questions that ask for further explanation of a topic often indicate that the questioner was listening but was not able to understand your full meaning. Questions that dig into or explore a topic you addressed, or questions that seek your thoughts on a related topic, can indicate a very high degree of listening and engagement; these are the best questions to get as it means that the people listening to you are engaging in critical thinking and want to explore your content some more. To learn more about handling audience questions, refer to the "Audience Matters" chapter.

How does emotion enhance a speech or presentation?

Emotion plays a critical role in communication during a speech or presentation. It enhances how memorable a speech is and increases how much someone remembers about the speaker and his or her content. It also gives important context cues, giving the audience subtext that can completely change how they understand a phrase or idea.

What are some indicators that people are listening?

Different signals can indicate different stages or levels of listening. Eye contact combined with eye movement and open body language are often indicators of listening and engagement. Hard, unmoving eye contact with closed or stiff body language may indicate hostile hearing but not true listening. Prolonged engagement with someone or something else—like lengthy whispering with the person beside you, staring at your smartphone, or shuffling through a meeting package—indicates a lack of listening. One of the best indicators that you can give to show you are listening, or that someone else can give you, are questions that expand on the topic being discussed or that check for comprehension of the information at hand. These questions demonstrate critical thinking about the subject at hand, which typically happens at higher levels of listening.

Our emotional states are influenced by the emotions we see other people having. Often, when we see someone expressing a certain emotion, we in turn will feel some of it ourselves. A speaker's emotional expression tells an audience what they should be feeling and how strongly they should be feeling it. Speakers can choose to express sympathy with their audience's emotions by reflecting the way the audience may be feeling. For instance, if the audience is upset by some news that the speaker is about to address, the speaker can use sad facial expressions or body language to show he or she feels that way too. Conversely, speakers can lead the audience to feel a different emotion by putting that desirable emotion on display. If an audience is lethargic or uninterested, a speaker could revive them by demonstrating great excitement and energy.

Within classical rhetoric, pathos—the appeal to an audience's emotions—is one of the best strategies to get people to commit to a course of action and then actually act on it. Even when an audience agrees with a speaker's line of reason or argument, they are unlikely to take any action on it unless the speaker engages their emotions and creates feelings of excitement and commitment. To do that, the speaker must use language that appeals to the audience's emotions but must also demonstrate emotional investment him- or herself in order to win his or her audience over.

How emotional should a public speaker be?

Emotional expressiveness is one of the strengths of public speaking; impactful speakers and orators tend to be highly emotionally expressive through both verbal and nonverbal signals. What is critical, though, is for the speaker to understand what and how much emotion is suitable for the situation. Asking what the audience wants and needs from the speaker can help determine what kind of emotion to show.

In situations of crisis, for example, people generally want to hear someone who is calm, controlled, and direct without being overly harsh. In this case, showing quiet strength and restraint is desirable. If someone is giving a toast at a wedding, the audience is likely wanting a light, friendly, and energetic mood. In this case, the speaker should be willing to laugh, to speak with lots of vocal variety, and to use energetic, open body language. The professional or personal role of the speaker will also give clues as to what emotions are appropriate and expected.

At all times, the emotion being shown should be plausible or genuine. When emotion is forced or overly rehearsed, it comes across to the audience as unnatural and phony. This rarely goes over well and tends to give the speaker a tiresome and patronizing air. Yes, emotional expression can and often should be amplified, but it must also be truthful; otherwise the audience won't accept the performance.

While audiences like to see emotional expression that feels natural and unrehearsed, there is also an element of control. The speaker must always be in control of what and how much emotion he or she expresses. Whether the speaker wants to show restraint, deep sadness, or buoyant exuberance, his or her emotional expression must be intentional, and the audience should be aware that the speaker is in control of his or her emotions and not the other way around.

It is unusual for speakers to show too much emotion. Most speakers tend to show too little, running the risk of being boring. Experiment with showing more emotion; the payoff of showing a little too much energy is greater than the risk of showing too little and being overly dull. That being said, speakers should not seek to emulate the high-strung, shrilly juvenile loss of control that we so often see from reality TV stars and pop celebrities on social media.

How can speakers who don't show a lot of emotion become more expressive?

It is more common for a speaker to under-emote than to go over the top. For speakers who are self-conscious or naturally more reserved, pushing through strong emotion can be difficult. Speakers often feel as though they're being more emotive than what the audience perceives. In these cases, what the speaker really needs to do is to express *more* emotion than he or she thinks necessary in order for his or her audience to pick up on it. Reserved speakers can use strategies like increasing their eye contact, increasing their vocal volume, using a wider stance, and adopting sharper, stronger gestures to increase their expressiveness as well as their own feelings of excitement.

Expressing emotions in your speaking can help convey the message, as long as you do so in a way that is natural and unrehearsed.

How can speakers who show too much emotion dial it back?

There are speakers who will go over the top and demonstrate too much emotion onstage. In these cases, it is important for the speaker to watch the audience closely and gauge how expressive he or she should be. If an audience seems uncomfortable, is avoiding looking directly at the speaker, or seems to be withdrawing or even shrinking back slightly in their seats, the speaker should dial down the emotion. Overexpressiveness usually results from an excess of nervous energy. An overly expressive speaker can help calm him- or herself down by using rhythmic, flowing gestures instead of agitated, choppy ones. This strategy still gives the nervous physical energy somewhere to go but has a calming rather than exciting effect.

Overly exuberant speakers also tend to speak too quickly. Using lots of pauses, breathing deeply, and slowing down their rate of speech will help them calm down and give their audience time to catch up with what the speaker is saying.

Why is humor an effective public speaking tool?

Humor is superb at creating a positive psychological state in audience members. Laughter relieves tension, especially when the subject at hand is difficult or uncomfortable. Humor can refocus lagging attention by introducing a new twist on how we perceive an issue. It can help the speaker and audience connect to one another by making them feel as though they think the same way about a topic and already share an understanding. This also works to create feelings of belonging and cohesiveness.

How can humor be used in a speech or presentation?

Using humor in public speaking doesn't mean relying on cracking jokes. Use of irony, wry observations, funny stories and anecdotes, or poking fun at yourself, members of the audience, or authority figures are all excellent ways to make an audience laugh. At all times, though, the humor must be relevant to the audience, appropriate to their values and context, and respectful of those listening to you. Using humor that is disrespectful to groups of people is risky, can cause an audience to turn against the speaker, and can seriously damage a speaker's credibility. Excessive use of humor might make the speaker seem flippant.

CONTEMPORARY PUBLIC SPEAKING

REVOLUTIONS IN RADIO, TV, AND THE INTERNET

How did early radio affect public speaking styles?

Early radio had poor quality sound, which, when combined with the lack of nonverbal communication, could make it difficult for listeners to understand radio speakers. Professionals and academics alike sought to establish a preferred voice presentation style specifically for radio. In order to deal with noise interference and the absence of visual cues and body language, radio speakers needed to enunciate more carefully and speak significantly slower than they would for a live audience. The speaker also needed to modulate his or her volume to make sure he or she didn't overload the microphone and create distortion. This created a fashion for slower, more deliberate speech that carried over into television. Radio speaking typically came in at a pace of 145 words per minute. This slower, more measured speech was taught by many public speaking programs, such as Toastmasters, Dale Carnegie, and 4H speech programs.

As audio recording technology improved, the pace of speech on radio and TV began to speed up. Modern recording technology can capture near-perfect recordings of human speech, and we can play it back with similar accuracy. This allows broadcast speakers to talk at a faster pace. Contemporary speakers are now speaking at an average of 165 to 190 words per minute—about the same pace as a normal conversation between two acquaintances.

How has podcasting contributed to contemporary public speaking?

The contribution of podcasting to public speaking lies in how it changed the distribution of radio-style shows and recorded programs. Podcasting—the distribution of radio-like shows over the Internet—has expanded access to talks and lectures for audiences and allowed speakers to reach potentially vast numbers of listeners. People wanting to create radio shows and programs, or who wanted to broadcast their talks to larger audiences, used to be limited to the whims and agendas of radio broadcasting agencies. If the person was technologically savvy, he or she could potentially create pirate (unlicensed) radio stations and programs, but the potential reach and audience of these programs were very limited. Now, people can easily record, upload, and freely distribute their talks online with minimal effort and no need to supplicate themselves to the demands of a broadcasting agent. In this way, podcasting gave content creators—such as speakers and lecturers—more control over their material and the means by which it is made available to their audiences.

Should a speaker treat a radio or podcast audience differently from a live audience?

Yes! Radio and podcast speaking has a more intimate audience feel than does speaking in front of large live audiences. Personal listening devices place the audience aurally closer to the voice of the speaker than a live audience. This increases the sense of closeness to the speaker. Because most radio and podcast consumers listen to talks as a solo activity, there is also a feeling that they are having a more intimate connection with the speaker or speakers, more so than if they were listening as part of a large crowd. These feelings of closeness mean that radio and podcast speakers should view their audience more like partners in a conversation.

When speaking for an audio-only audience, picture yourself talking directly to one other person, like you would talk with a friend over coffee. This carries through to your audience, and they will get that feeling of direct conversation that works so well in these formats. Another excellent way to take advantage of the intimate feeling of radio and podcasts is to use a dialogue with two speakers talking to each other. This is often done by having two regular hosts on a program or having a regular host who interviews a guest. Dialogue gives the audience the feeling that they are participating in a conversation. Radio and podcast speakers also benefit from a less formal style of speech with casual expressions and warmer, more spontaneous tones.

How does giving an audio-only speech differ from giving a speech where people can see the speaker?

Speakers working with an audio-only audience need to take into consideration the fact that their radio or podcast listeners get no visual or nonverbal information. Visual and nonverbal communication make it easier for people to understand one another; radio and podcast speakers need to slow down their speech slightly to make it easier for listeners to absorb what they are saying. It isn't necessary to go back to the old 145-words-per-minute pace; that would sound strange to listeners anyway. But speaking at the slower end of the conversational range—between 165 and 175 words per minute—will significantly increase the ease with which listeners can take in the speaker's words.

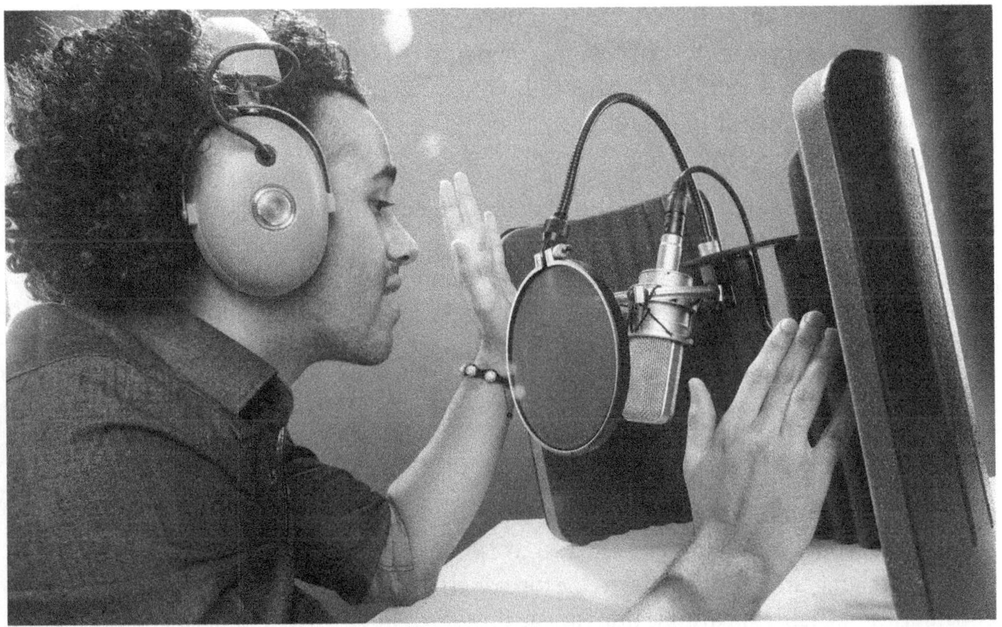

Radio broadcasting, when pre-recorded, can help make for a tighter presentation through skillful audio editing.

Speakers also need to make up for lack of body language by injecting more color and variety into their voice. A really vocally dynamic live speaker might not find this difficult, but people with a more restrained style of speech will find it necessary to dial up variations in speed, volume, and tone in order to send their energy and nonverbal vocal cues to listeners. We can't see your enthusiastic hand gestures through our listening devices, so you need to let us hear those gestures in your voice.

What are some of the advantages of radio or podcast speaking?

There are a few reasons why people may want to engage in public speaking through radio or podcasts. People with a strong desire to speak to an audience but who experience high levels of speaker anxiety might find this format more comfortable and liberating. Even for speakers comfortable with live audiences, recorded speech has advantages. Presuming the broadcast isn't distributed live, the speaker can edit out unwanted or unnecessary content. This creates a tighter, more succinct talk for the audience with few to no verbal flubs or errors. Radio and podcast recordings also have a wider geographic range and can potentially reach a global audience. This content is also often available on demand; audiences can listen to podcasts when and where they want, and more radio stations are adding online streaming or podcast recordings to their offerings.

What are some of the pitfalls of radio or podcast speaking?

Just as the lack of a live, in-person audience is helpful for some speakers, others find the lack of audience engagement difficult. Many speakers draw energy from their audience, and not being able to see the reactions of that audience can stifle spontaneity and make a performance feel more "forced." People who find it difficult to speak with considerable energy and variation might find the audio-only medium stifling, and their audiences could find them difficult to listen to.

Radio and podcast audiences also tend to expect the content creator—in this case, the speaker—to regularly create and distribute new content for them to consume. If a speaker releases his or her podcast or streaming content irregularly with wide gaps between new materials, he or she will find it difficult to attract a loyal listener base—especially as listeners have more choice of content than ever before. Many creators find the need to regularly churn out new content extremely tiring, and they may burn out or give up on creating new talks and speeches altogether.

How did speakers adapt to early television formats?

Television brought the new dimension of visual information to broadcasted public speaking. People who were previously used to working without cameras, such as campaigning politicians and public figures, found themselves having to take into new consideration their appearance and physical performance. Physical performance for TV is not the same as it is for a live audience—decisions had to be made such as whether to look directly at the camera or toward the people you are talking with. The size of the camera frame needed to be considered, and gestures had to be kept within that frame. The heat from stage lighting could be punishing.

Many speakers found this setting disconcerting, while others found that the added visual element worked in their favor. An excellent example of the effects television had on public speaking is in the famous 1960 presidential debate between U.S. senator John F. Kennedy of Massachusetts and Vice President Richard Nixon. Handsome, fresh-faced Kennedy performed brilliantly for the camera while Nixon—sweaty, pale, and uncomfortable with the format—was decried by many observers as the clear loser. (On the other hand, many who listened to the debate on the radio—without the visuals that hurt Nixon—believed the debate's results were much closer.) Much was made of the effect of Kennedy's photogenic, TV-friendly appearance and manner. Public speakers and politicians alike became more aware than ever of the importance of physical appearance and performance now that TV cameras were focused in on them.

What advantages did Internet resources like online video and streaming bring to public speaking?

Much like with podcasting, the main advantage of online video sharing and streaming was that it gave speakers new abilities to distribute their content. Where shows and recordings could previously only be distributed through TV networks or via physical recordings like DVDs, CDs, and videocassettes, anyone with a computer and Internet access can now start their own show or share their recorded material. Internet distribution has made it much easier for people to start public speaking careers as they can now show their talks to prospective audiences and clients worldwide.

The ease with which recorded content can be edited is also advantageous to people creating online content. Content can easily be edited for quality and content. A choppy, fast-paced editing style with lots of quick cuts has come into vogue. This speeds up the recording process; people don't need to take multiple long takes to capture good content. They simply choose the best bits in small chunks, break their recordings down into tiny snippets, and stitch them together.

What are some of the drawbacks of using Internet video as a public speaking platform?

A main drawback to Internet distribution is that the amount of material available to people is so large and dizzying that it's easy for someone's content to get lost in the noise. The push to be constantly creating and releasing new content leads to a lot of poor-quality, rushed content lacking in both substance and style. Content creators also need to be more aware of their appearance, performance for the camera, and other style considerations such as lighting and recording quality. This can lead to excessive agonizing over details that would normally be of lower priority to speakers. As a result, many speakers trying to reach an online audience focus on things like their appearance and video quality rather than on the quality of their actual talk or presentation.

Is public speaking on video or television different than public speaking to a live audience?

Speaking for the camera is a very different experience than speaking for a live audience. Many people find it difficult to perform for a camera lens, which can never give the speaker the boost and cues that a live, responsive audience can give. This can lead to flat or forced performances. To combat this, speakers need to be able to vividly picture an audience and perform to them, responding to this imaginary audience as if they were speaking to them directly.

The problem with broadcasting over the Internet is that there is so much competition for audiences that it is hard to get people's attention.

If the recording is of a speaker giving a talk to a live audience, the person watching the recording can see the social interaction between speaker and audience. In the absence of a live audience, certain social responses—for example, laughter or asking questions and waiting for answers—can seem downright odd to the viewer. Speakers wanting to record their presentations should keep this in mind if they aren't recording in front of a live audience. They might need to rework some of their content to make it work for the camera instead of for a group of responsive people.

The opportunity to do multiple takes of video recordings can both help and hinder many speakers. When a speaker does repeated takes, stopping and restarting a talk if he or she makes a mistake, he or she may lose the flow of his or her speech. Sometimes this doesn't create a problem; many people are able to pick up a talk where they left off relatively easily. Others, though, can find this problematic. In live performances, there is less opportunity to dwell on errors as the speaker simply has to push through them and carry on with his or her talk regardless of any desire to fix his or her mistakes.

Speakers performing for a camera need to be aware of the technical requirements and limitations. They need to know the actual space they have to work with in order to keep their movements and gestures within the camera's frame. They also need to be aware of the volume and pitch levels of the microphones and modulate their tone so they don't overload the audio devices. For speakers accustomed to projecting their voice from a stage or in a large room, this can be a tricky change from their normal performing style.

IMPORTANT SPEAKERS AND SPEECHES OF THE 20TH AND 21ST CENTURIES

What makes a speaker important?

It is not possible to provide a solid, consistent definition of what makes a speaker or speech important. The impact of a speaker on his or her social or political environment can vary greatly, as can his or her mannerisms and methods of delivery. The notion of what constitutes a "great" speaker on an individual level is strongly influenced by the tastes of the listener. The importance of a speech in a historical context often hinges on the speech contributing to actions taken by the audience following the speech or the speech providing vivid and widely broadcasted commentary on an issue of the day. Certain speakers become important because they set trends in their field or in the broader culture. All important speakers and speeches are marked by the ongoing attention they receive due to the combination of powerful, memorable composition and delivery.

It would be impossible within the scope of this book to list all the important speakers and speeches from the twentieth and twenty-first centuries. The people and speeches listed in this section are merely a small sample of significant speakers and important speeches since the start of the 1900s.

What sort of events usually lead to "important" speeches?

Speeches that embed themselves into history and continue to be studied and shared years after they were given are often related to major political or social issues. These issues provoke strong feelings and address topics urgent to the audience. They might have led to significant social changes, provoked action among a large group of people, or helped shift cultural norms.

How was British prime minister Winston Churchill a significant speaker?

Winston Churchill gave a large number of speeches during his career. He is most noted for the powerful, inspiring orations he delivered to the British Parliament, the British people, and the country's allies before and during World War II. Churchill was a master of English prose and rhetoric, and he was known for his skill in crafting vivid, climactic speeches capable of bolstering spirits and provoking decisive action among politicians and common people alike. Despite a stutter and propensity to mumble, the deep rumbling tone and gravity with which Churchill spoke amplified the seriousness of his words. His speeches were critical to maintaining the morale of the British people during the darkest periods of German invasion.

Among Churchill's many speeches, ones that are especially arresting are: "We Shall Fight on the Beaches"—June 4, 1940, British House of Commons; "Finest Hour"—June 18, 1940, British House of Commons; and "The Few"—August 20, 1940, British House of Commons.

How was German Nazi leader Adolf Hitler an important speaker?

Hitler's ability to stoke fires of discontent and fervent patriotism within a crowd are undeniable. He understood the importance of tapping into a crowd's feelings and made full use of body language and vocal mannerisms to create electrifying oratorical performances. Hitler understood the persuasive power of oratory and spent considerable time practicing each speech. Nazi propaganda minister Joseph Goebbels praised Hitler's ability to make his arguments and logic suit whatever crowd he was speaking to. Goebbels noted that "he has the ability to express things so clearly, logically, and directly that listeners are convinced that it is what they have always thought themselves." This telling statement describes Hitler's skills in using rhetoric to make his twisted notions resonate with his audience's logos (for a full description of rhetorical logos, refer to the "Rhetoric" chapter). The combination of persuasive rhetoric and charismatic performance made Hitler one of the most devastatingly effective public speakers on record.

World War II dictator Adolf Hitler came to power, in large part, because he was an extremely powerful and persuasive public speaker.

How did U.S. president Franklin Delano Roosevelt use radio and public speaking to connect with common Americans?

Roosevelt's "Fireside Chats" radio speeches, broadcast to the American public between 1933 and 1944, gave a new media face and unprecedented intimacy to presidential speech-making. Roosevelt had keen understanding of the reach of mass media and considerable insight into the style of speech and tone that would best work for the radio. By using simple language, plenty of personal and familiar pronouns, and folksy analogies, Roosevelt made the content of his radio speeches accessible to average Americans. His warm, friendly voice brought comfort to people anxious about global political and economic upheaval. Through application of a wide range of vocal performance techniques—tone, intonation, loudness, and speed—Roosevelt was able to use the radio medium with skill and virtuosity. While he also boasted considerable skill as a live orator, the goodwill and confidence that his "Fireside Chats" generated among the electorate undoubtedly contributed to his high approval ratings and multiple reelections as president. For more information about the "Fireside Chats," refer to the chapter "Contemporary Public Speaking."

Why was civil rights leader Martin Luther King Jr.'s oratorical style so effective?

King's soaring oratory contributed to the public visibility of the civil rights struggle, to the galvanizing of his civil rights supporters, and to King's own prominence among his fellow Civil Rights Movement leaders. Drawing strongly on his experience as a southern Baptist preacher, King infused his speeches with vivid imagery and rhythmic, mesmerizing cadence. King's use of biblical metaphor in his speeches contributed an air of Christian conservatism and historical gravitas to the movement. He employed a raft of oratorical devices when he spoke, such as balanced and rhythmic sentences, grand pauses, repetition of phrases (anaphora), and a unique style of intonation that drew out his vowels. These blended to create a soaring musicality to his speeches. King remains one of the most admired and studied orators of modern history.

British suffragist Emmeline Pankhurst was a rarity of her time, engaging in a lot of public speaking for her cause even though women of her day did not normally do that.

What was the importance of Emmeline Pankhurst's "Freedom or Death" lecture?

Emmeline Pankhurst (1858–1928), a militant leader of the British suffrage movement, traveled from England to the United

States to raise funds for the suffrage movement. It was unusual during that period for women to engage in public speaking, and Pankhurst used her status as both celebrity (she was frequently photographed) and curiosity to help draw attention to her cause. On November 13, 1913, she spoke to a crowd in Hartford, Connecticut, as a fundraising activity and to bolster the activities of American suffragists. While she could not outright incite civil unrest and disobedience among American suffragists, she sought to inspire such action by giving a powerful speech about the reasons behind the militant, violent, and often self-destructive strategies used by suffragists in England. In "Freedom or Death," Pankhurst legitimated militant tactics as rational, reasonable, and logical for the disenfranchised. Her soft-speaking mannerisms and strong words helped change the popular image of suffragists being frothing, Amazonian spinsters. Pankhurst's lecture, and others like it, helped to boost the activities of the American suffragists and increase the political attention being given to the movement.

How did Margaret Thatcher help us understand the relationship between voice and power?

Margaret Thatcher, prime minister of Great Britain from 1979 to 1990, demonstrated how conscious choices about vocal quality can affect a speaker's impression of power. As the only female leader in a Western democracy at the time, Thatcher faced working in an atmosphere rife with sexism and male dominance. In order to claim authority and leadership in this environment, Thatcher needed to adopt more dominant and masculine characteristics. Accused of sounding too shrill, Thatcher underwent extensive voice coaching to lower her voice and adopt a more authoritative speaking style. With a firmer and brighter quality and deeper tone, Thatcher's ability to speak with strength and power increased substantially. The effect of this vocal change on her speaking ability was remarkable and can be studied thanks to footage and recordings of her speaking before and after her coaching. Thatcher's conscious changing of her vocal tone through extensive coaching and practice has sparked many studies on the effects that power and vocal quality have on one another.

Why was Steve Jobs a significant modern speaker?

Steve Jobs, cofounder of Apple, turned business presentations into pop culture events. Considered a master presenter, Jobs melded together public speaking and visual presentations seamlessly. Known for theatrical tactics such as smashing old products or holding mock funerals for obsolete equipment, Jobs rejected traditional business presentations and sought to entertain and engage his audience as much as to inform them. As much of a trendsetter in public speaking and presentations as he was in technological innovations, Jobs influenced how business executives and professionals in diverse industries engaged with their audiences, customers, and stakeholders.

MAJOR PUBLIC SPEAKING ORGANIZATIONS AND EVENTS

What are public speaking organizations?

Public speaking organizations exist to promote the education and practice of public speaking and oratory skills. The focus of many public speaking organizations and clubs is to provide people with a welcoming atmosphere and supportive audience with whom to practice public speaking. Some organizations offer additional forms of training, such as leadership training, sales training, and management training.

Speech competitions and contests are often offered by public speaking organizations, particularly among not-for-profit clubs with national or international focus. Some charitable service organizations, such as Rotary International, Kiwanis International, and 4H, host public speaking competitions, often as part of their youth programs.

What is Toastmasters International?

Toastmasters International is a not-for-profit organization that offers members the opportunity to practice and receive feedback on their speaking skills. With over 15,000 clubs in 135 countries, Toastmasters is one of the foremost public speaking organizations worldwide. The organization was founded in 1905 by Ralph Smedley, director of education for the Young Men's Christian Association (YMCA), as a means to teach speech and leadership skills.

Toastmasters offers members a self-directed educational program with two tracks. The communication track focuses on the development of public speaking and group communication skills. The leadership track develops skills in managing and leading groups, committees, and teams. Meetings are run according to a standard procedure with speech presentations, impromptu speaking, and speaker evaluations, although the format of meetings may vary slightly from club to club. Toastmasters also holds regular local, national, and international speech contests, including the World Championship of Public Speaking.

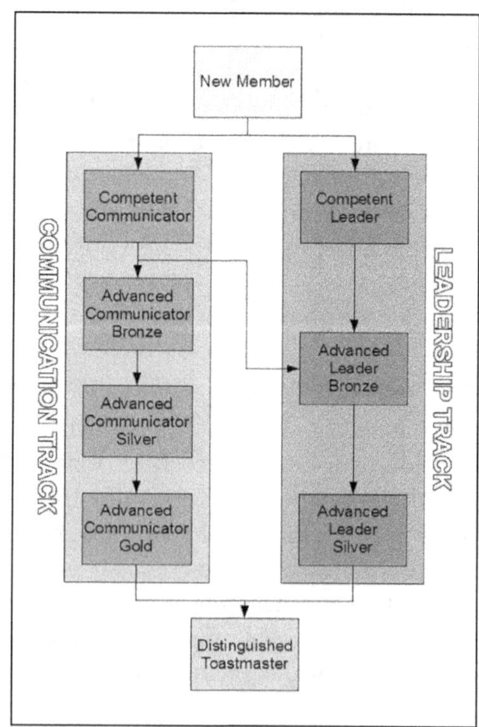

Toastmasters offers two educational tracks: one for leadership and one for communication skills.

What is Dale Carnegie Training?

Dale Carnegie Training is a franchise-based organization that teaches communication skills for businesses and organizations. Its programs include sales, leadership, presentation, management, and speech-related topics. Dale Carnegie Training grew from the teachings and educational work of Dale Carnegie, who taught personal development and public speaking skills in New York in the early 1900s. Carnegie's book *How to Win Friends and Influence People*, first published in 1937, remains a highly popular self-help and business skills development resource.

What is the American Forensic Association?

The American Forensic Association (AFA) was founded in 1949 to provide resources, support, and advocacy for directors of forensics programs. The AFA promotes public speech, discourse, and argumentation as a method for meaningful involvement in public and civic affairs. This organization holds tournaments at both local and national levels, culminating in the collegiate National Debate Tournament and National Individual Events Tournament.

What is the National Forensic Association?

Much like the AFA, the National Forensic Association (NFA) sponsors annual collegiate tournaments in speech and debate arts. The scope of speech competitions in an NFA tournament ranges across a variety of specialties, including poetry, dramatic interpretation, and duo speeches (speeches with two-speaker teams). Between 75 and 125 schools typically participate in national tournaments.

What is the National Speech and Debate Association?

The National Speech and Debate Association (NSDA), known as the National Forensic League until 2014, organizes competitive speech and debate events for school-age students. It provides additional resources for teachers and schools with limited access to speech arts programs. Teacher support programs provide professional development in critical thinking and analysis skills, encouraging such skills to be taught to students. Originally centered in the United States, the NSDA has expanded its programs internationally.

What is TED?

TED is a nonprofit, nonpartisan organization that hosts conferences and distributes media focused on sharing ideas and research in a wide variety of disciplines. TED stands for Technology, Entertainment, and Design, though the subjects addressed by TED speakers often expand beyond those themes. The first TED conference was held in 1984. The conference was not a financial success and lost money; six years passed before the second conference was organized. The conference was revitalized in the 1990s and operated as an elite event where speakers and audiences were chosen on an invitation-only basis. In 2001, the organization was acquired by Chris Anderson's nonprofit Sapling

What is Nerd Nite?

Nerd Nite is a speaker event hosted in cities worldwide. It follows a format similar to TED talks in that the speakers present talks eighteen to twenty minutes in length on a wide variety of topics and disciplines. The atmosphere of Nerd Nite is more raucous than TED, and speakers can range from researchers and university professors to amateur enthusiasts of a variety of topics and hobbies. Nerd Nite occasionally produces podcasts and distributes audio and video recordings of some of its events. All Nerd Nite events are locally organized and adhere to set rules and guidelines.

Foundation. The conference expanded to different locations around the globe, and in 2006 it began offering free recordings of TED talks online.

An expansion of TED known as the TEDx Program allows independent organizers worldwide to hold TED-style branded events. The TEDx program has significantly increased TED's reach and content.

TED generally presents content in the form of short talks or multimedia presentations, usually less than eighteen minutes long. It curates and distributes TED and TEDx talks on its website. While TED speakers are selected on an invitation-only basis, TEDx speakers are often chosen by local organizers through an open application process. Both TED and TEDx talks that present scientific or health information are expected to be based on peer-reviewed evidence and research.

What is PechaKucha?

PechaKucha is a presentation format and speaker event. As a speaker event, PechaKucha is hosted in over nine hundred cities worldwide. As a format, PechaKucha presentations follow the 20 x 20 rule, where a presentation is made up of a slide deck of twenty images, each of which is displayed for twenty seconds. The speaker does not have control over the slides; they advance automatically, and the entire presentation takes six minutes and forty seconds.

The PechaKucha format was developed by architects Astrid Klein and Mark Dytham as a way of promoting concise presentations. PechaKucha events are organized by city sponsors and are nonprofit events. Attendees can expect a wider range of speaking skills and experience than with TED or Nerd Nite; while speakers are chosen through an application process, there are no limitations in terms of topic or age of the speaker. The PechaKucha organization distributes videos of PechaKucha presentations online but encourages live attendance of PechaKucha events over social sharing of the online content.

The term PechaKucha is a phonetic spelling of Japanese words meaning "chit-chat."

SPEECHES AND PRESENTATIONS

STYLES AND TYPES OF SPEECHES AND PRESENTATIONS

What is a presentation?

A presentation is any kind of situation where someone delivers information by speaking to one or more people. Presentations can take place in person, online, or over the phone. Presentations can also be recorded and played back at the listener's convenience. They can be broken into many subcategories, such as speeches, lectures, demonstrations, and so on.

All presentations have a purpose, are usually planned, and are dominated by the speaker. While it's useful to view presentations as a conversation with your audience, it's going to be the designated speaker or presenter who does the majority of the talking. Presenters can allow audiences to speak, such as by asking questions or sharing stories, but it is the speaker who controls who gets to talk at any given point in time.

What is a speech?

A speech is a formal talk given to an audience. Speeches tend to be clearly organized and have a fairly defined structure, such as Cicero's classic six-part arrangement (please refer to the "Rhetoric" chapter and to questions that follow in this chapter for further description of this format). They are often given on special occasions, such as awards ceremonies, recognition events, and important social rite-of-passage events such as weddings, conventions, and campaigns.

What is a lecture?

A lecture is a formal educational presentation about a specific topic. These are usually delivered in an academic setting by a teacher, instructor, researcher, or professor. Many postsecondary institutions hold public lectures accessible to a general audience in addition to the regular private lectures given to classes of students.

What is a panel talk?

Panel talks (also called speakers' panels, panel lectures, or panel presentations) are presentations featuring several speakers, called panelists, giving their thoughts and ideas on a topic. Panels are hosted by a facilitator or moderator who controls the flow of the discussion by asking questions directly to individual panelists, providing transitions between questions, and expanding on the ideas put forward to keep the discussion going. Facilitators might also take questions from the audience and direct the questions toward specific panelists. Panel talks are typically unrehearsed, but panelists sometimes receive copies of the questions in advance so they can prepare answers. Panel talks are conversational in tone and often feel quite informal.

What is a motivational speech?

Motivational or "inspirational" speeches are talks intended to inspire and encourage the audience to improve some area of their life. The topics addressed by these speeches vary widely, but popular topics include achieving difficult goals, living one's "best life," following passions or interests, starting a business, losing weight, improving relationships, advancing careers, and attaining self-love. Motivational speeches are highly energetic and emotionally charged and are peppered with pithy one-liners and short, memorable statements. Speakers often describe overcoming great personal obstacles or barriers and use stories to demonstrate to the audience how they can overcome their own problems.

What is an informational presentation?

Informational presentations focus on giving the audience facts, figures, statistics, analyses, and other information necessary for making decisions or understanding a current situation. Informational presentations are extremely common in business and business-like settings like volunteer organizations or committees. Reports, summaries, press statements, and debriefs are all informational presentations.

What is an educational presentation?

Educational presentations teach audiences some new skill or knowledge. These presentations can be simple or complex and can take many forms, including formal lectures, hands-on demonstrations, training presentations, and workshops.

What is a persuasive presentation?

Persuasive presentations are intended to convince an audience to take a specific action or point of view. Nearly every presentation has an element of persuasion in it. Sales presentations, legal speeches, and motivational talks are obvious forms of persuasive presentation. Other types of presentations might have a persuasive element embedded in them. Many educational presentations are also intended to persuade people to adopt a new idea, process, or way of thinking. Speeches are often persuasive in nature, especially when being given for political reasons. Skill in persuasive presenting is highly valued in business settings.

What is a goodwill presentation?

Speakers are often charged with improving the reputations of the organization they are representing, the group to which they belong, or even themselves. Goodwill presentations are intended to bolster the opinion the audience has of the organization or speaker in question. They can also serve to forge a group identity and improve relationships among members of an audience. Much like persuasive presentations, goodwill elements can exist in other types of presentations. Training presentations and workshops often include a team-building element, meant to build good relationships between coworkers or colleagues. A formal speech at a political convention could be used to build media goodwill and strengthen a sense of group identity among the politician's supporters. Addresses, acceptance speeches, and press statements are other examples of presentations that could include a goodwill element.

What is a master of ceremonies, or emcee?

A master of ceremonies, often called an emcee or MC, leads a program of events at a large function. He or she is charged with keeping the audience engaged with the program, ensuring that things run on time, and providing the overall tone for the event. MCs provide a specific type of performance and presentation. Proper MCs will spend considerable time preparing for an event. As such, an MC should be considered as much a type of presentation as a role in an event.

An "emcee" (MC) or "master of ceremonies" is like a host who leads and introduces events at a function.

What is a facilitator?

A facilitator or moderator is someone who directs panel talks or who provides services to a speaker by taking questions from the audience and performing other duties related to a presentation. Like MCs, facilitators prepare material prior to the event they are facilitating and carefully plan out what they will say, just as with any other presentation. They often create questions for panelists, plan out who will answer a question and who will respond to that answer, lead or guide discussion, and take questions from the audience.

Can a presentation or speech involve several different styles?

Presentations often involve more than one style or purpose. A speech can be intended to increase goodwill, an informational presentation might need to also persuade a group on a course of action, and a motivational presentation could also be intended to educate. A master of ceremonies often provides informational content alongside growing goodwill among attendees at an event.

How do I know what kind of presentation I'm giving?

Thinking about the purpose or end goal of your presentation is an excellent way to figure out what type of presentation you are giving. If, for example, you are asked to give a toast at a wedding with lots of funny or touching stories about the married couple, then your goal is to be creating feelings of belonging among the guests and affection and congratulations for the married couple. This would be a goodwill presentation. If you need to teach a group of employees about a new software system with a view to increase their use of that software, then you are giving a combination educational-persuasive presentation. If you are giving a report so that your company's senior managers can make decisions about what course of action to take, then you are delivering an informational presentation. If you are inspiring a group of fellow volunteers to step up their efforts for a fundraising campaign, then you are giving a motivational speech.

What is impromptu speaking?

Impromptu speaking is when a talk is given, whether long or short, without the speaker having done a great deal of prior preparation. Impromptu speaking is often called "off-the-cuff" or extemporaneous speaking. In some cases, a speaker might have a general idea what he or she will be speaking about in advance but is still expected to talk in an unrehearsed manner with lots of opportunity for spontaneous content. A panel talk where panelists are given questions ahead of time but still give unrehearsed answers and impromptu responses is an example of impromptu speaking with prior preparation.

When might I have to give an impromptu talk?

Many people do impromptu speaking when they are expected to give answers to questions being asked of them. Any time a presenter has a question-and-answer session, they are engaging in impromptu speaking. Press and media scrums are examples of impromptu-speaking situations. Some people even find themselves in impromptu-speaking situations when they need to unexpectedly fill in for an absent speaker—such as someone who needs to give a report in a colleague's unexpected absence. The idea of impromptu speaking often fills people with a significant amount of anxiety. Others see it as an exciting challenge.

What makes a good impromptu speaker?

Good impromptu speech relies on being able to focus on an idea and statement and to follow through with supporting points. People who excel at speaking off the cuff are

One example of an impromptu-speaking situation is when a reporter stops someone for an interview on a newsworthy topic.

able to organize their thoughts as they are talking so that they don't muddle their message. Additionally, they avoid going off on tangents that don't meaningfully or directly contribute to their point. The quality of an impromptu speaker is strongly related to the fullness and relevance of his or her explanations or descriptions.

A skilled impromptu speaker focuses on the quality rather than the quantity of his or her speech. He or she has a good sense of timing and doesn't unnecessarily speak at length. He or she goes beyond terse "yes" or "no" answers but only gives as much explanation or support as necessary to back up his or her statement. Knowing when to stop is a key skill in impromptu speaking, and that generally comes with practice. When in doubt, follow the "less is more" philosophy.

How can I improve my impromptu speaking skills?

Start by finding the many opportunities for impromptu speaking throughout your regular life. Situations like answering questions in meetings, engaging the audience in discussion during or after a presentation, or talking about current affairs with friends are all opportunities to practice off-the-cuff speaking. When you have the chance to speak off the cuff, take a moment before you start speaking to decide on your main statement and a supporting point. At first, you can use the following formula to structure your impromptu speech:

1. Clearly state your main idea or response. *Example:* "I feel coffee is a much better choice than tea."
2. Tell the audience the reasoning behind your idea or statement—stick to one or two supporting points. *Example:* "Many recent studies have shown that coffee packs a better antioxidant punch than tea, and it gives a more efficient hit of caffeine."
3. Rephrase your main idea. *Example:* "For that reason, I would choose coffee over tea every time."

You can follow the above formula for short or long speeches. Stick only to talking about your main idea; avoid changing your views or going off on a tangent even if you think of something interesting halfway through. If you find yourself going off on a tangent, verbally bring yourself back on track. Focus on being relevant, focused, and clear rather than clever or funny.

KEY ELEMENTS OF SPEECHES AND PRESENTATIONS

What elements should always be present in speeches or presentations?

All presentations should have an introduction, a body, and a conclusion. Introductions set the frame for the presentation and clarify the topic of the presentation to the audience. The body contains the main information or content, and the conclusion summarizes what was covered in a memorable way.

How do I decide what to put into my presentation?

Deciding on the content of your presentation can be daunting. Presenters should always take an audience-centered approach to creating presentations and only put in information that is useful and helpful to the audience's immediate needs. To do this successfully, a presenter needs to analyze an audience's context, their surface and deeper information needs, their level of preexisting knowledge about the topic at hand, and how much information they actually need in order to get value out of the presentation. The process of doing an audience-needs analysis is discussed in greater detail in "Audience Matters."

How does storytelling fit into presentations?

Storytelling is a strong presentation technique that can provide the audience with context, analogies, and a narrative to help them understand the information they are being given. Stories help put data and insights into a relatable, more understandable flow. They also have the advantage of being highly memorable.

What sort of stories should I put into my presentation?

Stories should always be relevant to the audience's context, easy for them to understand, and relatable. There are some standard story structures that work well with presentations:

- The hero's journey: This narrative describes a hero leaving his or her known comfort zone and venturing into the unknown, encountering problems along the way that must be solved. After solving the problem, he or she returns to his or her comfort zone with new knowledge, skills, or outlooks. These stories are popular when describing overcoming adversity and are very common in motivational talks.
- Contrast stories: These stories contrast visions of an ideal world with descriptions of our actual, ordinary world. These are often used in persuasive and motivational talks.
- Parable: Parables provide a fictional narrative that has a simple moral or lesson.
- Humorous story: Humor is an outstanding way of relaxing an audience, introducing a story, and generating goodwill. Humor is often used in a self-effacing way by the presenter and can humanize him or her and make someone more relatable to the audience.

Do I need to introduce myself at the start of my talk?

Presenters rarely need to introduce themselves at the start of a talk. If the audience is already familiar with who you are—either because of your reputation or because of personal familiarity—then an introduction isn't necessary. Speakers often have a facilitator or convenor available to introduce them to an audience. In some cases, presenters might want to say a few words of context to establish their credibility. For example, a person giving a wedding toast might want to say how long he or she has known the bride or groom and how they met, or someone presenting a lecture might want to comment on the number of years he or she has been working in a particular field. These comments, though, are short and to the point and are usually woven into the rest of the

Should I open my talk with a story?

It is popular to open a talk with a story, and it is an oft-cited piece of advice for people preparing a presentation. Stories can be compelling openers as they launch the audience immediately into a memorable narrative that can create a setting and context for the presentation content. They can also be used to get the audience to warm up to a presenter. A story should only be used as an opener, however, if it helps build context for the presentation or credibility for the author. They should also be avoided if the time frame for a presentation is very short or if the agenda for the event is urgent.

talk. Don't rehash any introductions you have already been given as a way to launch into your presentation content—the repetition will annoy the audience. Even if you do need to tell the audience who you are, keep it brief and blended in with the rest of the content in your introduction.

What should go into an introduction?

An introduction is intended to set the stage for the main body of the presentation. In the introduction, the speaker raises the topic for discussion and provides the context of the presentation. In persuasive or motivational presentations, the introduction should contain a position or statement that the speaker will be supporting throughout the talk, much like a thesis statement in an essay. People giving informational or educational presentations might want to address why the content is necessary or useful to the audience.

What should go into the body?

The body of a presentation is where the actual presentation content lives. In the body, the presenter often introduces a problem, provides context, gives necessary background information, teaches or demonstrates skills and processes, and provides solutions to the audience. The body of a presentation can be arranged and organized in different ways, depending on the type of information being delivered and the needs of the audience. Organization strategies will be addressed in the next section of this chapter.

What are problems?

Within a presentation, a problem is the driving need behind the presentation itself. The problem may be obvious to the audience, or it might only be apparent to the presenter. In both cases, the problem provides the frame for what information the presenter covers in his or her talk. Identifying problems are a key part of the presentation development process and is discussed further in the "Audience Matters" chapter.

What are solutions?

Solutions are the presenter's recommendations to the audience or the information he or she provides that meets the audience's information needs. Solutions are always identified by the presenter for the audience, unless the speaker is delivering someone else's presentation content. Much like problems, solutions can either be very upfront and obvious, or they may be more subtly inserted throughout the presentation. When someone asks, "What does my audience need to know from me?", they are identifying the solutions. This topic is further discussed in the chapter "Audience Matters."

What should go into a conclusion?

A conclusion is a final summary of the presentation's content. It helps tie together all pieces of a presentation for the audience, giving them a big-picture view of what they have just heard. Conclusions are also an opportunity for the speaker to recommend a specific action for their audience to take, known as a call-to-action.

What is a call-to-action?

A call-to-action (CTA) is a statement made by a speaker at the conclusion of his or her talk that directs the audience to take some kind of action after the talk is over. The CTA often tells someone either the first step he or she needs to take to achieve some outcome or the next step he or she must take to further advance his or her progress.

Effective CTAs contain a clear, simple instruction or step that the audience members can implement quickly, ideally immediately after or within a few days of the presentation. The CTA must be easy and memorable; otherwise the audience is unlikely to carry through with it.

Why do I want a call-to-action at the end of my talk?

CTAs are superb for increasing audience retention of information and memorability of a talk. They increase a presentation's value by directly helping the audience achieve a desirable goal or outcome. People often don't get lasting benefit from a talk because they aren't sure how to implement everything they learned from the speaker. When a speaker gives an audience a CTA, he or she is providing them with a sort of map and putting the audience's feet directly on the path for improvement. Audiences who are given CTAs are often more satisfied with a presenter's performance and content.

What should a master of ceremonies include in his or her program or script?

A master of ceremonies (MC) needs to include all the basic components of a presentation into his or her script. He or she needs to have an introduction in order to get all audience members on the same page regarding the purpose of the event, the flow of the program, and to make them feel like a cohesive group. The body of his or her presentation will be made up of the event's program or proceedings, such as introducing speakers and key components, letting the audience know where they are in the event's presentation at various points in time, and keeping the audience engaged by telling stories and describing what is going on during the program.

How should a facilitator prepare for a panel talk?

A facilitator plays the important role of providing context for the talk to the audience, introducing the topics to be discussed, and introducing the panelists. Facilitators should prepare introductions and conclusions and be ready to adjust their conclusions on the fly so that they can incorporate points raised during the panel talk. They may be responsible for developing questions for the panelists to answer. These questions will generate all the content for the panel talk, so facilitators need to conduct audience-needs analyses similar to those done for standard presentations. This way they can be sure they are generating a discussion that is both relevant and interesting to the audience.

A facilitator, such as this one at a Moscow conference, introduces topics and keeps the discussion from going off subject.

STRUCTURE AND ORGANIZATION

Why does the structure or organization of a presentation matter?

Presentations need a clear, orderly structure if they are to go smoothly. Spending time organizing and structuring a talk means spending time evaluating which information is going into a presentation, why it is going in, and where it needs to appear to make sense with the rest of the information. A clear structure improves the logical flow of information and helps the audience follow the presenter's train of thought. From the speaker's angle, a clear structure makes it easier to stay on track during a presentation and to recover should the presentation go off the rails at some point.

Taking the time and care to properly organize a talk requires a presenter to evaluate what he or she is putting in a presentation and why. Doing this helps eliminate unnecessary or confusing content and helps ensure the presentation is completed in the time available. Information overload is avoided, the entire presentation is much tighter, and the speaker will appear more knowledgeable and competent than he or she would have with a disorganized or scattered talk. This holds true even if the speaker is giving his or her audience less information in a well-structured talk than if he or she gave more information badly organized.

How should I organize my presentation?

There are many choices for organizing and structuring presentations. The structure chosen depends a great deal on what kind of information is being given. Standard methods of structuring presentations are:

- Chronological
- Logical
- The Sandwich Method
- Ciceronian Arrangement
- Story Arc: This method follows a classic story arc with a rise and fall in tension as the presentation progresses. This method can be used in combination with other structures.

What is a chronological organization?

Chronological presentations organize information according to the chronological or historical order in which it happened.

This structure is excellent for analyzing series of events, performance reports and reviews, and any talk where a series of events is the focus. Reverse chronological organization can be an interesting twist on this structure, presenting facts from the most to least recent. This structure allows for a different sort of retrospective analysis of a situation, event, or outcomes.

What is a logical organization?

Presentations following a logical structure use an "if-then" or "first-this-then-that" structure. Content builds on itself, allowing for an accumulation of knowledge or facts. This is useful if the audience needs to understand one piece of information in order to understand the next bit of content. Educational presentations frequently need to follow this structure, and any presentation that is teaching a skill should organize the content logically.

What is the sandwich method?

When the information in a presentation can be given in any order, a good strategy is to "sandwich" the least engaging content in the middle—between the more engaging content. In this structure, the presenter saves the most engaging, surprising, or interesting content for the end of the presentation, delivering it right before the conclusion. The next most interesting piece of content goes at the beginning of the body of the presentation, right after the introduction. This structure allows the speaker to grab the audience's attention off the bat and then to reignite their attention at the end—which is the part of the presentation that audiences tend to remember the most.

What is a Ciceronian arrangement?

In his work as an orator, Cicero codified a standard formula for arranging speeches. As Cicero's oratory was usually performed in the senate or other political arenas or for the purpose of litigation, his formula for arrangement works extremely well for political- and legal-type speeches. A Ciceronian arrangement also works well for organizing defense speeches, such as a thesis defense presentation for a Ph.D. candidate.

A Ciceronian arrangement follows a six-part formula:

1. Introduction (*exordium*)

The speaker establishes his or her credibility or *ethos* to the audience and wins their trust.

Example: "I have been an obsessive coffee drinker and roaster for many years."

2. Narration (*narratio*)

The speaker states the facts and nature of the case at hand. This is often done in a narrative form and can include some storytelling and history. Stick to the most relevant and important details—don't bore or confuse the audience by getting bogged down in unnecessary facts.

Example: "For hundreds of years, coffee has been revered for its ability to boost energy, clarify the mind, and heal the soul. But now we see all manners of tea elbowing their way into health stores, denying valuable shelf space from coffee. It is time we stop this invasion, time we reclaim coffee's supremacy as our primary source of caffeine and antioxidants!"

3. Division (*partito*)

A description of what the speaker is about to argue and where the speaker agrees and disagrees with his or her opponent (the opponent may be a specific person or an undefined group of people). This gives the audience important context for the proofs that are to follow.

Example: "Now the tea growers will tell you that tea has outstanding levels of antioxidants. And that's true. They will say that tea can calm tempers. They will say that tea raises intelligence and good taste—and here I say they are going too far. It is coffee drinkers who are the truly erudite, the truly tasteful. And while tea may have many excellent properties, it is the coffee drinkers who are fortifying themselves with antioxidants and mellow feelings with far greater efficiency than those who consume tea."

4. Proof (*confirmato*)

This is the speaker's core argument and forms the main body of the speech. Proofs make a strong appeal to logos, and the arguments should be presented as logical, reasonable, and rational.

Example: "The following double-blind, peer-reviewed studies demonstrate without a doubt that coffee raises your IQ...."

5. Refutation (*refutatio*)

Now that the speaker has laid out his or her logical argument, he or she answers any arguments or rebuttals offered by his or her opponent. The speaker might present these rebuttals him- or herself and then immediately provide his or her own answers (a rhetorical device called *hypophora).*

Example: "My opponents from the International Tea Growers Association will tell you that the antioxidants and tannins found in tea leaves are more bioavailable, and that the roasting process of coffee destroys nutrition. Let me tell you why they are wrong...."

6. Conclusion (*peroratio*)

The speaker sums up his or her points and presents the audience with an emotionally charged conclusion, often building up his or her statements to a grand crescendo. This section of the speech makes use of pathos.

Example: "Don't be fooled by the marketing strategies of a frightened industry! You can, you must, reclaim your coffee habit. For the sake of your health and your sanity, you must drink coffee. For the sake of your relationships and career, you must drink coffee. For the sake of your quality of life, you must—*must*—drink coffee. So go immediately to your nearest local roaster, buy a kilo of the finest coffee they have available, and drink it in the knowledge that you are doing yourself and your world a favor!"

What is a story arc?

A story arc is a narrative flow used in most fictional stories that creates a rise in an audience's emotion and tension through problems or conflicts. These build to a climactic point, where the peak of excitement and action takes place. After the climax there is a path of falling action, where problems are resolved and loose ends tied up. This is then followed by a conclusion, which closes the story.

Nonfiction presentations and speeches can follow this same format of rising and falling tension. The story arc is extremely useful for motivational speeches, where much of the impact of the presentation hinges on building a state of excitement and emotion in the audience. It is also popularly used in persuasive presentations, such as sales talks and political speeches. Those engaging in oration or using a Ciceronian arrangement for their presentation can also use a story arc to plot out where to bolster the tension and emotion.

How can I use a story arc to organize a motivational or persuasive presentation?

When using a story-arc structure to organize presentations, the speaker builds tension and emotion by describing a problem (or series of problems) the audience has. The au-

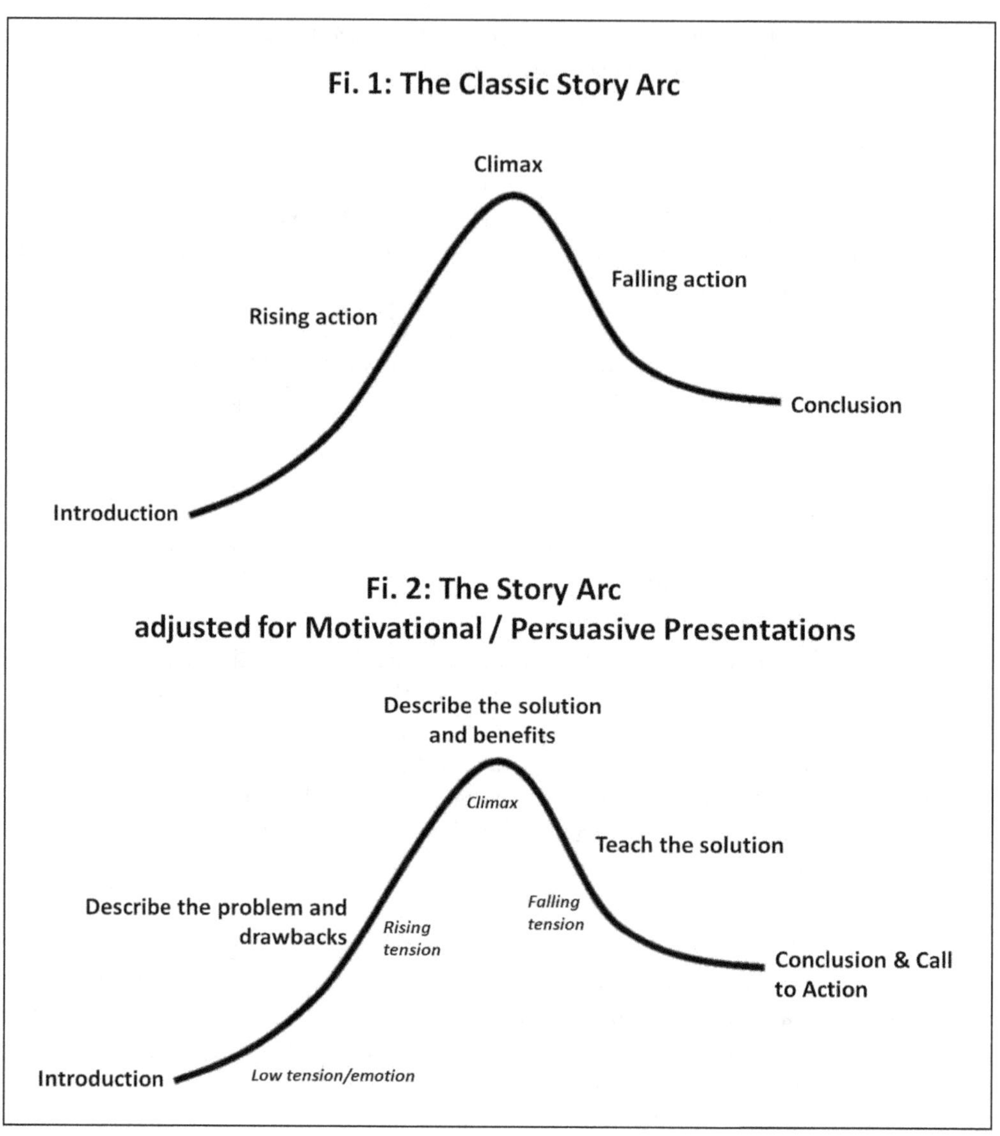

Two types of story arcs.

dience may know they have this problem, or it could be a problem created and introduced by the speaker. The speaker describes it in great, gory detail, building it up in the audience's mind so they become excited and emotionally charged. Then, at the climax point of the story arc, the speaker reveals a solution to the problem and describes the benefits—but does *not* tell the audience how to carry out the solution. Instead, he or she dwells on the benefits, painting a mental picture of how the solution will benefit the audience. This strategy leads the audience to picture themselves enjoying the benefits of the solution, which creates buy-in.

Once the benefits have been described, the speaker goes on to explain how the solution works and how to carry it out. He or she then gives the conclusion and a clear call-to-action that instructs the audience on the next step they need to take to implement the solution.

DELIVERY

What performance elements do I need to take into consideration when presenting?

There's a strong performance aspect to presentations and public speaking. Good performance technique helps gain and hold the audience's attention and can both clarify and amplify your message. The performance techniques that make the biggest impact on delivery are vocal variation, speed, body language, and audience engagement. Specific aspects of vocal performance and body language are addressed in the chapters "The Human Voice" and "Body Talk."

How can I be a more engaging presenter?

Engaging presenters are those who clearly demonstrate their personal investment in the topic at hand. This is done through nonverbal cues that show the speaker's energy and enthusiasm for the talk and his or her audience. Eye contact with the audience is critical to engagement as it communicates the speaker's interest in the people he or she is talking to. Forward-facing, open-body language is also important—being able to see the speaker move and gesture increases the audience's feeling of connection and familiarity with the speaker. This can't be achieved if the speaker is hiding behind a lectern.

Another way to engage your audience is to give them the opportunity to be active listeners or even participants in your talk rather than just passively listening to what you have to say. A conversational style of speaking lets the audience feel included in the presentation. Speakers can add to this by using direct audience-engagement tactics. Asking for answers to questions or having people participate in brief activities are excellent engagement techniques that can be used for small and large audiences alike. Questions or activities require verbal or physical responses, such as asking for people to say "yes" or "no," asking for a show of hands, or having people stand up and move around, are especially effective strategies for reengaging and reenergizing your audience.

How does unemotional or flat delivery harm the effectiveness of a presentation?

An engaging presentation does more than entertain an audience—it helps them maintain their attention and focus throughout the talk. If a presenter has a monotonous, flat delivery, they make it difficult for the people listening to them to pay proper attention. Flat deliveries also deprive the audience of vital information such as relative importance or urgency of certain parts of the presentation (often communicated nonverbally through cues like rises or falls in volume, pitch, and speed).

How can I tell if I'm underemoting or monotonous when I speak?

Even polite audiences will give off cues that a speaker is monotonous or emotionally flat. Look for signs of boredom in the audience, such as people looking around, long-lasting side conversations, lots of fidgeting, and glazed expressions. Speakers can also observe their own behavior for warning signs. If you notice that you are spending a lot of time reading from the notes, looking at your slideshow more often than you look at your audience, or not moving about and using physical gestures, it is very likely that you are delivering your speech in a monotonous, underwhelming manner.

Why are presentations less effective when the speaker is over the top with energy or emotion?

There are several reasons why delivering a talk with excessive energy makes a presentation less effective. Over-the-top performances can make a speaker seem undisciplined, which harms his or her credibility. They can also make a talk seem overly rehearsed and a speaker appear phony, both of which prevent the audience from connecting with a speaker. Often, speakers who are overly dramatic seem self-absorbed and more interested in their delivery than in engaging with the audience. The speaker also runs the risk of distracting the audience by their antics or drawing the audience's attention toward less important parts of the presentation.

How can I tell if I'm too over the top in my delivery?

Even though many people are afraid of showing too much emotion or seeming slightly crazy when they speak, it is far more common for presenters to be too repressed rather than too effusive. All the same, if you are a naturally energetic speaker or are trying to boost your expressiveness, it's helpful to watch for cues from the audience that could tell you if you are going too far.

When a speaker is going over the top with his or her expressiveness, the audience will give signs that they are overwhelmed or irritated. Examples of such signs are avoidance and distancing behaviors: avoiding eye contact, looking away, and shrinking back in their seats. Signs of irritation can include rolling eyes, closed body language such as tightly crossed arms, and laughing at inappropriate times during the talk.

How should a motivational speaker talk?

A key feature of motivational talks is the high level of energy that infuses both the presenter and the audience. People attending a motivational presentation will expect to engage as much through their emotions as through their reason. The delivery of these types of presentations rely on strong and frequent appeals to the audience's pathos (please refer to "Rhetoric") to gain their emotional commitment to what the speaker is saying. Speakers should expect to demonstrate a great deal of intensity and variety onstage, often swinging between sincere solemnities to exuberant joy in short periods of time. Large amounts of vocal variation, strong physical engagement, and lots of gesture and movement are key characteristics of these talks. The speaker should use a direct, conversational manner of speaking with frequent call-outs to the audience in the form of questions or instructions.

How should an informational or educational speaker talk?

Informational and educational talks tend to vary more in delivery than motivational talks. They are often conversational in nature, especially in training presentations or workshops. Speakers should seek to connect with the audience, establish their credibility as a speaker early on, and use language and terminology familiar to their audience. People delivering presentations like these don't often need to emote as strongly as in a motivational talk or as grandly as in an oration. Formal lectures tend to be slightly more restrained and distant in tone, although this isn't necessary and often not as effective as a more intimate style of talk.

All informational and educational speakers should still bring a sense of energy and interest in their talk and use cues like rises and falls in their speed and tone to draw their audience's attention to the most important points in their presentation. Humor and occasional levity are appreciated by the audience, even when the subject matter is serious. This helps refocus their attention and allows them to relax and take in the content with greater ease. Ideally, the speaker will balance a measured, reasonable tone with enough energy to draw in the audience's interest and sustain their attention throughout the talk.

For an educational speaker, such as a college professor, it is even more important to engage the audience. The speaking style is also more conversational in smaller groups, more formal in a large lecture hall.

How should I speak when giving a formal speech?

Formal speeches such as commencement addresses and acceptance speeches are often far more restrained in emotion than other kinds of presentations. These talks are not intended to be as intimate in feel as most other presentations, and it's more acceptable for the presenter to read from extensive notes. The speaker should look to match both the formality of the occasion and his or her level of familiarity with the audience. If the formal speech is being given to the speaker's colleagues, peers, or to people they know well, a more intimate tone can be used. If it is being given to an audience that the speaker doesn't have a prior or friendly connection with, a more removed, distant, and unemotional tone can be used.

How should I deliver an oration?

Orations are very grand speeches. The speaker will benefit from using a tone that is powerful and full of energy and emotion but with more appearance of restraint or self-control than a motivational speaker would use. Orations are intended to incite people to action, and that is most effectively done by appealing to an audience's pathos. An orator can make use of this by painting vivid verbal pictures, using rhythmic phrasing, formal or elegant language, and long pauses and silences. These delivery techniques have a strong emotional effect and will help the orator build up the emotional crescendo that is so typical of that style of speech.

What style of performance or delivery should a master of ceremonies use?

Masters of ceremonies (MC) need to maintain the audience's attention and enthusiasm throughout an event, so they typically need to bring quite a bit of energy to their performance. A light, conversational tone is best with stories or humorous bits liberally scattered throughout the script. The MC should be relatable to the audience with a bright, open voice and manner. As the "face" of the event, the MC can insert personal touches and references provided the audience can relate to those references or anecdotes. All the same, the MC is there to highlight the event and the audience and should present material that constantly focuses on the people gathered there rather than on themselves.

There may be the odd occasion when the event is a somber one, in which case the MC should take a respectfully neutral tone. Appearing overly saddened or grave in these circumstances may appear forced or inappropriate. Rather, a straightforward and formal style will give the proceedings the dignity and gravity necessary. In very solemn, formal events, the MC should avoid making personal references outside of his or her introduction at the start of the event.

What is a good style of delivery for a facilitator?

Facilitators are there to put the guest or panel speakers in the best light possible. Their delivery is similar to that of an MC, but in general they should be highlighting the speakers' presence instead of their own. A good facilitator will refrain from giving too many of his or her own ideas or input in the discussion and should always defer questions from the audience to the panelists.

A facilitator's manner is bright, open, curious, and likeable. He or she needs to balance a good amount of energy with a calm certainty that he or she is in control of the proceedings. Be ready to encourage participation from the audience in the form of asking questions, and be willing to manage audience questions by clarifying people's questions, rephrasing them, or politely cutting off someone who is monopolizing the question period.

Do I need to use humor in my talks?

Humor is effective because when people laugh together, they feel they understand one another. While it's a welcome addition to most talks, it isn't the most important part of an effective presentation. When creating a presentation, focus first on creating a clear, focused message with useful or informative supporting material and a well-organized structure. Once you have those in place, you can think about lightening and energizing the talk with a bit of humor. Worry first about the quality of your content. If your content is good, you can then safely worry about being funny.

I'm not a funny person—how can I put some humor in my presentation?

Many presenters are intimidated by using humor. They're worried that they just aren't funny or that their jokes will fall flat. Humor, though, takes many forms and isn't restricted to delivering comedy-club-style jokes, zingers, and one-liners. Using stories with unexpected twists, making wry observations, pointing out absurdities, and employing gentle self-deprecation are all examples of humorous content that doesn't rely on cracking jokes.

If you are struggling to insert some humor in your talk, think of a story or observation related to your content that you find funny. Then think if the reason you find that story or observation funny would also be funny to the majority of your audience. If you think it would make sense to most people listening to you, include it in your presentation. Keep it simple and light, and you'll have effectively used humor to boost your talk.

How do I decide what to say when I'm speaking off the cuff?

Generally, it's best to stick with the first idea that comes to mind. Even if you find yourself changing your mind about what you want to say while you speak, stay with the original thought until you have fully explored it. If you are speaking off the cuff because you were asked a question, focus on fully answering the question as simply and directly as possible. If you aren't sure what someone's question is or what someone wants you to speak about, ask him or her for clarification. Don't clutter your mind worrying about speaking for a long time or loading your listeners with as much information as you can conjure.

THE HUMAN VOICE

ANATOMY OF SPEAKING

How does my voice work?

When we speak, we push air from our lungs up the trachea and through the larynx, a triangular-shaped box made up of several cartilages. In the larynx are the vocal folds, commonly called the vocal cords, which vibrate to produce sound. A group of muscles, called the intrinsic laryngeal muscles, tighten in order to change the length and tightness of the vocal folds. This is what allows our voices to change in pitch. The tighter the vocal folds, the faster they vibrate, and a higher pitch of voice is produced. Loudness in the voice is created by forcing more air through the larynx. Whispering is made when air is passed through the larynx but without the force needed to make the vocal folds vibrate.

The air and sound then pass from the larynx into the mouth, where the speech muscles—the soft palate, tongue, jaw, and lips—change shape to produce different sounds and phonemes (the smallest units of pronounced sound). We string together phonemes to form words.

Why are men's voices deeper than women's?

The pitch of a voice depends on how fast the vocal cords vibrate. Anatomically, men have thicker, longer vocal folds. The size of their vocal folds means they aren't as tight as women's vocal folds and therefore vibrate more slowly, producing lower pitches. Both men's and women's voices tend to lower in pitch as vocal folds become looser with age (along with everything else).

How does breathing affect my voice?

The force and fullness of your breath, the amount of air you take in, and the strength and control you use when you push the air out all affect the pitch, richness, and loudness of your voice, as well as the length of time you can make a continuous noise. Relaxed, efficient breaths that use the diaphragm to pull air deep into the lungs and then to control how fast it is exhaled produce better sound; the speaker's voice sounds richer, with more depth and power. Speakers who breathe like this can also sustain sound for longer and can say more with each breath. Inefficient breathing—breathing that is fast, shallow, and mostly uses the upper chest muscles to pull air into the upper lungs—tends to be breathy and weak. When speakers breathe like this, they can't sustain a sound for long and often run out of air. This forces them to take more rapid, shallow breaths, which continue to produce poor sound.

What is the diaphragm?

The diaphragm is the primary breathing muscle. It is a sheetlike muscle, shaped somewhat like a parachute that stretches horizontally across the torso at the bottom of the rib cage. When the diaphragm is fully relaxed and we breathe out, it rises in the rib cage like a parachute, forming a dome. When it tightens and we breathe in, it flattens out, lowering toward the navel and pulling the lungs open. This creates a vacuum in our lungs, and we breathe in air to fill them. Full, relaxed, strong breaths are powered mostly from the diaphragm and are seen more in the lower torso and belly than in the upper chest and shoulders.

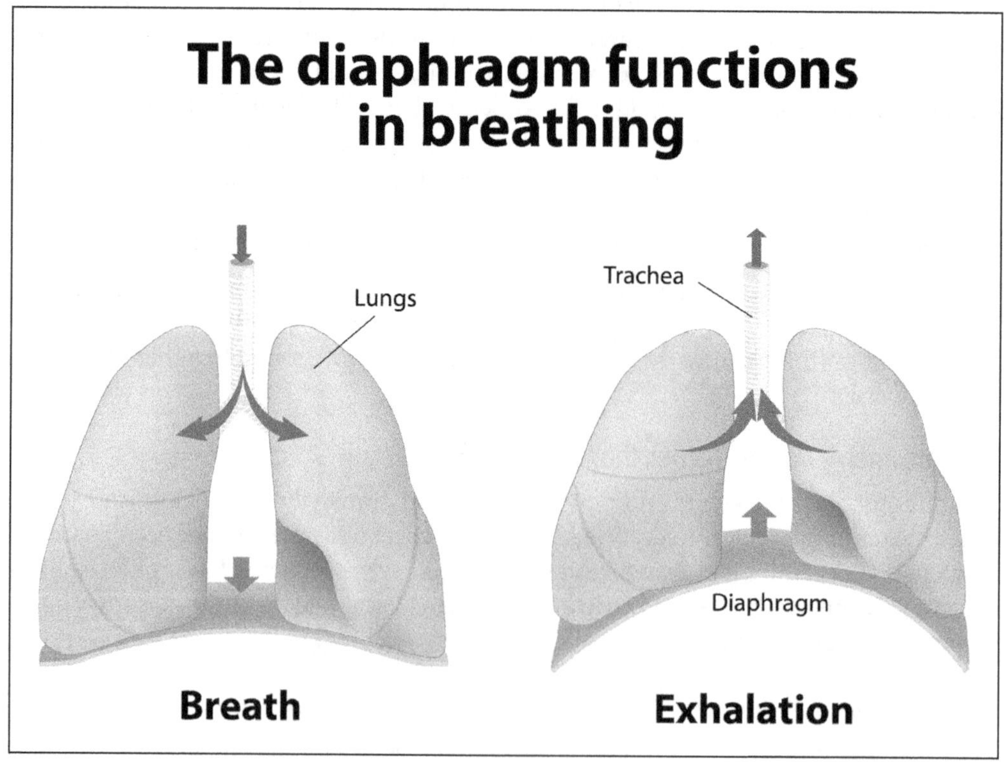

The diaphragm is a muscle under the lungs that controls breathing.

What other muscles help with breathing?

There are several additional muscles that help with breathing. The intercostal muscles between the ribs help the diaphragm pull the rib cage open and can rapidly contract to force air out more quickly. The sternocleidomastoid (which connects areas from the upper ribs, clavicle, and jaw) as well as the scalene (which connects the upper ribs, shoulder girdle, and neck) can also help with the breathing process by pulling the top ribs upward. These muscles are usually only involved in breathing when the person is under a great deal of stress of physical exertion.

While the abdominal muscles don't help us breathe in, they can help breathe out with sudden force by contracting and creating more pressure around the bottom of the rib cage, which will push out air. The abdominal muscles play a role in supporting and improving breath and voice by helping control how air is pushed out of the body. As such, they play a very important role in a speaker's ability to project and sustain a full, rich tone. This alone makes doing a few sit-ups or plank poses every day worthwhile.

What are the resonators?

Resonators are cavities (open spaces) in the body that help give tone and volume to the sounds we make. The main resonators are in our chest, pharynx, the sinus cavities in our face behind our eyes and nose, and the mouth. It is possible for some people to feel their resonators when they hum; it feels like vibrations in various places in their head, throat, and chest. While the resonators don't produce sounds, they can help modify it. It's useful for speakers to picture different resonators vibrating when they speak. The muscular movement that people experience when they try to figuratively "place" their voice in different resonators helps them learn how to gain better control over the pitch and tone of their voice when they speak.

Why do some people have louder voices than others?

Volume of air and size of resonators play a major role in how loudly people speak. People with larger bodies are able to push out more air and have larger resonators. They typically have naturally louder voices than more slightly built people. Other people speak with a great deal of abdominal support and breathe naturally from the diaphragm, either because they are naturally inclined to do so or because they have trained themselves to speak that way. They will have stronger, more powerful voices.

Why do people sometimes "sound tense"?

Muscular tension has a significant effect on the quality of our breathing and our voices. When people are tense, they often have tight muscles through their jaw, neck, shoulders, and ribs. They also tend to breathe less efficiently, taking short and shallow breaths in their upper rib cage rather than deep, diaphragmatic breaths that completely fill their lungs with air. This combination of tight muscles and poor breathing leads to tight vocal folds and less air with which to make sound. This leads to a voice that is weaker, more strained, and slightly higher in pitch than normal.

Why are some voices gravelly?

Some people have naturally gravelly voices, either due to inadequate air flow through the larynx or to relaxed or weakened vocal folds. Many people's voices tend to rasp slightly at the end of sentences or as they finish speaking, as they are already cutting off air or reducing the strength that they are pushing air through their vocal folds. Other people have gravelly, raspy, or hoarse voices due to long-lasting damage or injury to the vocal folds or larynx.

Why do we lose our voices?

When the larynx or the area around it becomes swollen, inflamed, or irritated due to illness or injury, the vocal folds can't vibrate properly. This can make the voice sound scratchy or hoarse. In some cases, the vocal folds won't vibrate at all, in which case the voice is lost completely and the person can only whisper. This is usually a temporary condition, and the voice returns to normal once the illness has passed or the laryngeal area has healed.

How do voices become injured or damaged?

There is a huge range of issues that can cause temporary or permanent injury and damage to a voice. Viral or bacterial infection, such as the common cold or strep throat, can cause laryngitis or other inflammations near or on the vocal cords. Other illnesses, like acid reflux or abnormal growths, can also contribute to damage.

Straining the voice by shouting or screaming for long periods of time can cause direct injury and trauma to the vocal folds in much the same way that excessive or repetitive use of a muscle or joint can result in injury. People who need to speak often or for very long periods of time, like teachers, can sustain overuse injuries to their voice.

Environmental factors like pollution can lead to irritation of the voice, as can smoking and secondhand smoke. Direct injury or trauma, such as that sustained by a blow to the throat or by surgery involving the laryngeal area, can result in temporary or permanent damage. Dry air can also contribute to vocal injury and is noticeable in many people living in dry climates or during cold winters.

Most people will experience temporary damage to their voices from temporary illness, overuse, or strain at some point in their life. If you frequently lose your voice, experience pain when you speak, have ongoing tenderness near your larynx, have hoarseness that doesn't resolve on its own, or are particularly bothered by the quality of your voice, you should consult with a doctor.

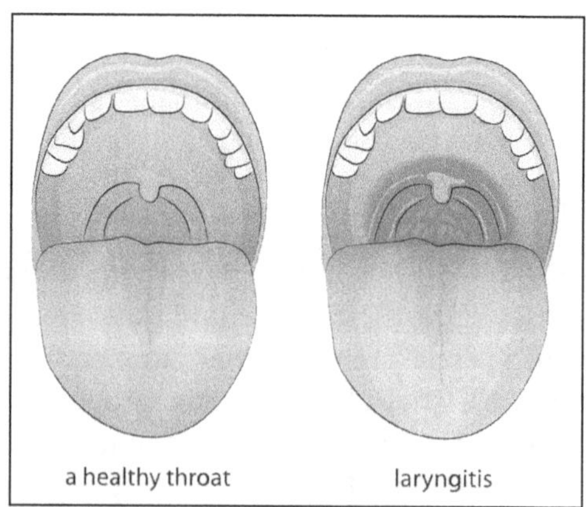

Laryngitis is an inflammation of the tissues in the throat that can make it difficult to speak.

How can I avoid straining my voice?

Speakers can take several steps to limit vocal strain. Learning how to relax the muscles in the jaw, neck, and upper chest will help the vocal folds move more freely. Breathing properly, with full, deep diaphragmatic breaths and good abdominal support, allows air to be used more efficiently, helping the speaker project without shouting or yelling. Proper enunciation can also help speakers be understood without needing to dial up the volume of their voice. Resting the voice is also very important for people who speak frequently. Speaking involves the use of many muscles and body systems, and giving them time to rest and recover is important. Complete rest—long periods with little to no talking at all—is sometimes necessary. If your voice is particularly injured from overuse or illness, even whispering can irritate it further.

DEVELOPING YOUR VOICE

Do we associate deeper voices with power?

Most people subconsciously associate deeper, stronger voices with power. Higher-pitched or breathy voices are usually perceived as juvenile or weak. What is considered to be a deep voice is subjective and depends on the person's gender. For a deep voice to convey power, it also needs to have strength and variability. If someone speaks in a low register but can't maintain his or her loudness, his or her voice will sound weak, and the impression of power is diminished. Voice researchers Sei Jin Ko, Melody Sadler, and Adam Galinsky conducted an experiment with 161 university students that showed that variability in loudness and a voice that was louder overall were better signals of power than pitch.

Should I speak in a deeper voice?

There are situations where external pressure or culture could lead you to want to deepen your voice. Workplace cultures with strong hierarchies and emphasis on status and power may warrant a stronger, richer tone of voice. The late British prime minister Margaret Thatcher worked with voice coaches to deepen her voice to improve her effectiveness within her party.

Some people find that the act of speaking in a lower register and the physical, muscular engagement that goes with it does make them feel more confident and helps them project a more powerful image. Others find that trying to drop their voices is too much of a strain and feels unnatural. The decision to try to deepen your voice by learning how to speak with a lower register should be a personal one based on whether or not the change makes you feel more confident or competent.

Whether or not you want to try to speak in a lower register, consider speaking with a better, fuller diaphragmatic breath and more muscular engagement through your abs. This will give you a stronger, richer tone and might give you the effect you want without having to speak lower than you normally would.

How can I improve my vocal tone?

Improving your vocal tone or developing a richer voice takes a fair amount of focus, concentration, and feedback. There are some basic exercises that you can practice on your own.

Focus first on breathing deeply from your diaphragm, pulling the air deep into your lungs without taking in too much air and straining your upper chest. This will help you take in enough air to produce a full sound.

Next, work on lightly engaging your abdominal muscles when you speak. This will give you the muscle support needed to control the amount of air you release when speaking and the force with which you push the air through your larynx and out of your mouth.

Then, focus on placing your voice in the front of your face, letting it resonate through your sinus cavities and mouth without blocking it and letting it become nasally. To figure out how to "place" your voice in the front of your face, make a humming noise as though you were agreeing with someone. Don't think about the pitch of your voice—just hum at whatever pitch comes naturally. Feel where the hum vibrates. If it is vibrating anywhere other than the front of your face and mouth, try sending the vibrations to your sinuses and mouth. Once you feel the vibrations happening in that area, open your mouth and speak, focusing on placing the sound in the same place as your hum. This takes a fair amount of visualization, and you may need to make several attempts before getting it.

If you are very serious about making dramatic or specific changes in your voice, you might consider hiring a professional voice coach.

Improving your vocal tone and quality can be tricky. If you are looking at making substantial or specific changes to the way you use your voice, hiring a professional voice coach is strongly recommended.

How can I improve my vocal range?

Increasing your natural vocal range is not necessary for speakers. Trying to speak in an unnaturally low or high register can strain and damage your vocal cords. While singers might benefit from an improvement in range, there isn't any reason for a speaker or presenter to do so. Instead, aim for speaking with more support and strength in your natural register by working on breathing from the diaphragm, supporting your breath through your core abdominal muscles, and letting your voice flow out from you freely and openly.

USING YOUR VOICE EFFECTIVELY

What makes a person sound confident?

When someone is praised for "sounding confident," he or she usually has a pleasantly rich voice and uses plenty of variety in his or her pitch. Confidence is also expressed in a person's volume. Somebody who sounds confident uses a volume suitable for the space and occasion and will vary that volume to give color to what he or she says. Overbearing, insecure, or angry people speak with inappropriate volume—either too quiet or too loud. Confident voices often convey a feeling of relaxed certainty, whereas anxious voices are tight and strained due to muscle tension in the speaker's face, neck, shoulders, and chest.

A confident voice is often accompanied by confident body language. Confident people tend to stand and move in a way that gives better vocal support and more freedom in expression.

What is upspeak?

Upspeak is a vocal habit of ending sentences on a rising note as if asking a question. While everyone uses upspeak from time to time, doing it often is very undesirable. It indicates a sense of apologetic uncertainty or insecurity, as though the person speaking needs validation or agreement from those he or she is speaking to. It's also considered a juvenile vocal trait and can diminish a person's credibility or authority. If you have this habit and want to change it, focus on finishing your sentences with a firm tone, presenting what you say as indisputable fact. Visualize the period at the end of the sentence, and think of putting a vocal period at the end of your sentences.

What is vocal fry?

Vocal fry is the drawing out of the final few words or sounds in a statement accompanied with a dramatic drop in pitch and volume. The "fry" is the gravelly, creaky sound made by the speaker when doing this. Vocal fry is an affectation—a style or behavior of speech adopted for fashion. It hit news headlines in 2014 as one of the more annoying speech mannerisms used by young people. This speech fad was popularly credited to Kim Kardashian, but many pop stars of that time used vocal fry in their speech.

Celebrity Kim Kardashian is credited with making the speech fad of vocal fry popular.

Vocal fry is different from the natural gravelly edge many people have when they speak. When people speak with a naturally rough voice, the gravelly sound occurs regardless of the pitch or strength with which they speak. Vocal fry happens specifically at the end of statements along with the drop in pitch and strength, and is very laconic in tone. It generally makes the speaker seem bored, lazy, or world-weary.

How can I stop running out of breath when I speak?

When presenting, many people experience the feeling of running out of air halfway through their sentences. Public speaking requires deep, frequent breathing and efficient use of air. Drawing in full breaths using the diaphragm rather than the muscles of the upper chest will help you take in enough air with each breath.

Another key to not running out of breath is to take frequent breaths, likely far more breaths than you think you should. You want to avoid squeezing out every last drop of air you have in an effort to make it to the end of a sentence before breathing. Rather, as soon as you feel that you are low on air, pause briefly and breathe before continuing. Breathing in the middle of sentences is perfectly acceptable. Speaking more slowly and becoming comfortable with pausing while you speak will help you breathe more frequently without it sounding odd or unnatural to your audience.

How can I stop saying things like "um" and "ah"?

Throwaway noises like "um" and "ah" are normal parts of speech. When we are trying to compose our next few words, these involuntary noises slip out as a way of filling the gap while we think. "Um," "ah," and other nonmeaningful sounds aren't a problem unless they prevent someone from understanding what you are saying or cause you undue stress. If you are determined to reduce how often you make such sounds, slow down how quickly you speak in order to give your brain time to catch up with your mouth. If you feel the urge to "um," or you can't seem to stop saying it, then pause and take a breath. This can kick your brain back into gear and let you carry on with your next sentence.

If you are giving a planned presentation, being very comfortable with your content will significantly reduce the frequency of these meaningless sounds. Spend plenty of time preparing your talk, paring down your content, and practicing. When speakers are comfortable with what they are saying, bothersome "ums" and "ahs" tend to melt away.

What are crutch words?

Crutch words are similar to "um" and "ah"—they are meaningless units of sound that help speakers transition to a different thought or think about how they want to express themselves. "Like" is a common and oft-maligned crutch word, as are "you know" and "anyway." "So" is a crutch word often used at the beginning of sentences or when someone is transitioning to a new thought.

Eliminating crutch words is similar to eliminating "um" and "ah" sounds. Slow down your rate of speech, and if you find yourself struggling to think of what to say next or are using a crutch word frequently, pause and give yourself time to think about what you want to say next. Pay attention to your own speech, and see if you can figure out any patterns to your use of crutch words. If you can identify when you're most likely to use crutch words, you can be extra vigilant and use pauses or changes in pace instead of your favorite crutch.

How can I learn to enunciate more clearly?

Effective speakers are clear speakers. Enunciation makes it easier for people to understand you and increases your impression of confidence and competence. Speakers often start to mumble when they are speaking too quickly, so slowing down your pace of speech is an important step to enunciation. In addition to slowing down your rate of speech, you can practice some easy enunciation exercises. Tongue twisters make outstanding enunciation drills. Do an online search for tongue twisters and practice saying them as slowly and as clearly as possible. Clarity is the goal, not speed. Go slowly and overenunciate every sound, especially the vowels. Different tongue twisters focus on different sounds, so some will be easier for you than others. Tongue twisters are easily found online, and many children's classics such as Dr. Seuss's *Fox in Socks* are ideal for enunciation exercises.

Another simple enunciation exercise is to bite a cork or chunk of carrot approximately one inch in diameter between your front teeth with the cork or carrot about a quarter to a half inch inside your mouth. Then, practice reading some text or reciting tongue twisters slowly while enunciating each sound as clearly as possible. This will increase your awareness of how your lips and tongue move to pronounce words while working all the muscles of the mouth and tongue. Do *not* do this exercise by filling your mouth with objects like marbles, as you run the risk of choking. A cork held between the teeth works just as well and is much safer.

How fast should I speak?

Speakers need to be able to talk at a pace that is interesting to listen to, that allows them to clearly enunciate their words, and that gives the audience time to process what they are hearing. A comfortable rate of speech for public speaking is approximately 165 to 190 words per minute. This is about the range in which people speak when they are having a conversation with acquaintances such as work colleagues.

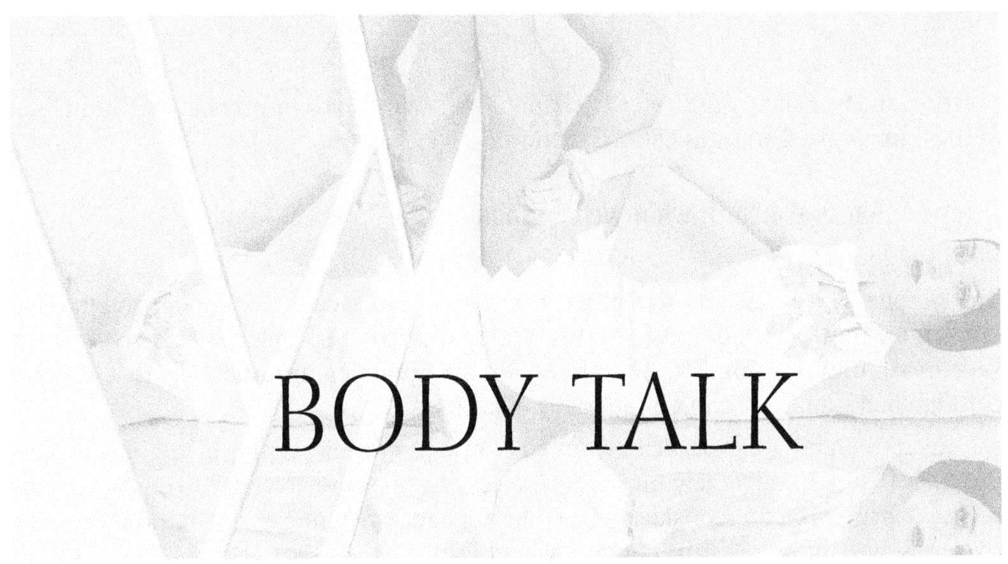

THE EFFECTS OF BODY LANGUAGE

What is body language?

Body language is a form of nonverbal communication that includes gestures, physical movement, and facial expressions. It can be informal and natural or highly choreographed and rehearsed. Most body language is performed spontaneously, but presenters and speakers may find it useful to roughly plan and rehearse their body language when practicing their talk.

Are there specific gestures or postures I should use when I give a presentation or speech?

Some aspects of body language are recognizable across cultures, such as protective movement like slouching or folding arms or powerful postures like standing up straight and taking up space. Most meaning-specific gestures, however, are cultural in nature. Signals like the North American "OK" sign—a circle made with the thumb and forefinger—means "zero" in France and is a rude gesture indicating a bodily orifice in countries such as Brazil and Russia. A good rule of thumb when using body language for different audiences is that if you are indicating an emotion or state of mind, it is likely to be understood across cultures. If it has a specific interpretation or symbolic meaning, it could mean different things in different cultures and you would be safest to avoid using that gesture.

What are universal expressions?

Research has indicated that there are universal facial expressions that indicate specific emotional states, regardless of culture. For more information about universal facial expression and body language, refer to chapter one, "What Is Communication?", and look at the "Nonverbal Communication" section.

Is it true that over half of what we communicate is done through body language?

The famous figure that fifty-five percent of our communication is done through body language is based off dubious interpretations of Dr. Albert Mehrabian's research in human communication. The actual percentage of our communication that is done through body language can't be so easily quantified.

Even though it's debatable how much of our communication is based in body language, it is still an extremely important aspect of a presenter's ability to engage an audience. It's important to consider your body language when presenting but unnecessary to obsess over minute gestures and movement.

What is mirroring?

Mirroring is the subconscious act of imitating another person's body language. This social behavior increases our agreeability and helps people synchronize their mood and feelings. Public speakers can make use of mirroring through body language by demonstrating the body language that is in line with how they want their audience to feel. A motivational speaker trying to energize an audience can get people excited by demonstrating excited, energetic body language. A presenter trying to soothe and calm an audience should use more relaxed body language and calming gestures; his or her audience will mirror that body language and begin to settle down as well.

What makes body language effective?

Effective body language clarifies and amplifies a speaker's message and engages the audience's attention without overwhelming them. Speakers who are skilled at using body language use it intentionally but without excessive planning or choreography. An extremely important characteristic of effective body language is that it is congruent with what the speaker is saying. Congruence is when the body language, expressions, and gestures match the meaning of the words being spoken. This can clarify meaning and enhance understanding between the speaker and the audience. Speakers can also use incongruous body language purposefully to indicate

"Mirroring" is when you imitate another person's body language subconsciously.

irony or hidden meanings. Incongruous body language is acceptable as long as it is done intentionally and in relatively small doses.

When is body language ineffective?

Ineffective body language might be distracting, underwhelming, or out of sync with the speaker's meaning.

There are two types of distracting body language. The first is unconscious or unintentional movements, such as pacing, fiddling with papers or pocket items like keys or coins, and gestures that communicate anxiety or tension. Presenters need to be aware of these habits and consciously correct them when they happen. The second type is over-choreographed body language and gestures. When speakers choreograph very specific or overly flamboyant body language throughout their speech, their movement usually seems bizarre, unnatural, or melodramatic. This puts off the audience and can create a barrier between the speaker and the audience as the speaker often seems more interested in themselves than in their audience.

Underwhelming body language is overly restrained or lacking in energy. This is ineffective because the presenter is not giving any nonverbal information indicating how much energy or emotion the audience should be feeling. It strips meaning from the presentation and makes it more difficult for listeners to pay attention.

Incongruous body language is out of sync or at odds with the speaker's intended meaning. Although incongruous nonverbal signals can be used intentionally for specific effect, such as irony, when it is unintentional, it can confuse the audience. This kind of ineffective body language tends to show up when the speaker is:

- overly tense or anxious,
- uninterested in his or her audience or material,
- feeling contempt for his or her audience or material, or
- unfamiliar or uncomfortable with his or her material.

What is confident body language?

Confident body language is open, honest, and relaxed. Confident speakers face their audience, limit turning away to face props like their slideshow, and avoid standing behind lecterns unless necessary. They avoid self-protective or apologetic nonverbal cues such as slouching or crossing their arms. Appropriate body language fits the situation at hand and demonstrates a suitable level of emotion; this is a signal that the presenter is comfortable with their ability to judge both the circumstances surrounding their talk as well as the overall mood of the room. Relaxed movement demonstrates the speaker's comfort with his or her role and with being the center of attention along with his or her own personal confidence in what he or she is saying. When combined, these nonverbal cues give a strong impression of confidence. A skilled performer can use these signals to cover up any anxiety, nervousness, or uncertainty he or she may actually be feeling.

What is nervous or tense body language?

Tension and anxiety are easily seen through a speaker's body language. Tight muscles restrict movement and make gestures choppy instead of smooth. Facial expressions are usually restrictive or frozen, jaw tension can give a harsh edge to words, and the presenter might avoid making eye contact with the audience. Many nervous speakers will engage in self-soothing behavior, pacing, or avoidant body language like folded arms, crossed legs, or hiding behind a lectern.

What is pacing?

Pacing is repetitive, aimless, unintentional walking movements. It's often done subconsciously and is usually rather rhythmic. What sets pacing apart from other movement is that it is done without intention and usually goes on at a steady speed and without pause. Common pacing movements are walking back and forth, standing in place but visibly shifting weight from one leg to the other, or stepping one foot forward and then back while shifting weight. Pacing is distracting to an audience and usually indicates anxiety.

Can we use body language when we present to increase our feelings of power or confidence?

Using powerful, expansive body language when you speak can increase both your own feelings of power and confidence as well as the audience's impression of such. Space use is a strong power cue—powerful people tend to be given more physical space. If you use large gestures, your audience will associate this with confidence and authority. Expansive, open gestures and proud posture also increase your personal sense of power. Playing up the size of your gestures and body language may increase your personal confidence in addition to the audience's confidence in you.

DEVELOPING YOUR BODY LANGUAGE

Do people have personal styles of body language?

People have distinct ways of moving that are as individual as the way they use their voice. One speaker might be extremely physically expressive and energetic, bounding from one space on the stage to the next and using sharp, staccato gestures. Another speaker could be graceful and elegant, holding to one area for a long time before purposefully moving to another and gesturing with flowing movements. When speakers try to use a style of body language and gesture that feels unnatural or uncomfortable, they won't move with the same degree of certainty and may find themselves getting distracted by the need to focus on their movement.

What is self-soothing?

Self-soothing is repetitive, subconscious motion that usually happens when a presenter is nervous. Clenching, wringing, or rubbing one's hands are very common self-soothing motions. Other self-soothing often observed in anxious speakers are fiddling with papers or notes, frequently touching or stroking one's hair, jingling keys or coins in one's pockets, and tapping tables or other nearby surfaces with the fingertips.

All speakers need to use a wide range of gestures and plenty of varied movement when they speak. They should also figure out how they best like to move around. To begin developing your own body language style, you need to determine how you are naturally inclined to move and what sort of movements appeal to you. To do this, ask yourself questions such as the following:

- How do I move and gesture when I'm talking with close friends?
- When I'm feeling confident and assertive, how do I hold myself? What kind of hand and arm movements do I use?
- When I'm feeling nervous, how do I hold my body? How do my gestures change?
- What sort of physical activities do I enjoy?
- What speakers do I admire? How do they move?
- When I picture myself giving a top-notch presentation, what sort of body language comes to mind?
- If I were to describe my ideal body language, what words would I use?

Answering these questions will help you determine what kind of movement appeals to you and what already comes naturally. Practice blending your ideal and natural movement together, and see what happens. Play around with different ways of moving when you speak, and spend time trying different movement styles as you practice your presentation. You will find that, over time, you'll develop a dynamic body language style that is suitable, natural, and comfortable for you.

How can I become more comfortable with moving around?

Most presenters hold back their body language rather than overexpress themselves. But audiences usually need us to be *more* physically expressive than we think we should be; otherwise, our body language might be too subtle and be lost on them.

To become more comfortable moving around, taking up space, and making bigger, grander gestures, you need to be willing to get a bit silly and try some over-the-top gestures when you practice your talks. When you are practicing, be overdramatic and get a bit crazy with the gesturing. Feel the space and the extent to which you are able to move. Relax into it, and don't take the activity too seriously. Party games like charades or Pictionary can help people get silly and creative with their body language (especially when kids are involved).

When you are feeling more comfortable with this over-the-top movement, dial it back a bit and make your body language more natural but still more expressive than you normally would. Practice with these different degrees of body language, and over time, you will start to feel more comfortable and natural moving around enthusiastically in front of your audience.

Noticing your body language is a first step in changing it. For example, you might not notice you bite your nails when you are nervous.

How can I stop fidgeting or using nervous body language?

Becoming aware of emotional or mental states that trigger nervous fidgeting, pacing, or self-soothing is the first step to mastering it. Try to observe your own body when you speak or present, and see if you can catch yourself doing any of these actions. Consider enlisting someone's help; these movements are usually subconscious, and it is hard to notice ourselves doing them. If you have someone else watching, they can signal you when the undesirable body language starts. When you notice it, observe your mental and emotional state. Are you panicking or anxious? Are you uncomfortable with your presentation content? Is there someone in the audience making you nervous? If you are able to identify such triggers, you'll be better able to identify them and consciously manage the urge to use nervous body language.

Another way to help control nervous body language is to learn to manage your anxiety levels when you are giving a talk.

How can I be sure that my body language matches what I'm saying?

Practicing your movement, expressions, and gestures in front of a mirror is a highly effective way of learning whether or not your body language matches your words. When you are practicing a presentation, stand up and perform it in front of a mirror as if you were presenting to an audience. Do you make incongruous motions like shaking your head while agreeing with someone or slouching or wringing your hands when trying to speak with conviction? Do you plunge your hands in your pockets when speaking about openness, honesty, and transparency? Watching yourself speak will help you figure this out. For a particularly effective way of figuring out if your body language matches your words, have someone take a video recording of your presentation. When reviewing the footage afterward, you will be able to focus on observing your body language without simultaneously worrying about the content. Be forewarned—many people find watching themselves on video difficult. You may want to have a glass of wine or cup of tea in hand while watching your video.

Should I plan out my gestures?

Planning gestures can be useful if you want to use a very specific gesture at a specific moment or are trying to adopt a particular style of body language for your talk. But be careful not to choreograph all your movement. Most body language is spontaneous, and overly choreographed movement looks stilted and melodramatic.

What is a genuine smile?

The ability to give a genuine smile on cue is very useful and is a skill all speakers should develop. Smiles that look fake or insincere don't engage enough facial muscles. The smile appears only around the mouth, and the upper cheeks and eye muscles don't move. This gives the smile a forced or frozen look and can be quite off-putting. This is also the reason why cosmetic Botox treatments can make someone's expression seem frosty or aloof. When someone is giving a genuine smile, his or her whole face is involved—even if the mouth movement is very small. With genuine smiles, the apples of the cheeks raise up and the muscles around the outer corners of the eyes contract, causing the person to squint slightly and wrinkle the skin at the corners of his or her eyes. The eyebrows will often raise, and a slight creasing on the forehead may occur.

An insincere smile can make you appear untrustworthy. A genuine smile involves muscles in the entire face, not just the mouth.

How can I learn to smile on cue?

Developing better control of your facial muscles will not only help you give genuine-looking smiles on cue but will also help you increase your overall range of facial expressions. You will need to get in touch with the muscles in your upper cheeks and surrounding your eyes—this is where most of the work will be done.

Place your index fingers on your upper cheeks about one inch below the outer corner of your eyes. Using your cheek muscles, try to move your fingers upward.

Next, move your fingers to the outer edge of your eye socket, immediately below the outer corner of your eye. Using the muscles around your outer eyes, try to move your index fingers upward (it will be a small movement).

Now move your fingers to the outer third of your eyebrows. Using the muscles around your outer eyebrow and a bit in your forehead, try to move your fingers upward.

The three spots where you placed your fingers are the muscles that are engaged with a genuine smile. Do this exercise several times and then try engaging those muscles all at the same time while also smiling with your mouth. Practice this in the mirror and work with the smile until it looks and feels natural.

How can I avoid looking tense when I'm speaking?

When a speaker "looks tense," it is because he or she is using body language with movements or postures that are visibly tight and rigid. Tension most often manifests itself in the shoulders and hands; presenters will stand with their shoulders hitched up around their ears, or they will clasp and clench their hands together. The key to getting rid of that tension is to consciously relax the tense muscles and engage in gestures that are the opposite of the tense gesture.

Any time you are presenting or you find yourself in a stressful interaction with someone, observe your body and try to feel where you are carrying your stress. It might be in your shoulders, your hands, your jaw, or somewhere else. First, consciously relax those muscles; don't try to move them in an unnatural position—just let them go slack. Next, do a gesture that is different from the tense pose you were in. If you were clenching your jaw, say "ah" and nod or smile. If your shoulders were high and tight, shrug and then release them, letting them fall back down. If your hands are clenched or clasped, make a large, inviting gesture by opening your arms wide with your hands palms up and open. These opposing movements help to actively counter the tense body language you were previously using.

USING BODY LANGUAGE EFFECTIVELY

How much physical space should I use?

When moving about your presentation space, use as much physical space as is available to you. If you are presenting from a stage, podium, or at the front of a room, feel free to move around in the entire space. If you are presenting standing in front of a boardroom table, keep your movement to the width of the table. The edges of the table can act as a frame; you can walk around inside that frame, but avoid leaving it. If you are seated at a table during your presentation, gesture as widely as you can in the space around you without making contact with or invading the space of the person sitting next to you.

Is it okay for me to walk around when I'm presenting?

Walking around in your presentation space can make you seem more interesting and energetic. The key to good walking is that it is done with purpose and intention. An example of intentional movement is with changes in material or a transition between ideas: Use those as an opportunity to walk to a different area. This will give your audience a visual cue to the transition, which can help them move from one idea to the next. Another example is when using contrasting ideas such as pointing out differences between groups of people, move to one side when introducing the first idea and speak to the audience on that side, then move to the other when talking about the contrasting idea and speak to that audience.

Spend time in different areas of your presentation space, pausing regularly instead of moving constantly. Aimless wandering or pointless, nonstop walking rapidly descends into pacing, which is tiresome and distracting for the audience to watch. Just as with all body language, keep your walking relaxed, purposeful, and varied.

What do I do with my hands?

Your hands are important gesture and body-language tools, so use them! Avoid holding them limply at your sides, clasping them behind your back, or jamming them into your pockets. A good rule of thumb is to keep your elbows at a minimum 90-degree bend and make the majority of your hand gestures between your navel and your lower jaw. Generally speaking, the lower you hold your hands, the less energy you are communicating, and the higher you hold your hands, the more energy or excitement your audience will perceive. Hands held below the navel usually give an impression of dullness, while excessive gesturing at or above the head makes the speaker seem unhinged or overbearing.

Don't worry about excessively planning your hand gestures. Think of how you move when having an animated conversation with your friends, and go for those sorts of motions when speaking to an audience.

Expansive gestures are wide and open, and they can be used to bring attention to the speaker.

What are expansive gestures?

Expansive gestures are wide and open, and they are excellent for drawing attention to big concepts or ideas. They can also be used to welcome or visually gather people together. When someone uses an expansive stance with their feet shoulder-width apart and arms mostly gesturing broadly from the sides of the body, they may be perceived as more powerful and authoritative. Large, sweeping movements, holding the arms out wide, gestures that move outward from the sides of your body, and a wide stance are all examples of expansive gestures and body language.

What are narrow gestures?

Narrow gestures are pointed, focused, and closed in. Narrow gestures are excellent for focusing an audience's attention on specific points or for creating a feeling of individuality among audience members. Closing motions, such as deliberately bringing the hands close together, can indicate a narrowing or focusing of an idea. If a speaker gestures with one hand and has a focused look toward a specific person or area in the audience, the audience members will adopt an individualistic instead of group frame of mind.

Narrow gestures are often choppy and may seem aggressive if backed up with strong material or a strident delivery. Avoid pointing with the index finger directly at people, as this is quite rude. If you want to point toward members of the audience, use your whole hand to do so.

What are contrasting gestures?

Contrasting gestures visually illustrate opposing points. These gestures move either from one side of the speaker's body to the other or from the speaker to the audience and vice versa. Full-body movement from one side of a presentation space to the other can also indicate contrast. Contrasting gestures help the audience focus on the differences between points and are useful in logical arguments and rebuttals.

How can I project authority without being overbearing?

Projecting authority through body language can increase the audience's receptiveness to what you are saying and can significantly boost a speaker's persuasiveness. A key to projecting authority is to have good posture and use plenty of relaxed, open body language.

To stand up straight without being too rigid or aggressive, start with a firm base by placing your feet shoulder-width apart and your weight balanced evenly between your feet. Then, lightly engage your abdominal muscles, as though you were preparing to pick up a heavy box from the floor. This abdominal engagement shouldn't be too harsh or restrictive—don't clamp your core as though you're doing sit-ups! Light abdominal engagement helps support your breath and releases back tension, allowing you to speak with more strength and stand with less stress.

Now, picture moving the center point of your chest upward without putting undue strain on your back. Don't puff your chest out (too aggressive), and don't allow yourself to collapse inward at your solar plexus (too submissive). Instead, think of holding your chest up and proud. Relax your shoulders without forcing them downward, feeling your neck naturally lengthen when you do this. Hold your chin parallel to the floor.

To compliment your strong, authoritative posture, gesture with your elbows away from your body instead of pinning them to your sides. Holding your elbows out and gesturing outward from your body expands the physical space you take up, which increases the impression of authority, confidence, and power you are giving to your audience.

AUDIENCE MATTERS

AUDIENCE NEEDS AND WANTS

What is a needs analysis?

It's easy for speakers to create talks that are more centered on the speaker's expertise and interests than on the audience's needs. A needs analysis is a process a presenter goes through to determine what he or she should include in his or her presentation. It is a crucial part of creating a presentation and helps the speaker ensure his or her talk is relevant and targeted to a specific audience.

An audience-needs analysis makes it easier to edit and refine presentation content by identifying what information the audience can do without. It can be difficult for a speaker to edit content that, from his or her point of view, is critical to the speaker's expertise or body of knowledge. An audience-needs analysis will help them identify what pieces of knowledge are most important and comfortably edit out the rest.

How do I do an audience-needs analysis?

To create a needs analysis, gather information about who will be in attendance, the reasons for the event or meeting, their current circumstances and problems, and any other information that can help you create a picture of who they are, what they need, and how you can help them. Try to make your answers as specific as possible.

Below are sample questions for an audience-needs analysis:

- Who will be attending this presentation?
- What roles do they have in their work or life?
- What demographics and psychographics do the audience members represent?
- What companies, groups, or associations are they representing (if any)?

- What is the purpose of the event/meeting/webinar, etc.?
- What are the attendees hoping to achieve by the end of this event or presentation?
- What is currently going on in their world that could be causing them difficulties or problems?
- How can your knowledge, expertise, or insight help them with this problem?
- What does the audience already know about your topic going into your presentation?
- What does your audience think they need from this presentation?
- What do you, as the speaker, think they need from this presentation?

These questions are just a starting point. As you answer them, you may think of additional questions to ask that will help you paint a clear picture of your audience's needs.

How can I gather information about my audience?

There are several ways to find out information about your audience. The most direct method is to get in touch with the event planner or the person hosting the event and ask them about the people who will be attending. If you're speaking at a regularly occurring event, you can look at programs or agendas from previous events to learn about who has been in attendance in the past and what sort of talks were offered. Check the websites of organizations that the attendees are representing; look online for their business or employer websites or for websites for their associations or clubs. If you are organizing the event yourself and you don't personally know the people in attendance, include questions such as "What is your job title?" or "What is your biggest worry about issue XYZ?" on registration websites or forms.

What are audience demographics?

Demographics are identifying characteristics of groups. Demographics can include age, income level, sex, ethnicity, gender, education level, and marital status.

What are audience psychographics?

Psychographics are the personal characteristics and personality traits of a person or group of people. They can include interests, attitudes, values, hobbies, and lifestyles. Demographics and psychographics are often combined in an audience-needs analysis.

How do I figure out what information my audience needs from me?

Asking questions about what problems or concerns your audience is facing will help you figure out what information they will most value from you. Consider what changes or shifts may be happening in their work or lives that relate to your area of expertise. Think about what current cultural, political, or economic issues might be affecting them. Frame these questions in terms of the audience's worldview: Are they here because they are concerned about issues that are affecting them on a small, local, or personal level or because they are exploring issues with a broader scope, such as national or international affairs?

It is important to know beforehand what kinds of people make up your audience, including such things as gender, education, age, and so on.

Once you have gathered some answers to questions like those recommended above, try to identify how your knowledge helps answer some of those questions. Be as specific as possible and hone in on your information or knowledge that most directly relates to a pressing problem or need the audience has. This will let you craft a presentation that is focused and highly relevant to a current need of your audience.

How much information should I give my audience?

When deciding how much information you should include in a presentation, the amount will be affected by the time you have to present and how much information the audience can take in before becoming overwhelmed or confused. To avoid causing your audience to feel overwhelmed, it's helpful to think of the medical practice of using the minimum effective dose: Give your audiences the smallest amount of information that will still meet their information needs. This usually means avoiding including extensive background information that is necessary to your own skill or expertise but would be too much for your audience to take in.

How can I make sure I stick to my allotted presentation time?

Most presenters put in more information than they have time to get through, even though the usual fear is that they won't have enough to talk about. It's always better to run a bit short than to go overtime, so avoid the urge to jam in too much content for your time frame. Audiences are unforgiving when people run overtime, and it's best to let them leave a little early rather than to keep them late. To make sure that you don't put in more information than you have time to deliver, practice talking through your content as you are creating it, and use a timer to track how long you take to speak about each point.

If you find yourself running overtime, you will need to cut out pieces of your presentation or possibly even change the focus of the presentation itself. Running significantly overtime means that your topic isn't focused enough, and you will need to narrow it down. Be ruthless in your editing process, and always keep in mind what information your audience will find most useful and how you can give it to them as simply as possible.

A further safeguard you can put in place is to make your presentation shorter than the time available to you. This will give you some wiggle room, which is important because most people speak for longer than they anticipated. Aim to give yourself between 5 and 10 percent of your total presentation time as flexible space in case you speak for longer than you intended. For a one-hour presentation, you might want to dedicate five minutes as flex time. For a shorter speech or presentation—five to fifteen minutes—consider between one and three minutes of flex time. Any time dedicated to questions and answers can also serve as flex time, but be careful not to cut too far into the Q&A time; don't completely eliminate the audience's time for asking questions.

At what level of knowledge or expertise should I start my presentation?

The level of information you put into your presentation will depend entirely on the level of knowledge your audience already has about your topic. As you have a limited time to present your information, avoid wasting time giving information that is either too basic or too sophisticated for your audience. If you are dealing with a beginner audience, you will need to start with basic information and won't be able to address too deep or complicated an issue.

For example, if you are giving a talk on retirement saving to a group of people with little experience in investing, you may need to avoid complicated subjects like how index funds are created and instead focus on basics like determining how much they need to save and what their risk tolerance is. If, on the other hand, you are talking about retirement planning to savvy, experienced investors, you won't need to cover simple topics like risk tolerance. You could instead start your presentation at a deeper level and delve into subjects like investment vehicle composition or self-directed portfolios.

How can I adapt an existing presentation for a new audience?

Many speakers give the same presentation to different audiences. Even if the bulk of the content is the same from presentation to presentation, the speaker should still strive to customize the content for individual audiences. This will increase their confidence in the speaker and help them relate to the content. To adapt an existing presentation for new audiences, look for opportunities to incorporate examples drawn from their interests, profession, or other things they share in common. Make sure that the language you use in your presentation makes sense to each audience; avoid jargon that is specific to one group of people or profession. Also consider whether the audience's context fits your material. You might need to change your focus or manner of expressing your ideas in order to work with the new audience's worldview.

ENGAGING YOUR AUDIENCE

How can I tell if my audience is engaged with me?

Engaged audiences indicate their interest through body language and behavior. Engaged audience members tend to sit up or lean forward in their seats. They make direct eye contact with the speaker and often indicate through facial expressions feelings such as surprise or agreement. Look for expressions like raised eyebrows or head nodding. They may also share brief comments with people sitting with them (if they start holding lengthy conversations, then they may be bored rather than engaged). When an audience is interested in the speaker, they will also respond in an appropriate way to cues the speaker gives. They laugh at jokes, nod or raise their hands when asked a question, and smile encouragingly.

Just as an audience can tell things about you through body language, the audience reveals how engaged it is to your talk through its body language.

How can I make my audience feel like they're having a conversation with me?

Making your listeners feel like they are part of a conversation with you is important to audience engagement. The first area to focus on is your manner of speaking. To make your presentation feel more like a conversation, limit your use of notes as much as possible so that you are speaking directly to your audience rather than reading from a script or slides. Use a natural, informal speaking style, rather than stilted or formal language. Picture how you would talk to your friends over coffee, and aim to use a similar but slightly more polished speaking style than that.

The next thing to consider is your body language. If there is a lectern available to you, avoid using it. The more your audience can see of you, the more they can read your body language and the more comfortable they'll feel. Lecterns dial up stiffness and formality, and they create a physical barrier between the speaker and the audience; these are all good reasons to not use them, even if they are there for you. Using plenty of relaxed, open gestures also helps create that conversational feel. Think about how you gesture when having an animated chat with your friends. You likely use your arms and hands to decorate your words, not worrying about how they look and allowing them to move in a natural, unplanned way. Ways of improving your body language are discussed in the "Body Talk" chapter.

What sort of interaction activities work well with a large audience?

There is plenty of opportunity to interact with a large audience. Activities that allow for simple group responses are ideal—asking for everyone to answer "yes" to a question, for instance, or getting a show of hands, or asking certain types of people to stand up. These are quick, easy, and give an observable effect for the audience. Another option for creating interactivity with a large audience is to have them interact with each other. Asking people to introduce themselves to the person sitting beside them, or asking them to take thirty seconds to share an idea or story with the person next to them, give the feeling of participation and contribution. If the room setup permits, easy physical state and space changes—such as asking people to change seats with someone else—are excellent ways to interact with and revive a large audience. Regardless of what interaction or activity you choose, pick something that is quick and easy for everyone to do.

Can I ask for volunteers from the audience to contribute stories, answer questions, or participate in an activity during my presentation?

Asking for volunteers to contribute stories or ideas works well in small audiences ranging from a handful of participants to approximately fifty people. Usually, the larger the group, the more hesitant people will be to step forward. Using audience volunteers also works better in fun or informal settings rather than in serious or formal presentations. When the point of a presentation is team building, entertainment, group sharing, or training, audience members will be far more willing to volunteer than if the presentation is a report to board members or a formal sales proposal. Before deciding whether or not to ask for volunteers during your presentation, consider the following questions:

- What is the purpose of this presentation?
- How big is the audience?
- Is the tone of this presentation energetic and informal, or is it more serious?
- Are the people attending likely to be willing to participate?
- Is having individual volunteers necessary, or can the activity work with a simple group participation?

Should I allow people to ask questions during my presentation?

Many speakers allow audience members to ask questions during their presentations. This can give the impression that the speaker is both considerate of the audience and comfortable with their material. Sometimes it also makes sense to allow the audience to ask questions during the presentation, especially if you are presenting to a small group or one with whom you are very familiar.

But this strategy can easily backfire. Unless you are very comfortable directing the audience and controlling the amount of time spent with questions, it's easy for the presentation to get sidetracked and go well over time. It's also common for audience members to ask questions that would have been answered later in the presentation. It can get annoying for both you and the audience to repeat "I'll be getting to that soon" whenever someone asks a question that you are about to address in your planned material.

The safest, most predictable route is to simply take questions at the end of the presentation. You usually don't need to tell the audience that this is what you will be doing; most people assume this is the case unless the speaker encourages them to ask questions throughout. Dedicate about twenty-five percent of your presentation time to a Q&A. Once you have finished speaking, encourage the audience to ask questions. If, however, you are:

- comfortable taking firm charge of the audience so they don't take too long asking their question,
- are able to limit the amount of time you spend answering questions, or
- are giving a presentation where it makes more sense to have people ask questions throughout,

then let the audience know they can ask you a question at any point.

When it comes to audience questions, it is often best to keep that portion of the presentation at the end of your talk.

Is it bad if people don't have any questions for me after my presentation?

A lack of questions at the end of a presentation can mean different things. If the audience doesn't have any questions, it's possible that you covered everything to their complete satisfaction. It's also possible that they are overwhelmed with information and don't know what to ask. Other circumstances could be that they need to leave immediately and don't have time for questions or that they were disengaged throughout the presentation and have no interest in furthering the conversation.

To figure out the reasons why people aren't asking questions, ask yourself the following:

- Did they seem engaged throughout my presentation? Were they making eye contact with me, nodding, leaning forward in their seats, or smiling?
- Did people rush out of the room after my presentation, or did they take their time, linger, or chat afterward?
- Did my presentation run over my allotted time?
- Were there lots of whispered conversations during my presentation? Did people look confused or glazed over?

If, when you ask yourself these questions, you get the feeling that the audience was engaged with your presentation or enjoying themselves, then the lack of questions could mean that you covered the topic to their satisfaction. On the other hand, if the answers to the above questions leave you feeling that the audience didn't enjoy the presentation, were bored, or were in a rush to leave, then it could mean that you overloaded them with information, didn't address the topic they actually wanted, or took too long.

If, on the other hand, people are asking lots of questions, it could be that you didn't cover the information they actually needed or that they didn't understand what you were presenting.

What does it mean if people have lots of questions at the end of my presentation?

If there are lots of questions at the end of a presentation, it usually means that either the audience is very engaged with your presentation and wants to explore your topic further or that they are confused or didn't get the information they need. The types of questions they ask can indicate which of these situations it may be.

If the questions being asked are predominantly clarifying questions, where they are asking you to go over information you already explained, then it is likely they are confused or missing other pieces of information necessary to understand what you were talking about.

If the audience is asking lots of probing questions, where they are asking for deeper levels of information, exploring different aspects of your topic, or initiating a discussion, then it's more likely that your presentation engaged them and piqued their curiosity.

What should I do if I don't understand someone's question?

If someone asks a question and you aren't clear on what they are asking, you have a couple of options. You can either ask them to state their question again, or you can paraphrase the question for them and ask them to confirm whether or not you paraphrased it correctly. The paraphrase strategy is usually the most effective. If you ask them to state their question again, you might just get a repeat of the same confusing question. If you paraphrase and are able to successfully put their question in your own words, you can be certain that the two of you understand each other.

What do I do if I can't answer someone's question?

There is nothing wrong with not knowing the answer to someone's question. Don't try to cover up the fact that you don't know the answer by making something up—that rarely reflects well on you. Instead, say flat out, "I don't know," and offer to follow up with him or her after you've had the chance to investigate the question. An alternative way to handle this is to say that you don't know and then ask the audience if anyone has any information or ideas about that question. It's entirely possible that someone else in the audience is able to answer it, and this strategy bumps up audience participation and increases discussion among audience members—both of which can increase audience satisfaction with your talk!

HECKLERS, SMARTPHONES, AND OTHER ANNOYANCES

What happens if I have a heckler in the audience?

It is very rare to encounter a true heckler in the audience. A true heckler is someone who simply flings negative comments or loaded questions at you without the expectation or desire for an answer. If you find yourself dealing with a heckler, understand that it is your responsibility as the speaker to shut him or her down. The audience is just as annoyed by hecklers as you are, so you are doing everybody a favor. Firmly thank the heckler for his or her comment, then say that you will be taking questions from other people in the audience. You must use a very firm voice and strong body language when doing this. Afterward, simply ignore his or her attempts to ask further questions or make further comments, and direct your attention to the other people there.

Be careful not to confuse someone who challenges your ideas with a heckler. Some people explore information by challenging it. These questions may come across as negative, but they can be an excellent opportunity for discussion. A challenger is willing to explore an idea and asks question that might be tough, but it opens the floor for discussion. A heckler isn't interested in discussion or exploration.

What should I do if someone in the audience is asking a question or making a statement but won't get to their question or point?

People who launch into monologues instead of asking questions or who simply never get around to their question are annoying for both the speaker and the audience. They also take away valuable Q&A time from other people. If someone isn't getting around to their question, interrupt them and paraphrase what you think their question may be. Then, answer that question and move on to the next person.

Using a mobile device during a talk is now considered acceptable. Often, audience members are posting about the talk on social media.

Should I tell people to put away their mobile phones or smartphones before my presentation?

It's now considered patronizing to ask people to put away their mobile devices. More people are aware of phone etiquette during live presentations and will have either put away their phone or have muted the ringer. Occasionally a phone may ring, but it is extremely unusual for that audience member to accept a call in the middle of someone's presentation.

Social media engagement and smartphones have also changed smartphone etiquette and behavior during live presentations. Many people will post comments on what they are listening to or learning to social media sites like Twitter or Instagram. These actions can be very positive for the speaker as the audience member is sharing your information with their own circles. Many speakers and event organizers encourage this activity by giving audience members their social media links or a hashtag to use to make it easier to share their information. This activity is more common in presentations with medium to large audiences than in small group presentations. If you are presenting to a medium to large audience and you see a few people tapping away on their phones, don't be insulted—it's possible they are enthusiastically sharing what you are saying through their social media channels.

If you are presenting to a medium or large group and your talk includes sensitive information or things that, for confidentiality reasons, shouldn't be shared, make that clear at the beginning of your presentation. This will help people avoid posting inappropriate things from your talk over social media.

What do I do if two or more people are having side conversations during my presentation?

It's not unusual for people to have brief side conversations during presentations. Often they're commenting on some bit of information you've just given. If, however, these conversations go on for any length of time, they can be distracting for both the audience and the speaker. In midsized to large audiences—over fifty or so people—it's usually best to just ignore the people talking, provided they aren't being too loud. In smaller groups, however, you can break up the conversation by asking them if they have a question. If they do have a question, they will ask it, and their conversation will most likely end. If they don't have a question, they will know that everyone is now watching them and will usually be embarrassed enough to stop their conversation.

TECHNOLOGY AND EQUIPMENT

AMPLIFIERS

What is a microphone?

A microphone, or "mic," is a piece of hardware used to either record or amplify your voice. In order to amplify the speaker's voice, the microphone must be attached or routed to an audio system that includes speakers. The microphone itself doesn't provide amplification but merely captures the voice and transmits it to the audio system and speakers.

Microphones can be wired directly to the audio system or can be wireless. Most wired microphones are attached to a lectern or to a microphone stand. Wireless microphones can be handheld, worn as a headset, or attached to the speaker's collar or lapel with a clip. Hands-free wireless microphones, such as headset mics, lapel mics, and body mics are also called "lavalier microphones."

Do all microphones help amplify my voice?

Not all microphones are used for amplification. Some are used purely to capture the voice for recording purposes. Microphones need to be connected either to an audio system for amplification or to a recording system for capture. Some audio systems can perform both amplification and recording.

Should I use a microphone?

The choice to use a microphone depends on the speaker's personal preferences and the size and setup of the room he or she is presenting in. Rooms the size of boardrooms or small classrooms that can accommodate between thirty and fifty people often don't require a microphone for the speaker to be heard. In small spaces, an amplified voice could easily overwhelm the audience and make it difficult to listen to the speaker.

In larger rooms—such as large lecture theaters, auditoriums, and ballrooms—it's advisable to use a microphone. A microphone will let you be easily heard without the need to waste energy trying to project your voice. The microphone will capture and project a wider range of nonverbal cues; you can use a greater range of vocal variety ranging from whispers to louder statements and still be perfectly audible to your audience.

If you are using a wired, standing, or handheld microphone, be sure you speak directly into it with your mouth about a hand's length away from the microphone. If your mouth is too far away from the mic, it may not pick up your voice. Too close to the mic, and you may overload the system and generate unpleasant audio feedback. Test the microphone before you start your talk. Hands-free and lavalier microphones are designed to be used further away from the mouth and tend to be a bit more forgiving.

RECORDING DEVICES

Can my amplification microphone also be used to record the audio for my talk?

Amplification microphones don't necessarily capture audio recordings. You will need to check if the audio system is also recording your talk. If you are using an audio system that amplifies but doesn't record audio, you may need to use a second microphone to capture and record your talk. This could be an additional separate microphone or a microphone combined with video recording equipment, such as the system microphone on a video camera.

I want to get a video capture of my live presentation. What sort of camera do I need?

There are many different options for capturing a video recording. The biggest determinants of what kind of camera you need will be what kind of quality of video you want and what sort of lighting is available. If you just want a basic video for reviewing, any sort of camera, such as a smartphone camera or point-and-shoot digital camera, will be sufficient. If you are wanting a crisper image for sharing, you may want to use a high-definition camera such as a DSLR (Digital Single Lens Reflex) camera or a camera intended for sports photography and videography, such as the GoPro series. Some high-definition (HD) webcams, like the Logitech HD Pro C920 webcam, can also provide good quality video recordings.

A good HD camera with an external microphone is a good idea for digitally recording a talk for a webinar or YouTube presentation.

If you want an extremely high quality video and audio recording for professional resale or a high-caliber speaker's portfolio, consider hiring a videographer to attend your talk. He or she will have the camera and audio equipment necessary to get the quality of video and audio you want as well as the knowledge to use the equipment and get tasteful, interesting shots.

I want to give online presentations like webinars and recordings for YouTube. What sort of camera do I need?

Many computers and laptops come with system webcams and microphones. If you are satisfied with the quality of recording your system camera and microphone produce, then you don't need to invest further in your equipment. If, however, you want a better image or sound, look for an HD (1080p or higher) camera and a dedicated external microphone.

For the camera, many people choose to invest in a good-quality DSLR camera with a 1080p or higher video capture system. These cameras can be expensive and may be overkill for your project. If you are a photography enthusiast or want to take videos in different locations without having to pack around a laptop, then this sort of camera might be a good choice for you. If, however, you are planning to take your videos in a location like your office or home workspace, a good quality HD webcam will do the job. The Logitech HD Pro C920 does a superb job of capturing clear video in a variety of different lights.

What is the difference between my system microphone and an external microphone?

A system microphone is one that comes embedded in your computer. System microphones often capture lower quality sound than external microphones. External microphones might be combined with your camera or on a headset. However, the best sound is captured by a dedicated external microphone. These usually plug into a recording device or computer through a USB cable.

Different external microphones have different sound capture capabilities. Unidirectional microphones are designed to only capture sound originating from right in front of the mic; these are useful for cutting down on background noises. Omnidirectional microphones are intended to capture sound from all around them; these are good if several people are speaking into the microphone, such as for a group online presentation or conference call. External microphones can vary greatly in price. A popular low-cost unidirectional external microphone is the ATR 2100-USB.

What equipment can make recording sound and video easier?

There are some pieces of equipment that make it much easier to capture good-quality audio and video recordings.

A pop filter is a piece of porous fabric set into a frame that sits in front of the microphone. It reduces "pops" of air (called plosives) when making sounds such as "p." These pops can lead to audio distortion and overload the recording levels of the microphone.

Tripods, camera stands, and microphone stands make it easier to adjust the height and angle of your capture devices. Different stands are suitable for different situations.

If you are recording in areas where there aren't any flat surfaces or you need to balance your camera or microphone on an uneven surface, a tripod with adjustable, flexible feet can be used. Tabletop stands are small and light and are excellent for situations such as sitting at a desk or boardroom table. Conventional tripods come in different sizes and weights, can be adjusted to different heights, and are usually sturdier than tabletop tripods. Microphone stands allow the angle of the microphone to be adjusted more readily and will help free up your hands for other tasks.

What software will I need to record sound and video?

Many computers and video recording devices come with recording software. Windows Movie Maker for PCs running Windows and iMovie for Mac or Apple devices both capture video and audio recordings and double as editing software as well. Other recording software may have more options for adjusting lighting effects, recording the computer's screen and cursor, and synchronizing with computer programs like PowerPoint. Popular recording software for those purposes are Movavi Screen Capture Studio, Camtasia Studio, and Adobe Presenter. There are many other types of recording software available in a wide range of prices. It is important to think of what kind of recording and editing needs you have and research what the different programs provide so that you don't overspend on features you don't need.

What do I need to edit my recordings?

In order to make cuts and edits to your recordings, you will need editing software. Most recording software can also be used to edit your audio and video recordings. The software listed in the question above all contain extensive editing software. These are software programs worth mentioning because of their popularity. Audacity is an open-source audio editing software available for free download. Because of its relatively short learning curve and fairly intuitive interface, Audacity has won a large number of awards and has remained highly popular despite the improvements in the editing software embedded in various operating systems. Audacity can be used on Windows, OS X, and Linus operating environments.

INTERNET APPLICATIONS

What are some popular sites where I can upload and stream my video or audio recordings?

Online sharing has enabled public speakers and presenters to reach wide, diverse audiences. In order to make their talks available, the talk needs to be uploaded and distributed through file sharing or streaming programs.

Streaming programs are very popular as they are generally easy to use, rarely require manually converting file types, and give the person who uploaded the content more control over its distribution. Streaming services that are popular among speakers and presenters of all types are:

One very popular site where you can stream your content is iTunes.

- YouTube: an extremely popular video streaming website. Most of the content on YouTube is either free or accessible privately. YouTube is currently expanding into paid content services. They embed advertisements in their videos either as banner ads or as ads that play before the actual video.
- Vimeo: a video streaming website and service and YouTube's main competitor. Vimeo is a popular way to distribute paid access content as it has more privacy settings than YouTube. Vimeo has different levels of membership with different features, such as advertisement-free streaming and integrations with other online software such as membership or email lists.
- Libsyn: a podcasting hosting service, Libsyn isn't used for listening to audio content but rather for uploading, storing, and distributing it to multiple platforms, including iTunes and Stitchr.
- iTunes and Stitchr: online audio-streaming programs popularly used for podcasting. iTunes allows for the distribution of free and paid content. Stitchr predominantly distributes free podcasts and radio programs.

What is livestreaming?

Livestreaming is video or audio content that is broadcast through the Internet and can be listened to live. Many livestreaming services also save recordings of the content that listeners/viewers can access at a later date.

What are some Internet applications I can use for livestreaming?

Livestreaming software has recently increased in popularity as new, simplified programs have become available. Two popular programs are:

- Blab—a video livestreaming app that lets multiple people participate in a livestream chat at once. Blab works in conjunction with social media platform Twitter. People watching a Blab stream can respond to the presenters.
- Periscope—a mobile video livestreaming app. Users broadcast themselves live through their mobile device, usually a smartphone. As with Blab, Periscope watchers can interact through social media with the presenter during the livestream.

MEMORY AIDS

What are speaker notes?

Speaker notes are written cues the speaker or presenter uses as a memory aid during his or her talk. Speaker notes should be very brief, outlining only the most important parts of the talk. While not using notes is seen as a mark of the speaker's skill, many professional speakers and lecturers regularly refer to notes during their talk.

What is the difference between notes and a script?

Notes are brief summaries of what the speaker is to address during his or her talk, usually written in bullet points. Scripts are complete records of what the speaker wants to say, written in full sentences and paragraphs. Most beginner speakers tend to bring scripts instead of notes, but this is unadvisable.

Scripts are difficult to use and should be avoided when presenting. It can be hard to quickly find your place in the script when you need prompting. It's also extremely tempting to simply read from the script. Once a presenter refers to a script to remind him- or herself of a point he or she forgot, he or she tends to read the whole thing as though he or she were reciting an essay.

Politicians (New York City mayor Bill DeBlasio is seen here in 2016) will often give speeches using a glass teleprompter. The scrolling text can only be read from one side, and audiences' views are not blocked by the screen.

How do I create good speaker notes?

Good speaker notes are brief, clear, and extremely easy to glance at and refer to. Avoid using long sentences or small fonts, and keep your notes to a single piece of paper. Your notes are not intended to tell you the exact words you want to use. Rather, they are there to remind you where you are in your presentation and get you back on track if you forget where you are in your presentation. Creating good speaker notes does not take the place of practice. Make sure you practice your presentation with your speaker notes in hand several times before your presentation. This way you will become comfortable with using them during your presentation.

Should I use index cards?

Using index cards for speaker notes is problematic. They are no less conspicuous than a piece of paper, and speakers tend to shuffle them, mixing them up. Even if you bind the index cards in order with a ring, it's easy to land on the wrong card and difficult to avoid the temptation to fiddle with them. Stick to using a single piece of paper with clear, simple notes in a large font.

A teleprompter is a screen placed in the speaker's line of sight that scrolls through the speaker's complete script. There is often a camera behind the screen so it looks like the presenter is looking directly at the camera instead of reading from something off-frame. When used in live settings, teleprompters may have a semitransparent screen so the audience can still see the speaker.

Teleprompters are commonly used by news anchors, politicians, and other people who do a large amount of speaking and may not have the time to commit their content to memory.

Just because a presenter makes use of a teleprompter, it doesn't mean they haven't practiced their content. Teleprompters help support the speaker, and reading from them takes a measure of attention and skill.

Should I use a teleprompter?

Most presenters won't have access to teleprompters. Even if you have the opportunity to use one, be sure you practice your content as much as possible ahead of time. Teleprompters can be tricky to use, so you will ideally want to practice with the teleprompter in place.

SLIDESHOWS AND VISUAL PRESENTATIONS

What slideshow software is useful for presentations?

Slideshow software is any kind of software that creates visual presentations for use during a talk. These presentations are projected onto a screen beside or behind the speaker.

Slideshows are also often used with online presentations and webinars. When presenting online, it's usually only the slideshow that is visible to the audience and not the speaker.

The three most popular slideshow software programs are PowerPoint, Keynote, and Prezi. PowerPoint is a Microsoft program and is so ubiquitous that many people use the term "PowerPoint" and "slideshow" interchangeably. Keynote is an Apple program, similar in offerings to PowerPoint. Both Keynote and PowerPoint let the user create graphs and charts, edit pictures, and create some animations. Prezi is a downloadable program that creates a mind map-type illustration of the slides and then lets the presenter "zoom" from one point on the map to another. Prezi does not have the same degree of flexibility as Keynote or PowerPoint and is more difficult to use. It is, however, a popular alternative to typical slideshow software.

It is extremely important to note that it isn't the slideshow software that makes a presentation good or bad but rather how the slideshow itself was designed. This tends to come down to the amount of care, attention, and planning the presenter or slideshow designer took in creating his or her visual presentation.

Should my presentation have a slideshow?

Slideshows can be useful but are often not necessary to a presentation. Slideshows should be used to visually support and enhance what the presenter is saying. If your presentation would be made more dynamic, more interesting, or clearer with some attractive visuals, then you might want to create a slideshow. If, on the other hand, your presentation would be just as interesting without big, splashy images or texts projecting behind you, then consider eliminating the slideshow so the audience can focus entirely on you.

What makes a slideshow good?

Good slideshows enhance rather than compete with the speaker. Bad slideshows are cluttered with too much information being displayed, usually in the form of excessive text or complicated graphs. These slideshows are difficult for the audience to read and extremely distracting for the audience. Ideally, a slideshow should place more emphasis on pictures than text. If a slide does contain text, it should show as few words as possible in large, easy-to-read font. Eliminate any unnecessary animations.

A good slideshow has graphics that enhance and complement the lecture; they should not overwhelm, compete with, or replace what you are trying to convey.

If your slideshow must contain a chart or graph, use that chart or graph to summarize information in a clean, simple illustration. The audience needs to be able to understand the graph quickly and easily; complex information doesn't work well for slideshows. If you need to present a complex chart or graph to your audience, consider distributing it as a paper or digital handout.

Why is it bad to have too much text on my slides?

Text is extremely distracting for both the audience and the speaker. As soon as people see text on slides, they immediately begin reading it, and it is impossible to read and listen at the same time. If your audience is reading a slide, it means they aren't listening to you. Additionally, the text on the slides is difficult for the speaker to ignore. Even if you don't intend to read from the slides, as soon as your eyes see the text on the screen, you will want to read it out loud. Reading from slides is a very disengaged way to present, it annoys the audience, and causes the speaker to lose his or her place or forget what he or she wanted to say once he or she stops reading.

How should I design a slideshow for an oral report?

Slideshows often accompany oral reports, especially if there is visual data such as charts or graphs to present. Slideshows should be clean, simple, and minimal so that the audience can focus on what you are saying instead of trying to read or interpret the slide. All slides should visually enhance what the presenter is saying and should favor high-quality graphics and images over cluttered text.

When creating a slideshow, avoid replicating a written report in slideshow format. Strictly limit the number of words on each slide. The slides should only be used to visually support what you are saying and should not act as a speaker's script or as handouts for the audience. When people see words on a slide, they will default to reading those words instead of listening to the speaker. Any words that do appear should be in very large font and be easy and fast for the audience to read so they can get back to listening to the speaker. Two popular guidelines for using text in slides are:

- *The 6 x 6 rule:* No more than six lines of text per slide, no more than six words per line.
- *The 30-point-font rule:* Text size must be no less than a thirty-point font. This rule will limit the space available for the text and ensure readability. Do not use condensed fonts just to squeeze more text into your slide.

If using a slideshow with charts or graphs, ensure the charts are clear and easy to read. This may mean simplifying or paring down the data being presented in the chart, but it will be more useful for your audience and easier for them to understand during the presentation. They can be provided a full version of the graphs in handouts or in a copy of a written report to accompany the oral presentation.

Can I use my presentation's slideshow as a handout?

Properly designed slideshows don't make good handouts. Slideshows should be dominated by pictures and graphics, and handouts are largely text-based. Well-designed slideshows rarely make sense without the presenter, whereas handouts should be easy to understand on their own. If you want to distribute handouts to your audience, create them as a separate document. It means doing more work, but it will result in a much better slideshow and handout set.

Can I put my speaker notes on my slideshow?

Slideshows can act as a type of cue to the speaker because they give a visual reminder of what is being addressed. That being said, you should *not* put your speaker notes on your slideshow. The text is distracting for the audience and doesn't provide any visual enhancement. What's more, the speaker almost invariably ends up reading off the slides instead of speaking to the audience.

What is a remote presenter?

A remote presenter is a handheld wireless device used to advance through a slideshow. The remote has a button that will let the presenter go forward or back through their slides. Some also allow the presenter to blank out the projector so the slideshow can't be seen. Many remote presenters have a laser pointer function, and some have a timer that counts down the minutes in the presentation. Remote presenters are excellent tools to use as they allow the presenter to move around without needing to be running back to the computer to advance to the next slide.

How can I get through my presentation if my slideshow doesn't work the way I expect it to?

Good planning can help you avoid slideshow disaster. When creating your presentation, try to create one that doesn't entirely depend on the slideshow. If you have content in the slideshow such as videos, think of how you could describe the meaning in the video verbally without playing it. This way, if your slideshow fails completely, you can still carry out your presentation without it. If you find that your slides are not advancing the way you intended—perhaps an animation doesn't carry through, the slides skip forward unexpectedly, or you forget to advance to the next slide—you can try to surreptitiously return to the slide you wanted. If, however, you aren't able to quickly and easily get back to the correct slide without interrupting your presentation, just carry on. Don't draw the audience's attention to the error or apologize for it.

BUSINESS COMMUNICATION

INTERPERSONAL RELATIONSHIPS AND ETIQUETTE

What is business communication?

Business communication is the sharing of information to drive forward the purpose, functions, goals, or commercial activities of an organization. The term "business communication" sometimes refers specifically to communication for commercial purposes, such as marketing or public relations, but may be more broadly defined to include all communication that needs to happen within a business or organization for it to function. This book uses the broad definition of "business communication."

What is organizational communication?

Organizational communication is the sharing of information among people working within an organization. While it may involve some aspects of organization–client communication, this is not its primary focus. Organizational communication places more emphasis on studying the social and interpersonal relationships within an organization than business communication.

How are organizational communication and business communication related?

Organizational and business communications exist as functions of one another. All business communication is affected by organizational behavior and communication as every business (even single-owner, single-employee businesses) interacts with other organizations in the course of their activities. Conversely, a business's functions impact the way people operate and communicate within an organization. People join or interact with commercial organizations in order to do business, so the two communication streams cannot exist independently of one another.

How do organizational communication and business communication differ?

There is no strict definition separating business communication and organizational communication; the line between the two is very blurry. Business communication tends to concentrate on the communication activities necessary to create profits or perform functions, while organizational communication is more focused on the nuances of how people within the company function with one another. Broadly put, business communication has an outward focus, while organizational communication's focus is more inward.

What communication structures exist within organizations?

There are two main types of communication structures in organizations: formal and informal.

Formal communication structures follow an established organizational structure. This guides the flow of information in terms of employees' defined roles and relationships to one another. An employee understands who he or she is to report information to and from who he or she will receive information and instructions. Formal communication structures help maintain the status quo within an organization and keep information-sharing practices clear and consistent. If a formal communication structure is too rigid, however, it may result in information getting bogged down and can hamper creativity and idea sharing.

Informal communication structures are developed more out of social consensus than by official direction. They arise between colleagues and do not necessarily follow a chain of command or the organization's hierarchy. Informal communication structures are impacted by friendships, history, and personality types. All work groups will create an informal communication structure. Some organizations encourage and foster informal communication structures, while others discourage employees from deviating from the formal organizational structure when sharing information. Generally, the more controlling the work environment is, the more likely it is that informal communication structures will be actively discouraged. Healthy informal communication can strengthen employee relationships and reduce stress, while dysfunctional informal communication can lead to gossip, rumor, cliquish behavior, and confused lines of communication.

How does organizational structure affect our ability to communicate?

Organizational structure has a direct effect on people's ability to access, share, and withhold information within an organization. Generally, those at the top of an organization's structure have access to more information and communication resources than those lower down. Within organizations, access to information can carry strong power implications, and people at certain levels may withhold or protect information in order to safeguard their position and power within an organization's structure. The subject of workplace power and communication is addressed further in this chapter.

Lines of communication typically follow an organization's structure. Large, hierarchical organizations tend to favor top-down lines of communication, which reinforces everyone's positions and creates a controlled, predictable communication environment. Flatter organizational structures have more open lines of communication. While different levels of authority still exist, there are fewer layers of authority than there are in large hierarchical organizations. Flat organizational structures encourage bottom-up and horizontal flows of information alongside top-down communication.

What is top-down communication?

Top-down communication refers to communication that flows down a chain of command from the top of a hierarchy to the bottom. Strongly hierarchical organizations tend to share information from the top down, often on a "need-to-know" basis as determined by an employee's superiors.

Organizations that rely on strict top-down communication structures may suffer from not meeting employees' actual information needs (not understanding what people really "need to know") while overloading them with information that is irrelevant or unnecessary. It may be difficult for employees to communicate information up the hierarchy as a person's supervisor will act as a gatekeeper for information that needs to reach higher levels in the organization. The more layers there are in an organization's hierarchy, the easier it is for information and communication to be stymied at different levels and get lost in bureaucracy.

What is bottom-up communication?

Bottom-up communication occurs when information flows upward within an organization's system with lower-level employees initiating communication with their supe-

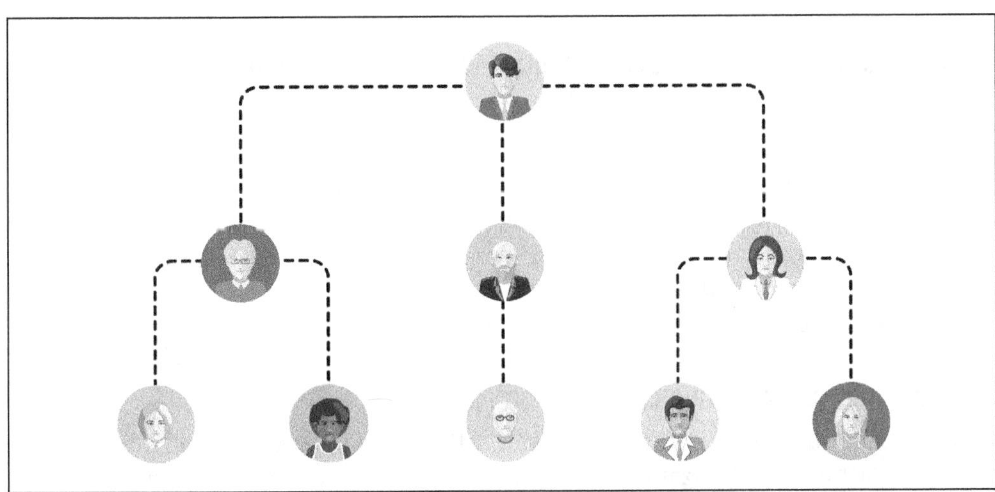

A strict, hierarchal, corporate chain of command can result in higher-ups communicating less frequently to employees, which can actually be inefficient and even harmful to productive efforts.

riors. Bottom-up communication may occur alongside top-down communication and is often more robust in flatter organizations. While organizational hierarchies and communication processes still exist and are still observed, organizations that encourage bottom-up communication generally give employees more access to information and better ability to reach superiors at different levels.

When bottom-up communication systems are functioning well, superiors benefit from more open communication from their employees about arising situations and new ideas. Open communication allows greater responsiveness and agility within the organization as a whole. If, on the other hand, superiors claim to value input and communication from employees but fail to listen or never take action on it, employees become dissatisfied, and the lines of communication may close down.

What is horizontal communication?

Horizontal communication occurs when employees at the same level as one another communicate across different departments or different functions. Organizations that allow and foster horizontal communication often allow for flexibility within the organizational structure and give employees more ability to determine their own work paths. Courses of actions that result from horizontal communication usually need to be approved, but that may be sought later in the communication process.

It does take some effort on the part of employees to engage in effective horizontal communication. If people are concerned about stepping on one another's toes or if rivalry or territoriality exists between groups, communication may not take place. Additionally, if employees are not able to readily connect with people in other departments, horizontal communication won't happen. If the effort of finding the proper people to communicate with horizontally outweighs the effort of simply speaking to a superior, then employees will most often opt to speak with their supervisor.

Do organizations without a clearly defined leader still follow these flows of information?

To a degree, the top-down, bottom-up, and horizontal information flows exist within all organizations. Even in flat organizations, where there is no formal structure that recognizes power or authority, social hierarchies will form with certain people deferring to others. These unofficial communication structures are known as "informal systems" and exist within organizations with strong, formal structures as well as those that follow a flatter structure with little to no defined hierarchy.

What are informal communication systems?

Informal communication systems evolve out of the social interactions and interpersonal dynamics within an organization. A popular term for an informal communication system is the "grapevine." Information exchanged through a grapevine tends to be more centered around the social or individual interests of the employees with an emphasis on

A classic stereotype of informal communication at the office is staff gathering around and gossiping by the water cooler. While such interactions still go on, social media is beginning to replace in-person interactions.

organizational news that either affects people's day-to-day lives or brings novelty to their working day (such as gossip). News travels quickly through grapevines and is most often spread through direct conversation, though social media is also a popular outlet for grapevine information.

Some people within an organization act as hubs and distributors of information, while others will not pass on anything they learn through the grapevine. People at all levels of an organization may participate in grapevines, although they tend to spring up more often within groups with stronger social ties, such as coworkers in a department or people at a certain level within the organization.

Grapevines can both reinforce as well as redefine hierarchies within an organization. For instance, information passed along a grapevine from a high-ranking manager will be more valuable than rumors coming up from a lower-level employee. The value of the manager's information reinforces his or her authority and position within the company hierarchy. On the other hand, people lower on a hierarchy but high up on the grapevine—such as executive assistants—can wield considerable informal power within an organization due to their ability to access high-level information and be a "fly on the wall" at important meetings.

How does an organization's ideology affect communication?

Organizational ideology rationalizes how an organization operates through beliefs about the way things should work.

Ideology can be used to encourage communication and creativity or to discourage employees from complaining or challenging the status quo. A positive ideology of "we think that it takes ten lousy ideas to hit on one great idea, so don't hold back" can encourage experimental or creative thinking and more open communication among employees. On the other hand, a superior who tells an employee "we all work really hard around here, and most people don't even stop for lunch" is communicating an oppressive ideology that employees should work excessive hours without comment or complaint. In that example, open communication is strongly discouraged.

What is power in business or the workplace?

Power in the workplace can be defined as someone's ability to get other people to carry out the actions they want. Those actions may be as obvious as sweeping a floor or as subtle as shifting their opinion about a new policy. Power may also include the ability to access and control resources that are valued by other people in the organization. Access to power and resources feeds and amplifies one another. People have access to resources because they are powerful, and they become more powerful because they have access to those resources.

How are power and communication connected in the workplace?

Power, information, and communication are intimately connected in all workplaces. There are many types of resources within an organization, such as money or human resources, and information is a highly valued and often tightly controlled resource. Those who have control over information and communication resources (including communication policies and technologies) can use it to build up and reinforce their power within a workplace. Communication styles and methods can be strongly influenced by the type of power someone holds.

What are the types of power people hold?

During the 1950s, psychologists John French and Bertram Raven conducted seminal studies on power constructs in social groups, including workplaces. They identified five bases of power:

- Reward: power based on a person's ability to give rewards to others
- Coercive: power based on a person's ability to punish people who don't follow their directives
- Legitimate: power granted to someone by virtue of that person being chosen or appointed by others to be in a position of power
- Referent: power based on social connections and affiliations with powerful people or organizations

- Expert: power based on someone having special knowledge, experience, or skills

These bases of power rarely work independent of one another. Depending on situation and circumstances, people will draw on different types of power to meet their communication goals. Someone with legitimate power might also draw on coercive or reward power. An expert could have strong referent power, and someone with referent power may obliquely use coercive power by threatening to influence someone with legitimate power.

How do the types of power affect the way people communicate?

Bases of power affect both the way a powerful person communicates and the way other people respond to them. Studies such as Virginia P. Richmond et al.'s 1980 investigation into how people use and respond to power-based communication showed that different types of power had varied effectiveness in organizational communication. Managers who relied on coercive or legitimate power typically engaged in "boss-centered" communication where employees were told what to do with little to no opportunity for input. Communication that used reward power was also boss-centered and didn't have much positive impact among employees. Managers who communicated through referent or expert power, on the other hand, engaged in much more employee-centered communication. Employees felt they had more input and engagement and reported higher levels of satisfaction when they interacted with those managers.

People who rely on legitimate, coercive, or reward power to communicate tend to place more emphasis on hierarchical relationships and top-down communication. Referent and expert power are more often used by people and organizations that operate with flatter organizational structures, promote meritocracy, and engage in more bot-

A business culture that is formal, stiff, and reliant on etiquette can provoke anxiety among employees.

tom-up and horizontal communication. It should be noted, though, that in any organization, managers and employees will use combinations of all five bases of power when communicating, depending on the circumstances at hand.

What role does etiquette play in business and the workplace?

Etiquette is a valuable communication tool. Far from being a series of stuffy rules designed to provoke anxiety, etiquette can make communication easier and more pleasant. It establishes norms of behavior that are socially acceptable within the setting at hand, which encourages respect and understanding. In the workplace, etiquette communicates important information such as your respect for behavioral traditions and standards, your interest in workplace or business culture, and what position and role you and others around you hold.

What are some important verbal or written expressions of business etiquette?

Common points of verbal business etiquette are how to address someone and the use of slang, informal language, or jargon. While many workplaces and businesses have moved to more informal manners of address, traditions of politeness and cross-cultural interactions mean that we still need to consider formal titles and language.

How should I address other people in a business or workplace setting?

Always address someone by their last name and title or honorific if they have one (e.g.: Mr. Jones, Ms. Smith, Dr. Watson) unless you receive indication to do otherwise. People who are older than you by many years, who are prominent or prestigious in their industry, or who have significant authority in your organization should be addressed by their last name. If the person introduces themselves by their first name or tells you to call them by their first name, you may switch to a first-name basis.

Etiquette regarding addressing juniors is less clear than that of addressing superiors. If the junior is significantly older than you, it is polite to call them by their last name and title. Generally, people with a high degree of power or authority within a company or organization have more latitude to call other people by their first name without being invited to do so.

If sending a letter or email to someone you haven't met or don't know informally, use their title (Mr./Ms./Dr./etc.) and last name in the greeting.

What is appropriate use of slang, informal language, and jargon?

Slang is usually unacceptable in business or work scenarios, unless the conversation is a casual one among good acquaintances or among people of equal rank. Avoid colloquialisms or trendy expressions. Aim for straightforward, plain, polite language—it is friendly, courteous, and makes it easier for the people communicating to understand one another. If speaking with people outside of your industry or area of expertise, avoid jargon and limit technical talk; they may not be able understand it.

What are some important nonverbal expressions of workplace etiquette?

Within business etiquette, three common nonverbal points of communication and etiquette are of particular note: clothing, personal space, and handshakes.

What does clothing communicate in terms of business etiquette?

Clothing is one of the most obvious etiquette expressions within business and work. It communicates unspoken values such as seriousness, conformity, individuality, and willingness to fit in. People with higher positions in an organization usually follow higher standards of dress than people below them. If the workplace favors traditional or formal attire, dressing casually might communicate lack of care about the business at hand or the other people involved. If the common dress is casual, formal businesswear could signal snobbishness or insecurity.

How do I know what to wear?

The best way to handle issues of clothing etiquette is to dress modestly and conform to the standards of those at or above your position. If you are uncertain what to wear in a business or work situation, research the company, look for online photos that may indicate a business's level of formality or informality, or contact someone in the company and ask about standards of dress.

What is communicated through personal space and space-related etiquette?

Personal use of space is a common way people communicate power in business settings. The most powerful person in a room will usually sit at the head of the table or near the head of the table if there is to be a presentation. Powerful people are given more physical space by those around them with the most junior people in a room being allotted the least amount of room in which to move. Superiors generally have permission to enter a junior's workspace without invitation, whereas most juniors would be committing a serious breach of etiquette if they were to do the same to their supervisor.

A good handshake is firm without being forceful or aggressive.

What is conveyed through handshakes?

Handshakes are an oft-cited point of etiquette anxiety. A limp, weak, or fingertip-only handshake conveys insecurity, anxiety, or aloofness. Overly hard or lengthy handshakes can be overbearing and signal a desire for control or possible power struggle. Firm, confident handshakes communicate sincerity, trustworthiness, and authority.

How do I give a proper handshake?

Proper handshakes make full palm-to-palm contact with elbows bent at or slightly over ninety degrees so as not to invade the other person's space. Avoid grabbing the other person's hand from above, which is an aggressive, dominant gesture. Limit the handshake to one or two seconds. Unless you know the person well, do not grasp their hand or arm with your free hand.

What communication skills are most important for leaders?

For leaders to communicate effectively, they must develop the following:

- *Deep understanding of the information needs of their employees or team members:* Many leaders underestimate the amount of information that employees need to do their job or to feel adequately informed about current circumstances. Leaders who communicate well do not hold back information unless there is a good, clear reason to do so.
- *Clear and concise speech:* Leaders must be able to communicate in plain, easily understood language
- *Close, objective listening skills:* Exceptional communicators spend most of their time listening to what other people have to say and withhold making judgments until they get the whole story. This holds true for leaders as well.
- *Skill in fostering connection between themselves and their audience:* Effective leaders are able to personalize the communication experience, whether they are speaking to one person or one hundred people. This is developed through intimate understanding of the needs and circumstances of the people they are talking to and then directly speaking to those needs.
- *Open body language and eye contact:* Body language sends important nonverbal information to the people you are interacting with and increases trust with the audience. Eye contact communicates personal interest and connection with those you are speaking to.

What communication skills are most important for followers?

Followers must also develop their communication skills if they are to work effectively with team members and their supervisors. Key communication skills for followers are:

- *Tact:* This is especially important when expressing disagreement with a supervisor's or leader's decision or opinion.
- *Clear and concise speech:* Like leaders, followers must be able to communicate in plain, easily understood language.
- *Ability to see and understand the broader picture:* This enables followers to put their ideas and contributions in a big-picture context, which increases the ability for leaders and supervisors to understand the potential impact of any ideas being contributed.

- *A nondefensive mindset:* It can be difficult for people with less power in an organization to avoid defensive thoughts. A defensive mindset, however, increases the potential to be inadvertently offended and may make someone reluctant to express their ideas.
- *Open body language and eye contact:* As with leaders, the body language and eye contact used by followers conveys important information about an individual's degree of caring or engagement with the matter at hand. Using engaged body language and eye contact will make supervisors and leaders more receptive to a follower's ideas.

How can I better communicate up the corporate ladder?

Communicating "up the ladder" can be stressful. First, it is important to note that many organizations have formal paths for when someone wants to communicate upward. These paths should be followed unless the situation is extreme and layers of authority need to be skipped.

When communicating up the ladder, it is critical to ensure that your message is focused and centered on the interests of the company. This puts your message into the context of the functions of the organization. The person you are communicating with should not have to do the mental work of figuring out how your message is relevant to the context and worldview of the company.

Ensure that you have honed your message or idea down to its clearest, most concise expression. This respects the time of the people you are speaking with and promotes clarity that your supervisors will appreciate. Be direct; passive aggression rarely goes over well and can undermine your credibility and purpose. Sometimes people mistake passive aggression with tact or subtlety. Evaluate the way you communicate as objectively as possible and keep your messages direct and polite.

Attempt to schedule a dedicated time to speak with your supervisor or the appropriate party, and let them know in advance what you want to speak about. This will give them the chance to enter the conversation already focused on the matter at hand.

If you need to take a message up multiple layers of authority in an organization, seek permission from your supervisor to address the higher authorities directly. This may not always be possible, but if you are given permission to do so, then you will avoid the garbling and miscommunication that occurs when messages are transmitted through multiple people. Seeking permission also avoids annoying your supervisor or higher authorities by going over other people's heads.

What is the best way to deliver bad news to my employees?

As the bearer of bad news, you must understand the circumstances that gave rise to it and anticipate questions regarding the situation. People are more willing to accept bad news if they believe there was sound decision-making behind it or reasonable attempts to mitigate it. Think how the news will affect the daily lives of the employees, and prepare a statement that acknowledges these difficulties.

When delivering the news itself, be as direct, clear, and accurate as possible. Sugarcoating unfortunate news does not make it any easier to take and may result in increased anxiety among everyone involved. Keep your language impersonal and emotionally neutral. While you can express disappointment with outcomes or acknowledge difficulties, refrain from providing your personal opinion on the matter. Stating any disagreement you may have with decisions that led to the bad news is not helpful to the employees or the managers and could potentially harm relationships and foster discontent.

Once the news has been delivered, change the focus of the conversation to what this means for the future. Direct people's attention toward next steps or upcoming tasks. This discourages people from dwelling on something that cannot be changed and gets them looking toward the steps they must take to deal with or improve the current situation.

Offer employees the opportunity to talk to you personally if they are particularly concerned or adversely affected by the news. It is important to show your people support by listening to their concerns and giving them a private avenue to express them. Although it is important to be emotionally neutral about the bad news, that does not prevent you from being compassionate toward the people the news affects.

How can I effectively deliver bad news to my supervisor?

Delivering bad news to supervisors is daunting. Even breaking bad news to supportive supervisors is among one of the more difficult workplace communication situations. Fears of punishment or insecurity over your job or position are normal.

The basics of delivering bad news to supervisors is similar to delivering bad news to employees. Think about the events that led up to the bad news, and be prepared to explain the course of action that led you there. It is likely that the supervisor will expect an explanation as to why the situation is what it is. Have a firm grasp of how the situation will affect the organization, its day-to-day functioning, and its ability to achieve its goals.

The direct approach that is recommended for supervisors addressing employees is the same for employees delivering bad news up the chain of command. Do not hide facts, do not deflect blame, and don't attempt to sugarcoat the situation. A straightforward approach that remains neutral in emotion and language is best.

If possible, prepare possible solutions or remedies to the problem. Be ready to present a recommended action plan detailing the next steps and actions necessary to resolve the situation.

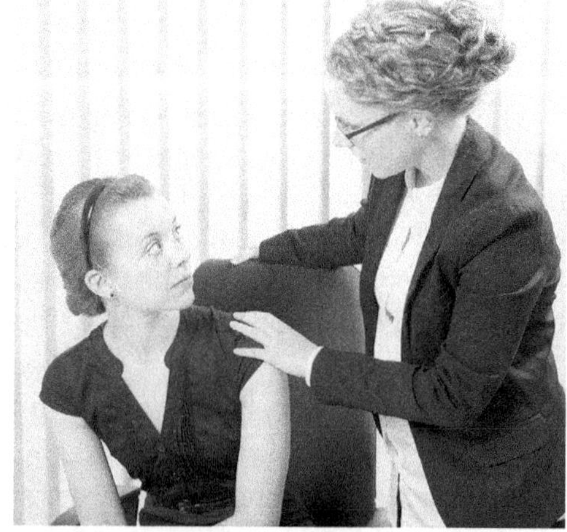

Delivering bad news is best done with sympathy and without sugarcoating. Talk to people on a personal level and talk about strategies for going forward.

How can I effectively deliver bad news to a client or to someone outside my organization?

Delivering bad news to clients or other people outside of your organization is all about focusing your attention on the impact and outcomes of this news for the external stakeholders. Direct your messaging around the interests of the client or stakeholder instead of commenting on effects internal to your organization. Clients are primarily focused on *their* interests and likely do not care much about how the problem impacts your organization, as long as you are seeking to resolve the problem for the client.

Again, delivering the news directly is the best approach. Even if you are not responsible for the situation, do not try to deflect blame. External stakeholders rarely care about who is ultimately responsible for bad news. Instead, apologize on behalf of the organization as a whole, and move on.

Clearly communicate the next steps that your organization will be taking to remedy the situation. Keep this simple with minimal detail. Inform clients or stakeholders of anything they may need to do or provide to speed along a resolution, but don't overburden them with excessive information about your plan of action.

How can I politely disagree with a coworker or superior?

Disagreement and debate is a reality of work. While power dynamics make it acceptable for a supervisor to disagree with someone at a lower level, disagreeing with equals or superiors requires more tact.

Keeping the conversation objective and focused on the task at hand is important. Disagreement can often come across as doubt about the other person's judgment or personal bias and preference. To remain objective and avoid personal offense, use as many neutral pronouns as possible. The words "you," "they," and "them" are particularly inflammatory as they are often used to assign blame and point fingers. "I," "we," and "us" can often bring down tension. Ideally, remove all personal pronouns and speak about the situation at hand as though it was as external and dispassionate as a discussion about where to put a postage stamp on a piece of mail.

How does bias affect communication in business or the workplace?

Bias significantly impacts communication in workplaces. It often causes people to form premature judgments about other people's ideas—such as them being particularly good or not worth listening to. It can lead to people becoming ignored or "voiceless," feeling as though regardless of what they say, their ideas go unnoticed or are even stolen by other people. Bias may come through clearly in the language that people choose to use and may incite upset or conflict. When people within an organization consistently experience bias, it may lead to reluctance in sharing thoughts or ideas, hampering innovation and positive group contribution.

Example:

Bad: "I don't understand why you want to recommend that account to the client. It doesn't meet their needs at all."

Good: "It seems this other account option ticks more of the client's boxes. Let's run a comparison before making a final recommendation."

Another tension-diffusing tactic is to offer your opposing viewpoints as options for discussion. This inserts your opinion or idea as an alternative for which you are seeking input and invites conversation, rather than just stomping over other people's thoughts or proposals.

Example:

Bad: "Italian restaurants are completely cliché for business lunches. Let's go to the Argentinean steakhouse—that will really wow the representatives."

Good: "Should we take the reps someplace a bit more unexpected like that Argentinean steakhouse? It might offer a change from the usual Italian."

When disagreeing with someone higher than you in an organization, there is a risk of coming across as insulting or dissenting, especially when dealing with people or professions that place high emphasis on rank. In these situations, a good strategy is to turn your disagreement into a request for instruction or help. This allows you to voice your thoughts and introduce a possible alternative without directly challenging the higher-ranking individual. It also allows the higher-ranking individual to save face by making corrections at a later date, should he or she not want to admit making any errors.

Example:

Bad: "That medication you prescribed will have a bad reaction with a drug this person is already on."

Good: "I was under the impression that there were bad interactions between that drug and this medication here, but maybe I'm mistaken. Are there situations where it's safe to combine the two?"

How can I get people at my place of work to better listen to me?

When people regularly feel that they are not listened to, there are usually critical flaws in their communication habits that make it difficult for others to pay attention. These flaws can be weak expressions, muddled messages, excessive talking, and speech that is difficult to understand. To make it easier for others to listen, ensure that you:

- *Have a clear purpose behind what you are saying:* Avoid irrelevant conversation or comments.
- *Present a clear, focused message:* Concentrate on conveying one idea at a time, and resist the urge to go off on tangents.
- *Speak with a firm, confident voice:* Weak or uncertain voices trigger the subconscious belief that what the person is saying is unimportant, thus increasing the

likelihood that you will be ignored. Use a volume appropriate for the size of the room and avoid apologetic language.

- *Make your point and then stop speaking:* Belaboring points, providing excessive information, or repeating yourself creates information overload and confusion for your listeners. Eventually, they will tune you out. If you do this on a regular basis, they will begin tuning you out very quickly. Get to the point of what you have to say and resist the urge to elaborate excessively or babble on at length.
- *Speak at a measured pace and enunciate clearly:* Speaking too fast or mumbling makes it difficult for people to understand what you are saying. This can mean that you are unable to clearly communicate your message. Monitor your speed, speak slightly slower than you think you should, and carefully enunciate your words.

What is bias?

Bias is a prejudice, belief, or inclination formed either in favor of or against a person or group. Everybody forms biases in different situations; it is a function of human thought and pattern recognition and can be consciously or unconsciously acted on. Some bias is relatively harmless, while others may create problems in workplace culture and career progression. Bias can create false impressions, such as an idea being better than it really is or a setback being a particular person's fault. It may cause us to jump to conclusions, ignore information, create cliques, or subconsciously treat people in ways we would never do consciously.

How can I deal with bias—such as gender, age, or race bias—in workplace communication?

Everyone deals with both sides of bias in the workplace—we all commit it, and we are all subject to it in some shape or form.

The first step when dealing with bias is to take an objective look at the communication that seems to be biased. Is there actual bias present? It is possible for people to become so sensitized to bias that they see it where none exists or so desensitized that they don't recognize when *they* are perpetuating bias. If so, what kind of bias is it, and how is it expressed? Be as specific as possible regarding the way the bias is communicated—the words used, the meaning, and the implications.

If there is indeed bias, ask yourself if it is affecting your ability to do your work. Is the bias leading you to hold back ideas? Does it lead you to unfairly discount or color what other people are saying? How does it affect people around you?

You then need to decide if you want to deal with bias on your own or bring it to the attention of others. If you want to deal with it on your own, look for alternative ways of expressing yourself. If you find that your ideas are being discounted because of your youth, consider dressing more formally. If you are overlooked because of your race or gender, start using more direct and forceful (but still polite) language. You could also seek out ways to speak up more frequently by giving reports or presentations where you are the center of focus. If you are imposing bias on others because you are not able to separate the contents of a report from the person who wrote it, request that people submit reports to you via anonymous file sharing and without their name on the front page.

If you determine that an organizational approach to managing bias is necessary, carefully communicate to the appropriate people the type of bias and the effects that concern you. You will likely be reporting to your supervisor, to a team, or to a human resources representative. Do not assign blame or point fingers; address this subject as neutrally and objectively as possible. Request that your organization takes measures to identify sources of bias and engage in active recognition and critical thinking about its occurrences and impact. Often, once people become aware of the everyday biases that occur in workplace communication, they are better able to identify and consciously limit or eliminate biased language and communication.

Organizations wanting to create a more positive, unbiased communication environment may want to get help from companies that specialize in workplace diversity and culture management. An objective third party can help employees change biases in a blame-free, productive way.

WORKPLACE CONFLICT MANAGEMENT

How does workplace conflict affect communication?

Workplace conflict strangles communication well beyond the individuals in conflict. Since workplaces have complicated group dynamics, conflict usually involves many people—those who are directly opposing each other, the people in the conflicting parties' "camps," and everyone else who relies on smooth, efficient communication between employees. When conflict arises between individuals, communication can:

- shut down, such as when those in conflict refuse to engage productively with one another,
- increase in complexity as shared information becomes muddied with agendas and internal politicking,
- decrease in reliability due to rumors and gossip, and
- degrade in other departments or parts of the workplace.

Is all workplace conflict bad?

Although disputes are rarely pleasant, when handled well, workplace conflict can lead to many positive outcomes. The clear, focused communication necessary for resolution can lead conflicting parties to discover shared values or goals, redefine or identify problems, and engage in creative problem solving and innovative thinking. For conflict to have a positive outcome, however, it should be identified and brought into the open as quickly as possible. Both parties involved should have equal interest in resolving the conflict and be open to frank, objective conversation about the issue.

How do workplace politics affect communication and conflict?

Workplace politics can have strong negative impacts on communication even when people aren't in active conflict. A politics-heavy climate can perpetuate poor communication practice, such as creating informal rules for who is "allowed" to talk about certain issues, not raising objections to certain people's ideas, or suppressing negative information or bad news. These practices can become entrenched in the organization's culture and be passed on to new employees. While internal politics are a reality in every organization, excessive negative politicking increases the likelihood of conflict between individuals by throttling healthy, productive communication.

Why do rumors develop in the workplace?

There tend to be three sources for rumors in a workplace:

- Misunderstanding in communication that spreads among employees
- A lack of information or communication with employees about important issues
- False information intentionally created and spread to advance a person or group's agenda

Rumors that are intentionally created and spread may range from out-and-out fabrication and lying to more insidious twisting of truths or manipulation of facts. The effectiveness of these rumors often depends on how much power or reliability the rumormonger has as these traits affect how likely people are to accept the rumors as truth. People who succeed at intentionally creating rumors are often skilled and subtle communicators as they're able to plant the seeds of rumors without overtly spreading them or being the obvious source of the false information. Rumors that that stem from misunderstanding or lack of information are far more common than intentionally created rumors.

Sometimes rumors are intentionally created to bring down one person and elevate another.

Misunderstandings can rapidly grow into full-blown rumors as the false information is passed from employee to employee, gaining momentum and often embellishment along the way. These rumors are extremely common and are often the least problematic and most easily solved of the three. When these rumors abound, an official clarification from the appropriate supervisor can usually put an end to the problem.

Rumors stemming from a lack of information are normal. Humans, much like nature, abhor a vacuum, and information vacuums are no exception. When there is a significant knowledge gap about important issues, people will fill it with speculation and educated guesswork, both of which can easily result in the creation of rumors. This kind of speculation and rumor development is natural as people attempt to make sense of developing situations, fragments of information, and feelings of uneasiness.

Workplaces that needlessly reinforce that communication is on a "need-to-know basis" are at high risk for rumors. While it is true that there will always be information that can't be shared freely with employees, organizations that apply the "need-to-know" rule for no good reason often have a secretive and paternalistic approach to employee management. This creates an atmosphere of mistrust, which can give momentum and credibility to rumors. In general, it's best to be open and share information with employees as freely as possible. Be cautious when telling people that they are on a "need-to-know" basis. Only apply that rule when absolutely necessary and give them a clear reason why they are not privy to the information in question.

How should rumors be dealt with?

Most rumors related to organizational performance or work-related issues are best dealt with through open clarification and refutation. This might be done in a staff meeting or through some other form of official communication. State what the rumor is and where the mistaken information lies, and provide the necessary details to clarify what is fact and what is fiction.

Rumors involving malicious intent or personal information should be dealt with privately with the parties involved. Breaches of confidentiality or slanderous comments could qualify as workplace harassment and may require intervention from your human resources department or legal advice, both which are beyond the scope of this book.

If you are able to identify the source or sources of the rumor, don't share their identity with other employees; assigning blame isn't helpful and may create conflict. People who habitually spread misinformation or who create rumors for malicious intent may need to be disciplined separately.

How can I express myself clearly without escalating conflict or creating more tension?

Using objective, neutral language when speaking with others and eliminating as many personal pronouns as possible can significantly decrease tension. This works by depersonalizing the conversation and keeping the conversation focused on an objective topic, separating the issues from the person or people involved. "I" and "you" statements easily set people up for opposition. Replacing those pronouns with neutral ones like "the" and "that" will help objectify opinions.

For example, to neutralize a potentially heated statement like "I don't think your proposed course of treatment will work," you could reframe it as a question: "Is there any reason that treatment wouldn't work here?" or as a neutral statement: "That course of treatment might not work because of these factors here." Both these statements keep the focus on an objective topic, avoid blaming or dismissing the other person, and ensure you don't force your own opinion on others.

Sometimes it's necessary to clarify your emotions to the person you're in conflict with, especially if feelings like frustration, upset, anger, or embarrassment are hampering communication. State your feelings simply and clearly so the other person can understand your mental state, but don't dwell on them. The more you can keep the conversation focused on an objective task or problem to be solved, the less opportunity there will be for emotions to muddy your message.

Asking questions to encourage the other person to tell his or her story and express his or her opinions helps create a two-way dialogue. It also demonstrates that you are listening and interested in the other person's views. This will encourage him or her to listen to you in return. Questions also help you understand the perspective of the person you are in conflict with and seek out mutually supportive goals or needs. Use open-ended questions that require more thoughtful answers rather than those that can be answered with a terse "yes" or "no."

In order to express yourself clearly, you must understand what the other person is saying. Paraphrasing statements made by the person you are in conflict with can help increase understanding for both parties. You will learn whether or not you fully comprehended the other person's message and can then improve your own phrasing and language to make your message clearer. When paraphrasing, avoid the phrase "What I hear you saying is…." This is patronizing, puts the onus for clarity on the other person, and implies that he or she isn't capable of communicating clearly. Instead, paraphrase his or her statement without preamble, and ask afterward if you understood correctly: "So instead of manufacturing a new blue widget, we should just repackage the red and purple widgets together—did I get that right?"

As leader or facilitator of a meeting that is addressing potentially contentious issues, it is your job to keep people focused on coming up with a solution and not simply arguing with one another.

How can I manage communication during meetings to be sure that discussion remains productive and conflict free?

When dealing with potentially contentious issues during meetings, productivity can get derailed as emotions run high. Your job as the leader or facilitator of the discussion is to keep people focused on an objective goal and steer the discussion away from fruitless bickering. There are several strategies that should be used before, during, and sometimes after a meeting to help keep things on track and productive.

Prior to the meeting taking place, ensure that the purpose and goal of the discussion is clear and that the group collectively understands what the point of the discussion is. If the discussion is part of a lengthier meeting, organize the agenda so that it happens when people are relatively alert, such as at the beginning of a meeting or after a break. Send out any necessary background information people may need in order to participate. Clearly state why they need to read the background information; many people don't review meeting packages prior to the meeting. You may want to issue reminders to them to read the documents.

During the discussion itself, your role is to keep everyone focused on its purpose and goal. Use neutral, objective language. If the language being used by others becomes heated or confused, step in and paraphrase people's comments so they are toned down and clarified. In order to minimize direct conflict between two or more people, have the meeting participants direct their statements toward you, much in the way that sitting politicians direct their comments toward a designated speaker. This prevents people from directly attacking one another's statements.

Should the conversation drift away from its intended purpose or tangential topics arise, bring everyone's attention back to the topic at hand. You may need to organize a separate discussion to address important tangents. If there is a particular individual creating difficulties or derailing the discussion, ask him or her to speak with you separately about his or her concerns after the meetings; you can organize a conversation between the relevant parties. It is possible you will need to tell them outright that the topics they're raising are not pertinent to this conversation and that you need to move on. This may create some tension, but the other participants will appreciate your management of the discussion.

After the meeting, create a summary of the discussion and the outcomes. If new meetings need to be scheduled to address unfinished business, a particular person's concerns, or important new issues, do so as soon as possible. These post-meeting summaries and follow-ups ensure that everyone sees and understands the progress that was made during the conversation. This will help set the tone for future discussions and allow people to approach difficult meetings with more objectivity and less trepidation.

Should I confront a colleague who is making comments that are offensive or unacceptable to me?

Before confronting someone who makes offensive, unacceptable, or insulting comments at work, first consider whether this is normal behavior for him or her. If the person in question doesn't usually make offensive remarks, it's possible this is a one-off situation due to some other source of stress in his or her life. If this is the case, it may be best to simply ignore the comment, provided that offensive remarks don't become habitual.

If the coworker regularly makes offensive comments, try to figure out why you find it inappropriate and what sort of response the degree of offense warrants. Also consider what you stand to gain by confronting this person. Would such a confrontation likely lead him or her to change his or her behavior, or would it set you up for further conflict or possibly even an escalation in the offensive statements? Speak to some trusted coworkers to get their input on the situation to ensure you are being objective.

Should your assessment of the offensive behavior be correct, develop a strategy for dealing with it. While it may be tempting to try to change someone's perspective or attitude, such efforts usually don't result in positive change. In many cases, simply ignoring the comments or verbally redirecting them toward the business at hand can be enough to discourage further comments. This demonstrates that such comments aren't appreciated while keeping everyone's dignity intact. If other coworkers are similarly bothered by the person's behavior, enlist their help and support in dealing with the problem.

Depending on the situation and the personality of the offensive coworker, you may want to speak with him or her privately and let he or she know directly that his or her comments are unwelcome and you want him or her to stop. For people who are good-natured and genuinely clueless that they are making people uncomfortable, this strategy works well. With other people, however, it may encourage or escalate the comments. If this happens, let them know that you will raise the issue with the suitable authorities.

Occasionally, offensive comments can affect people's sense of security or ability to do their work. Should this be the case, you may need to raise the issue with your supervisor, your human resources department, or your union. If the comments are coming from someone with significant power and you have no other support, you will need to consider whether the communication environment has made your work intolerable and what other employment options are available to you.

How can I talk about a problem with my team without the conversation turning into an attempt to assign blame?

If you find yourself needing to work through a problem with a feuding team, your role is to keep everyone's attention focused on the issue at hand rather than on individual slights or wounds. Identify the actual problem being encountered and work-related implications without drawing attention to individual responsibilities. Work with the group to find facts that everyone can agree upon, and frame discussions around those rather than around opinions or perceived insult.

Speak in future tense rather than past tense. In rhetoric, past tense is used to assign blame ("He did this." "You said that."). Future tense helps people switch to problem-solving mode ("How can we negotiate a better deal?" "What could the outcome of that strategy be?"). Be prepared for people to attempt to talk about past performances or outcomes. When this happens, guide the conversation back to future strategies.

I am in conflict with someone at work but still have a job to do. How can I communicate with him or her so that we are able to carry on with work in spite of our dispute?

Having conversations with coworkers you are feuding with can be difficult, even when the conversation has nothing to do with the conflict itself. To remain as productive as possible when working with your opponent, treat every conversation as a thing separate from your conflict. Before entering a conversation with your opponent, know what the purpose and goal of the conversation is. Focus on the goal and, just as with teams in the previous question, keep the conversation directed toward problem-solving. Encounters should be polite, impersonal, purposeful, and brief.

How should I communicate with a colleague who is angry?

Communicating through anger can be difficult. Often, it's necessary to allow a release of emotion or temper before a reasonable conversation can be had. A critical part of communicating with an angry coworker is to refrain from becoming angry yourself. If someone is angry, don't attempt to solve any problems in the moment. Let him or her know that you see and understand his or her frustration or upset, and suggest an alternative time to tackle the problem. Try not to take the anger personally; often, people direct angry comments at an individual rather than at the situation that made him or her

When faced with an angry coworker, it is vital not to return that anger. Much more effective is a strategy of calm in which you also don't try to resolve the problem right then when tempers are flaring.

upset. If needed, put some distance between you and your angry colleague to give you both time to cool off, then arrange a time to talk.

When should the help of a facilitator or mediator be sought?

Facilitators and mediators are useful in complex conflicts where clear communication or productive problem solving is difficult. Bringing in outside assistance can also be useful when a dispute has reached a stalemate or escalated to the point where work is seriously disrupted and communication is no longer taking place. Mediators and facilitators are not there to provide opinions or recommendations. Rather, they help guide conversations, maintain focus on the issue, clarify misunderstandings, and provide a neutral third party for people at which to direct comments and statements.

In some organizations, bringing in a mediator or facilitator can mean direct action or intervention from a union or workers' association and may have legal ramifications. For these organizations, formal facilitation is often a last resort. For problems that could still be resolved without outside intervention, it might be possible to have a coworker or manager facilitate the conversation as an informal facilitator. There is a possibility that the informal facilitator could get dragged into the conflict, though, so this approach should be used with caution.

PERSUASIVE COMMUNICATION

When do I need to persuade in business or work?

Persuasion affects all areas of work and business. While we often think of persuasion as being tied to sales, recruitment, or the promotion of new initiatives, it affects other areas as well. Whenever we attempt to influence someone's point of view, argue for an idea or course of action we want to take, or motivate team members or employees to push through a difficult task, we are actively persuading others.

Persuasive communication and argument is not always done with a view to sell or "win." It can also be used as a way to explore difficult issues and to thoroughly examine an idea. Used in this way, persuasion and argument are known as dialectic: People holding different points of view seek to find some sort of truth or consensus through rational argument. When this form of persuasive communication happens in the workplace or in business, it can help the parties involved make new discoveries, find alternative courses of action, and come to better conclusions and agreements.

How much information should I give when trying to persuade someone?

Many people will try to persuade others by overwhelming them with information. This may be done to demonstrate expertise or simply because of the view that "more is better" when it comes to information and persuasion. In reality, presenting too much information can make someone *less* persuasive. The listener may become confused and have a hard time making sense of the argument. It could also make the arguer seem unconfident, disorganized, or even desperate—all traits that dissuade people from being persuaded.

Instead of presenting all your persuasive information or arguments upfront, start with the piece of information that will be most relevant to both the situation at hand *and* to the person you are trying to persuade. This may not be enough information to convince him or her, but by presenting smaller pieces of information at a time, you will give the person listening to you a chance to process what you are saying. Additionally, it will start a back-and-forth discussion between you and those you are trying to persuade, allowing a more natural, fulsome discussion of the issue.

Using the smaller-dose strategy of persuasion is not about withholding information; it's about consciously deciding what is of greatest importance to the other person and giving him or her the courtesy of being able to respond to what you are telling him or her.

What is social proof?

Social proof is a persuasive tactic where the opinions or actions of others are used to back up the validity of your own argument. Humans look to other people to help them decide what is acceptable or desirable. This is as true in work and business as it is in our social lives.

Advertising campaigns frequently employ "social proof" as a way of persuading people to buy a product. In this Palmolive ad, the social proof is that doctors believe the product is good for women's skin.

The use of social proof frequently appears in business and workplace communication as a powerful advertisement strategy ("Nine out of ten pediatricians recommend RashEez soothing ointment"). It is also a superb persuasion tactic when convincing reluctant decision-makers to support a course of action. The actions of competitors can be used as social proof to convince someone to try a new process or technology ("All our competitors have Facebook ads, so we should too"). It may also be used in committee and board settings to speed the decision-making process. If other members on a board publicly lend their support to an idea, it becomes more likely that the individual holding out will change his or her mind. This strategy is at work when votes are taken publicly, such as by a show of hands.

If you are dealing with a team member or employee who is reluctant to accept your idea, proposal, or direction, try having other people on your team show their support. The reluctant employee may become more compliant if he or she sees that the larger group is willing to give the new idea a try.

Relying solely on social proof can be counterproductive. It is most effective when used in addition to other persuasive arguments, such a sound logic or evidence. If used on its own, the person making the argument runs the risk of being asked "And if all your friends jumped off a cliff, would you do it too?" (or some equally irritating variation thereof). Use social proof when someone needs an extra nudge toward your line of thinking.

How does power and authority affect persuasiveness?

First, we must differentiate between power and authority. Power is an individual's ability to make people take some kind of action or adopt a certain way of thinking. Authority is when an individual is granted power through designation or recognition of a third party. Authority is most strongly related to legitimate power (power assumed through someone's title or position) or expert power (power through having highly specialized knowledge).

In persuasive situations, having power or authority makes it easier to persuade someone to take an action or adopt a point of view. Power and authority can be used to shortcut the persuasive process by giving someone preexisting credibility. This is especially true with expert power or expert authority where a third party has declared someone to be particularly knowledgeable.

It should be noted that someone can have authority but no power, such as the manager that no one listens to or obeys. His or her title gives him or her authority, but his or her lack of actual power means he or she has a difficult time persuading people to do as he or she says. People can also have power without authority, such as the executive assistant who can restrict who has access to the CEO and knows all the office gossip. Despite their lack of authority, these individuals can be highly persuasive because their informal power gives them access to resources (the CEO and the gossip) that others value and are willing to negotiate for or defer to.

What is the relationship between likability and persuasion?

Likability is an individual's ability to have friendly interactions and quickly form social bonds. Likability creates a more positive impression of the thing about which someone is being persuaded. The persuader's likableness essentially "rubs off" onto the action or idea he or she is trying to convince the other person to adopt.

How can I be more likable when attempting to persuade someone?

When trying to be likable, look at all angles available to you. Physical attractiveness, such as good grooming and a neat appearance, increases likability. So do pleasant, agreeable manners. People respond very positively to flattery; if you are able to pay genuine compliments to the people you are trying to persuade, do so. Actions that are seen as helpful or generous—holding the door, buying someone a cup of coffee—also increase likability. The adage that we like people who are like us also holds true; we like things that are familiar. They comfort us and put us at ease. If you are going into a situation where you need to speak persuasively, try conforming to individual or organizational behaviors like dress codes and language or communication style.

NEGOTIATION

What is negotiation?

Negotiation is the process of coming to an agreement through exchanges of offers.

What is the purpose of negotiation?

On the surface, the purpose of negotiation is to develop a mutually agreeable offer or solution to a problem. At a deeper level, however, negotiation can be about relationship development, finding new solutions, managing needs and expectations, increasing buy-in, increasing collaboration or commitment, or creating other desirable outcomes.

What is win-win negotiation?

Win-win negotiation focuses on achieving outcomes that benefit both parties involved. In win-win negotiation, the notion of winning at the other person's expense is discarded. Instead, the parties focus on exploring solutions that advance both their interests. This is done with the understanding and expectation that there will be some give-and-take on both sides.

How might a win-win mindset affect communication and outcomes?

Win-win negotiation focuses on positive outcomes for both parties. As such, people enter the negotiation with more optimism and a greater willingness to collaborate on a solution. Communication increases, as does trust and nonselfish behavior. These kinds of negotiations are more likely to result in better terms and outcomes for both parties

U.S. Secretary of State John Kerry meets with Bulgarian President Rosen Plevneliev in this 2015 photo. Skilled diplomats should be able to negotiate deals in which both sides feel like winners.

involved. When directing students to take part in a negotiation experiment, noted business negotiator Joel Peterson found that those who were given win-win directions had "reasonable deals made, they were made quickly, they were relatively easy to understand and document, and there was a lot of camaraderie."

What is win-lose negotiation?

Instead of focusing on mutually beneficial outcomes, win-lose negotiations focus on one party achieving a significantly better outcome than the other. This usually is framed in terms of one person "winning" (getting what he or she wants) to the detriment of the other person. Win-lose negotiations are highly competitive with the goal of either making as few concessions as possible or of forcing the opposing party to make significant concessions in order to reach an agreement.

How might a win-lose negotiation mindset affect communication and outcomes?

A win-lose negotiation mindset encourages aggressive behavior, secrecy, and obstinacy. The people involved may use violent communication tactics like shouting, talking over others, and threatening body language. Collaboration is discouraged, and information is not readily shared. In the same experiment mentioned above, Peterson found that when students were given win-lose instructions, "fewer deals were made, they were made more slowly, [...] people were frustrated, and they hated their classmates." The deals that the students made were complex, often unworkable or unenforceable, and poorly documented. The interpersonal relationships between the students were also damaged.

What are some common situations where negotiation may happen?

Negotiation happens in a wide variety of situations, both formally and informally. Prospective employers and employees may negotiate terms of employment and compensation during the hiring process. Salespeople negotiate price and terms of service and delivery when making a business deal with a buyer. Coworkers will negotiate between each other to divide up tasks.

What are the signs of successful negotiation?

Identifying whether or not a negotiation is "successful" can be quite subjective. If an agreement was reached that heavily favored one party over the other, the unhappy party may consider the negotiations unsuccessful while the party that got what he or she wanted would think it a great success.

A more holistic idea of successful negotiations would be one in which both parties were satisfied with the outcomes. Successful negotiations can reduce animosity and hostility and build better interpersonal relationships. Agreements are reached in a reasonable timeframe, and both parties are clear on the terms of the agreement.

What are the signs of an unsuccessful negotiation?

Unsuccessful negotiations are those in which an agreement is not reached or in which the agreement makes one or both parties very unhappy. Working relationships may be damaged, resulting in lost potential for future service or collaboration. The agreements of an unsuccessful negotiation could be hard to interpret, carry out, or enforce.

What is anchoring?

Anchoring is a technique where one of the parties sets the terms or boundaries of the negotiation, such as the initial price or value of the negotiated item. Anchoring is a critical communication tactic within negotiation because it can establish a strong bias that makes the people involved interpret all additional information around the anchor. The anchor becomes the frame of reference for the rest of the negotiations. If you are familiar with the market or business you are negotiating with, speaking up first and setting the anchor is a good tactic, presuming the anchor you set (such as the price you want for an item you're selling) is realistic. If you aren't familiar with the market you are dealing with, you may want the other party to set the anchor as a means of discovering valuable information about the market in question.

What is framing?

Within business negotiations, framing is a rhetorical strategy that can define the way people perceive the thing being negotiated. It can also be used to rationalize decisions and courses of action or to focus people's attention on a specific aspect within the negotiation.

For example, someone might frame a price-related negotiation by referring to the item he or she is selling as an "investment" instead of talking about its "cost." This frames the item as something that will grow in value or give some kind of return to the purchaser. Another frame could be a negotiator referring to his or her competitor's team as "salespeople" while referring to his or her own team as "customer relationship managers," framing his or her team as being more invested in the happiness of his or her customers. Someone negotiating with a very environmentally conscious organization might frame the negotiation in terms of environmental responsibility rather than cost effectiveness.

What is trust?

Trust is one party's feeling that the other party will make good on their promises and fulfill the terms set out in the negotiation. It is also the sense a party has that the people they are negotiating with are taking everyone's needs and goals into consideration when making offers and proposals. Someone involved in negotiations should have a clear plan to communicate his or her trustworthiness, such as offering proof of past performance or indications that he or she understands the other party's goals and concerns. A degree of trust must be in place if people are going to be willing to communicate openly and honestly in a negotiation situation.

What are the components of trust in negotiating?

Joel Peterson states that for trusting, open communication to exist in negotiation, a person must have "character, competence, and power." Character refers to the individual's established reputation and record of behavior. Competence relates to the individual's level of knowledge and skill in relation to both the thing that is being negotiated and in the negotiation process itself. Power is the individual's decision-making capacity and whether or not he or she has the power to make a decision or take an action based on the proceedings or outcomes of the negotiation.

Because of the lack of trust Americans have for Russian President Vladimir Putin and vice versa, negotiations between the two nations repeatedly fail.

What is position-based negotiation?

Position-based negotiation, also called positional bargaining, is the practice of opening up a negotiation discussion with each party stating the concrete outcome they want, such as a price or specific terms of service. Positioning happens in both formal and informal business negotiations. You will know if you are engaging in positional bargaining if you are planning on starting a negotiation with the words "I want…." Position-based negotiations can often lead to a win-lose mentality as the negotiation process results in a whittling away or changing of the outcome or position that the negotiators initially declared. The negotiating parties are forced to compromise their positions, which usually results in more dissatisfaction with the outcome.

What is interest-based negotiation?

Interest-based negotiation focuses on the broader interests, circumstances, wants, and needs of both parties. The negotiating parties get together to look into the problem at hand, identify people's interests and concerns, then brainstorm possible solutions together. In this style of negotiating, specific offers are not made until later in the process. This form of negotiation is seen as more collaborative as the negotiating parties have the opportunity to see where their interests might merge or complement one another. Interest-based negotiation focuses more around a "win-win" mentality in which both parties are capable of getting what they want or need.

How does communication differ when engaging in position-based versus interest-based negotiation?

Position-based negotiation tends to foster stubbornness and a confrontational style of communication. As the parties have already made a decision on what they want, they are more committed to that specific outcome. Communication is further hampered by a desire to not "lose face" through concession, and listening tends to go down due to people focusing on planning their rebuttals more than on exploring the circumstances with the opposing party. This style of negotiation results in the parties viewing each other as adversaries and opponents, and their communication is accordingly closed and hostile in nature.

Interest-based negotiation begins with a more open communication process as the parties start by exploring the situation together. The people involved develop a better understanding of each other's circumstances and what is informing their wants and needs. Because underlying interests are discovered, the parties can be more flexible in determining their solutions and offers, often finding mutually acceptable outcomes that don't require unwanted compromises. This style of negotiation often leads the parties to feel more like partners collaborating on solutions rather than opponents vying for the prize, thus allowing for more open, productive, and efficient communication.

Should I communicate or demonstrate emotions when negotiating?

As with all communication, emotions can either derail a negotiation or help people arrive at a better conclusion. Using a poker-face strategy of negotiation, where you show no emotion because you don't want to "show your hand" or give the other party any information he or she can work with, is emblematic of a "win-lose" mentality. Demonstrating a controlled, reasonable level of emotion can help the other party determine your values, wants, and needs. It shows authenticity, sincerity, and openness, which can help increase trust between the negotiating parties. It also encourages the other party to be more open with you, allowing you to observe his or her behavior and figure out what his or her values and needs are.

The key to displaying emotion is to do it in a calm, controlled manner. It is possible to demonstrate a wide range of emotions—surprise, pleasure, frustration, anger, curiosity, and so on—in a rational and measured way. Demonstrating uncontrolled or explosive emotion is detrimental as it decreases likability and can come across as irrational and inflexible. Shouting, storming out of rooms, and cursing increase tension and stubbornness among everyone in the room, and any victory that comes of it can be chalked up to bullying. This behavior erodes trust, can inhibit positive outcomes, and ruins reputations. It is a lousy strategy and should be avoided.

What is a stalemate?

A stalemate is when neither party is willing to concede any ground to the other. Stalemates are often a result of win-lose negotiation. Communication comes to a standstill, and both frustration and stubbornness increases as the stalemate drags on. Reframing the negotiation to an interest-based conversation may help resolve stalemates by taking people's attention away from their entrenched position and redirecting it toward an analysis of the situation or problems. This reengages communication in a way that is focused on creative problem solving rather than on positions and offers.

When neither party in a negotiation will give ground, a stalemate results, and nothing is accomplished.

Who should I be speaking with in a negotiation situation?

Negotiating can be a frustrating, pointless activity if the person you are communicating with doesn't have any authority or decision-making power. In these cases, all conversation between the parties involved must be relayed to the person in authority. This is like playing telephone with the information and can easily result in mixed messages or errors in communication. It's also frustrating for one party to find out that he or she has been speaking with the "wrong person," and he or she may resent the time and effort wasted.

How do I know if I'm talking with the right person when negotiating?

If you want to be certain that you're communicating with the right person, ask the person you are to speak with in advance of your meeting to explain what kind of authority or decision-making capacity he or she has. If his or her reply indicates that he or she is a "representative" or "speaking on behalf" of a decision-maker, he or she might not actually have any direct authority him- or herself. If you are speaking to a representative, ask him or her what agreements he or she is able to make, how binding those agreements will be, and how information will be passed on to the actual decision-makers. Based on these answers, you can decide whether or not to negotiate with the representative or to push to speak directly with the decision-maker.

How much information should be shared when negotiating?

Anxious, insecure, or win-lose negotiators are often intent on revealing as little information as possible, which hampers communication and harms the negotiation. When involved in a negotiation, you should focus on sharing as much information as is relevant and/or helpful to the proceedings. What constitutes helpful or relevant information could change during the negotiation process itself as new information, interests, or other factors come to light. If the other party asks for information that is irrelevant, potentially harmful, or in violation of privacy rights or confidentiality agreements, you should refuse and be clear as to why you are refusing. It may be helpful to ask the other party why he or she needs that information and to see if you have other information to offer that would fit his or her needs.

What is the difference between written and oral reports?

Written reports typically involve more detailed information about the item being reported on. Written reports tend to be more technical in nature than oral reports. Oral reports usually paint a broader picture. The person giving the presentation provides a summary and interpretation of the data in a written report rather than actually going through the written report itself.

BUSINESS WRITING

What is reporting?

Reporting is a presentation of facts about different aspects of a business, delivered in either oral or written form. Reports are informative in nature and while they may be used to persuade at a later date, they should not contain any hidden motives or agenda. Avoid the use of highly subjective language that could change the reader's or audience's impression of the facts at hand.

For more on reporting and other business writing, see the chapter "Written Communication."

How should written reports be structured?

Written reports should begin with a summary of the scope of the report as well as its main points. The writer will then need to determine in what order to present his or her information. Many reports are chronological, but there are circumstances where a cause-and-effect organization scheme (where a situation or outcome is presented and then analyzed) is more appropriate. If there are statistical data or trends to report, the writer may wish to present them in a more visual format, such as a graph or chart.

If the report is to be accompanied by recommendations for action, the recommendations should appear at the end of the report and be backed up with clear reasons and evidence. Final summaries are usually not needed as a summary appears at the beginning of the report. Additional information that may be useful for the reader but too dense or not relevant enough to appear in the main body of the report can be attached to the end as an appendix.

To make reading the report as clear and as easy as possible, use headers to separate the main pieces of content and ideas into easily identifiable chunks. If the report is especially lengthy, a table of contents can be included.

How should oral reports be structured?

Oral reports follow a structure similar to written reports. The main difference is in how much information is presented in an oral report—they tend to be significantly shorter than written reports. Start with a summary of what is going to be presented, then the main body of information, followed by any conclusions or recommendations. Focus on delivering an analysis of the information and on interpreting the report for the audience. Avoid going into a huge amount of detail; this can overwhelm the audience.

NETWORKING

What is networking?

In business, networking refers to expanding the number of professional contacts you have by intentionally meeting new people. It increases business opportunities by establishing new relationships in a nonsales environment.

Networking can take place formally or informally, and opportunities for both can be readily found. Formal networking events include business association events, referral clubs, professional interest groups, and industry events. Networking events are often accompanied by a speaker or presenter, which gives the attendees something to discuss afterward. Informal networking happens just about anywhere but is most effective at social events and parties. These include dinner parties, weddings, and other occasions where you are able to have a long conversation with someone you don't see often or have just met.

Do I have to network in person, or is online networking good enough?

Online business groups abound, especially on social media sites such as Facebook. While these are an easy way to connect with a group of people, they can be fairly inefficient networking tools. Engagement and commitment to regular participation among group mem-

Business dinners, conferences, business association functions such as parties, and so on are among the places where networking occurs. It is important not to ignore these if you wish to make new business contacts.

bers tend to be low, and the bonds formed are often fairly weak. They do have value, but you need to participate very frequently in the group discussions to see any real benefit.

In-person networking creates a more dynamic, intimate interaction. Because both verbal and nonverbal communication are being shared, we can form a more complete picture of the person we just met. Bonds are formed more quickly, and individual follow-up meetings are arranged more often. As with online networking, you need to engage repeatedly with in-person networking groups and with the people you meet to get any benefit. Usually, though, the engagement can happen less often than with online groups.

Social media is an excellent way to extend your in-person networking activities. If you know people who are going to a networking event and you especially want to connect with them, consider connecting with them through social media before the event takes place. This can help break the ice, exchange some introductory information, and let you start an in-person conversation on a slightly deeper level. You can also use social media to stay in closer contact with the people you meet at networking events.

I'm an introvert, and talking to new people makes me nervous. How can I get more comfortable with networking?

Many introverts are nervous about networking. The idea of having to quickly connect with lots of different people can be overwhelming, especially if you are worried about not knowing what to say. If you find networking overwhelming or anxiety provoking, shift your focus from meeting lots of people to only meeting a couple of individuals. Establishing a goal—such as having a ten-minute conversation with two new people—will help bring the scope of networking down to something more comfortable and manageable. If talking about yourself makes you uncomfortable, focus the conversation on those you have just met. Ask them questions about themselves and let them do the talking; this will help you find commonalities and feel more comfortable sharing information with them. You may also want to consider bringing a friend to the event with you—someone you enlist to go with you and help you along in the conversations and small talk. Having a backup person can help you break out of your shell with the added benefit of also expanding your friend's network.

Networking feels phony and self-serving. How can I make the experience more real and enjoyable?

It's true that many networking events feel like attending a meat market in a business suit. To increase the enjoyment and effectiveness of your networking efforts, don't focus on handing out dozens of business cards (the spray-and-pray method) or hunting for new clients and leads. Rather, concentrate on learning about other people and discovering small ways to help them. Maybe you could introduce them to someone they might want to know or send them an article you think they would find interesting. A curious and helpful frame of mind will enable you to make more real connections and identify better prospective clients or partners. You'll hand out fewer business cards, to be sure, but the new relationships you'll make will be far more valuable and are more likely to result in future business.

How do I know to whom I should talk?

It can be difficult to know who to talk to at a networking event. If the event has a publicly available RSVP list, look over the list to identify people of interest to you. Aside from that, it's good not to worry too much about trying to strategically read a room" and instead just try to have some good conversations with a few people. Sometimes you'll connect with people who can help you out, sometimes you'll meet people who need your help, and sometimes you might not make any decent connections. Each time you go to a networking group or event, spend some time talking to people you haven't met before. That will increase the likelihood of meeting people who are "right" for you.

What are some good ways of introducing myself?

Instead of immediately introducing yourself using your job title, try talking about a hobby you are involved in or describe the sort of client you help. If your role or business doesn't fit any traditional title or description, consider telling a short story or analogy that describes what you do. This sort of information lets people see you in a light that isn't completely defined by a job title and can springboard you into more interesting conversations.

Are there some things that shouldn't be brought up when networking?

There are no hard-and-fast rules about what topics are "safe" when networking. Some people like to establish personal rules for avoiding topics that can easily become heated—usually politics and religion. If, however, you are comfortable discussing those things and are able to talk about them in a neutral, nonconfrontational way, then they're fair game. If you choose to bring up potentially touchy issues, watch how the person you are talking with responds; if he or she seems uncomfortable, change the subject. A good practice to follow is to avoid subjects that are overly personal, such as your kid's grades or your aunt's gout. Go for topics that everyone in the conversation can participate in.

How do I get better at small talk?

Getting better at small talk is a combination of practice and preparation. If you are going to a networking event, read up on news and current affairs that might be related to the sort of people in attendance. Find out what is trending on social media and think of some conversations you could have about that topic. Adopt a curious mindset and ask questions about the person you are chatting with (people love to talk about themselves). Practice these strategies with friends, family, and coworkers, and the networking small talk will become much easier.

When should I follow up with new contacts?

The purpose of a post-networking follow-up is to cement your identity in your new contact's mind. It's best to follow up with new contacts as soon as possible after you meet them, while memory of your meeting is still fresh. Usually, this means sending the new contact an email within one or two days. You don't need to send a lengthy message—a simple email saying that you enjoyed meeting and chatting with them about XYZ will be sufficient. Try to think of an extra piece of helpful information you can include in the email, such as a link to an interesting article or a book or restaurant recommendation.

How can I strengthen relationships with new contacts?

Regular communication is key to strengthening relationships with new contacts. Consider establishing a schedule and communication strategy for your business network, such as sending people a friendly email on their birthday or every two months sending them an article that might be of interest. If you have an exciting new venture or business development that may pique their curiosity, share it with them. These regular communications don't need to result in a reply from that person, but it will remind them of you and let you stand out as an engaging, helpful person.

PITCHING

What is pitching?

Pitching is any kind of direct explanation of a business offering with the intention of making a sale. Pitching takes many forms—from a short "elevator pitch" to a full-blown sales meeting that lasts several hours. Not all descriptions of products or services are pitches; what differentiates a pitch is that it is done with the specific intent of soliciting someone's business.

An elevator pitch is a concise blurb explaining what you are offering and why the potential client would want it.

What is an elevator pitch?

An elevator pitch (also called an elevator speech) is a short blurb about what you offer, who you offer it to, and how it helps your clients. Most elevator pitches are less than two minutes long, and many people believe that the shorter the pitch the better. An elevator pitch must be extremely clear and as specific as possible. There are many ways to give a short, compelling elevator pitch. You could tell a story about how you helped a client or ask the person you are speaking with to describe a problem related to your business.

Because the pitch needs to be very clear, it's often best to stick with a straightforward description. A popular formula for creating elevator pitches is the "I help (type of client) do (action or activity) so they can (achieve outcome)" template.

Examples of this template in action are:

- *Public speaking coach:* "I help professionals and businesses increase their presentation skills so they can stand out in their marketplace."
- *Real estate lawyer:* "I help home buyers navigate through the negotiations and contracts so they can purchase their homes worry free."
- *Homecare provider:* "I give seniors high-quality, in-home care so they can safely and comfortably live in their own homes for as long as possible."

This elevator pitch theme can be adapted endlessly. Consider this template as a useful starting point and then develop alternatives until you hit on one that you feel strong delivering.

What information should I include in a business pitch?

As with any presentation, you want to provide your audience with just enough information without overwhelming them. The information will vary slightly on whether you're pitching something a person can buy outright or an opportunity to invest in your business.

When describing a good or service someone can buy, focus on describing benefits rather than features. A feature is something like the length of an educational module or the different attachments that come with a widget. Benefits are the positive outcomes that the item will confer on buyers—some way that it makes their life easier, saves them time and money, or how it makes their hair more lustrous and bouncy. You can bring up features, but keep them to a minimum and frame them in terms of the benefit they bring. Other pieces of information buyers will want to know are price, availability, and any guarantees you offer.

Investors will want to see information such as a reasonable valuation of your business, a business plan, past performance metrics, and assets such as existing clients, contracts, or patents. Most will also want you to demonstrate your understanding of the market. You will need to present a plan for how you'll use the investment money and any related business models that affect your use of their investment. Some may ask to see an exit plan in case they want to sell their investment or the company folds.

Information to avoid is excessive, expert-level descriptions of precisely how you built the widget or developed the service or business. It's tempting to give this information when pitching, as we all tend to be personally invested in how we created the thing we're offering—a lot of time, money, energy, and thought went into it. From a buyer's or investor's perspective, however, the pitch is more about what your product, service, or business offers him or her than how you created it. It might be useful to give prospects an overview of the development process, but keep it relatively basic and avoid overly technical information or jargon. If they want more information, they will ask for it at some point in the investing process.

How can I increase my credibility?

A pitch should not be about the person giving the pitch but rather about the business, product, or service offered. While it's important to appear credible, you can achieve this by presenting solid, rational, and clear information about your offer and your past performance. Establishing your credibility when pitching has less to do with rattling off your formal credentials and more with proving past business success. You can do this through information such as positive client outcomes and sales performance. It's fine to open with a brief story about how you came to develop the thing you're pitching, but quickly shift the focus away from yourself and toward your offer. If your prospect wants to know more about you as an individual, they'll ask.

How can I boost the likelihood that someone will accept my pitch?

While it's impossible to craft a pitch that guarantees a sale or investment, having thorough knowledge of your prospect's individual context will help you develop a pitch that fits their needs. If you are speaking with buyers, gather as much information as possible about their demographics and be sure you can clearly explain intersections between their needs and your offering.

When speaking with investors, have an understanding of who they are, what sort of companies they have invested in, and what markets or resources they have access to. It's also helpful to know whether or not they tend to be a "hands-on" investor who will want to be involved in decision-making or if they are more likely to just provide financial backing. This will help you describe the sort of relationship you are seeking with them. Be certain that you can clearly describe how investing in you can boost the investor's portfolio and complement their other investments.

What style of presenting should I use when pitching?

Any kind of business pitch is a persuasive presentation, and as such, you will want to incorporate a strong appeal to the audience's pathos. You will need to excite them about your offer while demonstrating your own conviction and dedication to your products, services, or business idea. Show controlled enthusiasm, one that balances your excitement with clear-headed rationality. Use intelligent but relatively informal language; using excessive jargon or sounding like you're giving a thesis defense can confuse and alienate prospects.

WEBSITES AND SOCIAL MEDIA

Does my business need a website?

For many businesses, a website is the first point of communication with customers. Businesses large and small use websites to provide descriptions of their company and what they do, enable online sales, and direct people to the best way of contacting a representative. Websites are a critical contact point even for businesses with a small scope or no online services, including small businesses, one-person shops, traditional brick-and-mortar shops, and individuals selling local products and services offline.

It's important that businesses reach out to their customers in the manner the customers prefer. It isn't a matter of whether or not *you* want to set up a website but whether your customers want to see your website. And it's safe to assume that they do: as Internet searching has outstripped traditional forms of consumer outreach such as newspaper advertising and telephone directories, it is more likely that prospective customers will look for you online than anywhere else. Websites are now so ubiquitous that to not have at least some form of online presence is seen by customers as a red flag. It indicates that business owners either don't have basic computer literacy or are uninterested in making it easy for customers to find them.

What are mobile-friendly websites?

Mobile-friendly websites are those designed to work well within the confines of various mobile devices, like smartphones and tablets. Often called "responsive design," these sites will

In the early days of the Internet, you needed to hire a web designer or know how to code yourself. Today, a businessperson can subscribe to web host companies that offer easy-to-use templates and other design services.

change in appearance depending on the sort of device the viewer is using. Images and text may be resized, navigation usually changes to a pop-out menu, and some website features might be suppressed if they can't be displayed properly. These changes improve the user's experience and allow them to take in your information more easily than if they were attempting to navigate around a website that didn't display properly on a smaller screen. Mobile-friendly and responsive websites improve communication by allowing stakeholders, clients, and prospective clients to access your website through their preferred technology.

Does my business website need to be mobile friendly?

Most businesses will benefit from having a mobile-friendly version of their website. In 2015, Americans spent fifty-one percent of their online time with mobile devices versus forty-nine percent of their online time using desktops. Search engines such as Google have also increased the impetus for companies to have mobile-responsive websites. Websites that are deemed mobile unfriendly are forced lower in search rankings when the user is searching from a mobile device, downgrading your site's ability to get traffic through organic searches.

What should be on my website?

Good business websites run the gamut from simple landing pages with few features to vast sites with complex offerings, such as online shops and membership-only sections.

A website doesn't need to be complicated to be effective. The important thing is to understand what it is you want your website to do. Is it a place for you to simply display your basic business and contact information? Do you want it to be a portal for directly engaging or interacting with your market? Is it a storefront for your goods? A platform for you to provide free content such as articles or videos for people interested in your business? A good website is one that fulfills its purpose cleanly and elegantly, no matter how simple or complicated that purpose may be.

There are a few things that all business websites should communicate to their customers or stakeholders:

- *Value Proposition*—All websites should clearly and prominently state the business's value proposition—a description of what benefit the business gives its clients. The value propositions help orient website viewers to the purpose of your business, describe who you serve, and pique their interest about how your business can help them. An elevator pitch is an example of a value proposition (please refer to "What is an elevator pitch" earlier in this chapter for more information). You should state your value proposition prominently on the main page. It can be communicated in other ways as well, such as the website address you choose or the headers you use throughout the website.
- *"About" Page*—"About" pages describe the company and the people involved in it. It is one of the most frequently accessed sections of websites after the home page, and it plays a key role in establishing your credibility, ethos, and trustworthiness

with website visitors. This is where you can go into a fuller description of what your organization does, describe your values, give a compelling story about how and why you do what you do, and introduce visitors to the person or people behind the business. This humanizes the experience and makes visitors feel as though they are communicating with real people while building a feeling of trust in your business and your team.

- *Contact Information*—Contact information should appear in multiple areas of your website. It's good practice to place one piece of contact information—such as an email address—prominently in the header or the footer of each page and have a separate dedicated "Contact" page. On your contact page, you should provide several methods of contacting you. Always provide an email address, and consider giving a phone number as well. Contact forms can be convenient and can be kept on the contact page to minimize clutter on other pages. Other contact methods include physical location addresses, interactive maps, and social media handles (social media should be secondary to direct contact methods such as email and telephone).

What is discoverability?

A website's discoverability is its ability to be found online through search engines or other means. For a website to be of value as a communication tool, it needs to be discoverable by the people the business needs to reach. The discoverability needs of a website will depend on what type of audience the business is seeking. If the audience is limited to people an owner meets at networking events, then simply listing the website on a business card may be sufficient. If, on the other hand, the owner wants to draw in prospective clients from a broader audience, then online discoverability may need to be increased through search engine optimization, social media use, and backlinks.

Increasing the discoverability of a website can be a specialized and time-consuming activity, so carefully evaluate the breadth of audience you need to reach in order to determine how many resources you should devote to it.

Among the website pages that are must-haves is the Contact Us page.

What can help my website be discoverable?

Improving website traffic by increasing discoverability is a highly specialized subject beyond the scope of this book. It is, however, useful to know about some of the factors that affect it in order to decide whether to make website discoverability part of your business communication plan.

Discoverability is affected through a variety of means:

- *Metadata*—The hidden information on your website that tells search engines and other Internet crawlers what your website is about.
- *Keywords*—The words Internet users type into search boxes. Site crawlers search for keywords when matching websites with search results. Keywords can appear in a website's visible content as well as in its metadata.
- *Search Engine Optimization (SEO)*—Improving a website's unpaid ranking in search engine results. SEO involves determining the best strategic placement of keywords on your website to improve your search engine ranking. An SEO specialist compares the results of Internet searches using keywords relevant to your business, sees how highly ranked websites uses those words, then develops a strategy for integrating those words into your own site. SEO also involves increasing the likelihood that other pages will link to content on your page. This may be done by actively soliciting other websites to link to yours or by increasing the amount of "shareable" content—such as blog posts—on your site. Because online search trends and behaviors change quickly, SEO needs to be updated on a frequent basis, and the cost effectiveness of SEO is being increasingly debated.
- *Original content*—Frequently updating original content, often in the form of blog posts or short videos, increases discoverability by keeping a website refreshed and increasing its keyword use.
- *Paid advertising*—Search engines, social media, and some websites offer paid advertising services that increase your website's visibility. Paid advertising through search engines will put your website at prominent parts of search engine results pages, such as at the tops of lists or in sidebars. Social media sites integrate paid advertising with other content so it is visible to users. Websites may feature "sponsored content," which links to a paying client's website, or simply display advertisements on their pages.

How should my website be organized?

Website content should be organized in a way that makes it easy and intuitive for users to navigate. Usually, business websites begin with a description of what it is they do and who they help (the Home page), then progress to a brief history or description of the company and people behind the business (the About page). Next, a means of contacting the business is provided (the Contact page). Additional information, such as resources, a blog, a portfolio, or additional pages breaking down the business's offerings or activities usually appear in a navigation menu between the About page and the Contact page.

What is content?

Content is the intellectual and creative work presented on a website to catch and keep a visitor's attention. It is information that's of use or interest to your audience, like demonstrations, opinion articles, research, tips, images, graphics, recipes, art, personal

> ### What parts of website design should I be concerned about?
>
> Visiting your website should be a pleasant and easy experience. Visual communication aspects such as page dimensions, font types and sizes, color schemes, use of images, and navigation menus can help or hinder someone's ability to engage with your content. Creating a well-designed website can be complicated. Many website-hosting services and creation tools offer templates that make it easier for people to create attractive, serviceable websites. Depending on your needs, however, it may be worth hiring a professional website designer or developer to help you with this intricate process.

stories, advice, and more. Content can be delivered either through text (such as articles and blog posts) or through multimedia content (images, infographics, podcasts, and videos).

Free content such as blog posts and articles is frequently offered to visitors. This gives you the opportunity to establish your credibility by communicating your expertise, interests, and personality in a format that is interesting and helpful. Many businesses choose to have paid content, euphemistically called "premium content," available to those willing to pay for access. An excellent example of premium content models are online newspaper websites such as the *New York Times*, which allows free access to a limited number of articles and charges a subscription fee for unlimited access to the rest of its content.

What is content marketing?

Content marketing is a strategy where businesses use content such as blogs, articles, videos, and other resources to communicate with their audience. Their aim is to build trusting relationships with existing and prospective customers by regularly providing information that is interesting, valuable, or useful. To be effective, content marketing must be predictable, reliable, and of reasonable quality. New content should be published on a regular schedule and distributed through whatever means the business's audience is likely to engage with. Many businesses distribute their content in several ways, such as publishing it on their blogs, sending out newsletters to people subscribed to their email list, and promoting the new content through their social media channels.

Due to the sheer volume of information flowing through people's email in-boxes and social media feeds, updates should be relatively frequent if they are to be noticed. Daily, weekly, and biweekly updates are popular publication schedules, but most important is that the content is updated predictably. Sticking to a schedule shows reliability and investment in your followers. It builds trust among your audience and demonstrates your active interest in bringing them new information relevant to their interests.

What is copy?

Copy is the text or multimedia used on your website to tell visitors who you are, what you do, and how they can purchase your goods or services. Much of your persuasive communication and selling will be done through copy. If content is used to get visitors interested in your business and convince them of your competence, copy is used to get them to buy. Contrary to frequently updated content like blog posts, copy is more static in nature and only changes when there is a change in the offering—such as a promotional campaign—or a change in the business's desired audience. Copy contains clear references to value propositions, as well as descriptions of offerings and prices. A crucial component to copy is an explicit Call-to-Action such as a "Buy Now" button that links to a shopping cart or statements like "Call us today for your free consultation."

Do I need to have a blog?

You may have experienced some pressure to start a blog to help promote your business. If you enjoy writing or recording videos, have lots of ideas to share, and like the idea of regularly sending your audience updates, then a blog could be a good choice. However, there are many reasons to keep your website blog free. Blogs require considerable time and diligent attention to be useful. Infrequent or unpredictable posting can erode the audience's interest and trust rather than build it by communicating the blog author's lack of interest in keeping it up-to-date. Many blog authors hire ghostwriters to create new content for them, just to keep up with demand and expectations. If you find writing to be an onerous chore, don't have the resources to hire a freelance writer, or don't believe your audience would respond well enough to make it worthwhile, then you may want to avoid adding a blog to your website.

Alternative ways to provide useful information to prospective clients without being tied to a frequent blog publication schedule is to create a section on your website with links to content you produce on occasion, like white papers, video recordings of presentations, occasional articles, or bibliographies of books that may be of interest to your target market. You might also want to consider alternative blogging formats, such as vlogging, podcasting, or microblogging on social media sites like Pinterest or Instagram. For more information on vlogging, podcasts, and microblogging, refer to "A Brief History of Communication" in the section "How the Internet Changed Everything."

Does my business need to have a social media presence?

Many businesses large and small have social media as a core part of their communication plan. Your decision to do so will be based on several pieces of information. First, you need to know what you want your business or organization to get out of social media engagement. Do you want to attract new clients? Create a positive public image for your company? Gain media attention? Build a community? Share information? Recruit? Based on these answers, you will need to see if there is a social media platform that is well suited to your goals and that has sufficient traction in the online world to make the effort worthwhile.

You also need some idea of the information-seeking practices and Internet behaviors of your audience or target market. Does your key market embrace social media? What platforms do they tend to favor? How do they use those platforms? These questions will give you vital information about whether the people you most want to reach are likely to engage with content such as yours through social media.

These days, yes, your business should have a presence on at least a few of the popular social media sites and apps.

Just because one type of audience might not be the right fit for a social media communication strategy doesn't mean that social media isn't of benefit to your company. It's possible that a different stakeholder or audience type will take well to connecting with you through social media. A baked goods company, for example, might not benefit from using social media to reach out to potential distributors, but the company could use it to build awareness and goodwill among end customers in its markets.

How often do I need to update my social media content?

Like blogs, social media profiles need to be maintained, usually with a high frequency of activity. A corporate social media account must also engage directly with its audience; otherwise, the company will seem uninterested in building relationships with the people following it. The frequency of updates will depend on the social media platforms. Posts in Twitter only last a short time before they appear too far down a user's feed to be noticed. Businesses successfully using Twitter usually post multiple times per day. Facebook posts have a bit more staying power, but daily activity is recommended. Posts and articles shared through LinkedIn Pulse or through LinkedIn groups have a much longer life span and can be found by users for several days or even weeks. Should you decide to use social media as part of your business communication strategy, be prepared to spend the resources necessary to keep your profiles active, up-to-date, and engaged with your followers; otherwise there will be little payoff.

What do different social media platforms do for business communication?

Different social media platforms offer very different user experiences and target different types of visitors. Over the past few years, the following social media platforms have proven particularly useful for businesses:

- Facebook: Businesses seeking to build communities where clients, prospective clients, and stakeholders can gather together in a common space should consider Facebook. Facebook groups allow people to create discussions, share information, and connect in a focused community space. An organization with a Facebook profile can create a group for prospective and current customers to join. Group members and company staff alike can "meet" in a dedicated area where they can chat about something they share in common—their interest in your company. If you establish a Facebook group for your business, make sure you have a regular presence and interact frequently with the group members.

Engagement and interaction on Facebook is best done in a casual, friendly tone. Facebook has an extremely wide audience demographic, ranging from young teenagers to senior citizens.

- Twitter: Twitter's short, 140-character limit for posts makes it an excellent platform to send breezy, sound bite-style updates to your market. It may be used to develop your organization's online "personality" by sharing interesting information, linking to other resources, and providing chatty, conversational updates. Through strategic use of hashtags and growing your network by following others, you can make their offerings visible to a very wide audience. This platform is excellent for sharing other people's content to your followers and for promoting your own content to your audience. Interactions on Twitter are rapid and pithy, often having the feel of a back-and-forth conversation. Posts on Twitter have a very short shelf life, often only being useful for about thirty minutes after they have been posted. For Twitter to be effective for your business, use a social media scheduling software or service to post tweets several times a day. Twitter is particularly popular among college-educated adults under fifty.
- LinkedIn: LinkedIn is billed as a professional, work-and-business-oriented social media network. It is popular among recruiters, organizations, and individuals wanting to build their career. Many LinkedIn members use it primarily as a sort of online resume, but it can also be used to create groups and communities and as a publishing platform through Pulse (used for text-based content) and SlideShare (used for content presented in a slideshow style). LinkedIn's primary user base is adults between thirty and sixty-four, college graduates, and those earning high, middle-class incomes and above.
- Instagram: A social media platform dedicated to sharing photos, Instagram can allow businesses to showcase images of their products, their people, and their activities. While posting images of products is an obvious way to use this platform, the visual medium is a great way to communicate corporate culture by featuring images of employees, company celebrations, charitable activities, customers, and more. Instagram's user base is mostly made up of American teenagers, although it is gaining popularity among adults as well.
- Pinterest: Pinterest is a social bookmarking and curation platform. On it, people share links to content they like, which is accompanied by an image fetched from the website. Users may promote content from their own website. This platform is ideal for artists, crafters, and lifestyle- and food-related businesses. While Pinterest is

centered around images, much like Instagram, its outbound linking function makes it a good discovery tool. Women are the dominant users on this platform.

Pinterest is a social bookmarking site great for sharing favorite Web content with friends and business contacts.

How many social media platforms should I use for my business?

Not all platforms are suitable for all organizations, and without significant human resources, it would be difficult to maintain a presence on a large number of platforms. Also, not all platforms appeal to all users. A good practice if you are part of a small organization is to go for social media platforms that you genuinely enjoy using yourself, and see if that platform also fits your organization's personality and culture. Investigate other popular platforms that appeal to your target demographic, and after trying them out for a few months, stick with the top two or three performers in terms of audience engagement. Ultimately, don't spread yourself too thin. It's better to have good presence and engagement on just a couple of social media platforms than to be sporadically and shallowly active on several at once.

How can I write a good social media post?

A key to creating good social media posts for your business is to provide a variety of content for your followers. If your content is limited to updates on upcoming products, new projects, or business performance, it will seem dull and overly self-promotional, and people will quickly lose interest. It is definitely acceptable to post your organization's offerings and activities, but scatter these posts in with other content, such as links to interesting news stories or articles. Think of information or resources that can help your audience improve some little piece of their lives, and share that with them; it will help you build relationships with them and increase goodwill.

Posts should be easy and quick to consume. Some platforms restrict post length, like Twitter's 140-character limit. Others will allow you to create longer posts but will hide content exceeding a certain length, requiring the user to click to reveal the rest of the post. Try to keep the post within the limit that allows it to be fully displayed in the platform's feed. Embedding images into social media posts often results in more shares among users.

Social media is a great way for your organization to show its personality and demonstrate its culture and values. Consider creating posts about your organization's activities, staff parties, milestones, and charitable activities. You can also share customer testimonials, hints about new developments, and "behind-the-scenes" information. These glimpses into different aspects of your corporate culture will help humanize your business.

Certain post formats are easy to create, easy to share, and popular among social media users. Quotes, polls, funny photos or jokes, and quick tips perform well and are easy to produce. Watch for trending content, such as hot news topics or popular hashtags, and create content about those subjects.

What is a social media policy?

Social media policies are guidelines for the use of social media within an organization. These policies seek to protect the company by ensuring that social media activity is consistent with the organization's brand, good for its reputation, and reflects its values. Many organizations limit who is allowed to post on behalf of their company and have definitions of what information its employees can and can't share online. Policies can also establish style guidelines for social media posts that will give the business a clear and

My business is being trolled on social media! What should I do?

First, you need to determine whether your business is actually being trolled. Not all negative commentary on social media is trolling; complaints, challenges, and poor reviews may be justified (albeit unpleasant). You should respond to these individuals and help them to the best of your ability. Trolling, on the other hand, is repeated, malicious, and devoid of any interest in engaging with you or seeking for a solution to a problem.

In most cases, the best way for businesses to deal with a social media troll is to offer a neutral, formal reply inviting the person to contact you with his or her complaint. If the trolling continues, don't try to engage directly with the negative person; acknowledgment fuels trolling behavior. When an Internet troll doesn't receive a response from the person he or she is attacking, he or she usually turns his or her attention elsewhere. This strategy may take time, and you might have to deal with repeated attacks, but it's often very effective.

You may choose to document the trolling with screenshots. If the trolling is severe and gaining momentum or undue attention, screenshots can help in case future legal action is necessary. Some may feel compelled to release a statement addressing the issue. This should be a last resort as it might encourage more social media abuse. If your organization has a social media policy or communications department, consult with it before deciding on a response. Depending on the size and nature of your organization, you may wish to consult with your legal department or lawyers before issuing any statements or engaging with the social media abuser. Any threats should be reported to the police.

consistent online "voice." This helps reinforce brand identity while building trust with its audience. Such guidelines can also help businesses have strategies for dealing with unwanted social media behaviors or attacks from outside individuals, such as trolling.

IN-PERSON PRESENTATIONS

What different kinds of business presentations are there?

Most business presentations are either informative or persuasive in nature. Informative presentations provide the audience with information necessary for decision-making or strategizing or for accountability and transparency purposes. Reports, briefings, analyses, professional development sessions, and seminars are usually informative presentations.

Persuasive presentations are intended to sway people to a particular course of action or to sell products and services to existing or prospective clients. Product launches and reveals, sales presentations, and demonstrations are examples of persuasive presentations. Many informative presentations have persuasive elements in them. A report may include a section where the presenter gives recommendations; in a presentation like this, much of the informative content will be written and organized with the intent to persuade the audience toward the recommended course of action.

While the majority of business presentations fall into the two categories above, there are many more types of presentations. For a more thorough investigation into other forms of presentations, refer to the "Speeches and Presentations" chapter.

How do I know what to focus on in my presentation?

In business presentations, you must focus on what is most important to the audience's decision-making process. Determine what your goal and purpose are in delivering the presentation, what needs and context your audience has, and what actions they might be taking that are related to the topic of your presentation. Based off this information, figure out what piece of information you have that will most influence any actions or decisions your audience will take after your presentation. Remember that you must focus your content on the information that your *audience* will find most useful, as opposed to what *you* may think is most useful or interesting.

What sort of tone is appropriate for business presentations?

The tone of a business presentation is affected by the nature of the presentation as well as the audience's notion of proper corporate culture. All presenters should demonstrate interest and engagement in what they're saying. Presentations that address accomplishments, milestones, or lighthearted news can have a more buoyant, celebratory, and casual tone. Sales presentations benefit from an additional boost of energy. Presentations that address more serious or critical topics should have a sober, straightforward tone—

one that does not attempt to sugarcoat bad news but that is still respectful to the realities of the situation at hand.

Audiences coming from nontraditional organizations with an informal corporate culture often favor presentations that are themselves more relaxed, more casual, and possibly more energetic and emotional in nature. Audiences from traditional businesses, on the other hand, usually prefer a more formal tone and controlled manner of delivery. If you are giving a presentation to people from outside your organization, investigate their corporate culture—it may be very different from your own, and you need to be able to adjust the tone of your presentation to meet their values and expectations.

Should I use personal stories in business presentations?

As in any presentation, personal stories can add wonderfully persuasive and engaging elements to a talk. Business presentations can be greatly enhanced by personal stories, provided the stories are relevant to the topic at hand. Only use stories that directly explain or complement the material within your presentation; it's better to leave out stories than to tell ones that are only peripherally relevant. When using personal stories in business presentations, be sure that you are not violating any confidentiality or nondisclosure agreements. Identities of individuals or companies should not be revealed unless the story is flattering for them. It is usually inadvisable to tell stories that directly slam competitors. If your stories involve members of your competition, don't identify them, and keep the focus of the story on positive aspects of your company rather than on negative aspects of other businesses.

I don't have the authority to change the presentation slide deck, but I don't like or use all the slides. How can I work around this?

Many organizations create approved presentations and slide decks, and presenters don't always have the authorization to change the content of their presentations. It is, how-

How should I present complicated data?

Presentations are ideal for providing simplified interpretations of complicated data. A common error in business presentations is to project dense, illegible charts and graphs on a slideshow while the presenter describes every data point being displayed. This practice tends to overwhelm the audience, leaving them unable to make sense of what it is they are seeing and hearing. Instead of giving a blow-by-blow account, use your knowledge to extract the most important points and interpret their meaning for your audience. Any charts or graphs displayed should be drastically simplified, containing only a few data points that summarize overall trends. A full account of the data can be provided to your audience as a handout or a document in a meeting package.

ever, possible for a presenter to draw attention toward the parts they find most useful or relevant and brush past the bits they don't think are necessary. When you are scheduled to give a "canned" (premade and approved) corporate presentation, spend time reviewing the content and figuring out what you think should be emphasized. Practice your delivery so that you are comfortable and familiar with emphasizing the items you identified as most important. This practice will also help you figure out your own style of delivering the content and let you take some ownership over the presentation.

Simply skipping past slides with no explanation as to what they are will distract your audience; they'll be left wondering what was on those slides and why you didn't show them. Instead, check with your supervisor to see if you are allowed to blank out slides you don't feel are necessary. Presentation software like PowerPoint allows people to "hide" slides so that they don't appear when giving a presentation. Many companies will allow presenters to hide slides as it doesn't change the slide deck itself.

If you aren't allowed to hide slides, develop very brief verbal summaries of the unnecessary slides—fifteen seconds or less—and move through them quickly when delivering the presentation. This will satisfy the audience's curiosity about the content of the slides while keeping the time spent on them to a minimum. Be sure you practice delivering these summaries and skimming through the unwanted slides. This part of the presentation should be as carefully crafted and practiced as the rest of the talk if you want to integrate it seamlessly.

I'm giving a presentation created by someone else. How can I make my delivery seem natural?

Presentations are often prepared by someone other than the presenter. The presentation may have been created for you by an assistant, or it may be a canned talk created for use by several presenters. If the presentation is being created for you, be involved in the creation process. Be sure the person drafting the presentation understands your own goals and what you think is more important to communicate. Review the drafts, and be sure to practice the content several times before delivering it.

If you are giving a canned presentation and have no input in content creation, you can still add your own touch. Review the presentation, and see what original information or interpretations you might add into your talk to increase its value. Remember that you bring your own knowledge and expertise to this presentation. Even when the material is created in advance, there are unique pieces of insight you can provide to your audience. Add interpretations or analogies that are helpful to your audience or that liven up the prewritten material. Tell stories relevant to the material to connect with the audience and add depth to the content. This will help you personally engage with the material while inserting your own style and context. Practice the presentation several times so that you are deeply familiar with the content and aren't reliant on someone else's speaker notes or script. These steps will help you give a presentation that sounds and feels natural to you as well as your audience.

I need to create a presentation for my manager to deliver. How can I make it easy for them to give the presentation?

Involve your manager as much as possible in the presentation-development process. At minimum, get their input on what the key message of the presentation must be, along with a selection of points they want to discuss. Keep the presentation narrow, focused, and clearly organized so that the presenter can easily see the logic and flow of the content. The same follows for speaker notes; create notes that are as brief as possible so that the presenter can see at a glance what part of the presentation he or she is at and what is coming up. Stick with large fonts and short bullet points rather than writing a full script. Highly detailed scripts are tiring to read, difficult to deliver, and can create problems if the presenter loses his or her place in the script.

Encourage your manager to review the material as often as possible. You can do this by seeking approval for several drafts and revisions, asking for input and ideas for slideshow design (if a slideshow is being used), and requesting approval of the final speaker notes. Practice is a critical component to presentation success but is often neglected—especially by busy managers and executives. If your manager is willing to practice, schedule specific times for he or she to do so and protect that time from interruption. If the manager is not interested or willing to put in any practice time, request that he or she run through the presentation with you so that you can listen for any errors or awkward moments.

Should I spend time in my presentation going over the materials already distributed in the meeting package?

Meeting packages are intended to communicate information that participants need to know prior to the meeting itself. Reviewing material during the meeting in order to bring those who didn't read it up to speed defeats the purpose of distributing it in advance, wastes time, and annoys those who did review it. A better option is to include information about how the meeting package materials are relevant and necessary to discuss. This gives the attendees more motivation and urgency to review them. You may want to send out reminders to review the package close to the meeting date although excessive nagging should be avoided, no matter how tempting it may be.

Should I stand or sit during my presentation?

The size and tone of the meeting will indicate whether it is best to sit or stand. With very small groups, anywhere from three to five people, sitting is usually preferable to standing. Standing in front of a small group can seem overbearing, especially when the meeting is among colleagues who know each other well. Small meetings (around eight people) usually benefit from the more intimate, conversational feel of a sit-down presentation. Midsized meetings are more flexible; in groups of ten to twenty, you can still be easily seen and heard if you present sitting down, but standing up will

When deciding whether to sit or stand, consider the size of the audience. Usually, it is fine to sit in the more intimate setting of a small group, but you should stand for a larger audience.

give you greater presence and help the attendees focus on you. You should always stand when speaking to groups larger than twenty people; this will make you visible to everyone in the room and help you be heard more clearly. Standing during a presentation is useful in groups of any size when energy is flagging and attendees need a boost.

How do I use good body language if I'm sitting during my presentation?

Body language is just as important when presenting while sitting as while standing. Use good sitting posture with your feet placed evenly on the floor and your torso held straight, engaged, and proud. Do not slouch back in your chair. Good abdominal engagement even while sitting will give you better vocal tone and energy throughout your presentation.

Use as much space as is available to you when gesturing; using lots of physical space for body language is a sign of power, openness, and confidence. Gestures need to happen where people can see them. Keep your movements between the tabletop and your chin, and keep your hands visible even when you are not speaking or moving around. If you are able to gesture to the sides, go as far out with your arms as you are able without invading the space of the person sitting next to you.

PHONE AND VOICE-ONLY PRESENTATIONS

What is a webinar?

Webinars are real-time online meetings held over an Internet software application. These meetings may be for discussions, demonstrations, presentations, professional development, or any other purpose that could warrant an in-person meeting. The webinar host chooses the software to be used, and attendees log in to the webinar site at the scheduled meeting time. Popular webinar and videoconferencing tools are GoToWebinar, EasyWebinar, Google Hangouts, Skype for Business, and Instant Teleseminar.

Webinars are conducted with an audio connection that allows attendees to speak with one another. This connection may be through the Internet, via a teleconference dial-in number, or both. Many webinars also have a visual component, such as a webcam video of the person speaking or a slideshow for the attendees.

Interactivity plays an important part in webinars. Attendees are often muted by the host during a webinar presentation to prevent any interruptions, but other methods of interacting or communicating with the host are possible. Chat boxes allow attendees to send text comments or questions to the host. Individual attendees may be unmuted by the host, allowing them to speak directly with the host or presenter. Functions like a "Raise Hand" button lets participants indicate to the host that they have a question or comment. Many webinar programs have polling or survey functions. Some applications have chat rooms where attendees can interact with one another.

What is a teleconference?

Teleconferences are meetings held over telephone conference lines. Teleconferences are organized by the designated host through a teleconferencing service. Multiple participants in different locations dial in to the teleconference. The host can mute and unmute attendees to prevent interruptions or to control the flow of discussion. Many webinars combine Internet audio connections and teleconference connections to give participants access to different audio connections.

What equipment do people need in order to host or participate in a webinar or teleconference?

Teleconference requirements are fairly straightforward. As teleconferences take place through phone connections, participants will need access to a phone or to a compatible VoIP (Internet phone) service. The host will need access to a teleconference service to host the meeting or event. Speakerphones may be desirable if multiple people from one location are participating.

The technology and equipment requirements for webinars are higher than teleconferences. Both webinar hosts and attendees need a computer, a reliable Internet connection, and a browser that is compatible with the webinar software. The host needs webinar software from which to run the meeting. Attendees can usually access the webinar through a free download or web application. Both the host and attendees will need functioning speakers, though the host may offer a teleconference connection for attendees who don't have good audio on their computers. The host and presenter will need a microphone, as will any attendees who may want to speak during the webinar (a teleconference connection can take the place of a computer microphone).

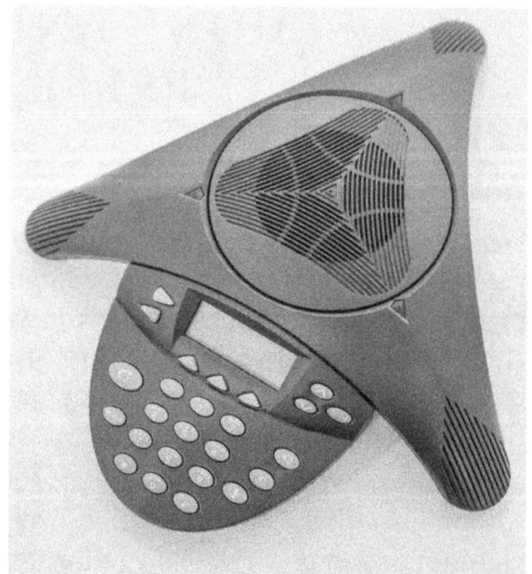

IP phones like this one use the Internet instead of the public switched telephone network; they are ideal for teleconferencing.

How is presenting through a teleconference or webinar different from presenting in person?

Audio-only presentations have some key differences from in-person presentations. The lack of a visual connection has some advantages—it is easier for the presenter to refer to his or her notes or even to read from a script if necessary. Anxious speakers may find it less intimidating to present knowing that people aren't looking directly at them. That lack of visibility also creates some problems. The absence of body language makes listening to a lengthy presentation more tiring. Even when the presenter is visible to the attendees through a webcam connection, body language is not as visible as it would normally be. As the speaker can't see nonverbal communication from the audience, it is more difficult to detect and respond to shifts in listeners' attention or mood.

Webinar and teleconferencing technology can be temperamental. Software compatibility issues happen frequently. Changes in the Internet connection of the host or attendees can result in lags or in loss of connection. Teleconference phone lines may get overloaded, and phone receivers don't always properly pick up voices, especially if more than one person tries to speak at once. Audio quality on both webinars and teleconferences can be distorted. Video and webcam broadcasts can significantly strain the bandwidth needed for a proper broadcast, creating further lags or distortion.

How can I improve the clarity of my speech when presenting through a webinar or teleconference?

Presenters should speak more slowly and with greater enunciation to compensate for technology issues and lack of body language. A speech rate of 151 to 165 words per minute is usually slow enough to improve clarity without irritating attendees. For more information and guidance on rate of speech, refer to "The Human Voice" chapter.

How important is vocal variety when giving a voice-only presentation?

Vocal variety and expressiveness are extremely important in voice-only presentations as the audience doesn't have body language or gesture to help them understand you. Expressiveness and variety not only help hold people's attention and make the presentation more interesting, they convey meaning and subtext while increasing the clarity of your message. Lack of tone and emphasis can result in people paying attention to the wrong things, misinterpreting your meaning, or even completely misunderstanding what you are saying.

When giving a voice-only presentation, increase the amount of vocal variety you normally use. Sit up straight and use plenty of facial expressions and gestures when you speak. This will help guide your voice and increase vocal expressiveness.

How can I check to see if my audience understands what I'm saying?

Because you can't rely on body language from your audience for clues to their comprehension (or lack thereof), you will need to ask them directly. Asking for verbal input or running a poll through webinar software are excellent methods of checking for understanding. Avoid simply asking if people understand you as many will reply "yes" just to be agreeable. Instead, ask the audience at regular intervals if they have any questions or if there is something they would like to revisit. Ask them questions that require thoughtful answers, or run a poll through the webinar software to gather people's opinions. The way people answer your questions or polls will give you a good idea of whether or not they are picking up on what you're saying.

How long should a voice-only presentation be?

Listening to voice-only presentations can be tiring, especially when the talk involves a lot of technical data or reporting. Audience attention flags more quickly than with in-person presentations, and it is easier for people to become distracted by other things like side conversations or mobile devices. In order to take these factors into account, voice-only presentations should be as brief as is reasonable, involving frequent check-backs with the audience and interactive components. Business presentations such as reports should be ten minutes or less, while professional development and other educational presentations may be up to an hour in length.

Avoid speaking without interruption or some form of interactivity for any longer than ten minutes at a time. You can also schedule in mini-breaks to allow people to stand up and refocus; this strategy works well with presentations that are an hour or more with two-minute mini-breaks happening every half hour to forty-five minutes.

How should I manage questions from the audience during a voice-only presentation?

Decide in advance of your presentation whether you want to hold off taking questions until the end of your presentation or whether you will address them during the presentation itself. Questions from the audience can be moderated by someone other than the presenter or saved for a specific time during the presentation. If you are using webinar software and want to allow people to ask questions during the presentation, have someone else act as moderator and keep an eye out for questions from attendees. It is next to impossible for presenters to give an effective talk and moderate questions over chat at the same time. Attendees can send questions to your moderator using the webinar tool's chat or Q&A text boxes, and the moderator can signal that there is a question or ask the question on the other person's behalf.

If you are using a teleconference or would rather questions be held to the end, inform the audience and then open the floor to questions afterward. If you are using webinar software, have attendees raise their hands or send their questions to the moderator so you don't get multiple people trying to speak through the audio lines at the same time.

During the presentation, always keep the attendees muted. It is highly disruptive to have someone try to cut in over a phone or Internet audio line, and it can cause problems with audio quality. To prevent this from happening, webinar and teleconference tools have the option to put attendees on mute or in "listen only" mode. This disables their microphone unless the organizer or host unmutes them. Choose in advance whether you want people to ask questions by unmuting them and allowing them to speak or by typing their questions into the webinar's chat or Q&A boxes.

ACCEPTANCE SPEECHES AND ADDRESSES

I am a member of a professional association and am accepting a personal award. What should I say in my acceptance speech?

Award and recognition ceremonies help associations reinforce group identity by acknowledging people who demonstrate their common values. As the recipient of the award, you are, in essence, a chosen representative of the best aspects of everyone in the room. Acceptance speeches are epideictic speeches (also known as ceremonial or demonstrative speeches), intended to praise a person or group of people.

The goal of your acceptance speech is to praise the association by reflecting a positive image of the group and its members back to them. Your speech should refer to shared values, what it means to belong to the association, and the work the association does. Express gratitude for being part of the group, and make a statement as to what it means to be a member of the association. Proper etiquette requires you to thank key supporters and mentors; do so, but keep it brief. A sample outline for a personal acceptance speech is as follows:

1. Statement about how you felt upon joining the association/profession.
2. Describe values and work done by the association.

3. Describe what it means to you personally to be a member of the association/profession.
4. Thank supporters, mentors, and association.
5. Conclusion—call to members to further the association's mission or uphold its values.

I am accepting an award on behalf of my organization. What should I say?

When accepting an award on behalf of an organization, you are again giving an epideictic speech. In this case, however, the focus of the praise is the organization receiving the award and the people within it. These speeches are an excellent opportunity to recognize your team and organization's corporate culture, along with how that culture reflects the values of the association granting the award. A sample outline is:

Fashion designer Marc Jacobs is shown here accepting an award in 2010. An important part of acceptance speeches is acknowledging those who helped you and reaffirming the values of the award-granting organization.

1. Statement about the values and mission of the association granting the award.
2. Describe the values and mission of your own organization.
3. Describe how employees or members of your organization uphold those values.
4. Describe some specific accomplishments of your team.
5. Conclusion—state how future activities of your organization will continue to uphold your own values as well as those of the association granting the award.

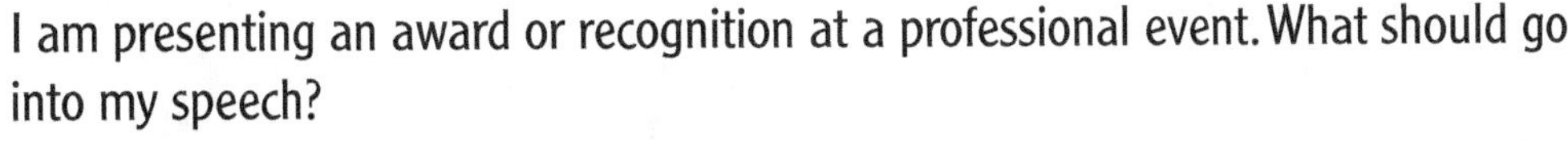

I am presenting an award or recognition at a professional event. What should go into my speech?

The presenter of an award is responsible for giving the audience important context about the award and the recipient. Although a presentation speech is usually shorter than an acceptance speech, there is a lot of ground to cover in terms of describing the award, the recipient, and the reasons for giving it to him or her. In order to cover these items while still keeping the speech short, try to describe the strengths and admirable qualities of the recipient as briefly and precisely as possible. A sample outline for an award or recognition presentation speech is:

1. Describe the mission and values of the organization or association granting the award.
2. Describe the purpose of the award itself and what achievements it recognizes.
3. Describe the person or organization receiving the award, and provide a brief background of their work and achievements.
4. Describe the characteristics of the award recipient and how he or she embodies the values represented by the award.
5. Congratulate the recipient and invite him or her to the stage to receive the award.

I'm giving a toast at a retirement celebration. What should I say?

Retirement and lifetime-achievement toasts allow companies to establish organizational legacy while building group identity. In these praise speeches, the focus is on the career of the retiree and how his or her work improved his or her current organization and the profession with whom he or she is associated. These speeches are personal, light in tone, and contain funny stories that most of the audience would be able to relate to. Light roasts of the retiree are common. A sample outline for a toast to a retiring colleague is:

1. State how you first met the retiree and what your impressions were.
2. Give a brief synopsis of the retiree's career. Spend the most time on parts of his or her history to which the majority of the party attendees would be able to relate. Include any funny stories or roasts here.
3. Describe any notable accomplishments.
4. Describe admirable personal qualities of the retiree, especially as a colleague or coworker.
5. Congratulate the retiree and state that he or she will be missed. Make the formal toast. If applicable, invite the retiree up to give a speech after the toast.

Retirement speeches should be light in tone, personal, and full of gratitude.

I have to make a speech at my retirement celebration. What should I say?

Your retirement celebration is a time to reflect on aspects of your career to which the audience can relate or aspire. This speech should inspire them to continue on with their work and seek to make meaningful contributions to their organization, profession, or society. The tone of this speech should be light, warm, and affectionate (even if you can't wait to empty out your desk and hightail it to a beach in the Bahamas). Funny, self-effacing stories are appropriate. Lightly roasting other attendees is acceptable, provided that the people being mentioned are of the same or higher seniority than you; it is impolite to pick on your juniors. A sample retirement speech outline is:

1. Reflect on how you entered your profession or line of work and your initial impressions.
2. Describe how you grew in your work and what your career taught you. Include any funny stories here.
3. Describe how your organization or profession will continue to grow. Provide advice and encouragement for younger audience members on how to grow in their own careers.
4. Thank your colleagues, your family, and any mentors for their support throughout your career.
5. Concluding remark (e.g.: a comment about going fishing or some other vacation-type hobby; offering a toast to those present for continuing your organization's good work).

I've been asked to introduce a speaker at a conference or event. What should I say?

A host or session convenor is responsible for giving the audience a brief description of the speaker, along with their background and any relevant credentials. You should explain how the speaker's topic is relevant to the work or interests of the attendees. While these introductions are short, they play a major role in establishing the speaker's credibility with the audience. A sample outline for a speaker introduction is:

1. State the topic of the session, talk, or keynote.
2. Explain how the topic is important to the attendees' current work, lives, or interests.
3. State the speaker's name, how long he or she has been working in his or her field of expertise, and any relevant credentials, significant accomplishments, or publications.
4. Invite the speaker to the front and lead the audience in a welcome applause.

My organization is hosting an event. Who should act as host or master of ceremonies?

A good master of ceremonies (MC) can ignite the audience's interest, engage their attention, and help keep the event program on track. As the MC may also need to provide on-the-spot announcements, whoever is acting as MC shouldn't have any additional duties during the event.

Large or complex events, or formal events like galas, opening receptions, and awards ceremonies, will benefit from the services of a professional MC. Professional MCs are skilled entertainers and will be able to make the event more engaging and memorable for the attendees. They are also accustomed to doing some crowd control, getting people's attention, and keeping the agenda on track.

If your event is running over the course of several days, such as a conference or retreat, you may want someone from within your organization to serve as MC for the majority of the event. This person should be relatively recognizable to the audience and have some authority within the organization. Executives and senior managers should not act as MC though they may give speeches, introductions, or present awards. Choose someone with an engaging personality who is comfortable speaking off-the-cuff and interacting with an audience. If someone like that isn't available in your company and you don't have the budget to bring in a professional, choose whoever is least likely to flee in terror when it is time to step up to the microphone.

I'm being interviewed about my business on local TV. How should I speak when I'm on the air?

Being interviewed on television can be both exciting and nerve-wracking. Advance preparation and practice go a long way to reduce nervousness and help you perform naturally and confidently. If possible, get a list of possible questions from the interviewer ahead of time so that you can prepare and practice your answers. If you aren't able to get any questions, draft questions they are likely to ask based on the purpose of the interview, any current affairs that might be relevant to your business, and questions that other people commonly ask you about your business or organization.

When on camera, be sure to speak to the interviewer and avoid looking at the camera, unless instructed otherwise. This can be hard to do as cameras are distracting. A useful trick to avoid getting distracted by cameras during an interview is to get a good, long look at them before filming begins. This will help acclimate you to the camera's presence and let you focus more easily on your interviewer.

Use plenty of relaxed gestures. Ask the camera operator how much of your body will be visible in the camera frame. Will they be showing your whole body, or will the frame be tighter, such as from your navel up or focused only on your head? This will let you know what kind of gestures will be visible to your audience. Sit or stand straight and proud to convey energy and confidence.

Be aware of how nervousness or anxiety affects your speech. Nervousness often causes people to speak more quickly or to mumble or trip over their words. Speak slowly and deliberately on camera, taking care to enunciate your words. Finish your thoughts, and speak in full sentences instead of trailing off. Avoid giving overly brief "yes"- and "no"-type answers; always elaborate and explain *why* your answer to a question is "yes" or "no."

Television professionals are used to dealing with nervous guests. They are there to help you come across in the best light possible and will help make you feel comfortable. If you have any questions for them prior to filming, don't hesitate to ask.

I'm going to be taking questions from the media. How can I prepare responses if I don't know what they're going to ask in advance?

Media questions don't come out of the blue. If you know that you will be taking questions from the media, spend some time drafting potential questions they could ask. These will likely involve current events that are directly related to your business. Think of why the media would be interested in your organization or in hearing from you. Make a list of questions that people are currently asking you about your business. Based off these, you will be able to anticipate questions with some accuracy.

Plan out what message you want to convey to the media and to your prospective audience. Instead of crafting highly scripted answers to specific questions, practice a variety of responses to themes or to broader issues. This will give you more mental flexibility during the actual media session. Prepare standard responses for questions that you can't or won't answer.

SOCIAL COMMUNICATION

WEDDING TOASTS AND OTHER COMMON SCENARIOS

When might I be expected to give a speech for social reasons?

Social speeches cover a variety of circumstances. Most commonly, speeches are given at social celebrations for major life milestones. Examples of traditional social speeches are a celebrant's speech at a bar or bat mitzvah, the "welcome to the family" speech from parents of a bride or groom, the best man's toast at a wedding, or a eulogy at a funeral or memorial service.

Are toasts or social speeches limited to formal events?

Occasions for informal, brief, or spontaneous speeches abound in social situations. Toasts are particularly well received, and celebrations and parties are often enhanced, when the host or person of honor gives a toast to their friends. Casual toasts don't need to be lengthy, preplanned, rehearsed, or even remotely formal. Once one person takes the lead and says a few words on the occasion, more are likely to join in and offer a few words of their own. If you want to take the plunge and offer a toast, simply make an observation about the occasion and the people gathered there, share a happy thought regarding your own feelings about the event, and invite people to raise their glasses. Job done.

Are there some general rules that should be followed when giving a toast or social speech?

The following guidelines will help make your social speech more successful and enjoyable:

- *Keep it short:* Go for quality of words rather than quantity. Most speeches and toasts should be under five minutes. Two minutes is an excellent average length for a toast or speech.
- *Don't read your speech:* Don't read from a page full of lengthy, full-sentence, script-like content. Using very brief, bullet-point-style speaker notes is acceptable. Practice your speech in advance so you are comfortable with your content.
- *Lead with a brief story:* A story related to the event or guest of honor will set the mood and context for the rest of your speech. The story should be short, and the point or punchline should be reached quickly.
- *Focus on the audience:* Social speeches are meant to create feelings of belonging. Talk to the audience about the audience. Use stories they can relate to and observations they can share with reasonable ease. Avoid making too many references to yourself.
- *Avoid inside jokes:* This is related to the above point of focusing on your audience. Inside jokes are shared by only a few people. The audience will feel left out if they aren't "in" on the joke.
- *Never use more than one famous quote:* Quotes, unless extremely suitable to the event, tend to be dull or awkward and often come across as a way of padding the speech.
- *Don't try too hard to be funny:* Humor often comes through better in wry observations or anecdotes than in canned or prepared jokes.
- *Keep humor or roasts tasteful:* Avoid jokes or stories that are raunchy, distasteful, or potentially hurtful. Any teasing of the guests of honor should be gentle and not smear their character or reputation.
- *Be true to your natural style:* If you are naturally gentle and soft-spoken, be gentle and soft-spoken. If you are down-to-earth with a folksy sense of humor, don't try to be overly formal or elegant. Audiences respond best to authenticity, and you will feel more comfortable and confident if you speak in your usual manner.

I'm giving a toast at a wedding—what should I say?

The content of wedding toasts depends on your role in the wedding. All speeches should express happiness at the occasion, an optimistic outlook for the new couple's future, and an observation about the couple or the event that everyone in the audience may share.

Parents of the bride or groom: You may wish to share a story about your child's youth that reveals a funny, likable, or admirable aspect of his or her character. Praise an aspect of your new son-in-law or daughter-in-law's character or personality. A blessing or expression of approval is customarily given though this can be discreetly skipped if it feels phony. Welcoming your child's new spouse to the family is an excellent way to close the speech.

The best man and maid of honor: You are typically called on to give the opening toasts during a wedding. Your toasts may be separate or combined into a single speech. Your goal is to bring together everyone with a sense of shared celebration. Your toast should be very light in tone and give the guests a feeling of ease and familiarity with one another. Stories you share should be easy for any guest to understand and should illustrate a positive or funny aspect of the bride or groom's character. Don't ramble on with stories about your misadventures that no one but the bride or groom can understand; these events may have been important in your friendship, but they exclude the rest of the guests. Praise or admiration should be expressed for a characteristic of each of the newlyweds. Observations on married life can be funny and teasing but never derogatory or crude.

When it comes to toasts at a wedding, that of the groom should be one of the shortest.

The newlyweds: Even though you are the focus of the celebration, your speech is usually the shortest. Welcome your guests and thank them for celebrating with you. You may share a story that illustrates your bond as a couple, your shared values, or a key moment in your relationship. Invite your guests to join you in your celebrations. You may offer a generic toast to your guests or to a suitable ideal like love, friendship, partnership, or families.

I'm giving a toast at a religious celebration—what should I say?

Many religions have important coming-of-age ceremonies or other spiritually significant celebrations. Speeches may be expected from the celebrant and from their mentors, parents, or other key figures. The topics of these toasts are usually joyful in nature but have greater gravitas or solemnity than in nonsecular events or weddings. When giving a toast or speech at religious celebrations, the focus of the speech is on the spiritual aspect of the occasion. Divine thanks or praise is given, and the spiritual importance of the event on daily life should be explained. Praise for the celebrant should tie one of their personality traits to the theme of the event. At a bar (bat) mitzvah or confirmation, for instance, the celebrant's wisdom or maturity may be commented on. Piety, humility, dedication to service, and generosity are other excellent character traits to praise in a religious context. Check with your religious leader or literature to see if there are any traditional phrases or statements that should be incorporated into your speech.

I'm giving a eulogy or memorial speech—what should I say?

Eulogies and memorial speeches are typically longer than many other social speeches. The focus is on the deceased. Your opening remarks should include a brief statement on how you knew the deceased so that guests may understand the context of your speech. Give any important facts about the person's life such as:

- Date and place of birth
- Names of parents and siblings
- Schooling and related achievements
- Names of spouse and children or other significant relationships
- Career or profession and any related achievements
- Interests, hobbies, and related achievements
- Significant historical events that affected their life
- Personal traits and quirks, such as likes and dislikes

Eulogies tend to be quite long because you are memorializing someone's entire life. It is a time to not only include biographical facts about someone but also meaningful, personal stories.

Some personal stories about the deceased should be shared. These should illustrate admirable or praiseworthy aspects of their personality, character, or life.

I'm hosting a party; how can I encourage guests to chat with one another?

Facilitating conversation and helping guests mingle is a more important job for the host than making sure the drink table is well stocked. You are, in effect, the party's communication facilitator. To encourage conversation among guests, be prepared to introduce people and start group conversations. In advance of the party, think of who is likely to get along with each other, what commonalities partygoers might share, and any topics or current events that are likely to spark conversation.

As people arrive, walk them over to guests you think they would get along with and either join in an existing conversation or casually start one about a subject of general interest. Ask everyone gathered plenty of open-ended questions in order to get the conversation going. As the conversation develops, you will be able to step away, greet other guests, and steer them toward interesting conversations.

Once people have arrived, it's good to encourage groups to break up and re-form so that partygoers interact with a variety of new people throughout the evening. If it seems like some conversations are winding down, feel free to politely interrupt and tell someone that you would like to introduce him or her to another person at the party. Make the introduction, briefly tell them why you wanted them to meet, and participate in the new conversation for a few minutes. Then, go to other people and make more introductions in a similar manner. Be ready with topics you can use to start conversations.

If you see someone not participating in any groups or conversations, take them under your wing and guide them to a group that may suit them. Join in the conversation and then insinuate the new person directly into the conversation by asking them questions about the topic. This will get the new person actively participating in the conversation without awkward silences or fear that they won't have anything to say. This strategy also works for blending two groups of people together into one larger conversation.

You will likely move rapidly from conversation to conversation, never really settling anywhere for more than five or ten minutes at a time. Don't be afraid to interrupt, join in, and leave conversations—doing this is important to your success in helping people meet and mingle.

How can I be a better conversationalist?

Being a good conversationalist is not about being the outgoing and witty center of attention. The true traits of strong conversationalists are openness, curiosity, and a keen interest in other people's views and experiences. People who excel at conversation have excellent listening skills. They ask questions more often than they give opinions. They take in what other people are telling them instead of trying to think of what they should say in response. They listen more than they speak.

In order to develop your conversation skills, look for learning opportunities around every corner. This will expand the topics you can discuss with others. Explore a variety of subjects through reading, social media, hobbies, and by talking to people. Ask yourself plenty of "why" questions so that you can foster curiosity about the world in general. Seek out other people's opinions and insights on a variety of matters. In particular, develop interest in other people's stories and contexts; this is what makes people's in-

I never know what to say to other people at social events. What should I do?

Conversations often fall flat after the standard ritual of sharing names and job titles. To avoid the inevitable awkward pause, spend time prior to the social event reading up on local affairs, current events, and lifestyle topics (these topics make for easy conversations). Pick some subjects you are interested in and that other people are likely to have an opinion about, such as the local restaurant scene, current diet or exercise trends, the latest political scandal, or vacation plans. Mention a topic, provide your own brief thought on the matter, then ask for the other person's opinion. As the other person speaks, listen for comments that you find interesting or for things you have in common. Ask follow-up questions about those comments, and let the conversation flow naturally from there.

sights unique. Being able to look at topics with other people's worldview in mind will make it easier to have interesting conversations about a variety of topics.

Finally, don't shy away from the opportunity to meet and talk to people. Like most skills, conversation becomes easier with practice. Speak to people in the checkout line, on public transportation, and at parties and meetings. These spontaneous conversations don't need to be deep, elaborate, or lengthy. Ask your waiter about his favorite item on the menu, then ask him why he likes that dish so much. Ask parents at your child's soccer game what they like to do on family vacations, then ask them what their dream vacation would be. Follow up questions with more questions, pay attention to others, and encourage them to speak. Eventually, you'll find that you become everybody's favorite person to talk to.

How can I start a conversation?

Conversations don't need to begin with a brilliant observation on a major social issue. Instead, go for the simple route of learning a bit about somebody or about what he or she thinks of a common interest. Begin with general observations, then move to more specific questions. The following table lays out some sample conversation scenarios, possible starter questions, and follow-up questions:

Scenario	Starter questions	Follow-up questions
Conference or convention	"What did you think of the keynote speaker?"	"What did you like/not like about XYZ?"
	"What sessions have you signed up for?"	"Why did those sessions catch your eye?"
Social celebration	"How do you know [guest of honor]?"	"Are you still involved in XYZ?"
	"What brought you here today?"	"Do you do that often?"
Generic group event (e.g.: hobby groups, classes, kids' sports activities)	"What keeps you busy these days?"	"What made you sign up for this?"
	"How did you get into that?"	"What about this do you most enjoy?"

How can I end a conversation?

All conversations must come to an end. The easiest way to end a conversation gracefully is to make an excuse as to why you have to leave, thank the person for the conversation, and—if suitable—wish him or her well with some future endeavor. Avoid hinting at the fact that you need to leave; being direct will result in better closure. Avoid any long-winded excuses for why you must go, and don't overdo any expressions of regret. Keep the parting short, simple, and positive.

Sample conversation enders:

- "Excuse me, I must run, but it's been great talking with you! Enjoy the concert next week!"

- "I need to say hello to this person before leaving. Great chatting with you! I hope your event goes smoothly!"
- "I have to go check on the (parking meter, kids, etc.). I'm glad we were able to catch up. Best of luck with that meeting!"

Not everyone will stop talking to you when you end a conversation, so you may need to repeat the fact that you have to go. Keep it simple, say goodbye, and offer a friendly wave as you walk away.

COMMUNICATING ACROSS CULTURES

How can I develop my cross-cultural communication skills?

Intercultural communication can be tricky. On the one hand, differences should be recognized and explored. This helps us develop better understanding of other worldviews, gives more context to what people say and do, and makes it easier to navigate difference in communication style. On the other hand, we want to avoid stereotyping, overgeneralizing, or assuming that we understand other people's cultural context.

Developing good cross-cultural communication skills means developing your ability to be inquisitive without judgment about cultural practices. Take note of behavioral customs, such as bowing instead of shaking hands or accepting something with two hands instead of one. Listen for repetitive expressions or turns of phrase that seem somewhat odd in your vernacular—these may be culturally specific expressions that the other person is translating directly. Use of names, who stands where, styles of dress, and other observable traits should be taken in with neutral objectivity. Don't make assumptions about why members of a group communicate or behave the way they do—just note that they do it differently from you. Encourage your own curiosity and knowledge by reading up on different cultures, and ask questions about another culture's communication norms and traditions.

Communicating with someone from a foreign culture can be a challenge. You can prevent embarrassing mistakes by avoiding stereotyping and making assumptions. Make an effort to learn about the other culture, too.

When engaging with someone from a different culture, avoid taking offense if they behave differently from you. You also shouldn't fret about drastically changing your behavior to match theirs. Adapting some general, broad behaviors to respect other people's level of comfort is a better strategy than trying to match their own cultural customs. For example, if someone appears uncomfortable with physical touch such as a handshake, greet them by nodding or giving a slight bow instead. This is respectful of someone's personal space whether the avoidance of touch is culturally driven or simply because they don't like shaking hands.

In culturally diverse groups, it might be necessary to mutually agree on definitions of terms, behaviors, and expectations. These can reduce friction and uncertainty between people in the group. Establishing communication protocols (such as everyone being on a first-name basis or using titles and last names like Mr. Smith) and behavioral expectations (such as bringing up problems freely instead of remaining politely silent) can make it easier for you and everyone else in the group to communicate clearly and smoothly.

I'm attending a wedding from a very different culture. How can I socialize without worrying about saying or doing something awkward?

Attending a wedding or social event from a different culture can be exciting, interesting, and intimidating. Realistically, holding conversations with people from different cultures is no different from having a conversation with anyone you just met. Take an interest in people around you. Talk about common subjects, such as the host who invited you, local events, upcoming vacations, and so forth. Feel free to ask those you have met about any customs or traditions you observed that day. Healthy curiosity is usually appreciated, and most people are keen to explain their cultural traditions. Don't shy away from taking part in some customs if it seems appropriate to do so. If everybody is getting up do a dance, join in, and don't worry about not knowing the steps. If everyone is presenting gifts to the guests of honor, bring yours up as well. If you aren't sure what to do, ask another guest for help—you will likely find yourself enthusiastically guided through the process.

Is it appropriate to ask people questions about their culture or cultural experience?

When asked with judgment-free curiosity, questions about culture and individual experiences are appropriate and usually welcome. Seeking to understand people encourages communication and builds relationships. To be sure that your curiosity is well-received make open-ended inquiries, and avoid leading questions. Don't make value judgments or criticize unfamiliar practices. Your goal is to learn about others, not to weigh them based on your opinion or beliefs. You'll learn more, encourage more sharing, and have a better experience with an open, observational approach.

How can I make myself more easily understood when talking with people who speak a different language?

When working around language barriers, slow down your speech considerably and dial up your enunciation. Use the sort of speed and pronunciation you would use with a young child; if your tone of voice is respectful and you use accurate vocabulary, you won't sound patronizing. Avoid using contractions, and stay away from slang and jargon altogether. Slang usually translates into nonsense, and jargon is confusing (even for native English speakers).

COMMUNICATING ACROSS GENERATIONS

Why can it be difficult to communicate with people of different generations?

Intergenerational communication can be very complicated. People's worldviews and personal contexts vary dramatically at different stages in life, even when they are members of the same family or work closely together. This can make it difficult to relate to the opinion or viewpoint of someone who is several years older or younger. There are also variations in status, responsibility, and authority between generations, even when no direct authority is acknowledged. This can create frustration when one or both parties feel they are not being spoken to with the respect or consideration they deserve.

Styles of communication can also complicate matters. Language and expression are as subject to changes in fashion as wardrobes. Vocabulary and word meaning are more

Children have short attention spans and a limited vocabulary, so you need to change your conversational style to communicate effectively with them.

changeable than might be expected. This is especially noticeable in slang terms and technological jargon in which words are invented and meanings morph over short periods of time. What is "sick" to a SoCal Millennial is not what is "sick" to her Boomer grandfather.

How can I help young children understand what I'm saying?

Short attention spans, limited vocabulary, and a tendency to take everything literally can make communicating frustrating for both you and children. Speak slowly and deliberately, giving them time to listen and understand. Use lots of color and variation in your voice; this helps kids interpret your meaning.

Keep sentences relatively short and uncomplicated. Watch out for confusing language like double negatives ("You don't want any more potatoes, do you?"), indirect commands ("Can you take off your shoes, please?"), and nonliteral expressions such as irony, sarcasm, or hyperbole. Be prepared to repeat yourself several times in succession. If you give a command, threaten a punishment, or make a promise, be sure to follow through with it. This teaches children that communication has meaning, value, and consequence.

How can I improve the way I communicate with teenagers?

Teenagers are negotiating a tricky phase of communication development. The straightforward, childlike literal mind is no longer there, but the regions of the brain governing logical and rational thought aren't fully developed. They are sensitive to truth and fairness (even when they are practicing neither). Authenticity is important when communicating with a teen.

The combination of seeking independence and fear of judgment can lead teens to be silent rather than forthcoming. When teens are talking to you, avoid interrupting or making judgmental remarks—let them tell their side of a story. Use specific, open-ended questions to stimulate or deepen conversation. Open communication and independent thought can both be encouraged by allowing teens to talk through problems and find their own conclusions instead of bombarding them with advice. Rather than providing solutions, simply ask how you can help. This will strike a balance between the parental support they need and the autonomy they crave.

Take an interest in current pop culture and technology trends. These are common sources of new vocabulary, slang, and expressions. By keeping on top of them, you'll be fostering shared interests with your teen and actively learning the current teen culture lingo. You don't have to speak like your sixteen-year-old, but understanding what he or she is saying will drastically improve your ability to communicate with him or her.

What issues should I consider when communicating with seniors?

Sensory changes that come with age, such as hearing and vision loss, can make it more difficult for seniors to understand quiet or fast speech. Cognitive changes are also a normal part of aging that can affect communication, particularly if memory and reasoning are affected. The Public Health Agency of Canada notes that "in general, sharp brains tend to stay sharp; cognitive processing may take a little longer, but this is normal aging, not a sign of 'senility.'" Emotional changes may also affect communication. Feelings of insecurity, loneliness, or loss of independence can make anyone anxious or short-tempered, regardless of age. Many seniors face these challenges, and they should be kept in mind if your interaction feels strained.

How can I communicate more clearly with seniors?

When speaking with seniors, watch for signs that they are having difficulty understanding or hearing you. These may include vague answers, nonresponses such as nodding instead of replying, and responses that are out of context or unsuitable to the conversation.

Speak slowly at a suitable volume. As hearing loss tends to be more pronounced at higher pitches, women and youths may find it helpful to consciously lower their vocal pitch. Be sure your lips are clearly visible; many people make up for loss of hearing by lip-reading. Rephrase overly long or complex sentences, and break them down into smaller, clearer chunks. Don't confuse speaking clearly with "dumbing down" your language; you may need to speak more slowly, but that doesn't mean you need to use overly simplified words and expressions.

Respectful communication is very important. Many seniors are treated as though they are infirm or invisible—this is never appropriate. Talk to them in the same way you wish to be spoken to. Make eye contact and speak directly to the senior, even if he or she has an assistant or caregiver present. Find out how seniors want to be addressed; some people wish to be called Mr./Mrs./Ms. Last Name, while others prefer first names. Address them by name so they know you are speaking with them and not with their assistant or caregiver.

How do I know if I'm "talking down" to someone of a different generation?

It's possible to inadvertently "talk down" to someone of a different generation without realizing it. Seniors and young children receive this treatment more frequently than other age groups. When talking to people of different generations (or anyone else, for that matter), be aware of the following behaviors and correct or eliminate them:

- Speaking about someone as though they aren't in the room or are unable to answer
- Directing questions about someone's preferences to their companion, assistant, or caregiver
- Needlessly simplifying your language or providing unnecessary explanations
- Using condescending or sing-song vocal mannerisms
- Interrupting or finishing the other person's sentences

If you catch yourself doing any of these, simply take note of it and carry on the conversation while making a conscious effort to change your manners. Communication habits can be hard to break, but with practice, you will become adept at communicating with greater awareness and respect.

NEGOTIATING WITH AND PERSUADING FAMILY AND FRIENDS

What is the difference between a disagreement and a conflict?

According to communication scholars Mark Knapp, Linda Putnam, and Lillian Davis, interpersonal conflict can be described as something that arises from "incompatibilities or opposition in goals or activities [between] two or more interdependent parties." Disagreements, on the other hand, don't always affect an end goal or a shared activity and usually represent lesser differences in viewpoint or opinion. It's possible to have a disagreement without being in conflict with someone.

Is it possible to be in conflict without fighting?

Conflict is a natural part of relationships and doesn't have to culminate in a fight. While hostile conflict usually results in fighting, friendly conflict can lead to improved relationships and creative problem solving. The following steps can help keep a conflict friendly and bring about a positive resolution:

- Acknowledge that a conflict exists and agree on what it's about
- Commit to positive, respectful communication
- Explore one another's points of view
- Work together to find win-win solutions

How do we communicate when we're in conflict with family or friends?

When we're in conflict, we tend to fall into certain manners of communication. Different people will favor either cooperative communication, competitive communication, or avoidance. Depending on the conflict at hand, we will use different styles or combinations of styles to handle the situation.

Cooperative communicators look for ways they can collaborate with or help the person with whom they are in conflict. They are often interested in "making things better" and are more interested in finding a solution than in winning a dispute. Cooperators can sometimes be pushy in their efforts and may not always take the other person's needs or contexts into consideration when looking for solutions. It is also possible for unassertive cooperators to become doormats, willing to sacrifice their interests far more than they should in their hunt for a solution. Cooperation is sometimes avoidance in disguise.

Competitive communicators like to win an argument. For some, the game of arguing their case is enjoyable. They argue without malice and with willingness to accept

Are there ways I can speak to help me keep calm when I'm in conflict with a friend or family member?

Using neutral, objective language and eliminating personal pronouns such as "I" and "you" can help stop emotions from running too hot. These strategies depersonalize the conversations, letting you focus on the issues at hand rather than on personal slights or hurt feelings. This manner of speaking also helps you avoid attacking or blaming other people, which helps them remain calm as well.

An important thing to remember when communicating while in conflict is that you can only take responsibility for your own behavior. You can't "make" someone be calm, see things a certain way, or look for common ground. If the other party continues to be combative or unreasonable despite repeated and realistic attempts to foster positive communication, you may need to accept that progress might be impossible and cut your losses. Some people are simply incapable or unwilling to take a positive approach to conflict management.

alternative solutions or outcomes. For others, winning is important to their sense of power, confidence, or security. In this case, the competitive person might be more interested in victory than in finding a reasonable solution. This focus can lead to unfair fighting, unnecessary or harmful stubbornness, and damaged relationships.

Avoiders prefer not to deal with conflict directly. Avoidance can be carried by agreeing with whatever the other person says, by not bringing up the conflict or problem, by changing topics whenever the conflict arises, or by putting off dealing with the conflict outright.

How can I communicate productively when in conflict with a young child?

Children are impulsive and live in the moment. They are interested in their own comfort and have difficulty seeing things from other people's perspectives. It can be difficult for young children to express their emotions, and "big feelings" can quickly overwhelm their communication abilities. Acknowledge their feelings of hurt, anger, or frustration, and describe those feelings back to them. This not only gives young children the words they need to tell others how they feel, but it shows that you are listening to them.

Try to understand what is really upsetting them. Avoid using sarcasm or teasing them, no matter how tempting it may be. Kids take things literally and will only become more upset at your provocation. Try using their natural curiosity about the world to distract them from the problem and find a solution. If necessary, use time-outs or other forms of household discipline as a consequence for any rule breaking. After the conflict is over and your child has calmed down, talk to him or her about it. Discuss how the conflict started, why it went the way it did, and what the outcome was.

If the child is in the middle of a full-on tantrum, take him or her to a quiet place and let the tantrum run its course. He or she isn't able to listen, take instruction, or think reasonably when in so much emotional upheaval. Give him or her the space and security necessary to calm down and talk to him or her about the conflict afterward.

How can I communicate productively when in conflict with a teenager?

Remember that even though they may display the bravado and stubbornness of a Hollywood diva, teenagers still need your help managing conflict. Try to find out as much as you can from them about their point of view and feelings on the matter that's causing conflict. Put yourself in their shoes, and make an effort to understand their view. Realize that they are in the process of forming identities, values, and beliefs separate from your own; don't assume that you know their mind or that your views and values are more important than theirs.

Exercise significantly more self-restraint than your teen; you are still the adult in this situation. Your teen is still relying on your ability to manage your emotions and possibly even help him or her manage *his or her own* emotions. This may be difficult in the face of a raging, insolent storm, but it's important for successful communication.

Teens are sensitive to insult; while they may hurl sarcastic comments at you, using sarcasm with them will only escalate tension. Acknowledge their feelings, and avoid invalidating them by saying they shouldn't feel a certain way. Ask open-ended questions about their opinions and desires. Regardless of what you think about their answers,

Communicating with teens takes more work than with children. You really need to try to understand their point of view and their personal struggles.

don't downplay or mock them. This will shut down their willingness to communicate with you, especially if they think they're being laughed at.

Give teens the time and privacy necessary to cool down. They will be more willing to open up if they don't feel as though they're being badgered or bullied into talking. While you may need to be the one to bring up the conflict for discussion when teens start talking, give them your undivided attention. Don't interrupt, and don't immediately jump in with value judgments or advice. Often, the catharsis of simply talking about a problem can go a long way for helping both teen and parent to overcome it.

(If conflict turns to aggression or violence, contact the National Domestic Violence Hotline at 1-800-799-7233 or visit their website at www.thehotline.org.)

Why should I communicate assertively?

Assertive communication helps you increase your clarity of communication while standing up for your own rights and interests. Assertiveness is an important part of healthy communication. It helps lower your levels of stress, increase your confidence, improve relationships with others, and earn respect. It also is a very honest, forthright way of communicating.

Passive communication, such as giving in, always agreeing with others, or undermining your own thoughts and opinions can create resentment and dissatisfaction in relationships. Aggressive communication can lead to bullying and damaged relationships. Assertiveness, on the other hand, helps people understand one another better. You are more likely to find win-win solutions to problems and encourage more open and respectful communication from others.

How can I be assertive without being rude or aggressive?

Assertive communication is neither rude nor aggressive. Rudeness and aggression ignore other people's needs and feelings, relying on intimidation and brow-beating to achieve the desired ends. Assertiveness, on the other hand, is very respectful. It is considerate of other opinions, views, and needs and seeks to build relationships rather than gain control. To communicate assertively without crossing the line into aggression or rudeness, try the following:

- *Treat others with respect:* Politeness goes hand in hand with firmness.
- *Clearly understand your goal or desired outcome:* You can't stick up for what you want unless you know what you want.
- *Learn about the other person's wants and needs:* Knowing their context helps you find solutions without sacrificing your interests.
- *Don't give unnecessary apologies:* These can appear submissive or insincere and may decrease your confidence.
- *Say yes only if you genuinely agree or want to do something:* Sacrificing your interests or opinions for the sake of agreeableness not only lowers confidence but is dishonest as well.

- *Say "no" directly and firmly:* Don't provide unnecessary excuses. If you don't agree with someone or don't want to do something, say "no" with polite firmness and leave it at that. If you must give a reason, keep it short and simple.

What strategies can we use to persuade family or friends?

Many different persuasive strategies exist. The three most effective persuasive strategies concentrate on knowing the best *appeal*—appeal to logic (logos), appeal to character or reputation (ethos), and appeal to emotion (pathos). To learn more about logos, ethos, and pathos as well as other persuasive techniques, refer to the chapter "Rhetoric."

To ensure your persuasive efforts are ethical and effective, always be honest about your intent and your goals. Take an objective look at the other person's needs and wants, and consider whether or not the thing you want to persuade him or her of is truly to his or her benefit.

What persuasive tactics should be avoided?

There are several persuasive strategies that we use with family and friends that may be convenient and effective but are often neither sensible nor ethical:

- *Deception:* Deception is sometimes light and harmless, such as convincing your toddler to eat his or her carrots by telling him or her it will make his or her eyes glow in the dark. However, it also involves overblown or hyperbolic promises, such as persuading friends to join a network marketing scheme by promising them easy income. At its worst, deception involves outright fraud or harmful intent, such as persuading someone to sign over his or her financial control by saying he or she is signing a document for a different purpose.
- *Coercion:* This strategy persuades through the use of force or threats. Low-level coercion could be threatening to send your child to his or her room if he or she doesn't apologize for hitting his or her sibling. It could also be refusing to go to someone's wedding unless you are seated at a table on the other side of the room from your nemesis. Coercion can rise in severity to physical and emotional harm.
- *Manipulation:* Manipulative persuasion is using artful, unfair, or insidious strategies to get others to do what you want. Emotional manipulation tactics can include playing the victim, guilt-tripping, and throwing tantrums. Political manipulation includes the classic childhood strategy of seeking permission from one parent before asking the other parent ("Mom, can I ride my bike on the garage roof? Dad said it's okay!") or getting the more powerful member of the group to argue your case for you. Manipulation often incorporates elements of deceit and coercion.

All three of these persuasive strategies have dark sides and in some instances may indicate an abusive situation. If you believe you or someone else is at risk, contact the National Domestic Violence Hotline at 1-800-799-7233 or visit their website at www.thehotline.org.

What's the difference between persuading and negotiating?

Persuasion involves bringing someone around to your way of thinking or convincing him or her to take a specific action. Negotiating means coming to an agreement with someone else about a solution or course of action that both parties must take.

Persuasion tends to be more one-sided than negotiation; there is a persuad*er* and a persuad*ed*, and the persuader is not offering to change his or her own position or interests. Negotiation goes two ways; both parties need to come together to find an agreement, and the negotiation process will involve concession or shifting of demands on both sides.

When might I have to persuade on behalf of family members?

Caregivers often need to advocate or persuade others on behalf of the family member for whom they are caring. The persuasion might be related to courses of medical treatment, legal matters, or family decisions associated with care or estate planning. If you find yourself in this situation, be sure that you have any information or documents necessary to help you speak clearly and truthfully about the interests and wishes of the family member in question. Information may include living wills, estate information, existing agreements, records of informal agreements, and anything else that may help you build and defend your arguments.

What are some good negotiation practices to use with family or friends?

Negotiating with family and friends is extremely similar to negotiating in business and at work. The language may be more informal and the interests more personal, but the principles of win-win negotiating, respectful communication, framing, and so on still apply. For a discussion on principles and strategies of negotiation, refer to the "Business Communication" chapter and review the "Negotiation" section.

ACADEMIC COMMUNICATION

STYLE AND CONVENTIONS

What manner of writing or speaking should I use in my academic writing and presentations?

Style and manner of expression in academic work vary considerably depending on the faculty, specialty, and academic discipline. In general, an academic style of writing and speaking is more formal, precise, and complex than what is used in everyday work and life. This is especially true for written academic work, which is even more formal than spoken presentations.

Contractions like "won't" or "don't," as well as abbreviations like "TV" and short forms like "the 'net," are avoided in favor of complete words ("will not," "do not," "television," "the Internet"). The correct technical or specialist language for the discipline must be used and colloquial expressions or slang avoided. Language should be nondiscriminatory and as gender-neutral as possible.

"Hedging" language frequently appears in academic communication, particularly when conclusions are being drawn and opinions offered. Expressions like "it appears that," "in some situations," and words such as "many," "some," "generally," "broadly," "may," and "suggest" let the writer or speaker avoid making overly definitive statements. This leaves room for error, disagreement, or outliers. Passive voice is frequently used as a means to hedge statements and distance the author or speaker from research results.

The sciences and technology-driven faculties typically favor highly objective, neutral language. They are driven by quantitative data and statistics that are plainly and thoroughly presented. Many students and professors in these disciplines favor a brief, staccato-like communication style. Personal pronouns are not used, and sentences are structured to avoid the impression that personal opinion or bias is muddying any data or conclusions.

Social sciences and the arts and humanities usually incorporate more storytelling and narrative techniques into their writing and presentations. As qualitative research appears more frequently in these disciplines, the context provided through narrative and storytelling can be important to the clarity of their work. Quantitative research is also used in some studies; in these cases, more formal and distant expressions may appear. Due to the hybrid nature of work in social studies, arts, and humanities disciplines, communication styles may vary more than in the hard sciences.

Individual faculties will also have their own unique communication style. This will depend on the communication preferences of high-ranking faculty members and influencers, as well as the communication fashions and trends of that discipline at that time. Take your communication style cues from other people in your specific faculty and department. If a formal approach is favored, use formal expressions. If informal or narrative communication is more in vogue, brush up on your storytelling.

How do plain language and simple style fit into academic communication?

The dense, formal nature of academic communication means that plain language is extremely important. Unnecessary qualifiers, vague expressions, and poorly constructed sentences can further confound already complex communication. A clean and simple style is best, and the language should be adapted to the audience. Precise, technical terms are necessary when addressing other academics and specialists in your disciplines. When addressing a lay audience, the use of more accessible terms along with analogies and allegories will help create clear understanding.

What sort of language and style should I use when applying for grants?

Grants are critical sources of funding for many academics, and the conventions of language and style will vary between granting agencies. The style should be tailored to the people who are evaluating the grant. Some grants are evaluated and awarded using a judging panel made up entirely of academics. In this situation, a formal academic style with the appropriate technical language should be used. A granting agency, however, might include "learned laymen" in the decision-making process. Learned laymen are people from outside academia who still have specialized knowledge and insight into the disciplines the grant is targeting. Check the grant application requirements and find out who is sitting on the jury. If learned laymen are involved, keep the language at a level that is accessible to someone outside your field.

What is the difference between academic CVs and regular professional résumés?

The length and scope of an academic CV (*curriculum vitae*) is significantly broader than regular résumés. Academic CVs include extensive information about applicant's research activities, teaching assignments, grants and awards they have received, projects they've undertaken, committees they sit on, and a list of their publications and conference talks. While standard résumés often run between two and four pages, academic CVs may easily exceed ten pages in length.

How does the presentation of quantitative vs. qualitative research differ?

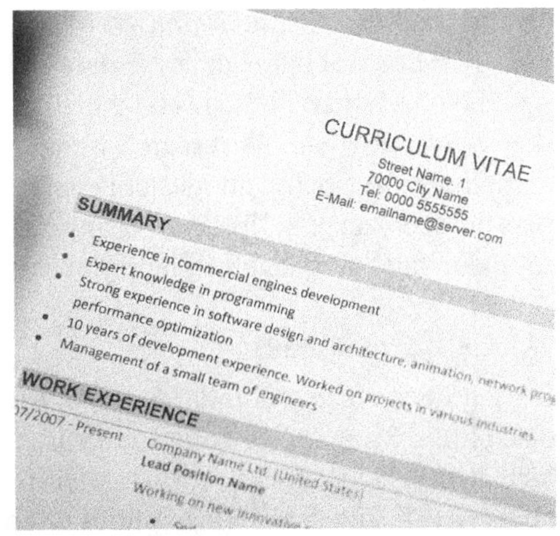

A CV or *curriculum vitae* is more detailed than typical work résumés and include such items as research and teaching assignments.

Quantitative research analyzes measurable phenomena. Data is collected using statistical techniques, and the information is analyzed with a view to find patterns and repeated processes. Quantitative research seeks to describe things that occur within large groups and general populations. Presentation of findings in statistical terms is required, and the statistical significance (or insignificance) of the findings is discussed. The research is presented in a straightforward, numbers-driven manner and does not present the opinions of the researchers.

Qualitative research involves deep, systematic investigation and exploration into aspects of human experience. It investigates reasons behind complex individual and social behavior and problems. Data is gathered through methods that provide flexibility within a specific structure. Data-collection methods include surveys, focus groups, interviews, embedded research, and observations. Qualitative research presentation is descriptive and often includes excerpts from interviews, focus groups, and other primary sources. Conclusions and findings demonstrate the researcher's explorations and analyses, and they create an understanding of an individual or group's context. Storytelling and skilled narrative can play a significant role in the researcher's ability to present his or her findings.

How can people within a multidisciplinary faculty work with the different communication styles present in different disciplines?

Communication is a challenge faced by students and academics in interdisciplinary departments. Traditions, fashions, and conventions in research, presentation, and communication can be so different that it may seem as though people from different disciplines are speaking completely different languages. Institutional barriers may also exist as cliquishness and insular behavior are not uncommon among people within their own specialty. Some may feel that their identity as a subject specialist and researcher is threatened by expectations to accommodate the academic traditions of other disciplines. This can lead to misunderstandings, disagreements, and even dismissal of the importance or validity of other people's work.

Overcoming communication issues in an interdisciplinary department is not much different from overcoming any other cross-cultural communication issue. Take an active interest in your colleagues and their work. Don't assume that the traditions of your discipline produce superior research—rather, be curious about different methods and approaches. Learn about people's research processes, the time it takes them to generate findings, how and where those findings are being used, and what developments or achievement they've recently had. As research processes and time frames vary considerably between disciplines, developing an idea of people's differences can reduce feelings of competitiveness or "scorekeeping" in terms of any one faculty member's output. Using common, easy-to-understand language will help you share your work more easily and enjoyably.

What are style guides?

Style guides outline standards for written communication within different academic disciplines. They create consistency in communication by laying out specific rules for formatting, structure, citations, references, and bibliographies. There are a variety of styles in use, and certain disciplines often follow one specific style. Check with your department, advisor, professor, or journal editor to learn which style you must follow in your own work.

What are the main style guides currently in use?

There are many style guides in use. Several disciplines have their own unique style guides. Some common style guides in use in different academic disciplines are:

- *Arts, humanities, and social sciences:* Modern Language Association (MLA) Style, American Psychological Association (APA) Style, Chicago/Turabian (Chicago) Manual of Style
- *Medicine and health-related disciplines:* American Medical Association (AMA) Manual of Style, Vancouver Style
- *Law:* The Bluebook Uniform System of Citation
- *Sciences:* American Chemical Society (ACS) Style, Institute of Electrical and Electronic Engineers (IEEE) Style, American Institute of Physics (AIP) style

The rules set out by style guides are extensive. Fortunately, there are plenty of easy-to-find online resources to help navigate them. You may also consult your postsecondary or academic library for assistance.

INSTRUCTIONAL PRESENTATION SKILLS

What role do public speaking skills play in effective instruction?

While developing performance and public speaking techniques may not be seen as an important part of academic work, it is critical to a person's ability to instruct. If someone can't present well, they won't get their message across. If they don't get their message across, learning will not take place. Lousy public speakers usually make lousy lecturers who hide behind their notes and bore students with long-winded monologues and brutally dense slideshows. Strong public speaking skills not only help make a lecture more effective and enjoyable for the students but for the instructor as well.

Academic instructors often give multiple lectures a day; proper speaking technique will help reduce vocal strain and physical fatigue. Having a firm grasp in the differences between spoken communication and written communication can help you choose the most effective words and expressions. Knowledge of speech structure and organization will let you create lectures that are easier to deliver, easier to follow, and more memorable. Finally, developing your public speaking skills will increase your confidence as a lecturer, reducing stress and pre-lecture anxiety.

For guidance on developing your public speaking skills, refer to the chapters on public speaking.

How much time should I reserve for questions and learning activities?

The best classes incorporate lecture with learning activities and discussion. Speakers often assume that at least twenty-five percent of their presentation time will be used for questions. If you are incorporating longer learning activities into your lecture, such as small group discussion and sharing, you may want to budget half your presentation time to the lecture and half your time to the learning activity, subsequent discussion, and questions. Assume that learning activities and discussions will take longer than anticipated.

How can I fit everything in the syllabus into my lectures?

Once you have factored in time to let the students settle in and account for questions and learning activities, the amount of time available in each class to actually instruct can seem extremely limited. For most syllabi, it would be impossible for you to cover everything the student needs to learn during class.

Of course, you will want to allow students to ask questions, which is an effective teaching tool. Allow for about twenty-five percent of class time for questions.

Experienced lecturers and staff developers Sally Brown and Phil Race recommend using lectures to only address the most important or complex parts of the syllabus in a series of "spotlights." Instructors can use part of their lectures to "include carefully formulated *briefings* about what [the students] are required to do under their own steam, which sources to select from, and (above all) how to check their learnings...." This model requires students to take responsibility for their own self-guided learning within certain areas of the syllabus. You facilitate this process by making it clear what they are expected to undertake on their own and how that fits into the larger course. It will be up to you to determine what content warrants valuable lecture time and what can be left for the students to work through on their own.

What sort of language style should I use when instructing?

Listening to lectures is hard work. A huge amount of information is being transmitted in a short space of time. The students are also taking in additional information conveyed through nonverbal means. They're often dealing with distractions from classmates, from laptops, and from mobile devices. The logical flow of information frequently gets interrupted by questions, comments, and discussions, and it can be difficult to get back on track afterward. On top of this, they are likely taking notes, simultaneously listening, paraphrasing, and transcribing what you are saying. Your goal is to make it as easy as possible for the students to listen to and understand you.

To do this, keep your language informal, simple, and clear. It's difficult and tiring to listen to some speak as though they're reciting from an academic journal. While you still need to be precise and technically sound, you should speak with a much more relaxed style than you would use when writing. Make use of analogies and metaphors to explain concepts. Tell stories and use plenty of vocal variation to help people pay attention. If you find yourself falling into expert-speak, using plenty of ten-syllable words and obscure jargon (you'll be able to tell thanks to the glazed expressions your students will take on), make a concentrated effort to speak more plainly. This doesn't dumb down your content; in fact, it will likely help the students extract *more* meaning from your words than they would have otherwise.

What visual style should I use for my slides?

Visual styles in slideshows can vary between faculties as much as language style and jargon. Slideshow trends among general audiences, arts, humanities, and social sciences are favoring bold images, strong, infographic-style visuals, and very limited text. This reflects their use of storytelling and narrative, which works particularly well in spoken presentations. Some science and technology disciplines are moving in this direction as well, especially when giving lectures for lay audiences or as keynote addresses.

High-level research presentations given in more traditional faculties often feature text-heavy slides with dense, complex charts and graphs. The effectiveness of these slides is highly debatable—the text, data, and graphs are often too small to be easily read. However, some still believe that this is a more professional look and better reflects the nature of academic research.

Ultimately, you should follow the conventions of your own faculty or department. If there is strong preference toward one style (image-heavy vs. text-heavy), go with the preferred type. If there seems to be no preference one way or another, an image-heavy style with limited text is strongly recommended.

How can I increase student engagement in my lectures?

Developing lectures with active engagement periods, such as learning activities and open discussion, gives students the opportunity to be involved in the material. Learning activities and discussion can take place in very large classes by having people break into groups to complete an activity and then reporting back. Mobile polling apps and "clicker" technology can allow for polls and surveys to be conducted during class.

In smaller classes and seminars, activities and discussions can involve the class as a whole. Some instructors enjoy dialectic styles of instruction where conversation and dialogue is as important to the learning process as lecture. In dialectic instruction, engagement from students is required.

In both large and small classes, think of creative ways to involve students in the learning and instruction process. Consider holding panel discussions with students as panelists. Organize debates. Develop unique group presentation assignments. Go to your colleagues for ideas. Take risks and experiment with different types of activities. Sometimes activities that seem silly or juvenile on the surface can result in a deep learning experience. Not every activity will be a winner, but you will find some that work especially well and are worth making a regular part of your courses.

Online discussion forums and social media groups provide further opportunity for engagement. Discussion, sharing, and collaboration can take place through means such as social media groups, learning management systems, and other mediated online spaces. You will need to be active in these online platforms if you expect students to engage. Students want and expect you to weigh in on at least some of their conversations. They will lose their enthusiasm for online discussion if you are never present; lack of activity on your part is easily interpreted as your lack of interest in the students. With your encouragement and participation, however, online collaborative spaces can be wonderful places for students and instructors to engage in dynamic, open conversation.

What are some tools I can use to enhance my lectures?

Lectures can be enhanced in a number of ways:

- *Slideshows:* Nearly everyone uses slideshows. Don't overlook them simply because they are a standard feature of instruction; slideshows are powerful enhancement tools. Learn the principles of good slide design, and take the time to dig into your slideshow software of choice. Create interesting, beautiful slideshows that complement what you're saying.
- *Online multimedia:* Websites such as YouTube make it easy to find relevant media to play during a lecture. Switching from lecturing to showing media helps refocus and reenergize the students, even if the media clip is only a few seconds long.
- *Classroom response systems:* These allow for real-time polling of students during the lecture. Students can answer multiple-choice questions and provide immediate feedback, which is then displayed to the class. These may be stand-alone technologies such as apps that are run through smartphones.

What are some tools I can use to encourage communication with and between students outside of the classroom?

Most institutions use learning management systems (LMS) to create virtual classrooms where students and instructors can engage in discussions as well as share, access, and submit course materials. In addition to an LMS, you may consider harnessing social media to further encourage nonclassroom communication. Facebook, Pinterest, YouTube, Vimeo, and other social media sites can act as collaborative online spaces.

- *Props:* Old-school props can make a big impact. Creative lecturers will use anything from costumes to toys to balls of string in order to make a point clearer and more memorable.

CONFERENCES, JOURNALS, BLOGS, ETC.

How long are most presentations at academic conferences?

Academic conference presentations can be anywhere from ten minutes to over an hour in length. Short talks are common as many presentations have multiple presenters or are done in a panel-discussion format. Even in hour-long, single-presenter sessions, the actual time the presenter has to talk about his or her findings and conclusions can be extremely short because of the need to describe research aims, methods, and other details along with reserving time for questions from the audience. Keynote speeches, featured talks, and plenary talks are typically forty-five to sixty minutes long.

Which conferences should I speak at?

There is no shortage of academic conferences at which to speak. When looking for speaking opportunities, start first with conferences specific to your discipline or subject expertise, then branch out to disciplines that are closely related to yours or to people who may have an interest in your research. Consider speaking at conferences outside academia as well. Industry, sector-specific, and special-interest conferences both large and small offer plenty of speaking opportunities for academics who are able to translate their work for a lay audience. Speaker events for general audiences can be a fun, gratifying way to reach out even further to people who would never otherwise know of your work. These may include events such as TEDx, PechaKucha, and Nerd Nite (for more information, please refer to the "Contemporary Public Speaking" chapter's section on major speaking organizations and events).

How do I figure out to which journals to submit my articles?

There are a staggering number of academic journals to which you could submit your articles. In order to figure out which ones might be a good match for your work, speak with colleagues from your faculty or discipline to find out where other people have published. Consider submitting your work to interdisciplinary journals or publications in different fields from your own, provided your content is related to their interests. Contact your institution's library and seek the librarians' help. Academic librarians work deeply with journals and databases, and they have significant knowledge about current publications' scope, prestige, and rank. Some major journal database companies, such as Elsevier, offer tools and services that can help match the content of your article or abstract with suitable journals.

Obviously, any academic will want to speak at conferences focusing on their field of study, but you should also consider conferences with business or political applications, if possible.

What is more important—writing journal articles or authoring books?

Both are very valuable to any academic. Science, technology, engineering, and medicine disciplines tend to place more emphasis on original articles and papers published in academic journals, but books also form an important part of their publication activities. Book publishing has special value in the humanities, arts, and social sciences because their length allows for stronger storytelling and better description of qualitative research and context.

What are original papers?

Original papers, also called original articles, describe the findings of original research. Publishing original papers tends to be more beneficial to an academic's publishing portfolio than review articles and book reviews.

What does "publish or perish" mean?

"Publish or perish" is a term used to describe the significant pressure placed on academics to publish their work in academic journals, books, and other peer-reviewed venues. The "perish" aspect comes from the threat—either real or perceived—that academics could lose their job or not advance in their career if they don't meet the publication demands of their faculty or institution.

The "publish or perish" practice has come under fire for creating unfair expectations and suppressing slower, more innovative research in favor of churning out articles for publication. A recent study by Jacob Foster, Andrey Rzhetsky, and James Evans, which analyzed thousands of biomedical abstracts in prestigious journals, indicated that the benefits of publishing novel, original research failed to outweigh the risks of not publishing frequently enough. This led academics to produce a greater number of lower-quality articles for publication. Despite dissatisfaction with "publish or perish," the implications that publishing has for both an academic's career and his or her faculty and institution's reputation makes it unlikely that the pressure will be lifted any time soon.

What do I need to be aware of when communicating my work to mainstream media?

Mainstream media is an excellent opportunity for you to distribute your work to a broad lay audience, including potential funders, donors, and political figures. It's important, however, to understand that mainstream media have their own agendas, interests, styles, and goals for spreading your story. Often, the goals are related to getting as many people as possible to look at the article, sometimes by sacrificing quality of content or faithfulness in reporting your work.

When working with mainstream media, be ready to explain your work and findings in extremely simple, attention-grabbing terms. You want to be able to excite a lay audience with a headline and distill complex research into a three-minute interview. Reporters are looking for sound bites that are easy to remember, easy to repeat, and easy to sell. If you don't provide those sound bites, the reporter might make some up, and there is no guarantee he or she will relay your words or work properly. Many academics have been frustrated by blatant misrepresentations of their research, conclusions, and insights for the sake of a catchy headline.

To limit misrepresentations, errors, or hyperbolic statements about your research, favor clarity and simplicity over depth and complexity. Be very concise in any explanations or statements you give and very clear on the implications of your findings and your conclusions. Think about how your work excites you and how you would talk about it to a savvy teen in order to excite him or her as well. That is the level and style of communication you want when dealing with mainstream media.

What factors can affect what research an academic or university communicates with the general public?

Only a fraction of the work produced at academic institutions is released to lay audiences. Many stories and reports are released to the public based on the amount of interest a story may have among a broad lay audience as well as the significance of the findings.

Bureaucratic and political realities also affect decisions regarding what stories and findings get communicated to the public. Political pressures from university administration may favor the communication of one research program over another. Funding demands may influence communication choices with certain findings being promoted

> ### What is a public information officer?
>
> Public information officers (PIOs) help arrange and coordinate external communication efforts for organizations and institutions. Academic institutions employ PIOs to help their faculty and researchers deal with media, reporters, and external stakeholders. PIOs help to spread and market research not only to the general public but also to governmental agencies, politicians, prospective funders, commercial and industrial entities, and more. Many researchers and academics work with PIOs to gain media attention and improve the visibility of their work with different lay audiences.

or suppressed in order to appease funding agencies. Academic communication can also be affected by the agendas of governments at the state or national level as administrators attempt to curry favor from the sitting government.

Certain fields have more restrictive practices than others when communicating research. Restrictions might be due to factors like the health, safety, or privacy implications of the findings. Science communication expert Dennis Meredith notes that the "Health Insurance Portability and Accountability Act severely restricts public disclosure of information about patients." Topics or practices that may raise the ire of special interest groups, such as animal rights activists, could face communication restrictions to protect the safety of the researchers and their projects.

How can I leverage social media to spread my research?

Social media is a popular way for people to discover news on academic research. Maintaining an active social media presence can help you grow and develop your audience. To properly leverage social media, first establish some type of website where you can share long-form articles with a lay audience. This may be a blog, a website, or a suitable social media space like a LinkedIn profile. Next, investigate several social media platforms and determine which ones are likely to attract your ideal audience and be fun for you to use. Stick to two or three social media platforms at the most, and become familiar with their tools, capabilities, and how people interact on them. Search for people you know on those platforms and connect with them so that you start building a following. Learn how to use hashtags to make your social media posts more searchable, then start posting! You'll need to post frequently to build an audience, but eventually your posts will gain traction, and you will attract more followers. Be sure to reply to people's comments on your posts and engage your followers in conversation.

Using social media to build an audience and spread your research can be extremely time consuming. There are many services that can take care of your social media posting and activity for you for a fee. If you feel that social media is an important part of your dissemination strategy, the cost may be worth the saved time and aggravation. An online search for "social media management," "social media marketing," or "social media services" will present you with a number of options to investigate.

APPENDIX 1: RHETORIC IN POLITICAL SPEECHES

We use rhetoric throughout our daily lives, whether we recognize it or not. Even though you don't need to memorize all the technical names and variations of rhetorical figures to speak or argue well, it's worth understanding some of the principles of rhetoric. Being able to see when they are being used and being able to use them ourselves gives us a leg up both in thinking critically about what we are hearing and in being able to achieve our own conversational goals.

When studying rhetoric, the political arena often provides the best fodder. Political speeches are highly crafted expositions, usually intended to persuade audiences to take a certain action or galvanize their collective belief in and commitment to the speaker. Speeches allow for some of the most spectacular oratorical performances and fanciest displays of rhetoric, particularly the stylistic tools of clever sentence arrangement and use of rhythm and repetition. While debates are improvised, the participants spend a great deal of time anticipating questions and planning and preparing their answers. This allows them to plan striking one-liners and sound bites, which are highly memorable and can help bolster the debater's final standing.

The analyses below dig into specific rhetorical aspects of three political speeches and one debate from two different periods: the combined period of the Great Depression and World War II and the period of the global economic recession of 1980. The speeches and debate were all very lengthy, so the analysis will examine an excerpt from each.

Rhetorical figures and strategies are rarely used one at a time—instead, we tend to pile them up, one upon another, using several at once. In order to better display and explain the rhetoric without becoming swamped or confused by detail, only a few rhetorical devices will be examined in each analysis.

NOTE: In the following analyses, the rhetorical notes and analysis appear beside the section of the speech where they take place. Some formatting of the original speech transcripts, such as paragraphs and breaks in text, have been inserted for clarity and readability. Each section or paragraph may have more than one rhetorical device appearing beside it in the notes, as multiple devices can be used at once.

BLENDING LOGIC AND EMOTION:

"We Shall Fight on the Beaches"

Excerpt from: Winston Churchill to the House of Commons, June 4, 1940

Context

Sir Winston Churchill, the late prime minister of the United Kingdom, delivered this speech during the height of World War II, shortly after an unexpectedly large number of the British Expeditionary Forces (BEF) were successfully evacuated from France to Dunkirk. Despite this reprieve, the situation in France was dire and Britain was at tremendous risk of invasion from German forces. Public morale was extremely low, but the unexpectedly successful evacuation of the BEF and a large number of Allied troops gave a badly needed boost to the spirits of the British people and politicians alike. There was a danger, however, that this jubilation could cloud the judgement of Parliament. In this speech—a significant portion of which was devoted to military events—Churchill needed to refocus the Parliament's attention on the peril they faced, while simultaneously bolstering morale and appealing to the United States for assistance in the war effort.

Overview

This analysis focuses on the final few minutes of Churchill's speech. Churchill, an enthusiastic student of classical rhetoric and oratory, frequently employed vivid descriptions and poetic stylings to his speeches. He understood the impact that dramatic prose and deft use of sound and rhythm had on audiences. Yet he needed to employ these strategies in a political arena, where the appearance of rationality and hard logic was important.

This excerpt was chosen to demonstrate how Churchill managed to weave his dramatic flair into logical arguments, and how he moved both his content and audience seamlessly from *logos* (appeal to logic) to *pathos* (appeal to emotion). The rhetorical tools outlined below were selected to demonstrate this movement from *logos* to *pathos,* along with the use of figures and expressions that amplify the stirring, emotional qualities of the prose. Many of the figures are stylistic, using rhythm, repetition, and sound play to heighten *pathos.* This speech was written entirely by Churchill himself (as were all his speeches—an unusual thing for a politician to do).

Rhetorical Devices, Figures, and Strategies Used

Accumulatio: summarizing various points made in a speech and presenting them in with increasing force, building up to a final, climactic statement. This is a method of emotional amplification.

Alliteration: repetition of the sound of the first letter in successive words (e.g., "clanged and clattered" and "slithered slowly and silently") A poetic technique with memorable and emotional effect.

Anaphora: repetition of the same word or group of words of one clause in the following clauses (e.g., "Look at that dress! Look at that hair, look at that ring, look at that smile!")

Concessio: concession, agreeing with a point against you or a point made by your opponent in order to strengthen your own position or argument.

Enargeia: use of especially vivid and descriptive language to paint an image in the audience's mind.

Expolitio: repeating the same idea but using different words. A form of amplification (e.g., "He spends money like water. As soon as a dollar is in his pocket, he goes out and buys something else.")

Logos: appeal to logic. Making one's argument through points that seem reasonable, logical, or consistent with the audience's world view.

Pathos: appeal to emotion. *Pathos* is highly persuasive and is often used to trigger an audience to take a desired action.

Phronesis: practical wisdom. The speaker uses this to persuade the crowd in ways that they think are realistic and practical.

Speech Transcript

We have found it necessary to take measures of increasing stringency, not only against enemy aliens and suspicious characters of other nationalities, but also against British subjects who may become a danger or a nuisance should the war be transported to the United Kingdom.

I know there are a great many people affected by the orders which we have made who are the passionate enemies of Nazi Germany. I am very sorry for them, but we cannot, at the present time and under the present stress, draw all the distinctions which we should like to do. If parachute landings were attempted and fierce fighting attendant upon them followed, these unfortunate people would be far better out of the way, for their own sakes as well as for ours.

There is, however, another class, for which I feel not the slightest sympathy. Parliament has given us the powers to put down Fifth Column activities with a strong hand, and we shall use those powers subject to the supervision and correc-

Rhetorical Analysis

Concessio—Here, Churchill agrees that loyal Britons may be negatively affected by war measures, but then he presents a logical argument as to why those measures are still necessary.

Speech Transcript	Rhetorical Analysis
tion of the House, without the slightest hesitation until we are satisfied, and more than satisfied, that this malignancy in our midst has been effectively stamped out.	
Turning once again, and this time more generally, to the question of invasion, I would observe that there has never been a period in all these long centuries of which we boast when an absolute guarantee against invasion, still less against serious raids, could have been given to our people.	*Phronesis*—Obviously rational statements made to increase the likelihood that people will agree with his later proposals of preparing for unthinkable tactics from their enemy.
In the days of Napoleon the same wind which would have carried his transports across the Channel might have driven away the blockading fleet. There was always the chance, and it is that chance which has excited and befooled the imaginations of many Continental tyrants. Many are the tales that are told.	*Enargeia*—Churchill creates the image of determined, crafty enemies from Britain's past and looming future threats from present enemies.
We are assured that novel methods will be adopted, and when we see the originality of malice, the ingenuity of aggression, which our enemy displays, we may certainly prepare ourselves for every kind of novel stratagem and every kind of brutal and treacherous maneuver.	*Expolitio*—Repetition of the idea of an inventive enemy who will use unexpected tactics.
I think that no idea is so outlandish that it should not be considered and viewed with a searching, but at the same time, I hope, with a steady eye. We must never forget the solid assurances of sea power and those which belong to air power if it can be locally exercised.	
I have, myself, full confidence that if all do their duty, if nothing is neglected, and if the best arrangements are made, as they are being made, we shall prove ourselves once again able to defend our Island home, to ride out the storm of war,	*Change in rhetorical appeal*—Here, Churchill shifts the focus of his appeals away from *logos* and fully onto *pathos*. Ending speeches by appealing to *pathos* is a common and very effective method of arranging a speech.

Speech Transcript

and to outlive the menace of tyranny, if necessary for years, if necessary alone. At any rate, that is what we are going to try to do. That is the resolve of His Majesty's Government-every man of them. That is the will of Parliament and the nation. The British Empire and the French Republic, linked together in their cause and in their need, will defend to the death their native soil, aiding each other like good comrades to the utmost of their strength.

Even though large tracts of Europe and many old and famous States have fallen or may fall into the grip of the Gestapo and all the odious apparatus of Nazi rule, we shall not flag or fail.

We shall go on to the end, we shall fight in France, we shall fight on the seas and oceans, we shall fight with growing confidence and growing strength in the air, we shall defend our Island, whatever the cost may be, we shall fight on the beaches, we shall fight on the landing grounds, we shall fight in the fields and in the streets, we shall fight in the hills; we shall never surrender.

And even if, which I do not for a moment believe, this Island or a large part of it were subjugated and starving, then our Empire beyond the seas, armed and guarded by the British Fleet, would carry on the struggle, until, in God's good time, the New World, with all its power and might, steps forth to the rescue and the liberation of the old.

Rhetorical Analysis

Accumulatio—Used throughout this final part of the speech as a method of amplifying emotional impact.

Enargeia—At this point, Churchill employs *enargeia* through to the end of his speech, painting a picture of ceaseless, tireless fighting until the enemy is vanquished.

Alliteration—The alliterations "grip of the Gestapo," "odius apparatus," and "flag or fail" create a memorable and poetic cadence that builds up emotions in the listener. This is a strong example of Churchill's use of alliteration.

Anaphora—This anaphora carries on for an extended period of time: "we shall fight…." This builds up to a final, climactic anaphora made even more impactful by its slight variation "we shall never surrender." This sort of repetition and accumulation creates huge emotional effect and is a strong appeal to the audience's *pathos*.

BUILDING A SENSE OF SHARED IDENTITY AND DETERMINATION:

"THE ONLY THING WE HAVE TO FEAR IS FEAR ITSELF."

EXCERPT FROM: FRANKLIN D. ROOSEVELT—FIRST INAUGURAL ADDRESS, MARCH 4, 1933

CONTEXT

At the time of Roosevelt's election, America was deep in the grip of the Great Depression. With unemployment at 25% and subsistence-level employment affecting millions more, the mood of voters was grim, even desperate. Roosevelt won the election on a platform based on government growth and the expansion of federal power. To make this type of platform work in a political culture traditionally averse to "big government" and resistant to widespread governmental social programming, Roosevelt needed to cultivate enormous public support of and pressure for the Democrat's policy plans.

OVERVIEW

The First Inaugural Address was largely penned by Roosevelt's trusted aide Raymond Moly, with some changes and edits by Roosevelt himself and a few additions by advisor Louis McHenry Howe. While this address doesn't have the same degree of poetic grandiloquence found in his contemporary Winston Churchill's speeches, Roosevelt's First Inaugural Address is famous for authentic emotional appeals and inspiring tones.

This excerpt is from the beginning of the speech and includes one of the most famous lines ever delivered by a president: "The only thing we have to fear is fear itself." The rhetorical strategies examined here are those used to forge a sense of collective identity among the listeners, to shift a group of very different people into a cohesive tribe. These strategies would help Roosevelt secure the popular support he would need to enable the expansion of federal powers in the face of the Great Depression, and are present throughout the speech.

Of note is the use of tense; Roosevelt shifts between present tense (used to create feelings of shared values, circumstances, and identity) and past tense (used to assign blame to a common enemy). This strategy helps focus the audience's attention on the things they hold in common. Enhancing this strategy is the use of rhetorical figures of repetition and amplification. The address uses simple words and straightforward ideas, then reinforces and enhances them to ensure that every person listening shares the same understanding of meaning, mental image, and emotional response created by Roosevelt's oration.

RHETORICAL DEVICES, FIGURES, AND STRATEGIES USED

Diacope: repetition of a word with only a few words in between. This figure of amplification creates emphasis and clarity in meaning. Diacopes may be simple ("Good boy! What a good boy!") or may add in successive descriptive words to elaborate or enhance the meaning, such as in Shakespeare's *Henry V:* "We few, we happy few...."

Enargia: use of especially vivid and descriptive language to paint an image in the audience's mind.

Past tense: the use of past tense conjugation. Past tense language assigns responsibility or blame, and is used for issues of justice. Used in forensic rhetoric.

Present tense: the use of present tense conjugation. Present tense language defines values—what is good vs. what is bad and can be used either to bond a group of people together or to separate and divide them into factions. Used in demonstrative rhetoric.

Pronoun change: Switching from first person (I) to second person (you, we) or third person (them, they) pronouns can affect people's feelings of belonging to a group. This shift in tense can be used by a speaker to single themselves out, to increase people's sense of cohesion, or to separate people or factions away from the group—a highly useful tactic when assigning blame.

Synonymia: using several words with similar meaning closely together to clarify meaning or heighten emotional effect.

Speech Transcript	Rhetorical Analysis
This is a day of national consecration. And I am certain that on this day my fellow Americans expect that on my induction into the Presidency I will address them with a candor and a decision which the present situation of our people impels.	
This is preeminently the time to speak the truth, the whole truth, frankly and boldly. Nor need we shrink from honestly facing conditions in our country today.	*Diacope:* "... the truth, the whole truth ..."
This great Nation will endure as it has endured, will revive and will prosper.	*Diacope:* "... will endure as it has endured ..."
So, first of all, let me assert my firm belief that the only thing we have to fear is fear itself—nameless, unreasoning, unjustified terror which paralyzes needed efforts to convert retreat into advance. In every dark hour of our national life a leadership of frankness and vigor has met with that understanding and support of the people	*Diacope:* "... the only thing we have to fear is fear itself ..." *Synonymia:* "nameless, unreasoning, unjustified terror"

Speech Transcript

themselves which is essential to victory. I am convinced that you will again give that support to leadership in these critical days.

In such a spirit on my part and on yours we face our common difficulties. They concern, thank God, only material things.

Values have shrunken to fantastic levels; taxes have risen; our ability to pay has fallen; government of all kinds is faced by serious curtailment of income; the means of exchange are frozen in the currents of trade; the withered leaves of industrial enterprise lie on every side; farmers find no markets for their produce; the savings of many years in thousands of families are gone.

More important, a host of unemployed citizens face the grim problem of existence, and an equally great number toil with little return. Only a foolish optimist can deny the dark realities of the moment.

Yet our distress comes from no failure of substance. We are stricken by no plague of locusts. Compared with the perils which our forefathers conquered because they believed and were not afraid, we have still much to be thankful for. Nature still offers her bounty and human efforts have multiplied it. Plenty is at our doorstep, but a generous use of it languishes in the very sight of the supply.

Primarily this is because rulers of the exchange of mankind's goods have failed through their own stubbornness and their own incompetence, have admitted their failure, and have abdicated. Practices of the unscrupulous money changers stand indicted in the court of public opinion, rejected by the hearts and minds of men.

Rhetorical Analysis

Pronoun change: Roosevelt moves from using the singular "I" to the plural "we," associating himself with the same difficulties faced by common Americans.

Enargeia: Here, Roosevelt vividly describes the effects of the Great Depression, using parallel structures for the descriptions and piling on scenarios to increase emotional impact.

Synonymia is also employed, using different terms to express the same meaning or idea, in this case, the notion of economic depression.

Past tense: A switch from present tense (which helps a group established shared values and identity) to past tense (which is used to establish culpability or blame on someone). This redirects voters' attention from the Great Depression towards an "other"—in this case, bankers and businessmen. Nothing bonds people together like a common enemy.

Speech Transcript

True they have tried, but their efforts have been cast in the pattern of an outworn tradition. Faced by failure of credit they have proposed only the lending of more money. Stripped of the lure of profit by which to induce our people to follow their false leadership, they have resorted to exhortations, pleading tearfully for restored confidence. They know only the rules of a generation of self-seekers.

They have no vision, and when there is no vision the people perish.

The money changers have fled from their high seats in the temple of our civilization. We may now restore that temple to the ancient truths. The measure of the restoration lies in the extent to which we apply social values more noble than mere monetary profit.

Happiness lies not in the mere possession of money; it lies in the joy of achievement, in the thrill of creative effort.

Rhetorical Analysis

Enargeia: Roosevelt creates a clear, shared mental image of the desperate, scraping bankers being blamed for the Great Depression. By doing so, he ensures that the people listening all have the same picture in their minds and are on the same mental and emotional page, reinforcing the audience's sense that they all belong to the same tribe.

Diascope

Present tense: Tense switches again, back to present tense. This encourages further bonding and feelings of collective will as he speaks of the action that they can now all take together to improve their circumstances.

Synonymia

DESTROYING ONE'S CRITICS:

"THE LADY'S NOT FOR TURNING"

EXCERPT: MARGARET THATCHER:
SPEECH TO CONSERVATIVE PARTY CONFERENCE, OCTOBER 10, 1980

CONTEXT

Officially titled "The Reason Why," this speech was given by British prime minister Margaret Thatcher at the Conservative Party Conference in October 1980. At that time, the United Kingdom was experiencing a period of economic unrest. Trade union strikes had plagued the country in the previous year, and the failure of Labour government to contain them was partially responsible for the vote of no confidence that triggered the general election that resulted in Thatcher's Conservative government coming to power.

Thatcher's own party was divided on her leadership and policy style, however. In an effort to control inflation resulting from a recession, Thatcher slashed government spending, privatized many industries, and closed down several coal mines and factories. As a result of her aggressive cuts, unemployment rose precipitously. Several members of the Conservative Party disagreed with her policies and called on her to perform a "U-turn"—a term popularized in the British news media. This excerpt directly addresses the "U-turn" in an outstanding play on words.

The speech was written by Sir Ronald Miller, a noted playwright and Thatcher's long-time speech writer.

OVERVIEW

This is a relatively aggressive political speech. Thatcher uses a wide variety of rhetorical attacks to discredit her critics and reinforce her position as party leader. This speech is very representative of the cut-and-thrust style of rhetoric necessary when politicians are actively facing down critics. It has a much different tone than grander orations given to a more united audience, such as the speeches by Churchill and Roosevelt examined earlier. Here, Thatcher doesn't attempt to woo her critics but rather separates them and their arguments from herself and the rest of the Conservative party. Thatcher directly attacks the characters of her critics and openly mocks their arguments, while still creating a grandness of speech through the use of metaphor, clever word play, and other striking rhetorical figures. It has the feel of a bar room brawl being conducted by an impeccably dressed fencing master.

RHETORICAL DEVICES, FIGURES, AND STRATEGIES USED

Ad Hominem: an attack on an opponents character, usually with the view of dismissing their argument as invalid due to a character flaw. This is typically frowned upon by logicians, but it is a useful persuasive rhetorical tool and an absolute must in politics (e.g., "You have no right to argue for environmental reform—you drive an SUV!")

Apodioxis: dismissing a person or a person's argument as being false, wicked, unnecessary, or otherwise absurd.

Apophasis: bringing up a subject by denying it or by denying that others should bring it up at all. It can also be used to define a thing or idea by stating what it is not.

Chiasmus: repeating a clause or idea in an inverted order. A figure of contrast, often used to dismiss one idea in favour of its contrasting or opposite idea (e.g., "Ask not what your country can do for you, ask what you can do for your country.")

Epizeuxis: successive repetition of words. May be used to create emphasis and amplify meaning (e.g., "Every time they get together at Thanksgiving, they just fight, fight, fight!")

Metonymy: Referring to a person or a thing via one of their attributes or characteristics (e.g., "The pen is mightier than the sword." 'Pen' is a writing implement and is used to mean all written words. 'Sword' is a weapon and refers to all forms military force.)

Refutation: one of the canons of rhetorical arrangement. In the refutation portion of a speech, the speaker destroys their opponent's arguments using a variety of rhetorical and oratorical devices and strategies.

Periphrasis: using a description to identify someone or something rather than naming the person or thing outright. Example: in J. K. Rowling's Harry Potter series, Lord Voldemort was usually referred to as "He Who Must Not Be Named." This is a form of circumlocution—a way of "speaking around" something.

Syncresis: using a parallel clause to compare or contrast two ideas. Hillary Clinton used syncresis during the 2016 presidential debates in her statement: "When they go low, you go high." Syncresis can take place across longer, more complex clauses and sentences.

Speech Transcript	Rhetorical Analysis
If spending money like water was the answer to our country's problems, we would have no problems now. If ever a nation has spent, spent, spent and spent again, ours has. Today that dream is over. All of that money has got us nowhere but it still has to come from somewhere.	*Refutation:* Thatcher briefly mentions the arguments for a liberal spending plan advocated by her critics within the Conservative party. She then spends the rest of this excerpt systematically tearing down their argument through strong *logos*-based points. *Epizeuxis:* "spent, spent, spent, and spent again"
Those who urge us to relax the squeeze, to spend yet more money indiscriminately in the belief that it will help the unemployed and the small businessman are not being kind or compassionate or caring. They are not the friends of the unemployed or the small business. They are asking us to do again the very thing that caused the problems in the first place. We have made this point repeatedly.	*Periphrasis:* Thatcher is calling out critics in her own party without actually naming them outright. Rather, she identifies them by speaking around their names and instead describes their economic policy positions. *Apodioxis:* she dismisses her critic's argument as false, uncaring, and stubborn.

Speech Transcript	Rhetorical Analysis
I am accused of lecturing or preaching about this. I suppose it is a critic's way of saying "Well, we know it is true, but we have to carp at something."	*Ad Hominem:* counters an *ad hominem* attack (that she is a lecturing nag) with another *ad hominem* (that her critics complain for the sake of complaining).
I do not care about that. But I do care about the future of free enterprise, the jobs and exports it provides and the independence it brings to our people.	*Apodioxis:* rejects her critics' comments as being not worth caring about.
Independence? Yes, but let us be clear what we mean by that. Independence does not mean contracting out of all relationships with others.	*Apophasis*
A nation can be free but it will not stay free for long if it has no friends and no alliances. Above all, it will not stay free if it cannot pay its own way in the world. By the same token, an individual needs to be part of a community and to feel that he is part of it. There is more to this than the chance to earn a living for himself and his family, essential though that is.	*Syncresis:* "a nation can be free but will not stay free"
Of course, our vision and our aims go far beyond the complex arguments of economics, but unless we get the economy right we shall deny our people the opportunity to share that vision and to see beyond the narrow horizons of economic necessity.	
Without a healthy economy we cannot have a healthy society. Without a healthy society the economy will not stay healthy for long.	*Syncresis (both sentences)*
But it is not the State that creates a healthy society.	*Metonymy:* "The State" refers to all aspects of a complex government.
When the State grows too powerful people feel that they count for less and less. The State drains society, not only of its wealth but of initiative, of energy, the will to im-	*Epizeuxis:* "less and less"

Speech Transcript

prove and innovate as well as to preserve what is best. Our aim is to let people feel that they count for more and more. If we cannot trust the deepest instincts of our people we should not be in politics at all. Some aspects of our present society really do offend those instincts.

Decent people do want to do a proper job at work, not to be restrained or intimidated from giving value for money. They believe that honesty should be respected, not derided. They see crime and violence as a threat not just to society but to their own orderly way of life. They want to be allowed to bring up their children in these beliefs, without the fear that their efforts will be daily frustrated in the name of progress or free expression. Indeed, that is what family life is all about.

There is not a generation gap in a happy and united family. People yearn to be able to rely on some generally accepted standards. Without them you have not got a society at all, you have purposeless anarchy. A healthy society is not created by its institutions, either. Great schools and universities do not make a great nation any more than great armies do. Only a great nation can create and involve great institutions—of learning, of healing, of scientific advance. And a great nation is the voluntary creation of its people—a people composed of men and women whose pride in themselves is founded on the knowledge of what they can give to a community of which they in turn can be proud.

If our people feel that they are part of a great nation and they are prepared to will the means to keep it great, a great nation we shall be, and shall remain. So, what

Rhetorical Analysis

Epizeuxis: "more and more"

Speech Transcript	Rhetorical Analysis
can stop us from achieving this? What then stands in our way?	
The prospect of another winter of discontent? I suppose it might. But I prefer to believe that certain lessons have been learnt from experience, that we are coming, slowly, painfully, to an autumn of understanding. And I hope that it will be followed by a winter of common sense. If it is not, we shall not be—diverted from our course.	*Metaphor:* The phrase "Winter of Discontent" was a metaphor used to refer to the period of trade union strikes during the winter of 1978–79. Here, Thatcher extends the season metaphor to refer to upcoming periods of trust building and reasonable action.
To those waiting with bated breath for that favourite media catchphrase, the "U" turn, I have only one thing to say. "You turn if you want to. The lady's not for turning." I say that not only to you but to our friends overseas and also to those who are not our friends.	*Metonymy:* Thatcher referring to herself as "The lady." This can create the impression of grand stature and power.

PERSUASION THROUGH INFLATION:

THE CARTER–REAGAN PRESIDENTIAL DEBATE

EXCERPT: CARTER–REAGAN PRESIDENTIAL DEBATE, OCTOBER 28, 1980

CONTEXT

Shortly after the above speech by Margaret Thatcher electrified the Conservative Party in London, former California governor Ronald Reagan electrified American voters during his presidential debate with President Jimmy Carter. The nation was on edge, having been through a wrenching recession that featured high inflation, high interest rates, and high unemployment. Global events were not favoring Carter's period as president. Increasing hostility from Iran, the 1979 oil crisis shock, and the lengthy problem of Americans being held hostage in Iran all cast doubts on his capabilities as president.

Reagan, on the other hand, was riding a wave of popularity, coming off his successful bid to be the Republican nominee. Despite the pejoratives launched at his policies by members of his own party, Reagan's promises to increase government revenue while lowering taxes were well received by voters, who were worn down by years of rising inflation and economic insecurity.

The October 28 debate was the only debate between Carter and Reagan. President Carter refused to participate in any debates that included independent candidate John Anderson, and it was not until the final weeks of the election that Reagan conceded to Carter's demands to hold a debate without Anderson present.

OVERVIEW

This excerpt of the Carter–Reagan debate begins approximately thirteen minutes into the debate. The issue at hand focused largely on the problem of inflation. As is typical in debates, the candidates spent a fair amount of time and energy jockeying for a favorable definition or framing of the issue. Within debate, defining issues and framing them in an advantageous light is a critical rhetorical strategy. It allows the speaker to craft arguments that put their best foot forward, while simultaneously making the other debater look as though they are avoiding responding to the issue at hand.

Reagan's background as a movie actor can be seen throughout this excerpt. His knowledge of theatrical flare helped him make emotion-triggering overstatements (hyperboles) without becoming so dramatic as to weaken his position. He demonstrates a deftness with words and gives his down-home style of speaking a memorable rhythm. In particular, Reagan had the ability to create memorable one-liners and sound bites that were easy to recall and repeat.

Carter, on the other hand, was primarily on the defensive throughout the debate. While he did attack Reagan's positions through various means, including raising Reagan running mate George H. W. Bush's comment about "voodoo economics," his responses included more statistics than emotion. Emotion and appeal to *pathos* is critical when running for office, as people tend to vote more emotionally than logically.

Both candidates made hearty attacks against each other's *ethos*, repeatedly calling into question the intelligence and intentions of their opponent, as well as the validity of one another's arguments and proposals.

Rhetorical Devices, Figures, and Strategies Used

Anthorism: redefining a term or issue to one that is more favorable to you. This may also appear as a reframing of an argument so that the context of the issue or connotation of a word is different than the one being used by your opponent.

Apodioxis: dismissing a person or a person's argument as being false, wicked, unnecessary, or otherwise absurd.

Hyperbole Erotreme: : deliberate exaggeration, usually achieved through metaphor or particularly colorful language.

Parallelism: separate clauses or phrases that are similar in composition. Parallelism covers a variety of rhetorical figures. It can be used for a variety of purposes, such as making comparisons or contrasts, creating pleasant rhythms, or making statements more memorable.

Speech Transcript

MR. [HARRY] ELLIS, CHRISTIAN SCIENCE MONITOR: Mr. President, when you were elected in 1976, the Consumer Price Index stood at 4.8%. It now stands at more than 12%. Perhaps more significantly, the nation's broader, underlying inflation rate has gone up from 7% to 9%. Now, a part of that was due to external factors beyond U.S. control, notably the more than doubling. of oil prices by OPEC last year. Because the United States remains vulnerable to such external shocks, can inflation in fact be controlled? If so, what measures would you pursue in a second term?

MR. CARTER: Again it's important to put the situation in perspective. In 1974, we had a so-called oil shock, wherein the price of OPEC oil was raised to an extraordinary degree. We had an even worse oil shock in 1979. In 1974, we had the

Rhetorical Analysis

Anthorism: redefines the issue by changing the perspective

SPEECH TRANSCRIPT	RHETORICAL ANALYSIS
worst recession, the deepest and most penetrating recession since the Second World War. The recession that resulted this time was the briefest since the Second World War.	
In addition, we've brought down inflation. Earlier this year, in the first quarter, we did have a very severe inflation pressure brought about by the OPEC price increase. It averaged about 18% in the first quarter of this year. In the second quarter, we had dropped it down to about 13%. The most recent figures, the last three months, on the third quarter of this year, the inflation rate is 7%—still too high, but it illustrates very vividly that in addition to providing an enormous number of jobs—nine million new jobs in the last three and a half years—that the inflationary threat is still urgent on us.	*Logic supporting the anthorism:* shifts the issue away from one about dire inflation and oil prices and towards one about mitigating even worse outcomes through prudent administration. Anthorisms must be pursued and reinforced if they're going to work.
I notice that Governor Reagan recently mentioned the Reagan-Kemp-Roth proposal. which his own running mate, George Bush, described as voodoo economics, and said that it would result in a 30% inflation rate.	*Apodioxis:* dismisses Reagan's economic proposals as false (voodoo) and so absurd that Reagan's own running mate speaks badly of them.
And *Business Week,* which is not a Democratic publication, said that this Reagan-Kemp-Roth proposal—and I quote them, I think—was completely irresponsible and would result in inflationary pressures which would destroy this nation.	*Hyperbole*: Carter uses terms like "completely irresponsible" and "destroy" to amplify the fears created by Reagan's proposal.
So our proposals are very sound and very carefully considered to stimulate jobs, to improve the industrial complex of this country, to create tools for American workers, and at the same time would be anti-inflationary in nature. So to add nine million new jobs, to control inflation, and	

to plan for the future with an energy policy now intact as a foundation is our plan for the years ahead.

MR. [HOWARD K.] SMITH [ABC]: [Mr. Ellis, do you have a follow-up question for Mr. Carter?

MR. ELLIS: Yes. Mr. President, you have mentioned the creation of nine million new jobs. At the same time, the unemployment rate still hangs high, as does the inflation rate. Now, I wonder, can you tell us what additional policies you would pursue in a second administration in order to try to bring down that inflation rate? And would it be an act of leadership to tell the American people they are going to have to sacrifice to adopt a leaner lifestyle for some time to come?

MR. CARTER: Yes. We have demanded that the American people sacrifice, and they have done very well. As a matter of fact, we're importing today about one-third less oil from overseas than we did just a year ago. We've had a 25% reduction since the first year I was in office. At the same time, as I have said earlier, we have added about nine million net new jobs in that period of time—a record never before achieved.

BLUNDER! Carter should have used an anthorism or euphemism to redefine "sacrifice" to something more palatable, like "challenge" or "tighten our belts." This would have put a more positive spin on Carter's words. No one wants to sacrifice, but people are proud of rising up to a "challenge" to "tighten their belts" for the greater good.

Also, the new energy policy has been predicated on two factors: One is conservation, which requires sacrifice, and the other one, increase in production of American energy, which is going along very well—more coal this year than ever before in American history, more oil and gas wells drilled this year than ever before in history.

Parallelism: repeated clause structure amplifying the collective results of his energy and economic policies.

The new economic revitalization program that we have in mind, which will be

Speech Transcript	Rhetorical Analysis
implemented next year, would result in tax credits which would let business invest in new tools and new factories to create even more new jobs—about one million in the next two years. And we also have planned a youth employment program which would encompass 600,000 jobs for young people. This has already passed the House, and it has an excellent prospect to pass the Senate.	
MR. SMITH: Now, the same question goes to Governor Reagan. Governor Reagan, would you like to have the question repeated?	
MR. ELLIS: Governor Reagan, during the past four years, the Consumer Price Index has risen from 4.8% to currently over 12%. And perhaps more significantly, the nation's broader, underlying rate of inflation has gone up from 7% to 9%. Now, a part of that has been due to external factors beyond U.S. control, notably the more than doubling of OPEC oil prices last year, which leads me to ask you whether, since the United States remains vulnerable to such external shocks, can inflation in fact be controlled? If so, specifically what measures would you pursue?	
MR. REAGAN: Mr. Ellis, I think this idea that has been spawned here in our country that inflation somehow came upon us like a plague and therefore it's uncontrollable and no one can do anything about it, is entirely spurious and it's dangerous to say this to the people.	*Hyperbole:* over-the-top inflammatory language ("spawned," "plague") to amplify the absurdity of Carter's comments. *Apodioxis:* dismisses Carter's as absurd and irresponsible.
When Mr. Carter became President, inflation was 4.8%, as you said. It had been cut in two by President Gerald Ford. It is now running at 12.7%. President Carter	

Speech Transcript / Rhetorical Analysis

also has spoken of the new jobs created. Well, we always, with the normal growth in our country and increase in population, increase the number of jobs.

But that can't hide the fact that there are eight million men and women out of work in America today, and two million of those lost their jobs in just the last few months.

Anthorism: refocuses the issue as not being about how many jobs were created, but rather about how many people are still jobless.

Mr. Carter had also promised that he would not use unemployment as a tool to fight against inflation. And yet, his 1980 economic message stated that we would reduce productivity and gross national product and increase unemployment in order to get a handle on inflation, because in January, at the beginning of the year, it was more than 18%.

Since then, he has blamed the people for inflation, OPEC, he has blamed the Federal Reserve system, he has blamed the lack of productivity of the American people, he has then accused the people of living too well and that we must share in scarcity, we must sacrifice and get used to doing with less.

Apodioxis: disputes Carter's arguments about the source of inflation by dismissing him as absurd and, by extension, dismisses Carter as a self-interested blame-dodger.

We don't have inflation because the people are living too well. We have inflation because the Government is living too well.

Parallelism: the memorable cadence and parallel rhythm makes this an easily remembered "sound bite."

And the last statement, just a few days ago, was a speech to the effect that we have inflation because Government revenues have not kept pace with Government spending. I see my time is running out here. I'll have to get this out very fast. Yes, you can lick inflation by increasing productivity and by decreasing the cost of government to the place that we have balanced budgets, and are no longer grind-

Speech Transcript	Rhetorical Analysis
ing out printing press money, flooding the market with it because the Government is spending more than it takes in. And my economic plan calls for that.	
The President's economic plan calls for increasing the taxes to the point that we finally take so much money away from the people that we can balance the budget in that way. But we will have a very poor nation and a very unsound economy if we follow that path.	*Hyperbole:* deliberately overstates the downsides of the plan by words like "finally" and "so much," then paints an exceptionally bleak outcome (it's as though America would have ended up a third-world country).
MR. SMITH: A follow-up, Mr. Ellis?	
MR. ELLIS: Yes. You have centered on cutting Government spending in what you have just said about your own policies. You have also said that you would increase defense spending. Specifically, where would you cut Government spending if you were to increase defense spending and also cut taxes, so that, presumably. Federal revenues would shrink?	
MR. REAGAN: Well, most people, when they think about cutting Government spending, they think in terms of eliminating necessary programs or wiping out something, some service that Government is supposed to perform. I believe that there is enough extravagance and fat in government.	
As a matter of fact, one of the secretaries of HEW under Mr. Carter testified that he thought there was $7 billion worth of fraud and waste in welfare and in the medical programs associated with it.	*Anthorism:* reframes the issue from government spending to government fraud and waste. This particular anthorism is quite subtle.
We've had the Central Accounting office estimate that there is probably tens of billions of dollars that is lost in fraud alone,	

Speech Transcript

and they have added that waste adds even more to that.

We have a program for a gradual reduction of Government spending based on these theories, and I have a task force now that has been working on where those cuts could be made. I'm confident that it can be done and that it will reduce inflation because I did it in California. And inflation went down below the national average in California when we returned the money to the people and reduced Government spending.

MR. SMITH: President Carter.

MR. CARTER: Governor Reagan's proposal, the Reagan-Kemp-Roth proposal, is one of the most highly inflationary ideas that ever has been presented to the American public.

He would actually have to cut Government spending by at least $130 billion in order to balance the budget under this ridiculous proposal. I notice that his task force that is working for his future plans had some of their ideas revealed in The Wall Street Journal this week. One of those ideas was to repeal the minimum wage, and several times this year, Governor Reagan has said that the major cause of unemployment is the minimum wage.

This is a heartless kind of approach to the working families of our country, which is typical of many Republican leaders of the past, but, I think, has been accentuated under Governor Reagan.

In California—I'm surprised Governor Reagan brought this up—he had the

Rhetorical Analysis

Hyperbole: inflating the likely amount of fraud and waste to play to voter desire for the near-impossible promise of a balanced budget, reduced spending, a tax cut, and no elimination of programs or services.

Hyperbole: words like "most" and "ever" are hyperbole red flags. Carter amplifies the threat of inflation, which voters were sensitive to due to a recent period of high inflation.

Speech Transcript	Rhetorical Analysis
three largest tax increases in the history of that state under his administration. He more than doubled state spending while he was Governor—122% increase—and had between a 20% and 30% increase in the number of employees.	
MR. SMITH: Sorry to interrupt, Mr. Carter.	
MR. CARTER: in California. Thank you, sir.	
MR. SMITH: Governor Reagan has the last word on this question.	
MR. REAGAN: Yes. The figures that the President has just used about California is a distortion of the situation there.	*Apodioxis*: rejects Carter's argument as false.
Because while I was Governor of California, our spending in California increased less per capita than the spending in Georgia while Mr. Carter was Governor of Georgia in the same four years. The size of government increased only one-sixth in California of what it increased in proportion to the population in Georgia.	*Anthorism:* redefines the increases in spending from an overall increase to a per capita proportional increase (which would result in very different and more favorable figures).
And the idea that my tax-cut proposal is inflationary: I would like to ask the President why is it inflationary to let the people keep more of their money and spend it the way that they like, and it isn't inflationary to let him take that money and spend it the way he wants?	
MR. SMITH: I wish that question need not be rhetorical, but it must be because we've run out of time on that.	

APPENDIX 2: SAMPLE SPEECHES FOR REAL LIFE

Many people find it useful to refer to examples when writing speeches. Below are sample speeches for several common speaking situations we may face at work and in life. These speeches follow the suggested speech templates that appear in the chapters "Business Communication" and "Social Communication." The sample speech text appears in the column on the left, while the associated speech component appears alongside it in the column on the right.

WEDDING TOASTS, THANK YOU SPEECHES, MASTER OF CEREMONIES, AND MORE

ACCEPTING AN AWARD OR OTHER HONOR

Sample Script	Speech Component
Thank you, everyone, for this incredible honor.	
When I first received my accountant's designation, I thought I was just getting a permission slip to work in this industry. Very quickly, though, I realized that being a member of this profession and this association means so much more.	Statement about how you felt upon joining the association/profession.
It means being part of a group of people dedicated to upholding the values of truth, honesty, and accountability to their clients. It means being held to a standard of excellence, not just in our work but in how we represent our entire profession to the public.	Describe values and work done by the association.

Speech Script	Speech Component
But to me, it goes even further. It means being part of a group of people who care for one another, who look to help lift each other up, make one another better, and provide support for each other when we stumble. And just as you helped me grow into the professional I am today, I'm proud to continue that tradition and help the new generation of accountants achieve their goals and dreams.	Describe what it means to you personally to be a member of the association/profession.
While I owe my thanks to everyone here, there are some that I would like to acknowledge individually. Sarah Morgen, thank you for being there for me from the beginning. Aleem Mumtaz, I will always be grateful for the generosity you showed me, both with your time and your knowledge. And Oliver Legsworth, you embody everything it is to be a mentor—I'm blessed that you were mine.	Thank supporters, mentors, and association.
I invite everyone here to continue your outstanding work, and continue representing the values of truth, honesty, and accountability. I also invite you to continue the tradition of this association of welcoming in new members and helping lift them up so they can reach even their highest goals.	Conclusion—call to members to further the association's mission or uphold their values.
Thanks again so very much.	

Accepting an Award on Behalf of an Organization

Speech Script	Speech Component
It's my privilege to accept this award on behalf of the Academic Libraries Consortium.	
The Southwestern Libraries Association has been supporting the development of libraries and library services in our region for many years. They represent excellence in our organizations and champion our commitment to freedom of information.	Statement about the values and mission of the association granting the award.
It's an honor, therefore, for the ALC to be recognized by the SLA as an example of those values. ALC has long strived to create an environment of inclusion and sharing. Our whole team is dedicated to improving the skills and knowledge of other librarians in our region.	Describe the values and mission of your own organization.
Even though I'm up here accepting the award, the praise goes to the staff of ALC. They take enormous pride and care in their work. They care about our members and are always ready to help in any way they can, whether it's though our programs and services or through enthusiastic participation in our professional community.	Describe how employees or members of your organization uphold those values.
Without their dedication, projects such as the development and launch of the first region-wide shared library management system would never be able to come to fruition.	Describe some specific accomplishments of your team.
We at ALC will keep working hard to help our region's libraries share knowledge, information, and resources. We'll live up to this award and to the honor granted to us by the SLA.	Conclusion—state how future activities of your organization will continue to uphold your own values as well as those of the association granting the award.
Thank you.	

Presenting an Award or Recognition at a Professional Event

Speech Script	Speech Component
For over 50 years, The Event Planners Association of Lincolnshire has promoted excellence and innovation in the event planning industry.	Describe the mission and values of the organization or association granting the award.
The Peter McKay Award for Innovation acknowledges a planner's use of forward-thinking designs and cutting edge technology to make their events come to life.	Describe the purpose of the award itself, and what achievements it recognizes.
This year's recipient has been inspiring our community with truly original event designs and inventive uses of new technology for over ten years. She has become one of the most sought-after planners in the Northeastern region, and has lent her talents to national and international events. Many here will remember the Interstellar Wonderland event, where she created an out-of-this world experience literally out of smoke-and-mirrors, along with thousands of lasers.	Describe the person or organization receiving the award and provide a brief background of their work and achievements.
The Peter McKay award honors those who bring an attitude of curiosity and originality to their work. Tonight's recipient is definitely both curious and original. She's always looking for fresh inspiration, whether it's from theatrical set design or the work of master magicians and illusionists.	Describe the characteristics of the award recipient and how they embody the values represented by the award.
Please welcome to the stage this year's recipient of the Peter McKay Award for Innovation, Brenda Lafontaine!	Congratulate the recipient and invite them to the stage to receive the award.

Giving a Toast at a Retirement Celebration

Speech Script	Speech Component
Almost 25 years ago, a not-so-young new detective walked into my office and asked if I could possibly lend him $1.50 for the coffee machine, because he owed his staff sergeant a cappuccino and had locked his wallet inside his station locker but couldn't find the key.	State how you first met the retiree and what your impressions were.
And I thought "uh oh, this is who we're letting into the force nowadays?"	
I later learned that Donovan's staff sergeant had put him up to it. He had dared a new recruit to play a prank on the station superintendent on his first day at work. And Donovan, not being one to fear a challenge, immediately agreed.	Give a brief synopsis of the retiree's career. Spend the most time on parts of their history that the majority of the party attendees would be able to relate to. Include any funny stories or roasts here.
Fearlessness and humor are two characteristics that have defined Donovan's career. He is totally fearless, having left a cushy desk job in his late thirties because, and I quote, "It was making me fat," and launching into a totally new and daunting line of work. And it's a darn good thing he has such a good sense of humor, otherwise I doubt that the rest of us would have been willing to put up with his non-stop practical jokes for the next 20-plus years.	
But even more striking than Donovan's jokes—or untamable enthusiasm for learning something new, or bravery in the face of danger—is his commitment to serving his community and our city through tireless work on case after case after case. It didn't matter what the case was, when it happened, or who else was involved—Donovan wanted to get to the bottom of it, do the right thing, and make his community better by it.	

Speech Script	Speech Component
Many of you may remember the arsons that held the city breathless five years ago. It was Donovan's determination, resourcefulness, and fearlessness that helped him lead his team in finding, arresting, and convicting the person responsible.	Describe any notable accomplishments
And yes, his humor helped out too, because I don't think any of us could have put up with the hours Donovan demanded if he hadn't been so darn charming about it. In our line of work, that's a trait we badly need, and something I'll always admire you for. You taught us how to laugh at ourselves and at everyone else without losing our compassion for the people we serve.	Describe admirable personal qualities of the retiree, especially as a colleague or co-worker
You've had an amazing career, Donny, and our station will be a little quieter without your laughter booming through the halls. But if Pam gets tired of your pranks at home, I hope you come back to the station and play a couple of them on us.	Congratulate the retiree and state that they will be missed.
Everyone, please raise your glasses to Donovan "Donny" Moreland—he may be retiring, but I don't think he'll ever be out of the game.	Make the formal toast. If applicable, invite the retiree up to give a speech after the toast.
Donny, will you come up and say a few words?	

Giving a Toast at a Retirement Celebration

(Written as a response to the sample retirement speech above.)

Speech Script	Speech Component
Thanks so much, Patrick, for that toast. You've been willing to put up with me since day one, and I think I still owe you that buck fifty.	
Patrick was right—my old desk job was making me fat. But I also wanted the opportunity for adventure, for excitement, and to make a difference to my community. They might be the dreams of a 10-year-old, but a 35-year-old can have them too. That's what joining the police force meant to me. And it brought me those things right from day one, when Sarah Jones dared me to ask Patrick for money for the coffee machine.	Reflect on how you entered your profession or line of work and your initial impressions.
Policing, and detective work in particular, has taught me things I didn't think I needed learning at 35—discipline, open mindedness, how to set aside my own biases and pre-conceived ideas. It also taught me that regardless what you think you know, or how prepared you think you are, you need to work your backside off otherwise you will have it handed to you by a bunch of 20-somethings with youth, endurance, and bald-faced naivety on their side.	Describe how you grew in your work and what your career taught you. Include some funny stories.
I always liked to joke around, but as a detective I learned how to joke with a purpose. I learned that a joke could help a witness relax, or help a victim get a little bit better.	
I learned that excitement comes in lots of different forms, and that waiting for your partner to discover that you re-arranged all the letters on his keyboard could be as exciting as finding a critical piece of evi-	Describe how your organization or profession will continue to grow. Provide advice and encouragement for younger audience members on how to grow in their own careers.

Speech Script	Speech Component
dence during a scene investigation. Learn to type with more than two fingers, Jordan, it's an important life skill!	
To the young officers who came here today, thanks for your willingness to put up with an old guy rambling platitudes at you. But in all honesty, I see a bright future for our force when I look at you. Stay straight and stay true. Work for the good of your community. Respect everyone in it. And never forget how to smile.	
Thanks to Patrick and Sarah for taking in a relatively old dog and teaching him some new tricks. Your faith and trust in me helped make me the detective I am. Thanks to my kids, for their belief in me and excitement for the adventure I chose, and especially to Pam, who is both the love and the rock of my life.	Thank your colleagues, your family, and any mentors for their support throughout your career.
As my first order of business after today, Pam and I will be jumping into an RV and reconnecting with some long highways. This road trip will be a great test of how long she can put up with me before making me sleep on the roof. But before we do that, I want to raise a toast to you for putting up with me, for making my career with the force an unimaginable honor, and for being my family away from home. Our communities are in good hands. Ladies and Gentlemen, please raise your glass to the Amryville Police Service.	Concluding remark (e.g., a comment about going fishing or some other vacation-type hobby; offering a toast to those present for continuing your organization's good work).

Introducing a Speaker at a Conference Event

Speech Script	Speech Component
Welcome, delegates, to the opening keynote of our conference.	State the topic of the session, talk, or keynote.
Surviving and thriving through organizational change is a topic on everybody's mind nowadays.	
In an unpredictable economy and a technological environment that seems to shift at the speed of light, being able to adapt, re-prioritize, and embrace change at organizational and operational level is critical to our success and mental well-being.	Explain how the topic is important to the attendee's current work, lives, or interests.
Shawnita Wallan has been a figurehead in the organizational change field for over 20 years. She boasts a Ph.D. in organizational behavior and a Master's in psychology, and has been the go-to change consultant for several Fortune 500 companies, including J.P. Morgan Chase, Costco, and Gap. She's authored 5 books, the latest of which, *How to Succeed at Change without Really Trying,* has hit the *New York Times* bestseller list.	State the speaker's name, how long they have been working in their field of expertise, and any relevant credentials, significant accomplishments, or publications.
Please join me in welcoming Shawnita Wallan.	Invite the speaker to the front and lead the audience in a welcome applause.

Opening Script for a Master of Ceremonies at a Professional or Corporate Event

(These opening comments were developed and delivered by Lauren Sergy for the Edmonton Event Awards gala in February 2016. All names and organizations have been omitted.)

Speech Script	Speech Component
Welcome, event professionals! Welcome planners and photographers, caterers and entertainers, hoteliers, decorators, technicians, designers! Welcome you magic makers and happy mongers to the first annual Edmonton Event Awards! My name is Lauren Sergy, and I'm delighted to be your MC for the evening.	Welcome delegates, identify different groups of people present, briefly introduce yourself as MC.
Tonight we celebrate the people who make the important moments in our lives shine by deciding who was able to bend backwards the furthest in an attempt to meet their client's outrageous expectations.	State purpose of the event. Include some light humor about the event and/or people present.
We get to tip our hats to the caterers who manage to make that gluten, soy, and dairy-free vegi-paleo feast not only edible but enjoyable. We applaud the venue owners and suppliers who put up with kleptomaniac guests pinching centerpieces and cloth napkins. We celebrate AV wizards who can wire a room up better than the Starship *Enterprise*, designers who can spin a budget of straw into something that looks like gold, and planners who manage to do double duty as both organizer and client therapist.	
This night is about the marvelous people in this crazy industry, people who have the skills of true masters, the panache of style mavens, and the patience of saints.	
Tonight we are honoring excellence across all areas of the event industry in the	Provide an overview of the event proceedings.

Speech Script	Speech Component
Greater Edmonton Region. These have been broken down into four categories of awards: • The Best suppliers category, which has 8 awards covering Event Décor, Floral Design, Event Entertainer, Event Photographer, Audio Visual, Caterer and Food Supplier, Function Venue, and Hotel • The Best Event category, which has 5 awards celebrating the best Trade Show or exhibition, Conference, Fundraiser, Wedding, and Special Event • The Best Innovative Idea category, with one award for the whole category, and • The Best Industry Professional category, with awards for Independent or 3rd Party Wedding Professional and Independent or 3rd Party Event Professional.	
It is time now to extend our warm acknowledgement and thanks to some of the best friends any event can have—our sponsors and supporters! Many people and organizations have made tonight possible (*name sponsors while their logos appear on slideshow*)	Thank event sponsors and contributors (if applicable).
We thank you from the bottom of our hearts and wallets for the funding and resources (and funding) to make tonight possible!	
All nominees and finalists were reviewed and evaluated by our panel of expert judges:	
Please join me in a big thank-you for the wisdom and effort of our judges!	Name judges and associated organizations. Lead applause
Now I will welcome to the stage _______ for some words on behalf of the judges. Welcome and thank any special guests (e.g.: adjudicators, industry leaders, executives of the host organization, politicians or other noted community leaders, etc.)	

Opening Script for a Master of Ceremonies at a Social Event

Speech Script	Speech Component
Welcome, everyone, and thank you so much for joining us tonight to celebrate the marriage of Anne and Steven! It's so wonderful to see so many friends and family members gathered together to share their love for the couple, help them start this new chapter in their lives, and try to outdo one another as Worst Dancer of the Evening. My name is Brent, I'm Anne's sister (officially your brother-in-law now, Steve, so watch it!), and I'll be your MC tonight.	Welcome wedding guests, make upbeat comment about the happy gathering. Introduce yourself briefly. Light humor throughout is encouraged.
When Anne and Steve asked me if I would MC this evening, I was pretty surprised. Anyone who watched Anne and I grow up knows that she's the brains of the family. But I'm proud to say that this time I didn't get her to do my homework and wrote every word of this MC script myself! In all honesty though, I'm honored to get to play a part in my little sister's special day, and am excited to finally be able to call Steve "brother."	Provide a very brief story demonstrating your fondness for the couple.
We're going to get going in just a moment, but first, I've got some important instructions. Anne and Steve are going to Vegas for their honeymoon, so we decided to bring a bit of Vegas here tonight. Over there is a green table with a big pair of dice on it. If you want Steve and Anne to kiss, you'll need to gamble. "KISS" is on those dice, but so are some other things too. So roll the dice, and whatever comes up is what you … or Anne and Steve … will have to do. We'll be watching you, so no cheating!	Provide a brief overview of the evening and any special instructions.

Speech Script	Speech Component
We're going to have a few speeches, then move straight on to dinner, then the dance. The couple will cut the cake at 10:30, so don't go anywhere before then.	
For the first speech of the evening, I'd like to welcome up brother of the groom and best man Gordon, to give a toast to the bride and groom.	Invite up people giving speeches.
(*Gordon gives speech. Lead applause after speech, then invite up the next person, and so on.*)	

SPEECH FOR NEWLYWEDS TO THEIR WEDDING GUESTS

(EACH PERSON MAY SAY A PORTION OF THE SPEECH.)

Speech Script	Speech Component
(Bride) Thank you so much, everyone, for being here with us today. We wanted this night and this hall to be full of love and laughter, and with you here it's bursting at the seams.	Thank guests for attending your wedding.
(Groom) Just about everyone here seemed to know that Anne and I would be walking down the aisle even before we did. Maybe it was the fact that we both owned matching *Star Wars* backpacks.	Share a story or comment about your relationship.
(Bride) Or that we both had the San Diego Comic Con on our buckets lists.	
(Groom) Or that we each preferred to spend evenings playing ultimate Frisbee on campus instead of going out to bars.	
(Bride) Or maybe you just saw two people who were so obviously made for each other that it wasn't obvious to them.	
(Groom) But whatever it was, all I can say is that when four different people come up to you independently and say "Steve, I found the perfect girl for you," you'd better believe them.	
(Bride) To my bridesmaids, thanks so much for keeping me sane throughout this whole thing.	Thank members of the wedding party and parents.
(Groom) To my groomsmen, thanks for helping me figure out what this whole thing even was.	
(Bride) To our parents, thanks for being there and loving and supporting us every step of the way.	
(Groom) And to all of you, for your love and friendship. We're so happy you're here to celebrate with us tonight, so let's start the celebration!	Thank guests for attending, provide concluding statement.

EULOGY

Speech Script	Speech Component
We're gathered here today to celebrate the life of Samuel Garcia, and to comfort one another in our sadness at his passing.	Opening statement regarding the purpose of the gathering.
Samuel was my older brother. He was there for me through thick and thin all his life, and I'm proud to be remembering him at the end of his.	Briefly describe your relationship to the deceased.
Samuel was born in Albuquerque on June 3rd, 1940, the first of three children of Maria and Santiago Garcia. He was followed by a brother, myself, and a sister, also named Maria. The three of us grew up in a happy household, and although our parents had to work extremely hard to give us the life they dreamed of, we were never lacking in love, care, or support.	State the deceased's date of birth and the names of their parents and siblings.
Samuel was a diligent student. His work ethic was obvious from a young age. He cared deeply about making our parents happy, I think because he saw them working so hard. He loved making things, cared about his work, and saw himself as a craftsman.	Describe some of the deceased's childhood, such as their schooling, hobbies, or interests.
Care and craftsmanship helped Sam get a dream apprenticeship right out of high school, at a time when such dreams were hard to come by. Around that time, Sam met Daniella and knew he had found the person to be by his side while he built his dream.	
It was an incredible dream they built. Sam grew the apprenticeship into a business at the same time that he and Daniella grew their family, having three wonderful children—Amelia, Daniel, and Estefan. Nothing gave Sam more delight	Describe other aspects of the deceased's life, such as any marriages or children, their interests, and their career or personal achievements. Include some stories that describe the deceased's personality.

Speech Script	Speech Component
then seeing his kids horsing around with the rest of the neighbourhood. To Sam, the people in his neighbourhood were part of his family, and he always made the time to bring that extended family together. For those of you lucky enough to have been at to one of Sam and Daniella's incredible block parties, you know just how much he loved throwing parties and inviting everyone along. No one outside the neighbourhood would have guessed that the person behind those huge parties was the guy with the quiet smile, calmly sipping a beer beside the pool.	
Sam's family grew, and his kids had kids of their own—ten grandkids in total. They were the apple of their granddad's eye. When Sam lost Daniella just a few years ago, he told me that he didn't know how he'd smile again without her. But he did smile, every time he saw his kids, every time he saw his grandkids.	Describe aspects of the deceased's later life, such as grandchildren or other accomplishments, as applicable.
And even though it's Sam who is now gone, we need to do what he did. Smile. Find the things in life that warm our hearts, that let us know that love is in us and around us. I'm going to miss Sam, we all will, but I know that whenever I see any of you smile, I'll also be seeing a bit of Sam smiling too.	Give a closing statement with a fond statement and final farewell to the deceased.

Further Reading

"About." *American Forensic Association.* n.d. (Accessed April 30, 2016). http://www.americanforensics.org/about.

"About." *Toastmasters International.* 2016. (Accessed April 30, 2016). https://www.toastmasters.org/About.

Adler, Ronald B., George R. Rodman, and Alexandre Sévigny. *Understanding Human Communication.* Don Mills, Ontario: Oxford University Press, 2015.

Alberta Health Services. *Healthy Parents Healthy Children.* Government of Alberta. http://www.healthyparentshealthychildren.ca/. (Accessed March 19, 2016).

Alberta Learning Information Service. *Let' s Talk: A Guide to Resolving Workplace Conflicts.* Government of Alberta, Human Services, 2007. https://alis.alberta.ca/pdf/cshop/letstalk.pdf. (Accessed June 10, 2016).

Allen, Craig. "Our First 'Television' Candidate: Eisenhower over Stevenson in 1956." *Journalism Quarterly* 65, no. 2 (Summer 1988): 352–359. Communication & Mass Media Complete, EBSCOhost (accessed March 17, 2016).

Anderson, Cameron, and Sebastien Brion. "Perspectives on Power in Organizations." *Annual Review of Organizational Psychology and Organizational Behavior* 1, no. 1 (March 21, 2014): 67. *Supplemental Index*, EBSCOhost (accessed May 6, 2016).

Anderson, R. C., and C. A. Klofstad. "Preference for Leaders with Masculine Voices Holds in the Case of Feminine Leadership Roles." *PLoS ONE* 7(12): e51216.

Andrejevic, Mark. *Infoglut: How Too Much Information Is Changing the Way We Think and Know*. n.p.: New York : Routledge,. University of Alberta Library, EBSCOhost (accessed April 5, 2016).

Baran, Stanley J. *Introduction to Mass Communication: Media Literacy and Culture*. New York: McGraw-Hill Education, 2015.

Baron, Naomi S. *Alphabet to Email: How Written English Evolved and Where It's Heading.* London: Routledge, 2002.

Bartlett, Kenneth G. "Social Impact of the Radio." *Annals of the American Academy of Political and Social Science*, 1947, 89, *JSTOR Journals*, EBSCOhost (accessed March 16, 2016).

Beauchamp, Christopher. "Who Invented the Telephone?: Lawyers, Patents, and the Judgments of History." *Technology and Culture,* no. 4 (2010): 854. *Project MUSE*, EBSCOhost (accessed April 1, 2016).

Bennet, Annmarie. *Social Media: Global Perspectives, Applications and Benefits and Dangers*. Hauppauge, New York: Nova Science Publishers, Inc, 2014. *eBook Academic Collection*, EBSCOhost (accessed June 13, 2016).

Beuick, Marshall D. "The Limited Social Effect of Radio Broadcasting." *American Journal of Sociology*, 1927, 615, *JSTOR Journals*, EBSCOhost (accessed March 16, 2016).

Bippus, A. M., and J. A. Daly. "What Do People Think Causes Stage Fright?: Naive Attributions about the Reasons for Public Speaking Anxiety." *Communication Education* 48, no. 1 (n.d.): 63–72. *Arts & Humanities Citation Index*, EBSCOhost (accessed May 10, 2016).

Blake, Brett Elizabeth, and Robert W. Blake. "Chapter Two: The Foundations of Literacy and Its Consequences." In *Literacy Primer*, 31. n.p.: 2005. *Supplemental Index*, EBSCOhost (accessed March 7, 2016).

Bodroghkozy, Aniko. *Equal Time: Television and the Civil Rights Movement*. n.p.: Urbana: University of Illinois Press, 2012. University of Alberta Library, EBSCOhost (accessed March 21, 2016).

Bonvillain, Nancy. *Language, Culture, and Communication: the Meaning of Messages.* Upper Saddle River, NJ: Pearson, 2014.

Bowden, Mark. 2010. *Winning Body Language: Control the Conversation, Command Attention, and Convey the Right Message—Without Saying a Word.* New York: McGraw-Hill.

Brazeal, Donald K. "Precursor to Modern Media Hype: The 1830s Penny Press." *Journal of American Culture* (Malden, MA) no. 4 (2005): 405. *Academic OneFile*, EBSCOhost (accessed March 8, 2016).

Brown, Sally; Race, Phil, *Lecturing: A Practical Guide.* Taylor & Francis, 2002. http://www.myilibrary.com?ID=7415 (accessed June 11, 2016)

Buchweitz, Augusto, et al. "Brain Activation for Reading and Listening Comprehension: An MRI Study of Modality Effects and Individual Differences in Language Comprehension." *Psychology & Neuroscience* 2, no. 2 (2009): 111–123. *MEDLINE*, EBSCOhost (accessed May 11, 2016).

Campbell, W. Joseph. *Getting It Wrong: Ten of the Greatest Misreported Stories in American Journalism.* Berkeley: University of California Press, 2010. eBook Collection (EBSCOhost), EBSCOhost (accessed March 16, 2016).

Campbell-Kelly, Martin, and Daniel Garcia-Swartz. "The History of the Internet: The Missing Narratives." *Journal of Information Technology* 28, no. 1 (March 2013): 18–33. Library & Information Science Source, EBSCOhost (accessed April 4, 2016).

Carawan, Edwin. *Oxford Readings in the Attic Orators.* Oxford: OUP Oxford, 2007. eBook Academic Collection (EBSCOhost), EBSCOhost (accessed March 21, 2016).

Carney, Dana R., Amy J. C. Cuddy, and Andy J. Yap. "Power Posing: Brief Nonverbal Displays Affect Neuroendocrine Levels and Risk Tolerance." *Psychological Science*, 2010, 1363. *JSTOR Journals*, EBSCOhost (accessed May 19, 2016).

Carayol, Valeérie, and Alex Frame. *Communication and PR from a Cross-cultural Standpoint: Practical and Methodological Issues*. Bruxelles: Peter Lang AG, 2012. *eBook Collection (EBSCOhost)*, EBSCO*host* (accessed June 28, 2016).

Carp, Harvey. *The Happiest Toddler on the Block.* New York: Bantam, 2008.

Carpenter, Frederic Ives. "Leonard Cox and the First English Rhetoric." *Modern Language Notes* 13 (5). Johns Hopkins University Press: 146–47.

Carroll, John B., and Princeton, NJ, Educational Testing Service. *Learning from Verbal Discourse in Educational Media: A Review of the Literature. Final Report.* 1971. *ERIC,* EBSCOhost (accessed May 11, 2016).

Canadian National Institute for the Blind: http://www.cnib.ca/en/living/braille/braille-system/Pages/default.aspx (accessed February 13, 2016).

Centre for Equitable Library Access. http://iguana.celalibrary.ca/ (accessed February 13, 2016).

Chen, Adrian. "The Troll Hunters." *MIT Technology Review* 118, no. 1 (January 2015): 50. MasterFILE Premier, EBSCOhost (accessed April 5, 2016).

Chelen, Dustin, Bill Connor, Gerda de Vries, and David Kahane. "What Is Good Teaching?" Vimeo video. Posted by University of Alberta Centre for Teaching and Learning. October 24, 2013. https://vimeo.com/78284413 (accessed July 2, 2016).

Chiaventone, Frederick J. "Taking Stock of the Pony Express." *Wild West* 22, no. 6 (April 2010): 28. MasterFILE Premier, EBSCOhost (accessed March 24, 2016).

Christopher, Elizabeth, ed. *Communication across Cultures.* New York: Palgrave MacMillan, 2012.

Churchill, Winston. "We Shall Fight on the Beaches." Speech, House of Commons, London, England, 04 June, 1940. The Churchill Centre. https://www.winstonchurchill.org/resources/speeches/1940-the-finest-hour/128-we-shall-fight-on-the-beaches (accessed 12 February, 2016).

———. "The Scaffolding of Rhetoric." November, 1897. The Churchill Centre. https://www.winstonchurchill.org/images/pdfs/for_educators/THE_SCAFFOLDING_OF_RHETORIC.pdf (accessed 12 February, 2016).

Cicero, Marcus Tullius, and H. M. Hubbell. *De inventione.* [electronic resource] ; *De optimogenereoratorum; Topica.*Cambridge, MA: Harvard University Press, 2014., 1949. University of Alberta Library, EBSCOhost (accessed April 11, 2016).

Coleman, Peter, Morton Deutsch, and Eric Marcus. *The Handbook of Conflict Resolution: Theory and Practice.*San Francisco: Jossey-Bass, 2014.

Corbett, Christopher. "The Pony Rides Again (and Again)." *American Heritage* 60, no. 1 (Spring 2010): 38. MasterFILE Premier, EBSCOhost (accessed March 24, 2016).

Coulmas, Florian. *Writing Systems: An Introduction to Their Linguistic Analysis.* New York: Cambridge University Press, 2003.

"Dale Carnegie Training." *Dale Carnegie Training.* (Accessed April 30, 2016).

Dahlgren, Peter. "Social Media and Political Participation: Discourse and Deflection," in *Critique, Social Media and the Information Society.* Edited by Marisol Sandoval and Christian Fuchs, n.p. New York: Routledge, 2014. *eBook Collection,* EBSCOhost (accessed June 13, 2016).

Davis, Stephen, and Jon Lukomnik. "Social Media Virality & the Ice Bucket Challenge." *Compliance Week* 11, no. 129 (October 2014): 46–47. *Business Source Complete*, EBSCOhost (accessed June 10, 2016).

DelliCarpini, Michael X. "Radio's Political Past." *Media Studies Journal* no. 3 (1993): 22. Academic OneFile, EBSCOhost (accessed March 17, 2016).

Diercksen, Michael, et al. "The Effects of Social Media in Today's Workplace." *Proceedings for the Northeast Region Decision Sciences Institute (NEDSI)* (April 2013): 946–952. Business Source Complete, EBSCOhost (accessed June 21, 2016).

Dietrich, Maria, and Katherine Verdolini Abbott. "Vocal Function in Introverts and Extraverts during a Psychological Stress Reactivity Protocol." *Journal of Speech, Language, and Hearing Research* 55, no. 3 (June 1, 2012): 973–987. *ERIC*, EBSCOhost (accessed May 10, 2016).

Dodd, Annabel Z. *The Essential Guide to Telecommunications.* Upper Saddle River, NJ : Prentice Hall PTR, 2002.

Dow, Clyde W. "The Personality Traits of Effective Public Speakers." *Quarterly Journal Of Speech* 27, no. 4 (December 1941): 525. *Communication & Mass Media Complete*, EBSCOhost (accessed May 10, 2016).

Duck, Steve, and David T. McMahan. *Communication in Everyday Life.* 2nd ed. Los Angeles: SAGE Publications, 2015.

Duggan, Maeve, Nicole B. Ellison, et. al. *Demographics of Key Social Networking Platforms.* Pew Research Center. January 9, 2015. http://www.pewinternet.org/2015/01/09/demographics-of-key-social-networking-platforms–2/ (accessed May 20, 2016).

Ekman, Paul, Wallace Friesen, et. al. "Universals and Cultural Differences in Judgements of Facial Expressions of Emotion." *Journal of Personality and Social Psychology.* 1987, Vol. 53, no. 4: 712–717.

Elwalda, Abdulaziz, Kevin Lü, and Maged Ali. "Perceived Derived Attributes of Online Customer Reviews." *Computers in Human Behavior* 56 (March 2016): 306–319. *Education Research Complete*, EBSCOhost (accessed June 21, 2016).

Encyclopedia Britannica Online, s.v. "Postal System." http://www.britannica.com/topic/postal-system. (Accessed March 22, 2016).

———. "Vladimir Zworykin" http://www.britannica.com/biography/Vladimir-Zworykin. (Accessed March 17, 2016).

Ene, Daniela, and Marian Panainte. "Beyond Language in Translation Theory: Translation and Nonverbal Communication." *Scientific Journal of Humanistic Studies* 6:11 (October 2014).

Fantham, Elaine. *The Roman World of Cicero's De Oratore.* Oxford ; New York : Oxford University Press, 2004.

Fast, Julius. 2002. *Body Language*. Revised and updated ed. Lanham: M. Evans & Company.

Federal Communicaions Commission. "711 for Telecommunications Relay Service." Web. https://www.fcc.gov/consumers/guides/711-telecommunications-relay-service. (Accessed March 7, 2016).

———. "Voice Over Internet Protocol (VOIP)." Web. https://www.fcc.gov/general/voice-over-internet-protocol-voip (accessed March 7, 2016).

———. "VoIP and 911 Service." Web. https://www.fcc.gov/general/voice-over-internet-protocol-voip. Last reviewed 11/2/15 (accessed March 7, 2016).

Fisher, Roger, William Ury, and Bruce Patton. *Getting to Yes: Negotiating Agreement without Giving In,* 2nd ed. Boston: Houghton Mifflin, 1991.

Forsyth, Donelson. *College Teaching: Practical Insights from the Science of Teaching and Learning,* 2nd ed. Washington: American Psychological Association, 2003.

Foster, Jacob G., Andrey Rzhetsky, and James A. Evans. "Tradition and Innovation in Scientists' Research Strategies." *American Sociological Review* 80, no. 5 (October 2015): 875–908. *Business Source Complete*, EBSCOhost (accessed June 29, 2016).

Founders' Constitution, The. Volume 5, Amendment I (Speech and Press), Document 8. Web. http://press-pubs.uchicago.edu/founders/documents/amendI_speechs8.html. The University of Chicago Press (accessed March 8, 2016).

Frederick, Peter. *Persuasive Writing: How to Harness the Power of Words.* Harlow: Prentice Hall/Pearson, 2011.

French, John, and Bertrand Raven. "The Bases of Social Power," in *Studies in Social Power*, edited by D. Cartwright, 150–167. Ann Arbor: University of Michigan Press, 1968.

Gearhart, Sherice, and Weiwu Zhang. "'Was It Something I Said?' 'No, It Was Something You Posted!'" A Study of the Spiral of Silence Theory in Social Media Contexts." *Cyberpsychology, Behavior and Social Networking* 18, no. 4 (April 2015): 208–213. *MEDLINE*, EBSCOhost (accessed June 20, 2016).

Goebbels, Joseph. "The Fuhrer as Speaker." 1936. *German Propaganda Archive*. Web. Calvin College, 1998. http://research.calvin.edu/german-propaganda-archive/ahspeak.htm. (Accessed May 5, 2016).

Gunderson, Erik, ed. *The Cambridge Companion to Ancient Rhetoric.*New York: Cambridge University Press, 2009.

Habinek, Thomas. *Ancient Rhetoric and Oratory*. Oxford: Blackwell Publishing, 2005.

Hanqi, Fang. *History of Journalism in China.* Singapore: Silkroad Press, 2013.

Hanson, Erin. "Oral Traditions." *Indigenous Foundations.* University of British Columbia. Web. http://indigenousfoundations.arts.ubc.ca/home/culture/oral-traditions.html (accessed March 11, 2016).

Hanson, Ralph. *Mass Communication: Living in a Media World*. 3rd ed. Washington: CQ Press, 2011.

Hargrave, Jocelyn. "Disruptive Technological History: Papermaking to Digital Printing." *Journal of Scholarly Publishing* 44, no. 3 (April 2013): 221–236. *Canadian Reference Centre*, EBSCOhost (accessed March 7, 2016).

Harper, Rebecca G. "Making Sense of Texts." *SRATE Journal* 23, no. 2 (June 1, 2014): 21–27. *ERIC*, EBSCOhost (accessed April 23, 2016).

Hearing, Gregory A., and Brian C. Ussery. "The Times They Are a Changin': The Impact of Technology and Social Media on the Public Workplace, Part I." *Florida Bar Journal* 86, no. 3 (March 2012): 35–39. *Legal Source*, EBSCOhost (accessed June 21, 2016).

Hickson, Clive, Candide Sloboda, and Alex Brown. "What to Do So That Your Course Doesn't Suck!" Vimeo video, posted by the University of Alberta Centre for Teaching and Learning, September 23, 2013. http://vimeo.com/75508876 (acessed July 2, 2016).

Hochfelder, David, and Muse Project. *The Telegraph in America, 1832–1920.* Baltimore: Johns Hopkins University Press, 2013. eBook Academic Collection (EBSCOhost), EBSCOhost (accessed April 1, 2016).

Hochmuth, Marie. "I. A. Richards and the 'New Rhetoric.'" *Quarterly Journal of Speech* 44, no. 1 (February 1958): 1. *Communication & Mass Media Complete,* EBSCOhost (accessed April 12, 2016).

Hosch, William L. "Smartphone." *Encyclopedia Britannica* (September 2014): *Research Starters*, EBSCOhost (accessed April 2, 2016).

Human Resources Council of Alberta. "Conflict at Work." *Workplaces That Work.* http://hrcouncil.ca/hr-toolkit/workplaces-conflict.cfm. (Accessed June 13, 2016).

Hwa-Froelich, Deborah A. *Social Communication Development and Disorders.* New York: Psychology Press, 2015.

Kato, Morimichi. "Significance of the Rhetorical and Humanistic Tradition for Education Today." *Asia Pacific Education Review* 15, no. 1 (March 1, 2014): 55–63. ERIC, EBSCOhost (accessed April 11, 2016).

Kennedy, George A. *A New History of Classical Rhetoric.* Princeton: Princeton University Press, 2011.

Kiefel, Barry. "Trends in TV and Internet Use: The Impact of Internet TV on Canadian Programming." Canadian Media Research, Inc, 2011. http://www.omdc.on.ca/Assets/Research/Research+Reports/Trends+in+TV+and+Internet+Use/Trends+in+TV+and+Internet+Use_en.pdf. (Accessed April 4, 2016).

Kim, Woo Gon, Jun (Justin) Li, and Robert A. Brymer. "The Impact of Social Media Reviews on Restaurant Performance: The Moderating Role of Excellence Certificate." *International Journal of Hospitality Management* 55, (May 2016): 41–51. *Hospitality & Tourism Complete*, EBSCOhost (accessed June 21, 2016).

Knapp, Mark, Linda Putnam, and Lillian J. Davis. "Measuring Interpersonal Conflict in Organizations:: Where Do We Go from Here?" *Management Communication Quarterly* February 1988 1: 414–429, doi:10.1177/0893318988001003008.

Ko, SeiJin, Melody Sadler, and Adam Galinsky. "The Sound of Power: Conveying and Detecting Hierarchical Rank through Voice." *Psycological Science*. 2015, Vol. 26, No. 1.

Kremmydas, Christos, and Kathryn Tempest, eds. *Hellenistic Oratory: Continuity and Change*. Oxford: Oxford University Press, 2013.

Lathem, Edward Connery, ed. *Meet Calvin Coolidge: The Man behind the Myth.* Battleboro: Stephen Greene Press, 1960.

Lee, Jayeon. "The Double-Edged Sword: The Effects of Journalists' Social Media Activities on Audience Perceptions of Journalists and Their News Products." *Journal of Computer-*

Mediated Communication 20, no. 3 (May 2015): 312–329. *Communication & Mass Media Complete*, EBSCOhost (accessed June 21, 2016).

Lev, Peter. *Transforming the Screen, 1950–1959.* [electronic resource]. n.p. New York: Charles Scribner's Sons, 2003. University of Alberta Library, EBSCOhost (accessed March 17, 2016).

Lewin-Jones, Jenny, and Victoria Mason. "Understanding Style, Language and Etiquette in Email Communication in Higher Education: A Survey." *Research in Post-Compulsory Education* 19, no. 1 (March 2014): 75–90. *Education Research Complete*, EBSCOhost (accessed June 10, 2016).

Lind, Nancy S., and Erik Rankin. "First Amendment Rights." [electronic resource]: *AN Encyclopedia.* n.p.: Santa Barbara, CA: ABC-CLIO, 2012. University of Alberta Library, EBSCOhost (accessed March 8, 2016).

Loviglio, Jason. *Radio's Intimate Public: Network Broadcasting and Mass-Mediated Democracy.* Minneapolis: University of Minnesota Press, 2005.

MacIntyre, Peter D., and Kimly A. Thivierge. "The Effects of Speaker Personality on Anticipated Reactions to Public Speaking." *Communication Research Reports* 12, no. 2 (September 1, 1995): 125–33. *ERIC,* EBSCOhost (accessed May 10, 2016).

Martimianakis, Maria Athina (Tina), and Linda Muzzin. "Discourses of Interdisciplinarity and the Shifting Topography of Academic Work: Generational Perspectives on Facilitating and Resisting Neoliberalism." *Studies in Higher Education* 40, no. 8 (October 2015): 1454–1470. *Education Research Complete*, EBSCOhost (accessed June 29, 2016).

McCafferty, Dennis. "Activism vs. Alacktivism." *Communications of the ACM* 54, no. 12 (December 2011): 17–19. *Business Source Complete*, EBSCOhost (accessed June 14, 2016).

McCormick, Horace. UNC Kenan-Flagler Business School. *The Real Effects of Unconscious Bias in the Workplace*. Chapel Hill, NC: UNC Executive Development, 2015. http://www.kenan-flagler.unc.edu/~/media/Files/documents/executive-development/unc-white-paper-the-real-effects-of-unconscious-bias-in-the-workplace-Final (accessed April 30, 2016).

McNeal, Marguerite. "One Writer Explored the Marketing Science behind Clickbait. You'll Never Believe What She Found Out." *Marketing Insights* 27, no. 4 (July 2015): 24–31. *Business Source Elite*, EBSCOhost (accessed June 19, 2016).

Meeker, Mary. *2015 Internet Trends Report.* Kleiner Perkins Caulfield & Byers. 2015. Web: Slideshare presentation. http://www.slideshare.net/kleinerperkins/internet-trends-v1 (accessed May 20, 2016).

Mehrabian, Albert. Personal website. http://www.kaaj.com/psych/smorder.html. (Accessed February 29, 2016).

Meredith, Dennis. *Explaining Research : How to Reach Key Audiences to Advance Your Work*. Oxford: Oxford University Press, 2010. *eBook Collection (EBSCOhost)*, EBSCO*host* (accessed June 11, 2016).

———. *Working with Public Information Officers: A Supplement to Explaining Research.* Web: Issuu.com, 2010. https://issuu.com/dennismeredith/docs/working_with_public_information_officers (accessed June 11, 2016).

Miller, Keith D. "On Martin Luther King Jr. and the Landscape of Civil Rights Rhetoric." *Rhetoric and Public Affairs* 16, no. 1 (Spring 2013): 167–183. *MLA International Bibliography*, EBSCOhost (accessed May 22, 2016).

Mills, Adam J. "Virality in Social Media: The SPIN Framework." *Journal of Public Affairs* 12, no. 2 (May 2012): 162–169. *Business Source Complete*, EBSCOhost (accessed June 10, 2016).

Morse, W. C., M. Nielsen-Pincus, J. Force, and J. Wulfhorst. "Bridges and Barriers to Developing and Conducting Interdisciplinary Graduate-Student Team Research." *Ecology and Society* 12(2): 8 (2007). http://www.ecologyandsociety.org/vol12/iss2/art8/ (accessed June 29, 2016).

Murphy, James Jerome, Michael J. Hoppmann, and Richard A. Katula. *A Synoptic History of Classical Rhetoric.* New York: Routledge, 2013.

National Association of the Deaf. "TTY and TTY Relay Services." https://nad.org/issues/telephone-and-relay-services/relay-services/tty. (Accessed March 7, 2016).

National Forensic Association. 2016. (Accessed April 30, 2016). http://www.nationalforensics.org

National Speech and Debate Association. 2016. Website (accessed April 30, 2016). http://www.speechanddebate.org/

Nerd Nite. 2016. Website. http://nerdnite.com (accessed April 30, 2016).

Obar, Jonathan A., and Steven Wildman. "Social Media Definition and the Governance Challenge: An Introduction to the Special Issue." *Telecommunications Policy*, Vol. 29, no. 9 (2015), 745–750. DOI: http://dx.doi.org/10.2139/ssrn.2647377 (accessed June 6, 2016).

Oetzel, John G., and Stella Ting-Toomey. *The SAGE Handbook of Conflict Communication: Integrating Theory, Research, and Practice*. Thousand Oaks: SAGE Publications, Inc, 2013.

Ong, Walter J. *Orality and Literacy : The Technologizing of the Word.* London: Routledge, 2002. eBook Collection (EBSCOhost), EBSCOhost (accessed March 10, 2016).

O'Rourke, Sean Patrick, et al. "The Most Significant Passage on Rhetoric in the Works of Francis Bacon." *Rhetoric Society Quarterly*, 1996, 31, *JSTOR Journals*, EBSCOhost (accessed April 11, 2016).

Orman, Hilarie. *Encrypted Email: The History and Technology of Message Privacy.* eBook: Springer International Publishing, 2015. DOI: 10.1007/978–3–319–21344–6 (accessed June 24, 2015).

O'Sullivan, Maureen, et al. "Universals and Cultural Differences in the Judgments of Facial Expressions of Emotion." *Journal of Personality and Social Psychology* 4 (1987): 712. *Academic OneFile*, EBSCOhost (accessed June 2, 2016).

Palau-Sampio, Dolors. "Reference Press Metamorphosis in the Digital Context: Clickbait and Tabloid Strategies in Elpais.com." *Communication & Society* 29, no. 2 (April 2016): 63–79. *Academic Search Complete*, EBSCOhost (accessed June 19, 2016).

Palmer, Erik. *Teaching the Core Skills of Listening & Speaking.* Alexandria, VA: ASCD, 2014.

Papa, Michael J., Tom D. Daniels, and Barry K. Spiker. *Organizational Communication: Perspectives and Trends.* Los Angeles: Sage Publications, 2008

Papers of John F. Kennedy. Presidential Papers. President's Office Files. Speech Files. Remarks on signing honorary citizenship for Sir Winston Churchill, 9 April 1963. http://www.jfklibrary.org/Asset-Viewer/Archives/JFKPOF–043–032.aspx. (Accessed Mach 13, 2016).

Pasquale, Frank. "How to Tame an Internet Troll," *The Chronicle of Higher Education* 5: 10. Academic OneFile, EBSCOhost (accessed April 5, 2016).

Patnode, Randall. "Friend, Foe, or Freeloader? Cooperation and Competition between Newspapers and Radio in the Early 1920s." *American Journalism* 28, no. 1 (2011): 75–95. *Communication & Mass Media Complete*, EBSCOhost (accessed March 16, 2016).

Pavlus, John. "How Ikea Designs Its (In)Famous Instructions," *Behind the Brand* (Blog). Fast Company. October 28, 2015. http://www.fastcodesign.com/3052604/how-ikea-designs-its-infamous-instruction-manuals (accessed June 26, 2016).

PechaKucha: 20x20. 2016. Website. http://www.pechakucha.org/ (accessed April 30, 2016).

Penney, Joel. "Social Media and Symbolic Action: Exploring Participation in the Facebook Red Equal Sign Profile Picture Campaign." *Journal of Computer-Mediated Communication* 20, no. 1 (January 2015): 52–66. *Communication & Mass Media Complete*, EBSCOhost (accessed June 14, 2016).

Peterson, Joel. *The 10 Laws of Trust: Building the Bonds That Make a Business Great.* New York: AMACOM, 2016.

———. *Conducting Effective Negotiations.* YouTube Video, Stanford Graduate School of Business, January 31, 2007, 29:10. https://www.youtube.com/watch?v=rCmvMDrCWjs. Accessed May 20, 2016

Priestman, Chris. *Web Radio: Radio Production for Internet Streaming.* n.p.: Burlington: Focal Press, 2013. University of Alberta Library, EBSCOhost (accessed April 5, 2016).

"Psychologist Dr. Eddie Murphy Gives Tips on Communicating with Teenagers." *Leinster Express* (Port Laoise, Northern Ireland), July 31, 2014. Canadian Points of View Reference Centre, EBSCOhost (accessed June 28, 2016).

Public Health Agency of Canada. *Age-Friendly Communication: Facts, Tips, and Ideas.* eBook. Ottawa: Division of Aging and Seniors, Public Health Agency of Canada. http://www.hss.gov.yk.ca/pdf/afcomm-commavecaines-eng.pdf (accessed June 28, 2016).

Quinn, Kelly. "Why We Share: A Uses and Gratifications Approach to Privacy Regulation in Social Media Use." *Journal of Broadcasting & Electronic Media* 60, no. 1 (March 2016): 61–86. *Academic Search Complete*, EBSCOhost (accessed June 21, 2016).

Radner, Karen. *State Correspondence in the Ancient World: From New Kingdom Egypt to the Roman Empire.* n.p.: New York : Oxford University Press, 2014. University of Alberta Library, EBSCOhost (accessed March 22, 2016).

Ray, Benjamin. "Your Tweet Half-Life Is 1 Billion Times Shorter Than Carbon–14's." Blog. Wiselytics. http://www.wiselytics.com/blog/tweet-isbillion-time-shorter-than-carbon14/ (accessed June 14, 2016).

ReachOut Australia. "Connecting and Communicating." https://parents.au.reachout.com/Skills-to-build/Connecting-and-communicating (accessed June 28, 2016).

Richmond, Virginia P., et al. "Perceived Power as a Mediator of Management Communication Style and Employee Satisfaction: A Preliminary Investigation." *Communication Quarterly* 28, no. 4 (Fall 1980): 37–46. *Communication & Mass Media Complete*, EBSCOhost (accessed May 6, 2016).

"Rhetoric," narrated by Melvyn Bragg, with Angie Hobbs, Ceri Sullivan, and Tom Healy. *In Our Time,* October 28, 2004, http://www.bbc.co.uk/inourtimeprototype/episode/p004y263. (Accessed March 18, 2016).

Robinson, Andrew. *Writing and Script: A Very Short Introduction.* Oxford: Oxford University Press, 2009.

Rodenburg, Patsy. *The Actor Speaks: Voice and the Performer.* New York: Palgrave MacMillan, 2002.

Rogers, Henry. *Writing Systems: A Linguistic Approach.* Malden, MA : Blackwell, 2005.

Rosenblatt, Louise M. *The Reader, the Text, the Poem: The Transactional Theory of the Literary Work.* Carbondale: Southern Illinois University Press, 1994.

Rosenzweig, Roy. "Wizards, Bureaucrats, Warriors, and Hackers: Writing the History of the Internet." *The American Historical Review,* 1998: 1530, *JSTOR Journals,* EBSCOhost (accessed April 4, 2016).

Roskos-Ewoldsen, David R., et al. *The Handbook of Communication Science*. Thousand Oaks, CA: SAGE Publications, 2010.

Ross, Howard. Diversity Best Practices. "Proven Strategies for Addressing Unconscious Bias in the Workplace." *CDO Insights* 2, issue 5. http://www.cookross.com/docs/UnconsciousBias.pdf (accessed April 30, 2016).

Sabath, Ann Marie. *Business Etiquette: 101 Ways to Conduct Business with Charm and Savvy.* Franklin Lakes, NJ: Career Press, 2010.

Sanderson, Jimmy, et al. "'How Could Anyone Have Predicted That #AskJameis Would Go Horribly Wrong?' Public Relations, Social Media, and Hashtag Hijacking." *Public Relations Review* 42, no. 1 (March 2016): 31–37. *Business Source Complete,* EBSCOhost (accessed June 14, 2016).

Schulaka, Carly. "David Meerman Scott on Breaking Marketing Rules, Newsjacking, and Authentic Storytelling." *Journal of Financial Planning* 28, no. 6 (June 2015): 14–19. *Business Source Complete,* EBSCOhost (accessed June 13, 2016).

Schumann, Sandy, and Olivier Klein. "Substitute or Stepping Stone? Assessing the Impact of Low-Threshold Online Collective Actions on Offline Participation." *European Journal of Social Psychology* 45, no. 3 (April 2015): 308–322 15p. *CINAHL Plus* with Full Text, EBSCOhost (accessed June 14, 2016).

Scott, Simon. "Chapter 1: Newspaper History of the United Kingdom." In *Insights into Understanding the Financial Media—An Insider's View,* 2–10. n.p.: Thorogood Publishing Ltd., 1998. *Business Source Complete,* EBSCOhost (accessed March 8, 2016).

Shakespeare, William. *Romeo and Juliet*. In *The Complete Works of Shakespeare,* 4th ed. Edited by David Bevington, 977–1020. New York: Longman, 1997.

———. *As You Like It*. In *The Complete Works of Shakespeare*, 4th ed. Edited by David Bevington, 288–325. New York: Longman, 1997.

Shields, Christopher, *Aristotle* (Routledge, 2014), http://www.myilibrary.com?ID=563322 (accessed April 11, 2016)

Shorey, Harry H. *Animal Communication by Pheromones.* [Electronic Resource]. New York : Academic Press, 1976.

Silvester, Richard D. "Why Are Lawyers and Legal Documents So Hard to Understand?" *Silvester Law Office* (blog). http://www.silvesterlaw.com/index.php?option=com_content&view=article&id=54:why-are-lawyers-and-legal-documents-so-hard-to-understand&catid=13:laws-and-lawyers&Itemid=14. (Accessed June 26, 2016).

Sindone, Mario, and Katherine O'Regan. "Full Federal Court Concludes That Online Simulcasts of Radio Programs Are Not a Broadcast." *Gadens,* May 29, 2013. Web. http://www.gadens.com/publications/Pages/Online-simulcasts-of-radio-programs-are-not-a-broadcasting-service.aspx. (Accessed April 2, 2016).

Smith, J. David, Margaret Wilson, and Daniel Reisberg. "The Role of Subvocalization in Auditory Imagery." *Neuropsychologia,* 33(11), November 1995. *Science Direct,* Elseveir. DOI: 10.1016/0028–3932(95)00074-D. (Accessed June 23, 2016).

Socolow, Michael J. "The Hyped Panic Over 'War of the Worlds.'" *The Chronicle of Higher Education* 9 (2008): Academic OneFile, EBSCOhost (accessed March 17, 2016).

Socha, Bailey, and Barbara Eber-Schmid. "What Is New Media? Defining New Media Isn't Easy." Web. New Media Institute. 2014. http://www.newmedia.org/what-is-new-media.html (accessed March 9, 2016).

The Social Net: Understanding Our Online Behavior. Oxford University Press, 2013. *Oxford Scholarship Online*, EBSCOhost (accessed April 6, 2016).

Statista. "Leading Social Networks Worldwide as of April 2016, Ranked by Number of Active Users (millions)." Statistic. http://www.statista.com/statistics/272014/global-social-networks-ranked-by-number-of-users/ (accessed June , 2016).

Steel, C. E. W., and Henriette van der Blom. *Community and Communication: Oratory and Politics in Republican Rome.*Oxford: Oxford University Press, 2013.

Steel, Catherine. *Roman Oratory.* Cambridge: Cambridge University Press, 2013.

Suler, John. 2005. "The Online Disinhibition Effect." *International Journal of Applied Psychoanalytic Studies* 2, no. 2: 184. EBSCOhost (accessed April 5, 2016).

TED. 2016. Website. http://www.ted.com/ (accessed April 30, 2016).

"Teenagers and Communication." *Better Health Channel: Healthy Living* (Website.) Victoria State Government, 2016. https://www.betterhealth.vic.gov.au/health/healthyliving/teenagers-and-communication (accessed June 27, 2016).

"Telegraph." *Funk & Wagnalls New World Encyclopedia* (2015): 1. *Funk & Wagnalls New World Encyclopedia*, EBSCOhost (accessed March 31, 2016).

Thomas, William G. III. "Television News and the Civil Rights Struggle: The Views in Virginia and Mississippi." *Southern Spaces,* November 3, 2004. http://southernspaces.org/2004/

television-news-and-civil-rights-struggle-views-virginia-and-mississippi (accessed March 13, 2016).

Thompson, Susan O. "Paper Manufacturing and Early Books." *Annals of the New York Acadamy of Sciences.* 314, no. 1: 167–176.

Tindale, Christopher W. "Ways of Being Reasonable: Perelman and the Philosophers." *Philosophy & Rhetoric* 43, no. 4 (November 2010): 337–361. *Humanities International Complete,* EBSCOhost (accessed April 12, 2016).

Troyan, Scott D. *Medieval Rhetoric: A Casebook.* New York : Routledge, 2004.

Trump, Donald. "Donald Trump Presidential Announcement Full Speech 6/16/15." YouTube video, 32:22, posted by "Donald J. Trump for President," June 16, 2015. http://www.youtube.com/watch?v=q_q61B-DyPk&nohtml5=False (accessed 10 April, 2016).

Turkle, Sherry. *Alone Together: Why We Expect More from Technology and Less from Each Other.* New York: Basic Books, 2011.

Twenge, Jean M. "Does Online Social Media Lead to Social Connection or Social Disconnection?" *Journal of College and Character* 14, no. 1 (February 1, 2013): 11–20. *ERIC,* EBSCOhost (accessed June 21, 2016).

United States Postal Service. "Publication 100—The United States Postal Service—An American History 1775–2006." *About.* 2012. https://about.usps.com/publications/pub100/welcome.htm. (Accessed 11 April, 2016).

VanCour, Shawn Gary. *The Sounds of 'Radio': Aesthetic Formations of 1920s American Broadcasting.* University of Wisconsin-Madison, 2008. http://wiki.transnationalradio.org/data/3/32/VanCour_SoundsofRadio.pdf (accessed March 10, 2016).

Van De Graaff, Kent. *Human Anatomy,* 5th ed. Boston: McGraw Hill, 2000.

VanMeter, Rebecca A., Douglas B. Grisaffe, and Lawrence B. Chonko. "Of 'Likes' and 'Pins': The Effects of Consumers' Attachment to Social Media." *Journal of Interactive Marketing* 32 (November 2015): 70–88. *Business Source Elite,* EBSCOhost (accessed June 21, 2016).

Wharton, Tim. *Pragmatics and Non-Verbal Communication*. New York: Cambridge University Press, 2009.

Wheeler, Tom. *Mr. Lincoln' s T-Mails: How Abraham Lincoln Used the Telegraph to Win the Civil War*. New York: HarperCollins, 2006.

Wood, Stephen C. "Television's First Political Spot Ad Campaign: Eisenhower Answers America." *Presidential Studies Quarterly,* 1990, 265, *JSTOR Journals*, EBSCOhost (accessed March 17, 2016).

Upton, C., & Davies, B. L. (2013). *Analysing Twenty-First Century British English: Conceptual and Methodological Aspects of the Voices Project.* Milton Park, Abingdon, Oxon: Routledge, 2013.

Zacharis, John C. "Emmeline Pankhurst: An English Suffragette Influences America." *Speech Monographs* 38, no. 3 (August 1971): 198. *Communication & Mass Media Complete,* EBSCOhost (accessed May 22, 2016).

Zafarani, Reza, Mohammad Ali Abbasi, and Huan Liu. *Social Media Mining: An Introduction.* New York: Cambridge University Press, 2014.

Zimmerman, Adam G., and Gabriel J. Ybarra. "Online Aggression: The Influences of Anonymity and Social Modeling," *Psychology of Popular Media Culture* 5, no. 2 (April 2016): 181–193. *PsycARTICLES*, EBSCOhost (accessed April 5, 2016).

Index

Note: (ill.) indicates photos and illustrations.

C

N

O

P–Q

R

S

T

U

V

W

X, Y, Z

www.ingramcontent.com/pod-product-compliance
Lightning Source LLC
Jackson TN
JSHW061646170426
101040JS00018B/390

* 9 7 8 1 5 7 8 5 9 5 8 7 7 *